UNCANNY X-MEN: WOLVERINE & CYCLOPS

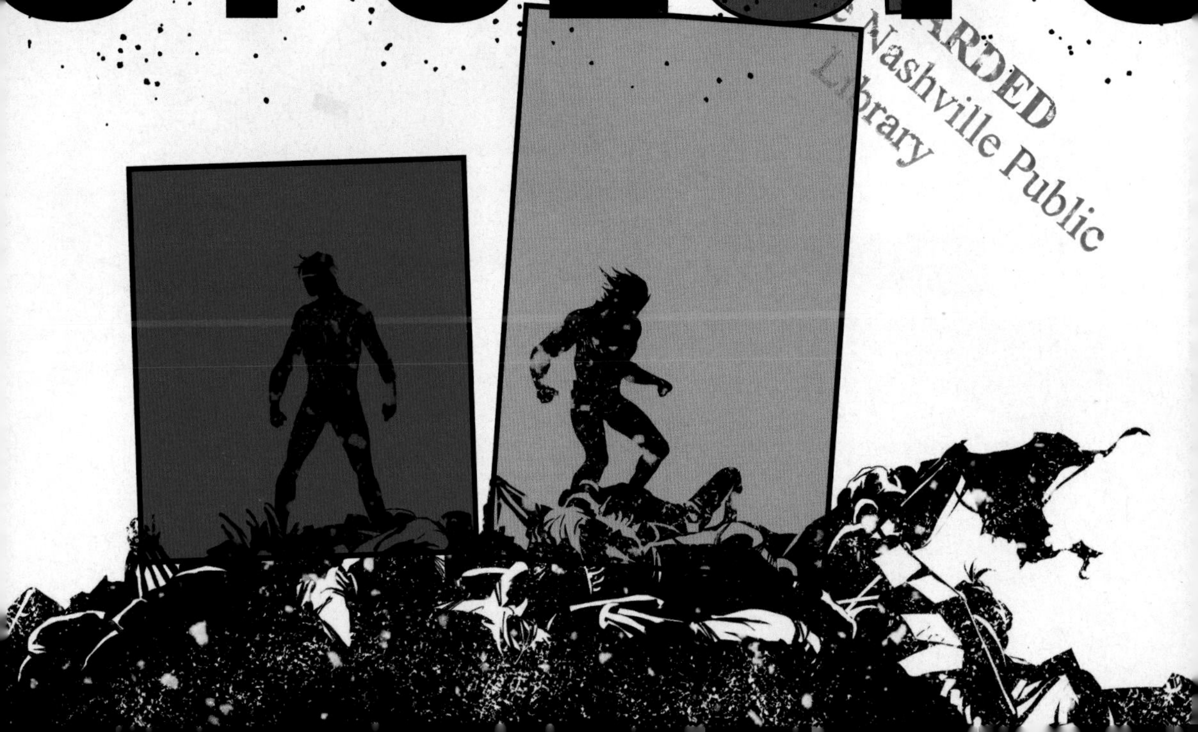

They were born mutants... possessing powers of a genetic origin that made them outcasts of society. But one man — Professor Charles Xavier — brought them together to learn to use their unique gifts in the service of a world that hates and fears them... They are Children of the Atom...

UNCANNY X-MEN:

WOLVERI

AND

&

X-MEN CREATED BY **STAN LEE** & **JACK KIRBY**

COLLECTION EDITOR/**JENNIFER GRÜNWALD** // ASSISTANT EDITOR/**CAITLIN O'CONNELL**
ASSOCIATE MANAGING EDITOR/**KATERI WOODY** // EDITOR, SPECIAL PROJECTS/**MARK D. BEAZLEY**
VP PRODUCTION & SPECIAL PROJECTS/**JEFF YOUNGQUIST** // BOOK DESIGNER/**JAY BOWEN**

SVP PRINT, SALES & MARKETING/**DAVID GABRIEL** // DIRECTOR, LICENSED PUBLISHING/**SVEN LARSEN**
EDITOR IN CHIEF/**C.B. CEBULSKI** // CHIEF CREATIVE OFFICER/**JOE QUESADA**

PRESIDENT/**DAN BUCKLEY** // EXECUTIVE PRODUCER/**ALAN FINE**

UNCANNY X-MEN: WOLVERINE AND CYCLOPS VOL. 1. Contains material originally published in magazine form as UNCANNY X-MEN #11-16. First printing 2019. ISBN 978-1-302-91582-7. Published by MARVEL WORLDWIDE, INC., a subsidiary of MARVEL ENTERTAINMENT, LLC. OFFICE OF PUBLICATION: 135 West 50th Street, New York, NY 10020. **Printed in the U.S.A.** DAN BUCKLEY, President, Marvel Entertainment; JOHN NEE, Publisher; JOE QUESADA, Chief Creative Officer; TOM BREVOORT, SVP of Publishing; DAVID BOGART, Associate Publisher & SVP of Talent Affairs; DAVID GABRIEL, SVP of Sales & Marketing, Publishing; JEFF YOUNGQUIST, VP of Production & Special Projects; DAN CARR, Executive Director of Publishing Technology; ALEX MORALES, Director of Publishing Operations; DAN EDINGTON, Managing Editor; SUSAN CRESPI, Production Manager; STAN LEE, Chairman Emeritus. For information regarding advertising in Marvel Comics or on Marvel.com, please contact Vit DeBellis, Custom Solutions & Integrated Advertising Manager, at vdebellis@marvel.com. For Marvel subscription inquiries, please call 888-511-5480. **Manufactured between 4/26/2019 and 5/28/2019 by LSC COMMUNICATIONS INC., KENDALLVILLE, IN, USA.**

10 9 8 7 6 5 4 3 2 1

NE CYCLOPS

After a pitched battle,
the X-Men were wiped out without a trace.
They are presumed dead.

WRITER / **MATTHEW ROSENBERG** ARTIST/ **SALVADOR LARROCA**

COLOR ARTISTS/ RACHELLE **ROSENBERG** (#11-12) & **GURU-eFX** (#13-16)

"WOLVERINE RETURNS"
ARTIST / **JOHN McCREA**
COLOR ARTIST/ **MIKE SPICER**

"THE LAST BLINDFOLD STORY"
ARTIST/ **JUANAN RAMÍREZ**
COLOR ARTIST/ **RACHELLE ROSENBERG**

LETTERER / **VC's JOE CARAMAGNA**

COVER ART/ **SALVADOR LARROCA**
& RACHELLE **ROSENBERG**

ASSISTANT EDITOR/ **CHRIS ROBINSON**   EDITOR/ **JORDAN D. WHITE**

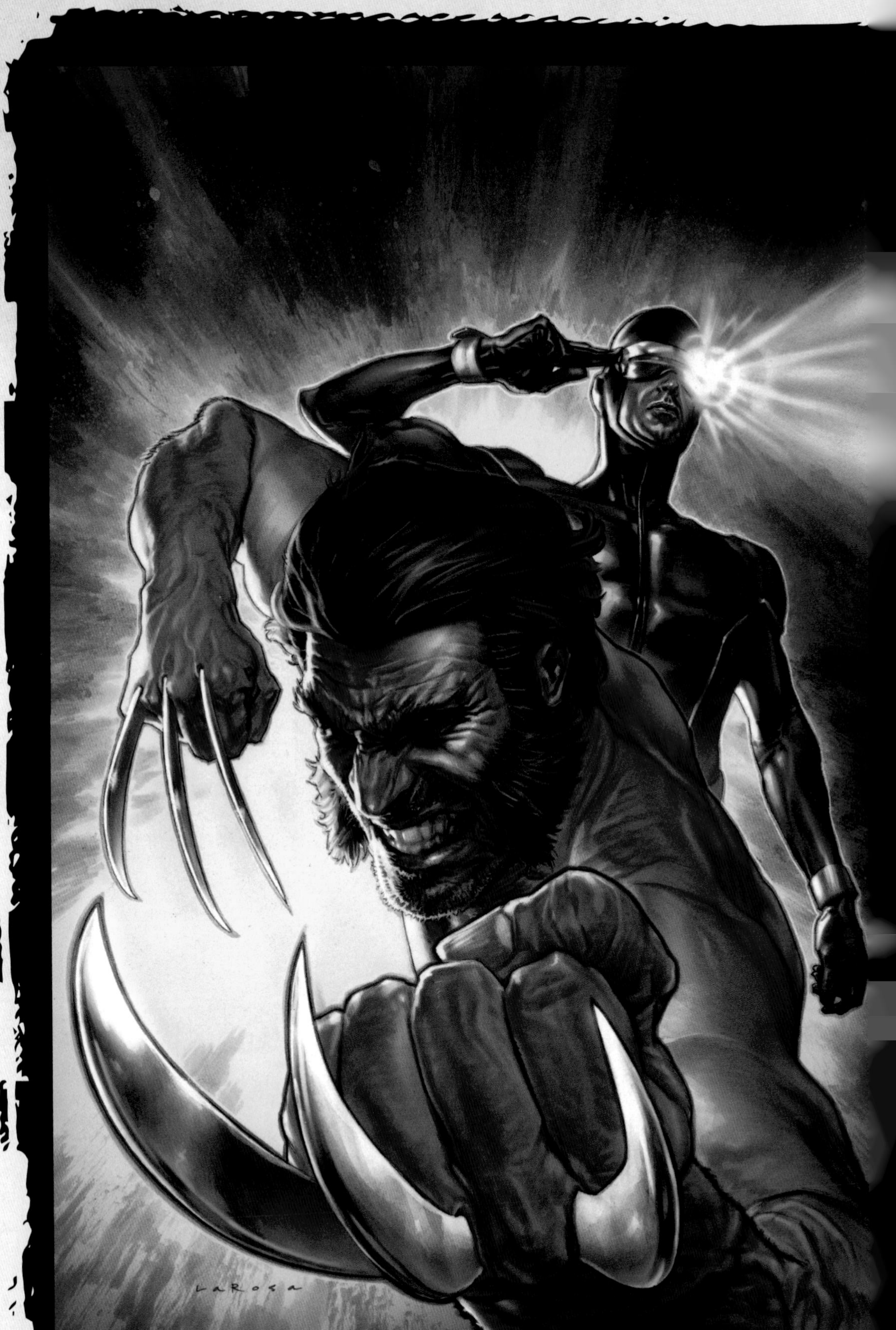
LAROSA

#11 VARIANT COVER BY **LEWIS LAROSA** & **DIEGO RODRIGUEZ**

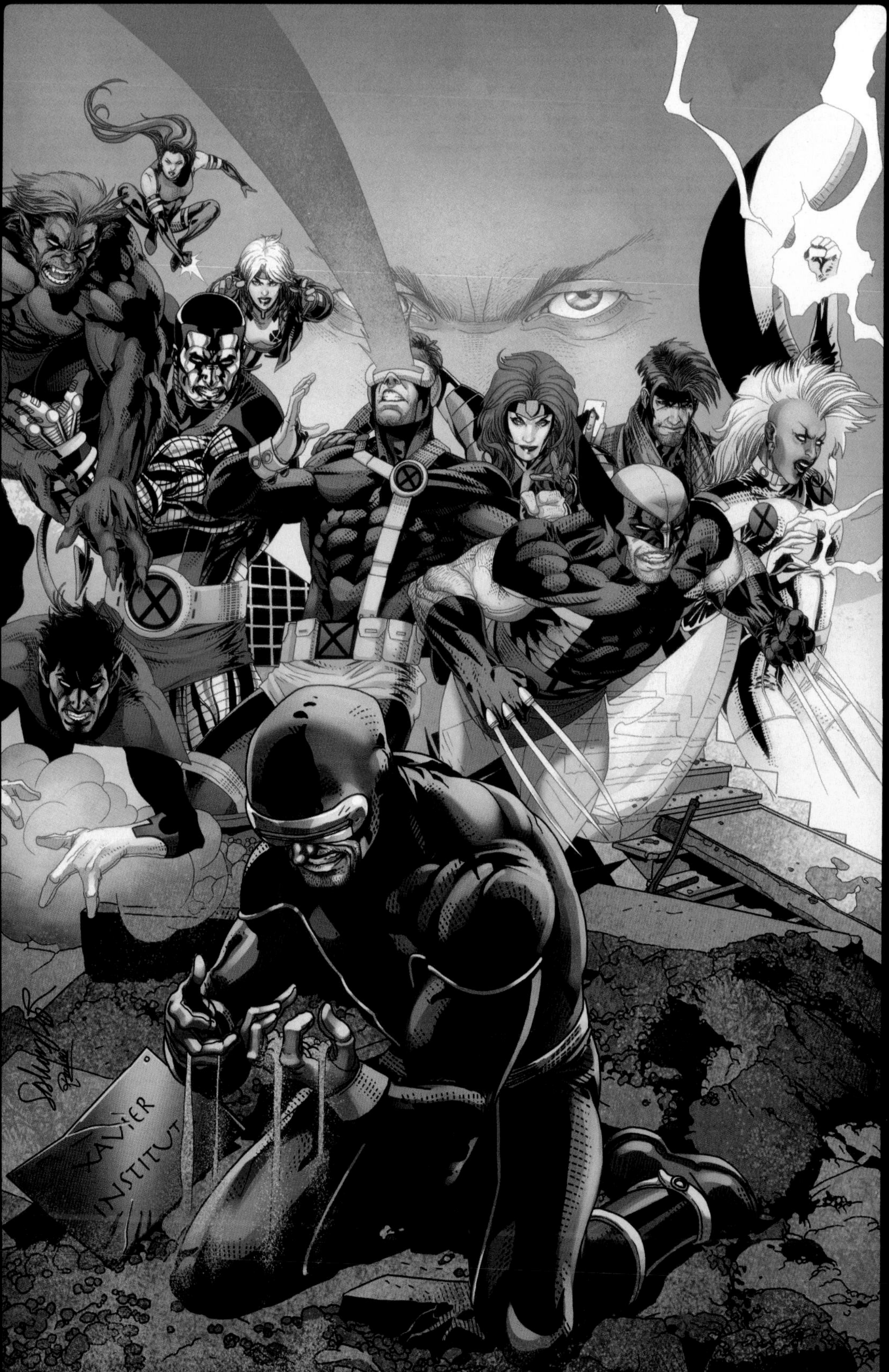
XAVIER
INSTITUT

11

This is Forever Part 1

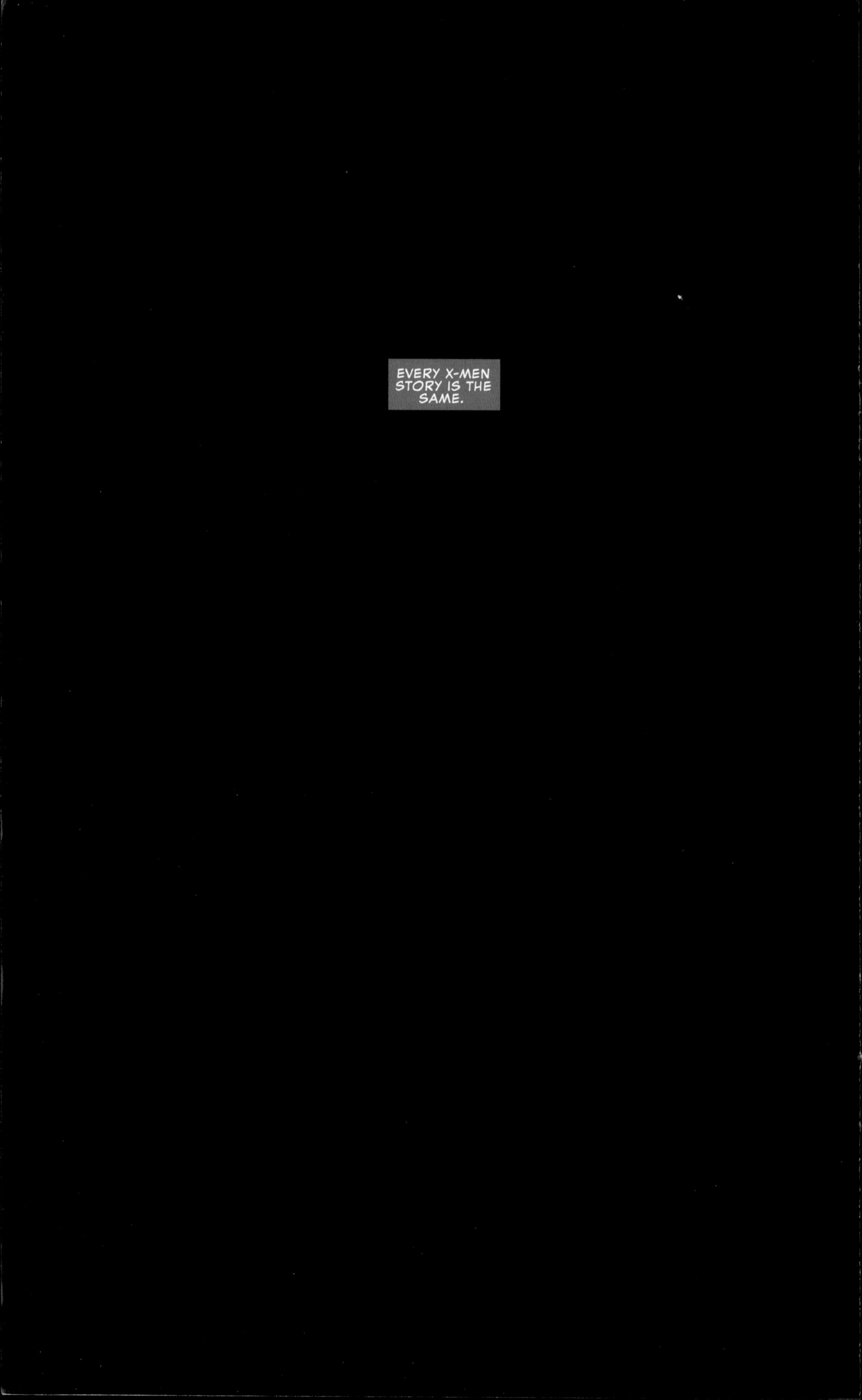
EVERY X-MEN STORY IS THE SAME.

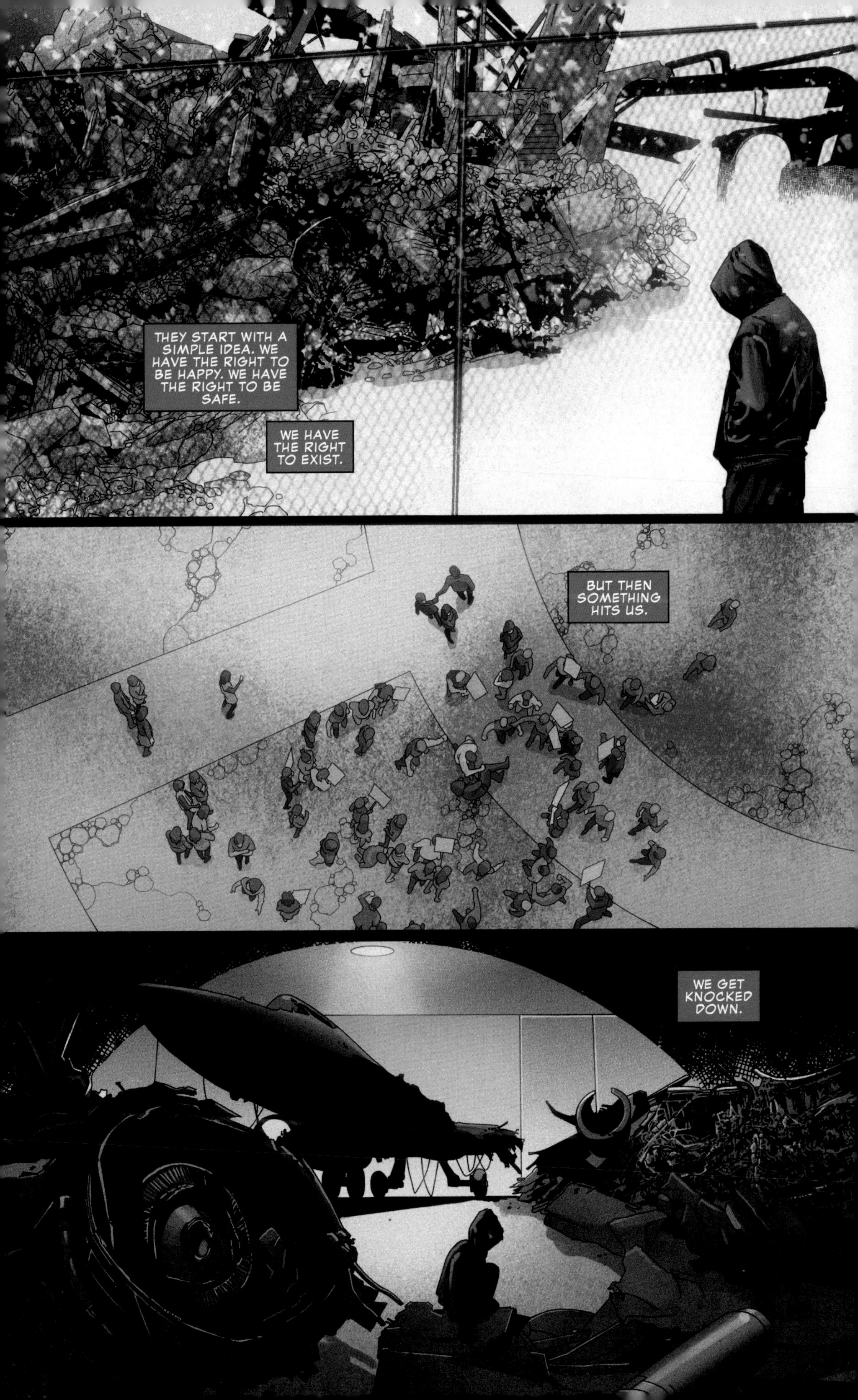
THEY START WITH A SIMPLE IDEA. WE HAVE THE RIGHT TO BE HAPPY. WE HAVE THE RIGHT TO BE SAFE.
WE HAVE THE RIGHT TO EXIST.
BUT THEN SOMETHING HITS US.
WE GET KNOCKED DOWN.

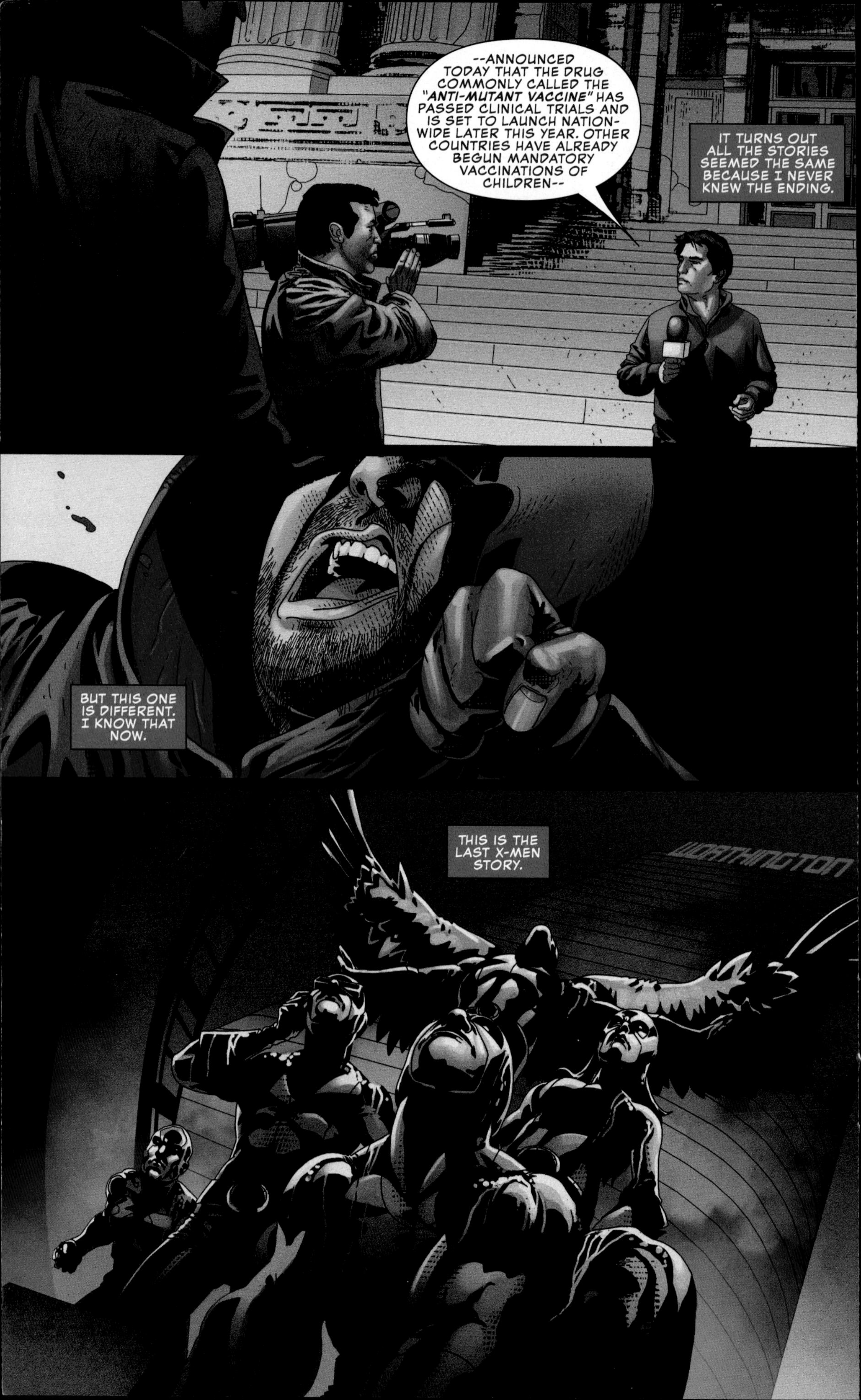
--ANNOUNCED TODAY THAT THE DRUG COMMONLY CALLED THE "ANTI-MUTANT VACCINE" HAS PASSED CLINICAL TRIALS AND IS SET TO LAUNCH NATION-WIDE LATER THIS YEAR. OTHER COUNTRIES HAVE ALREADY BEGUN MANDATORY VACCINATIONS OF CHILDREN--
IT TURNS OUT ALL THE STORIES SEEMED THE SAME BECAUSE I NEVER KNEW THE ENDING.
BUT THIS ONE IS DIFFERENT. I KNOW THAT NOW.
THIS IS THE LAST X-MEN STORY.
WORTHINGTON

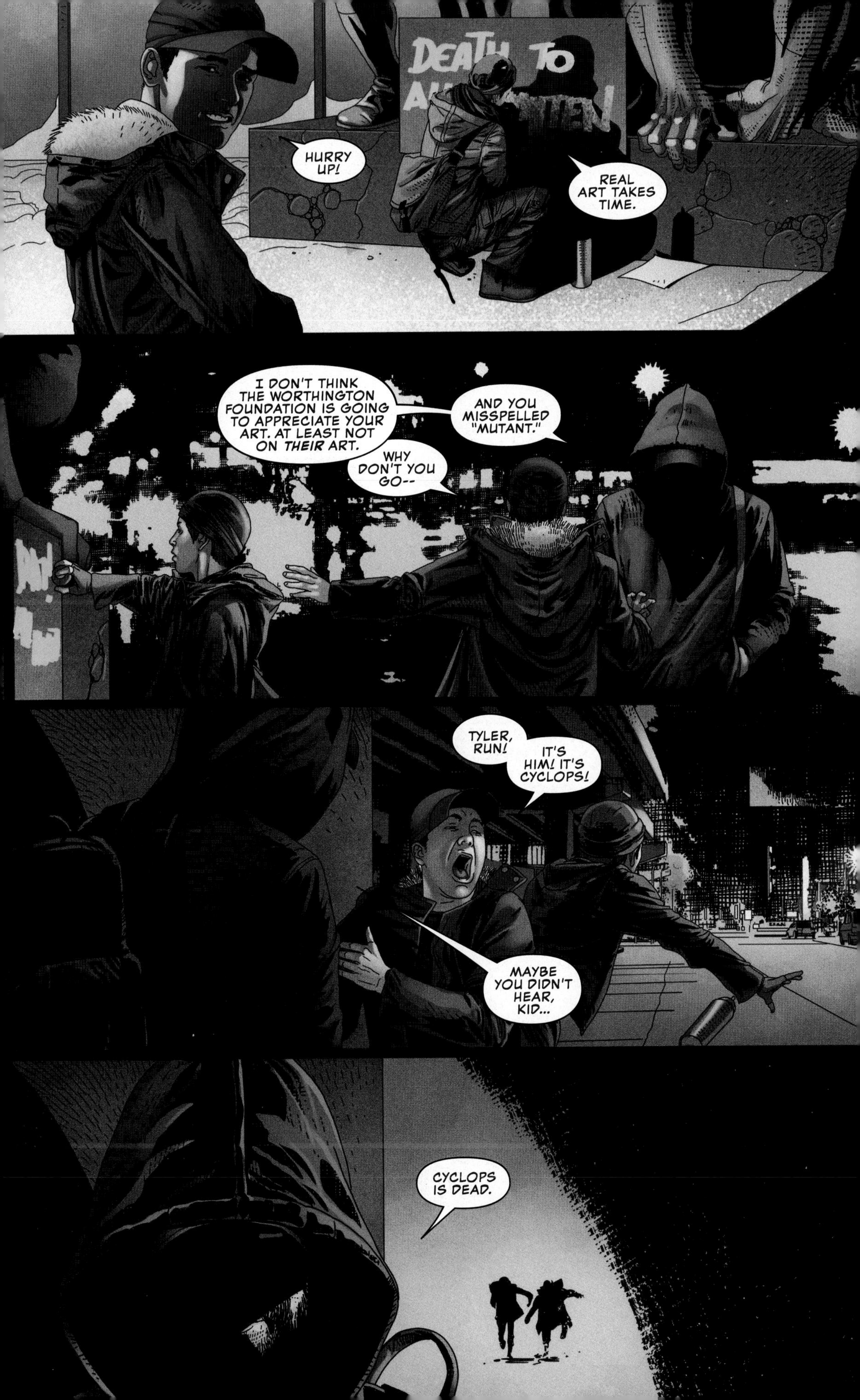
DEATH TO
HURRY UP!
REAL ART TAKES TIME.
I DON'T THINK THE WORTHINGTON FOUNDATION IS GOING TO APPRECIATE YOUR ART. AT LEAST NOT ON *THEIR* ART.
AND YOU MISSPELLED "MUTANT."
WHY DON'T YOU GO--
TYLER, RUN!
IT'S HIM! IT'S CYCLOPS!
MAYBE YOU DIDN'T HEAR, KID...
CYCLOPS IS DEAD.

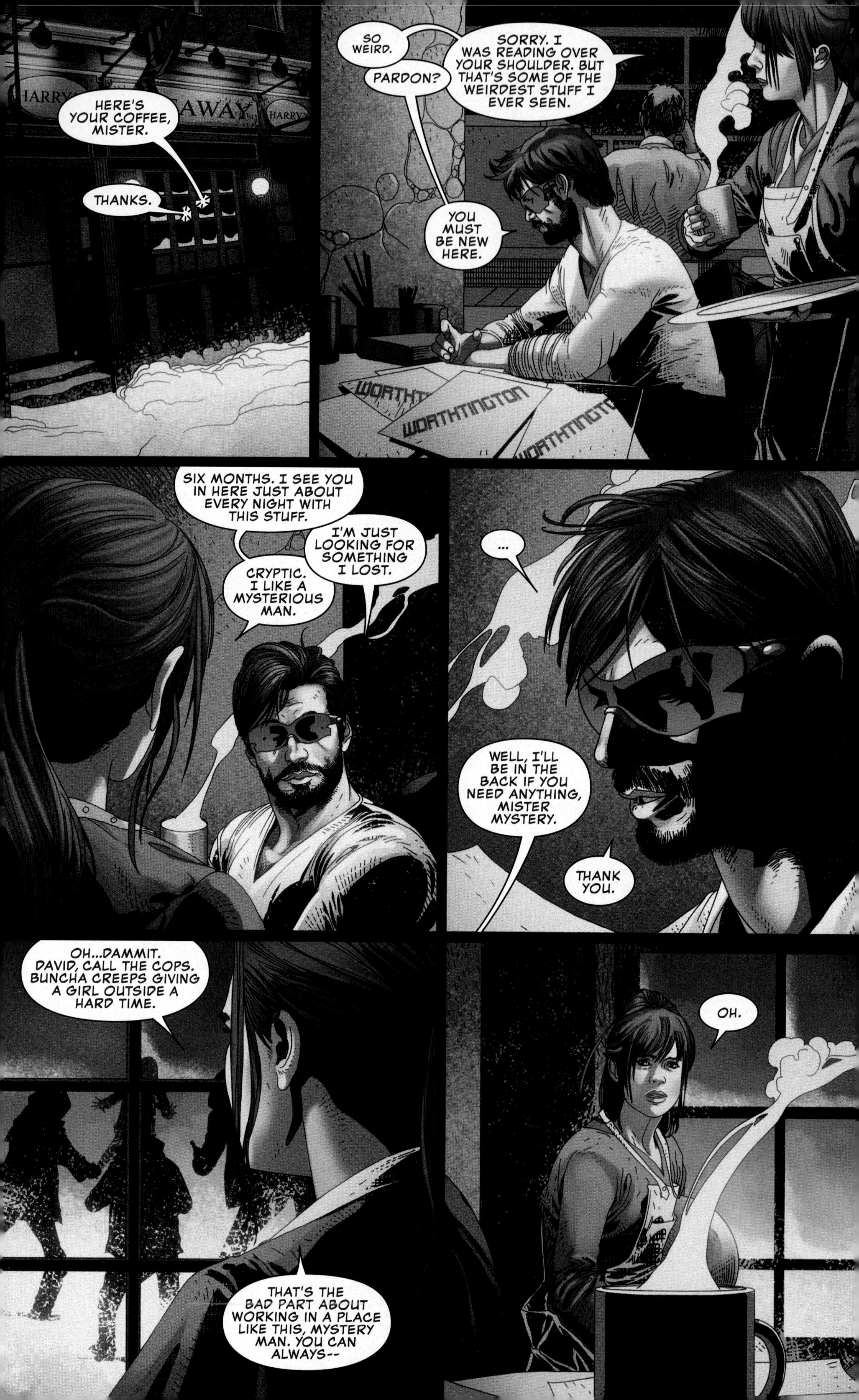
HARRY'S
HIDEAWAY
HERE'S YOUR COFFEE, MISTER.
THANKS.
SO WEIRD.
PARDON?
SORRY. I WAS READING OVER YOUR SHOULDER. BUT THAT'S SOME OF THE WEIRDEST STUFF I EVER SEEN.
YOU MUST BE NEW HERE.
WORTHINGTON
SIX MONTHS. I SEE YOU IN HERE JUST ABOUT EVERY NIGHT WITH THIS STUFF.
I'M JUST LOOKING FOR SOMETHING I LOST.
CRYPTIC. I LIKE A MYSTERIOUS MAN.
...
WELL, I'LL BE IN THE BACK IF YOU NEED ANYTHING, MISTER MYSTERY.
THANK YOU.
OH...DAMMIT. DAVID, CALL THE COPS. BUNCHA CREEPS GIVING A GIRL OUTSIDE A HARD TIME.
THAT'S THE BAD PART ABOUT WORKING IN A PLACE LIKE THIS, MYSTERY MAN. YOU CAN ALWAYS--
OH.

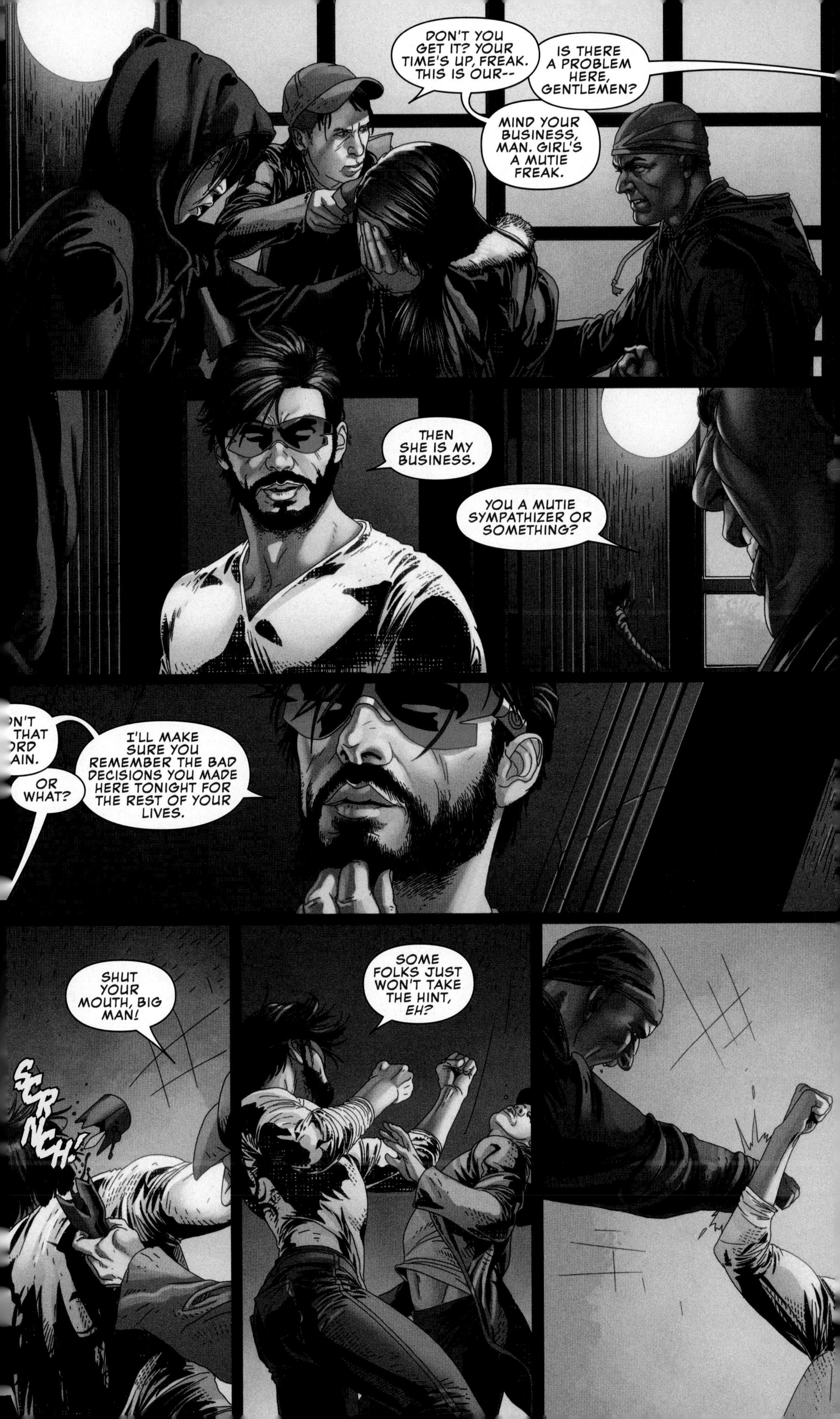
DON'T YOU GET IT? YOUR TIME'S UP, FREAK. THIS IS OUR--
IS THERE A PROBLEM HERE, GENTLEMEN?
MIND YOUR BUSINESS, MAN. GIRL'S A MUTIE FREAK.
THEN SHE IS MY BUSINESS.
YOU A MUTIE SYMPATHIZER OR SOMETHING?
OR WHAT?
I'LL MAKE SURE YOU REMEMBER THE BAD DECISIONS YOU MADE HERE TONIGHT FOR THE REST OF YOUR LIVES.
SHUT YOUR MOUTH, BIG MAN!
SCRNCH!
SOME FOLKS JUST WON'T TAKE THE HINT, EH?

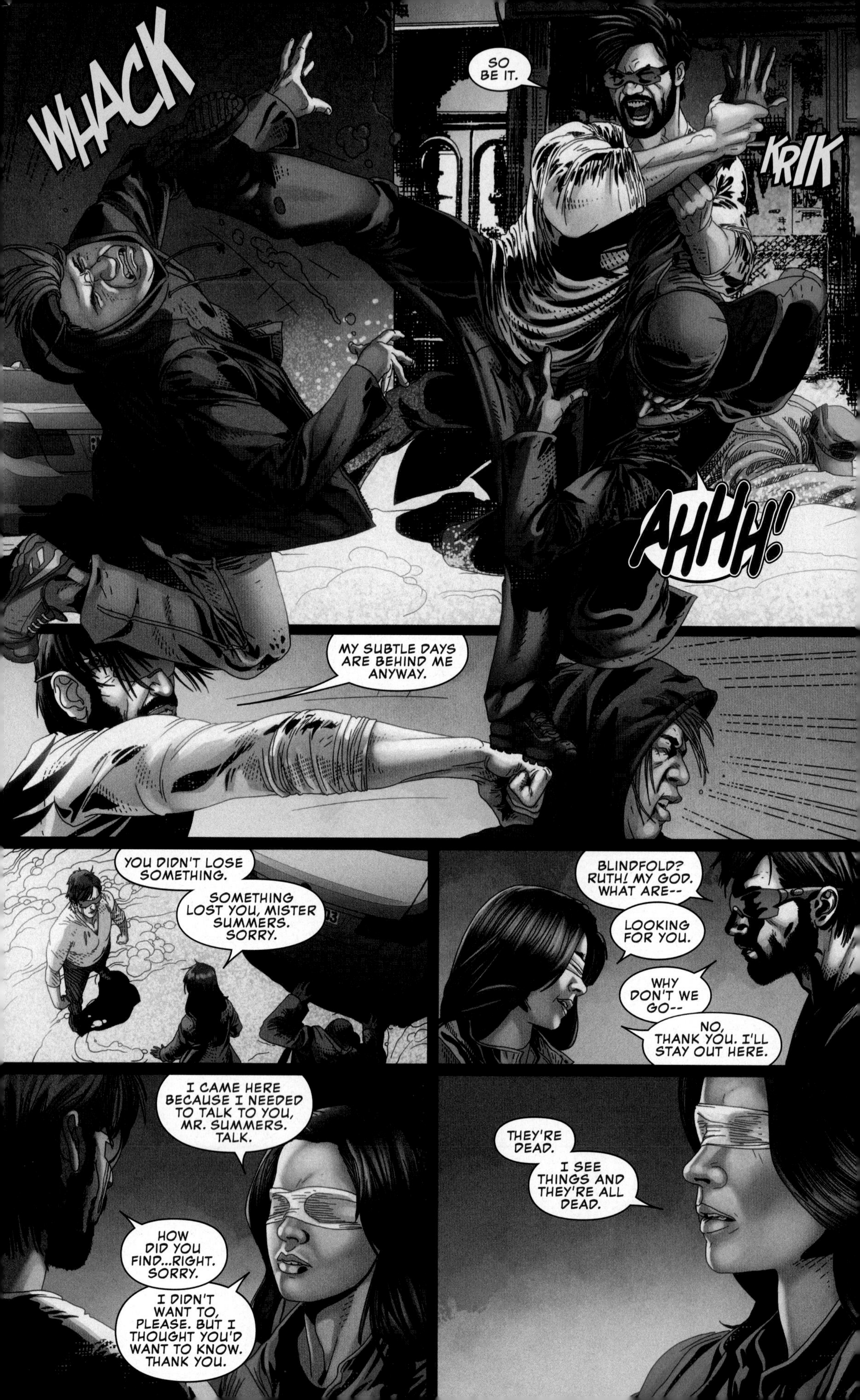
WHACK
SO BE IT.
KRIK
AHHH!
MY SUBTLE DAYS ARE BEHIND ME ANYWAY.
YOU DIDN'T LOSE SOMETHING.
SOMETHING LOST YOU, MISTER SUMMERS. SORRY.
BLINDFOLD? RUTH! MY GOD. WHAT ARE--
LOOKING FOR YOU.
WHY DON'T WE GO--
NO, THANK YOU. I'LL STAY OUT HERE.
I CAME HERE BECAUSE I NEEDED TO TALK TO YOU, MR. SUMMERS. TALK.
HOW DID YOU FIND...RIGHT. SORRY.
I DIDN'T WANT TO, PLEASE. BUT I THOUGHT YOU'D WANT TO KNOW. THANK YOU.
THEY'RE DEAD.
I SEE THINGS AND THEY'RE ALL DEAD.

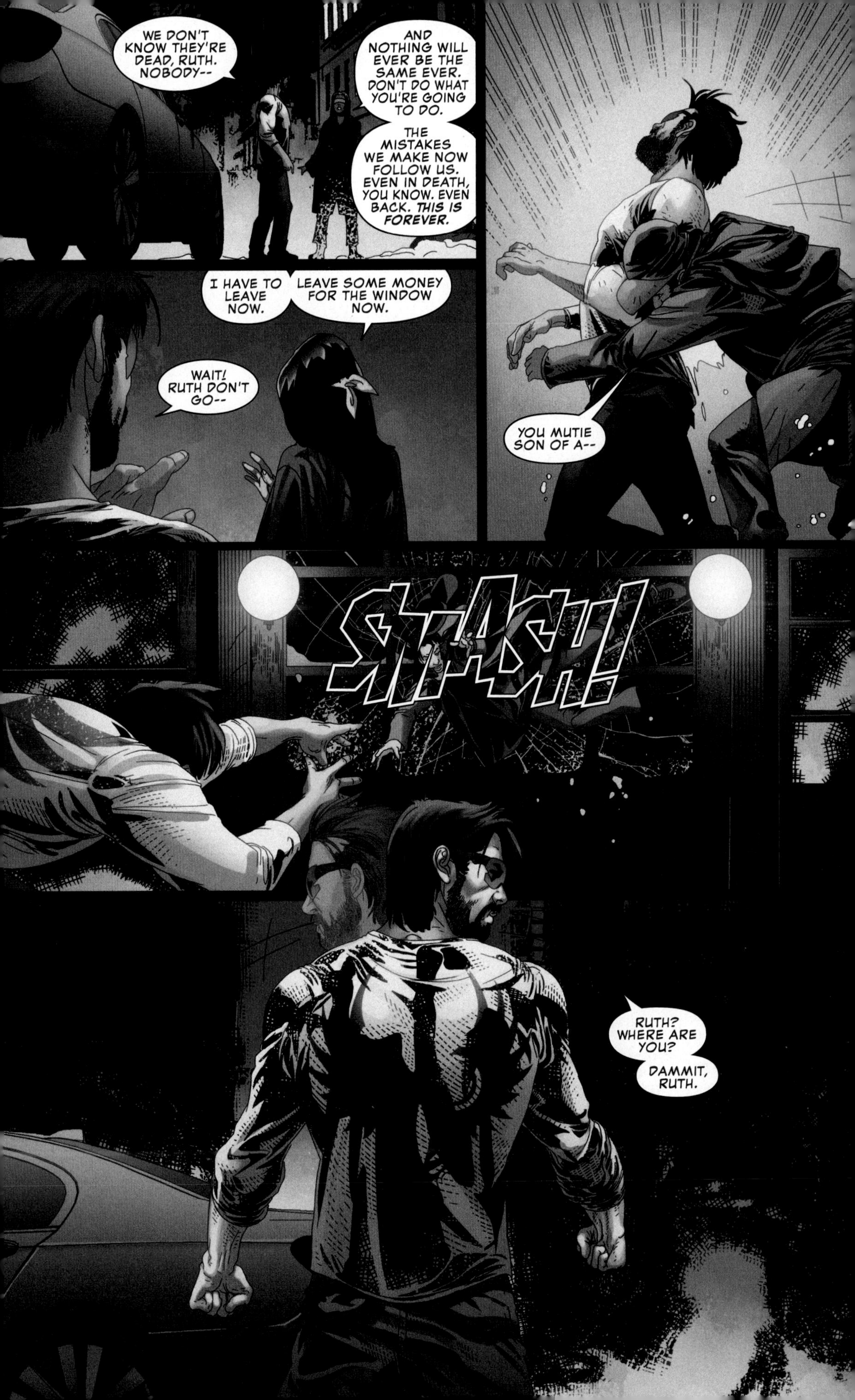
WE DON'T KNOW THEY'RE DEAD, RUTH. NOBODY--
AND NOTHING WILL EVER BE THE SAME EVER. DON'T DO WHAT YOU'RE GOING TO DO.
THE MISTAKES WE MAKE NOW FOLLOW US. EVEN IN DEATH, YOU KNOW. EVEN BACK. *THIS IS FOREVER.*
I HAVE TO LEAVE NOW.
LEAVE SOME MONEY FOR THE WINDOW NOW.
WAIT! RUTH DON'T GO--
YOU MUTIE SON OF A--
SMASH!
RUTH? WHERE ARE YOU?
DAMMIT, RUTH.

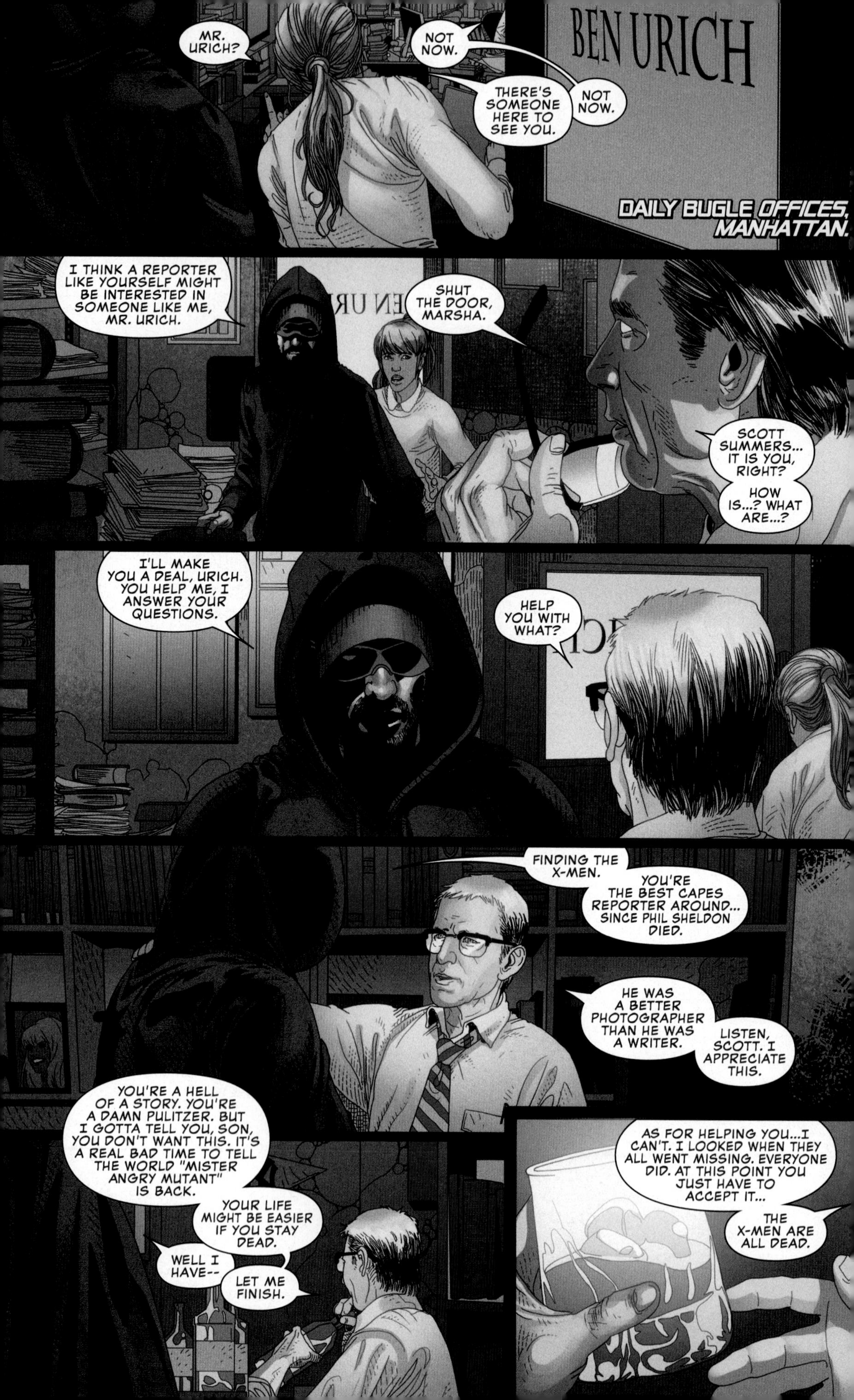
BEN URICH
MR. URICH?
NOT NOW.
THERE'S SOMEONE HERE TO SEE YOU.
NOT NOW.
DAILY BUGLE OFFICES, MANHATTAN.
I THINK A REPORTER LIKE YOURSELF MIGHT BE INTERESTED IN SOMEONE LIKE ME, MR. URICH.
SHUT THE DOOR, MARSHA.
SCOTT SUMMERS... IT IS YOU, RIGHT?
HOW IS...? WHAT ARE...?
I'LL MAKE YOU A DEAL, URICH. YOU HELP ME, I ANSWER YOUR QUESTIONS.
HELP YOU WITH WHAT?
FINDING THE X-MEN.
YOU'RE THE BEST CAPES REPORTER AROUND... SINCE PHIL SHELDON DIED.
HE WAS A BETTER PHOTOGRAPHER THAN HE WAS A WRITER.
LISTEN, SCOTT. I APPRECIATE THIS.
YOU'RE A HELL OF A STORY. YOU'RE A DAMN PULITZER. BUT I GOTTA TELL YOU, SON, YOU DON'T WANT THIS. IT'S A REAL BAD TIME TO TELL THE WORLD "MISTER ANGRY MUTANT" IS BACK.
YOUR LIFE MIGHT BE EASIER IF YOU STAY DEAD.
WELL I HAVE--
LET ME FINISH.
AS FOR HELPING YOU...I CAN'T. I LOOKED WHEN THEY ALL WENT MISSING. EVERYONE DID. AT THIS POINT YOU JUST HAVE TO ACCEPT IT...
THE X-MEN ARE ALL DEAD.

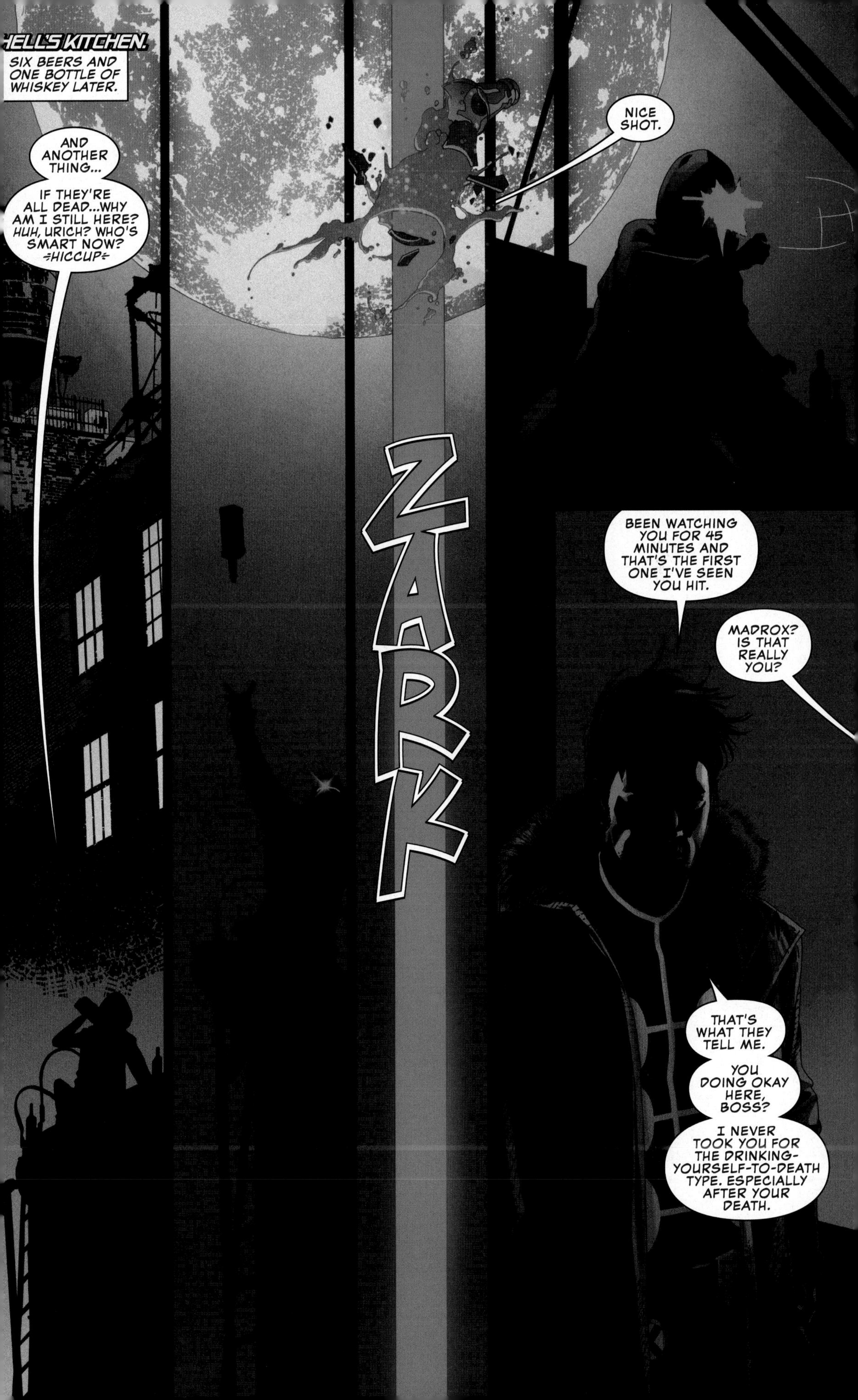
HELL'S KITCHEN.
SIX BEERS AND ONE BOTTLE OF WHISKEY LATER.
AND ANOTHER THING...
IF THEY'RE ALL DEAD...WHY AM I STILL HERE? HUH, URICH? WHO'S SMART NOW? *HICCUP*
NICE SHOT.
ZARK
BEEN WATCHING YOU FOR 45 MINUTES AND THAT'S THE FIRST ONE I'VE SEEN YOU HIT.
MADROX? IS THAT REALLY YOU?
THAT'S WHAT THEY TELL ME.
YOU DOING OKAY HERE, BOSS?
I NEVER TOOK YOU FOR THE DRINKING-YOURSELF-TO-DEATH TYPE. ESPECIALLY AFTER YOUR DEATH.

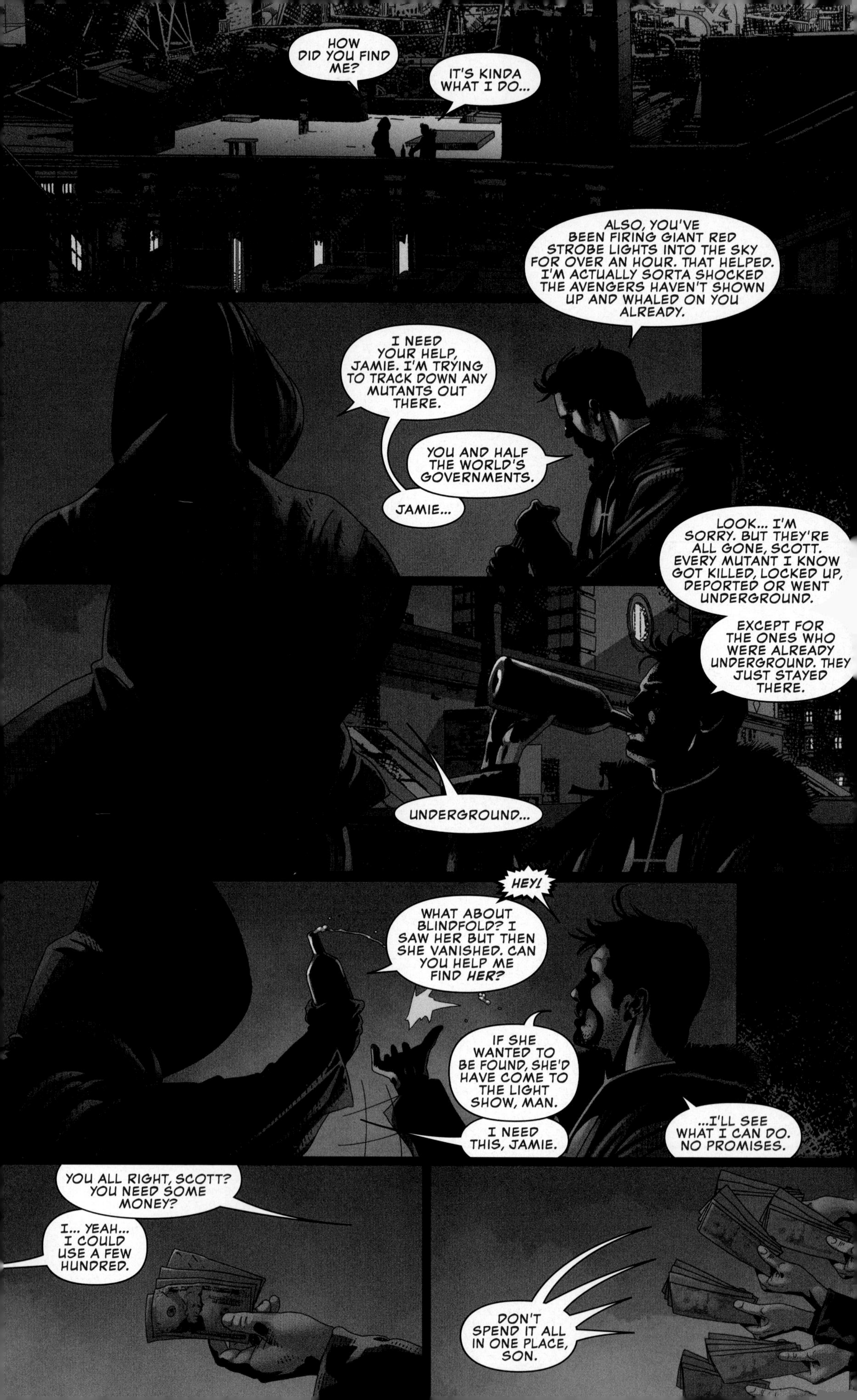
HOW DID YOU FIND ME?
IT'S KINDA WHAT I DO...
ALSO, YOU'VE BEEN FIRING GIANT RED STROBE LIGHTS INTO THE SKY FOR OVER AN HOUR. THAT HELPED. I'M ACTUALLY SORTA SHOCKED THE AVENGERS HAVEN'T SHOWN UP AND WHALED ON YOU ALREADY.
I NEED YOUR HELP, JAMIE. I'M TRYING TO TRACK DOWN ANY MUTANTS OUT THERE.
YOU AND HALF THE WORLD'S GOVERNMENTS.
JAMIE...
LOOK... I'M SORRY. BUT THEY'RE ALL GONE, SCOTT. EVERY MUTANT I KNOW GOT KILLED, LOCKED UP, DEPORTED OR WENT UNDERGROUND.
EXCEPT FOR THE ONES WHO WERE ALREADY UNDERGROUND. THEY JUST STAYED THERE.
UNDERGROUND...
HEY!
WHAT ABOUT BLINDFOLD? I SAW HER BUT THEN SHE VANISHED. CAN YOU HELP ME FIND HER?
IF SHE WANTED TO BE FOUND, SHE'D HAVE COME TO THE LIGHT SHOW, MAN.
I NEED THIS, JAMIE.
...I'LL SEE WHAT I CAN DO. NO PROMISES.
YOU ALL RIGHT, SCOTT? YOU NEED SOME MONEY?
I... YEAH... I COULD USE A FEW HUNDRED.
DON'T SPEND IT ALL IN ONE PLACE, SON.

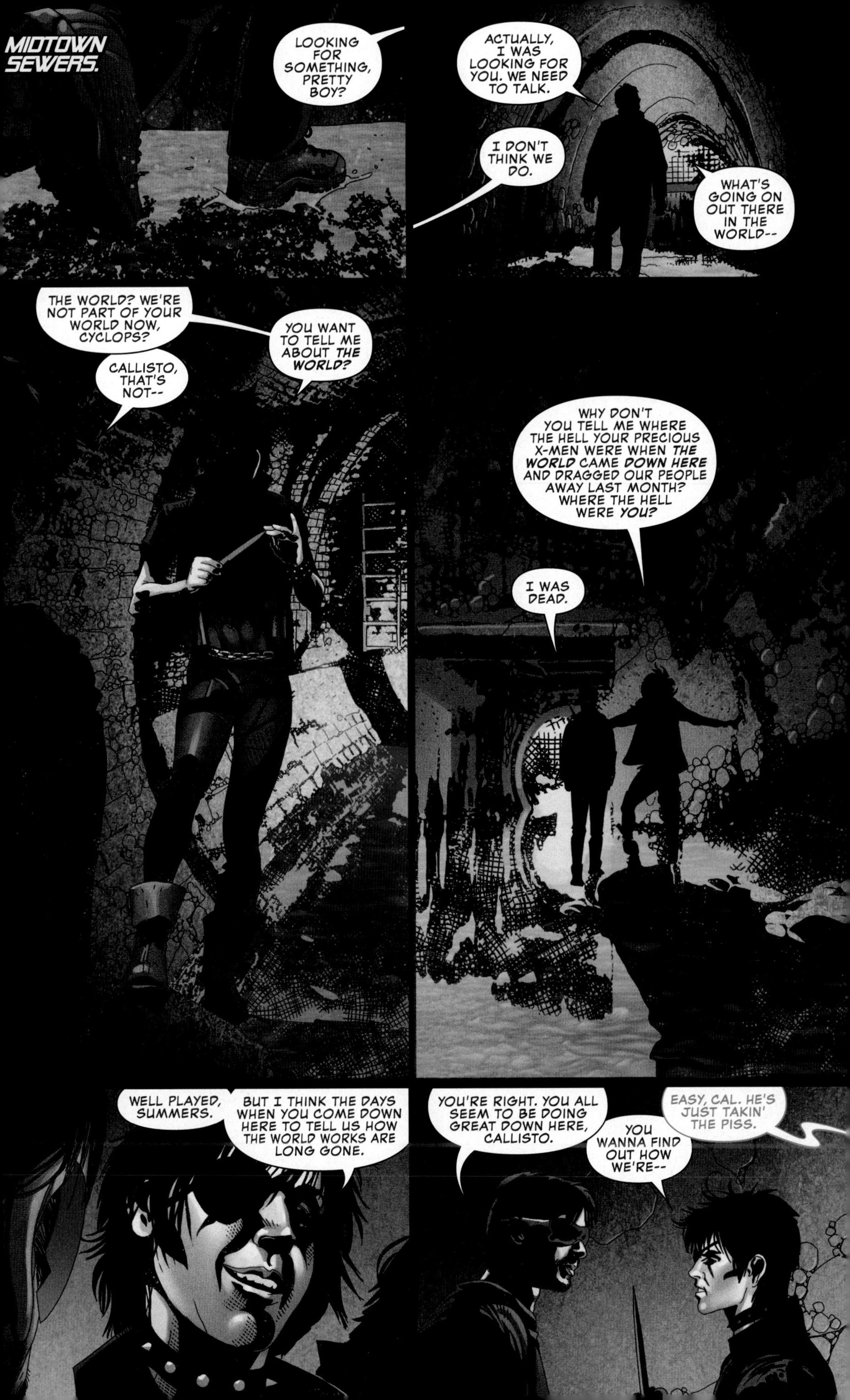
MIDTOWN SEWERS.
LOOKING FOR SOMETHING, PRETTY BOY?
ACTUALLY, I WAS LOOKING FOR YOU. WE NEED TO TALK.
I DON'T THINK WE DO.
WHAT'S GOING ON OUT THERE IN THE WORLD--
THE WORLD? WE'RE NOT PART OF YOUR WORLD NOW, CYCLOPS?
YOU WANT TO TELL ME ABOUT THE WORLD?
CALLISTO, THAT'S NOT--
WHY DON'T YOU TELL ME WHERE THE HELL YOUR PRECIOUS X-MEN WERE WHEN THE WORLD CAME DOWN HERE AND DRAGGED OUR PEOPLE AWAY LAST MONTH? WHERE THE HELL WERE YOU?
I WAS DEAD.
WELL PLAYED, SUMMERS.
BUT I THINK THE DAYS WHEN YOU COME DOWN HERE TO TELL US HOW THE WORLD WORKS ARE LONG GONE.
YOU'RE RIGHT. YOU ALL SEEM TO BE DOING GREAT DOWN HERE, CALLISTO.
YOU WANNA FIND OUT HOW WE'RE--
EASY, CAL. HE'S JUST TAKIN' THE PISS.

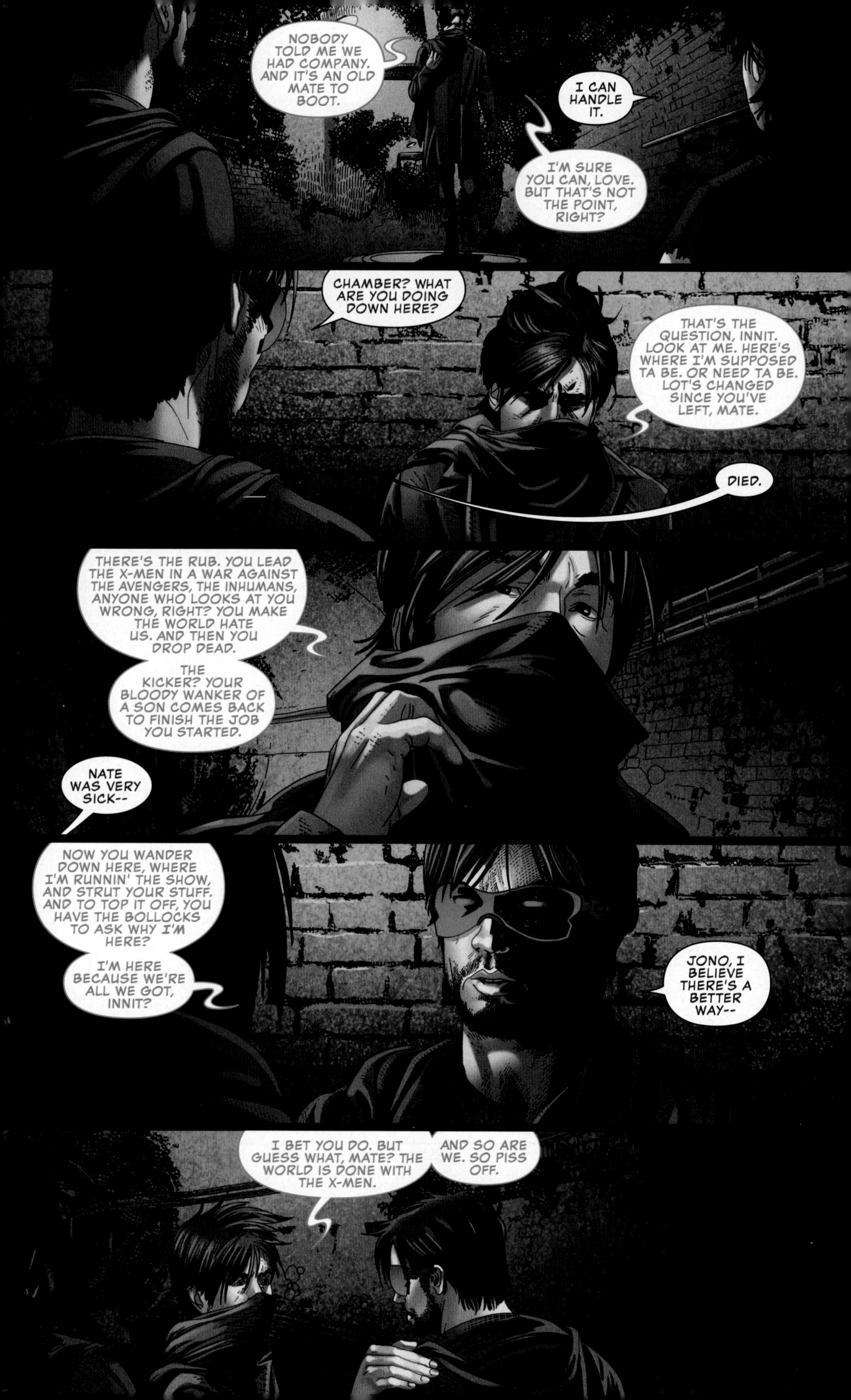
NOBODY TOLD ME WE HAD COMPANY. AND IT'S AN OLD MATE TO BOOT.
I CAN HANDLE IT.
I'M SURE YOU CAN, LOVE. BUT THAT'S NOT THE POINT, RIGHT?
CHAMBER? WHAT ARE YOU DOING DOWN HERE?
THAT'S THE QUESTION, INNIT. LOOK AT ME. HERE'S WHERE I'M SUPPOSED TA BE. OR NEED TA BE. LOT'S CHANGED SINCE YOU'VE LEFT, MATE.
DIED.
THERE'S THE RUB. YOU LEAD THE X-MEN IN A WAR AGAINST THE AVENGERS, THE INHUMANS, ANYONE WHO LOOKS AT YOU WRONG, RIGHT? YOU MAKE THE WORLD HATE US. AND THEN YOU DROP DEAD.
THE KICKER? YOUR BLOODY WANKER OF A SON COMES BACK TO FINISH THE JOB YOU STARTED.
NATE WAS VERY SICK--
NOW YOU WANDER DOWN HERE, WHERE I'M RUNNIN' THE SHOW, AND STRUT YOUR STUFF. AND TO TOP IT OFF, YOU HAVE THE BOLLOCKS TO ASK WHY *I'M* HERE?
I'M HERE BECAUSE WE'RE ALL WE GOT, INNIT?
JONO, I BELIEVE THERE'S A BETTER WAY--
I BET YOU DO. BUT GUESS WHAT, MATE? THE WORLD IS DONE WITH THE X-MEN.
AND SO ARE WE. SO PISS OFF.

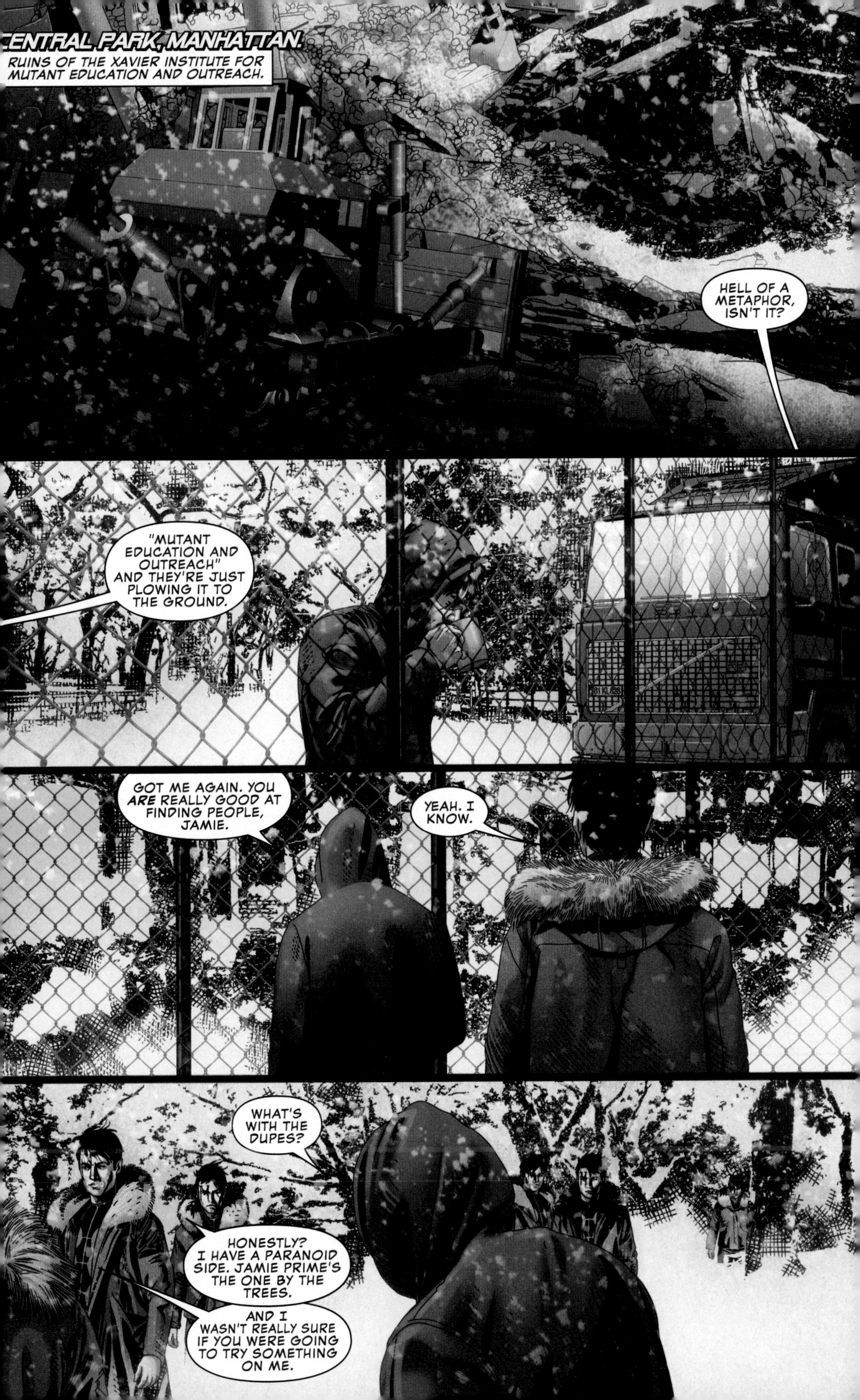
CENTRAL PARK, MANHATTAN.
RUINS OF THE XAVIER INSTITUTE FOR MUTANT EDUCATION AND OUTREACH.
HELL OF A METAPHOR, ISN'T IT?
"MUTANT EDUCATION AND OUTREACH" AND THEY'RE JUST PLOWING IT TO THE GROUND.
GOT ME AGAIN. YOU *ARE* REALLY GOOD AT FINDING PEOPLE, JAMIE.
YEAH. I KNOW.
WHAT'S WITH THE DUPES?
HONESTLY? I HAVE A PARANOID SIDE. JAMIE PRIME'S THE ONE BY THE TREES.
AND I WASN'T REALLY SURE IF YOU WERE GOING TO TRY SOMETHING ON ME.

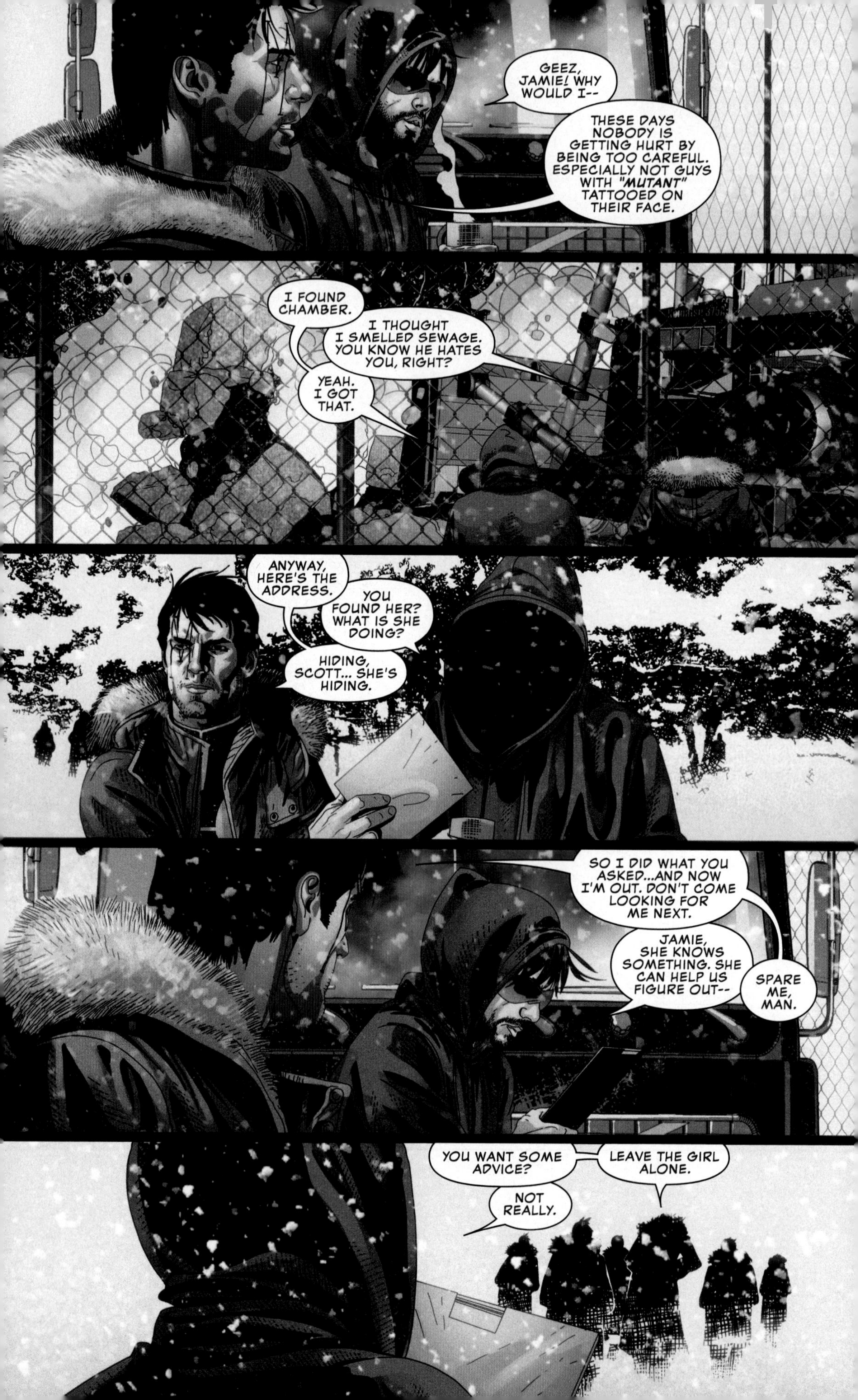
GEEZ, JAMIE! WHY WOULD I--
THESE DAYS NOBODY IS GETTING HURT BY BEING TOO CAREFUL. ESPECIALLY NOT GUYS WITH "MUTANT" TATTOOED ON THEIR FACE.
I FOUND CHAMBER.
I THOUGHT I SMELLED SEWAGE. YOU KNOW HE HATES YOU, RIGHT?
YEAH. I GOT THAT.
ANYWAY, HERE'S THE ADDRESS.
YOU FOUND HER? WHAT IS SHE DOING?
HIDING, SCOTT... SHE'S HIDING.
SO I DID WHAT YOU ASKED...AND NOW I'M OUT. DON'T COME LOOKING FOR ME NEXT.
JAMIE, SHE KNOWS SOMETHING. SHE CAN HELP US FIGURE OUT--
SPARE ME, MAN.
YOU WANT SOME ADVICE?
LEAVE THE GIRL ALONE.
NOT REALLY.

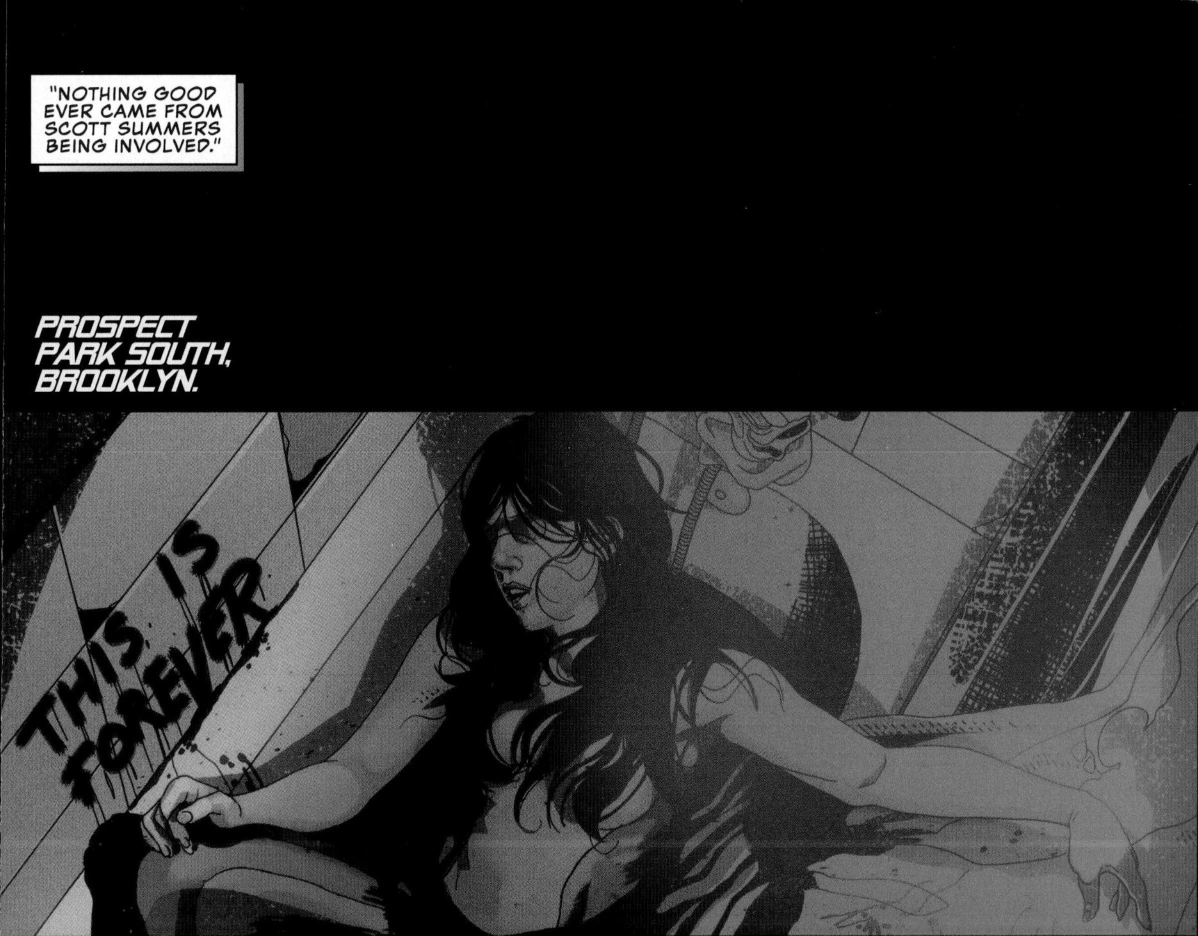
"NOTHING GOOD EVER CAME FROM SCOTT SUMMERS BEING INVOLVED."
PROSPECT PARK SOUTH, BROOKLYN.
THIS IS FOREVER

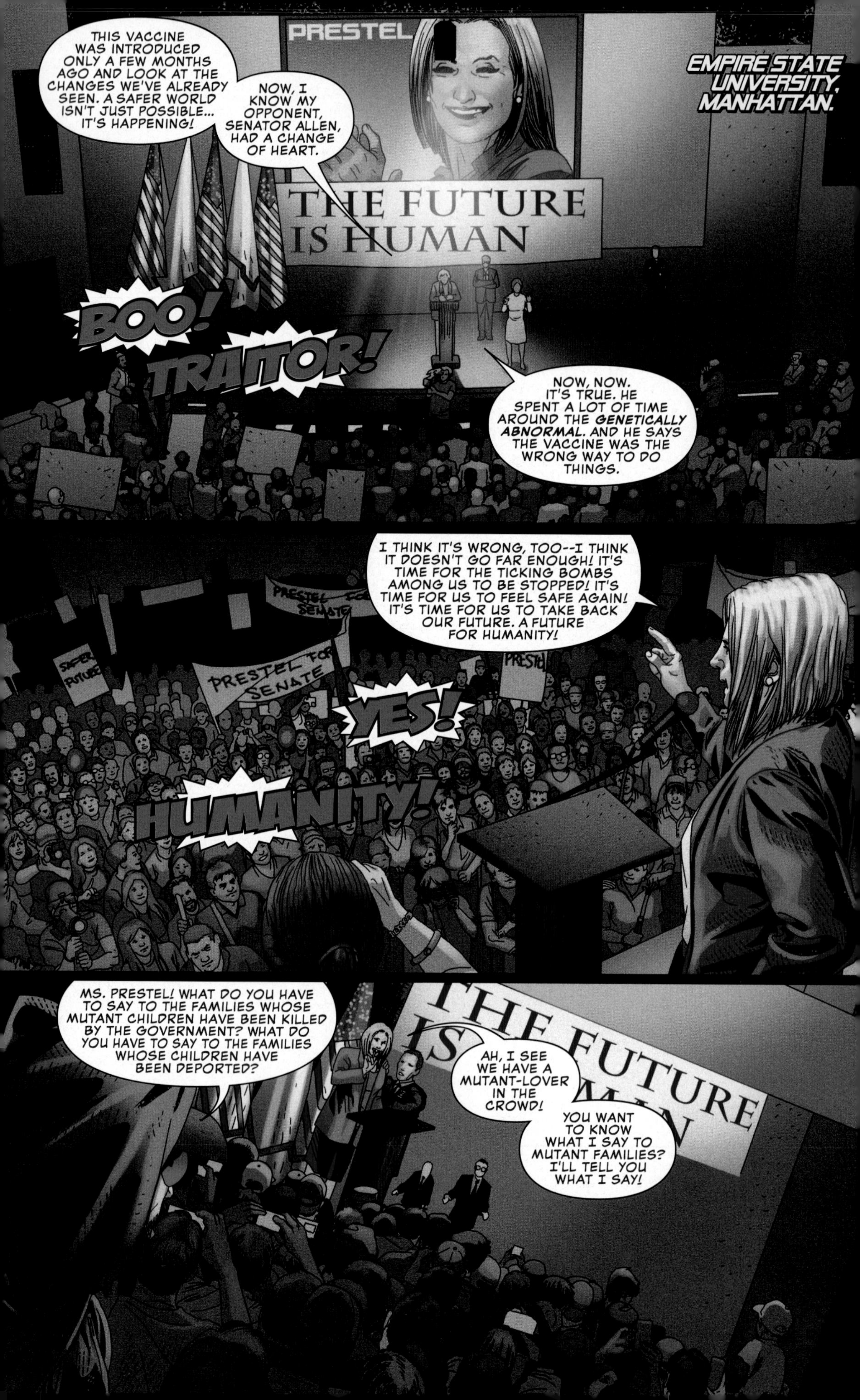
EMPIRE STATE UNIVERSITY, MANHATTAN.
PRESTEL
THE FUTURE IS HUMAN
THIS VACCINE WAS INTRODUCED ONLY A FEW MONTHS AGO AND LOOK AT THE CHANGES WE'VE ALREADY SEEN. A SAFER WORLD ISN'T JUST POSSIBLE... IT'S HAPPENING!
NOW, I KNOW MY OPPONENT, SENATOR ALLEN, HAD A CHANGE OF HEART.
BOO!
TRAITOR!
NOW, NOW. IT'S TRUE. HE SPENT A LOT OF TIME AROUND THE GENETICALLY ABNORMAL. AND HE SAYS THE VACCINE WAS THE WRONG WAY TO DO THINGS.
I THINK IT'S WRONG, TOO--I THINK IT DOESN'T GO FAR ENOUGH! IT'S TIME FOR THE TICKING BOMBS AMONG US TO BE STOPPED! IT'S TIME FOR US TO FEEL SAFE AGAIN! IT'S TIME FOR US TO TAKE BACK OUR FUTURE. A FUTURE FOR HUMANITY!
PRESTEL FOR SENATE
SAFER FUTURE
PRESTEL FOR SENATE
YES!
HUMANITY!
MS. PRESTEL! WHAT DO YOU HAVE TO SAY TO THE FAMILIES WHOSE MUTANT CHILDREN HAVE BEEN KILLED BY THE GOVERNMENT? WHAT DO YOU HAVE TO SAY TO THE FAMILIES WHOSE CHILDREN HAVE BEEN DEPORTED?
AH, I SEE WE HAVE A MUTANT-LOVER IN THE CROWD!
YOU WANT TO KNOW WHAT I SAY TO MUTANT FAMILIES? I'LL TELL YOU WHAT I SAY!

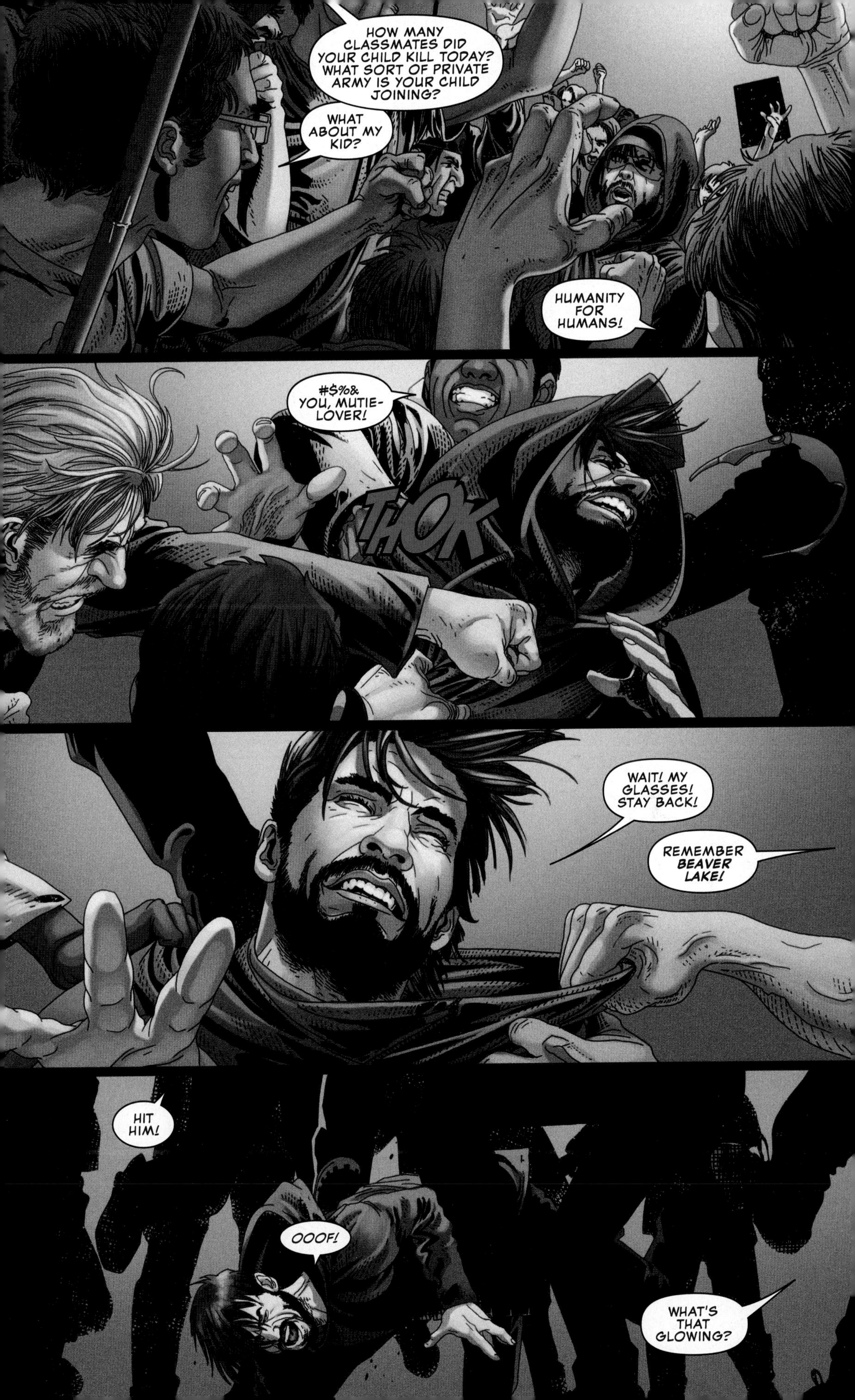
HOW MANY CLASSMATES DID YOUR CHILD KILL TODAY? WHAT SORT OF PRIVATE ARMY IS YOUR CHILD JOINING?
WHAT ABOUT MY KID?
HUMANITY FOR HUMANS!
#$%& YOU, MUTIE-LOVER!
THOK
WAIT! MY GLASSES! STAY BACK!
REMEMBER BEAVER LAKE!
HIT HIM!
OOOF!
WHAT'S THAT GLOWING?

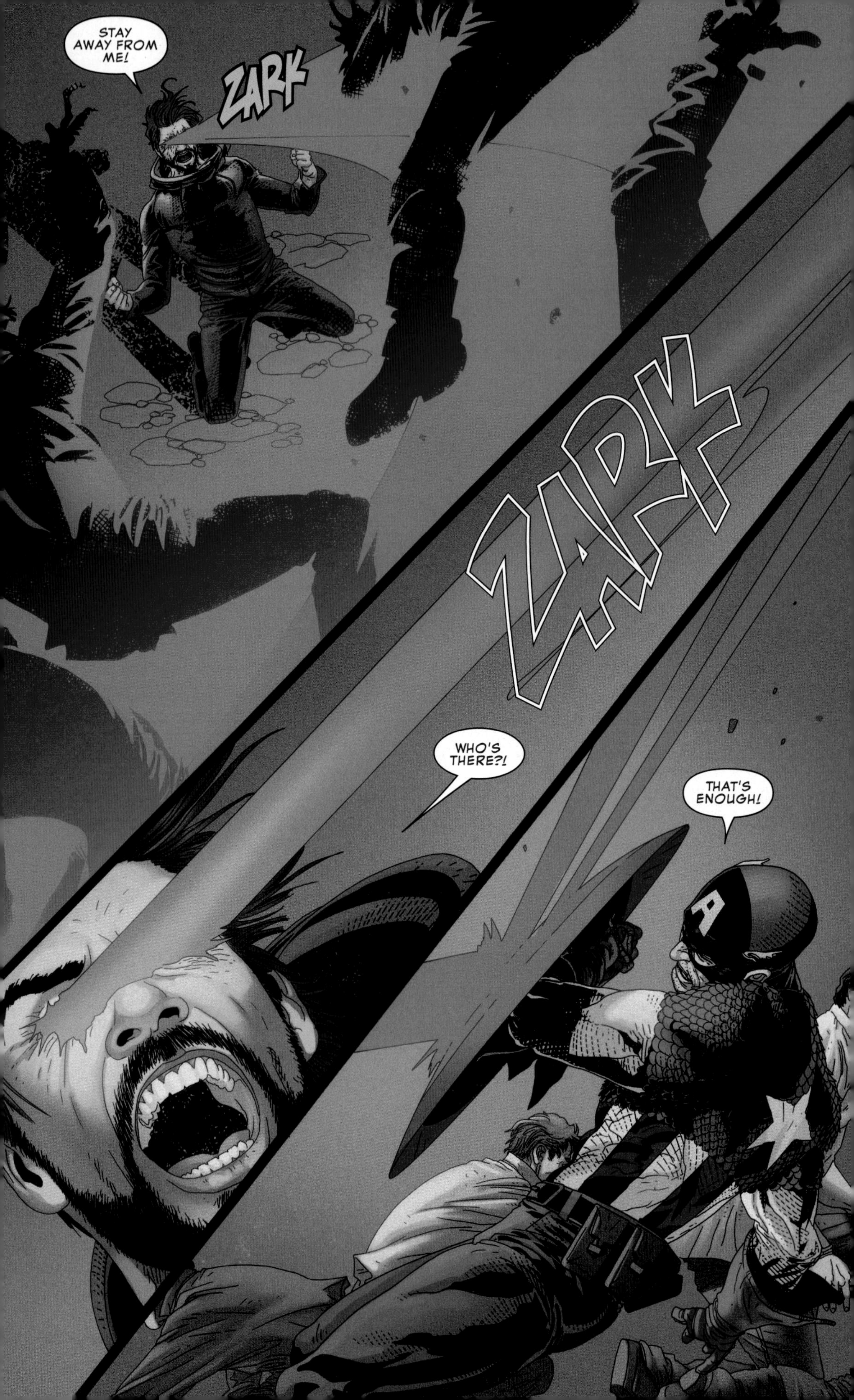
STAY AWAY FROM ME!
ZARK
ZARK
WHO'S THERE?!
THAT'S ENOUGH!

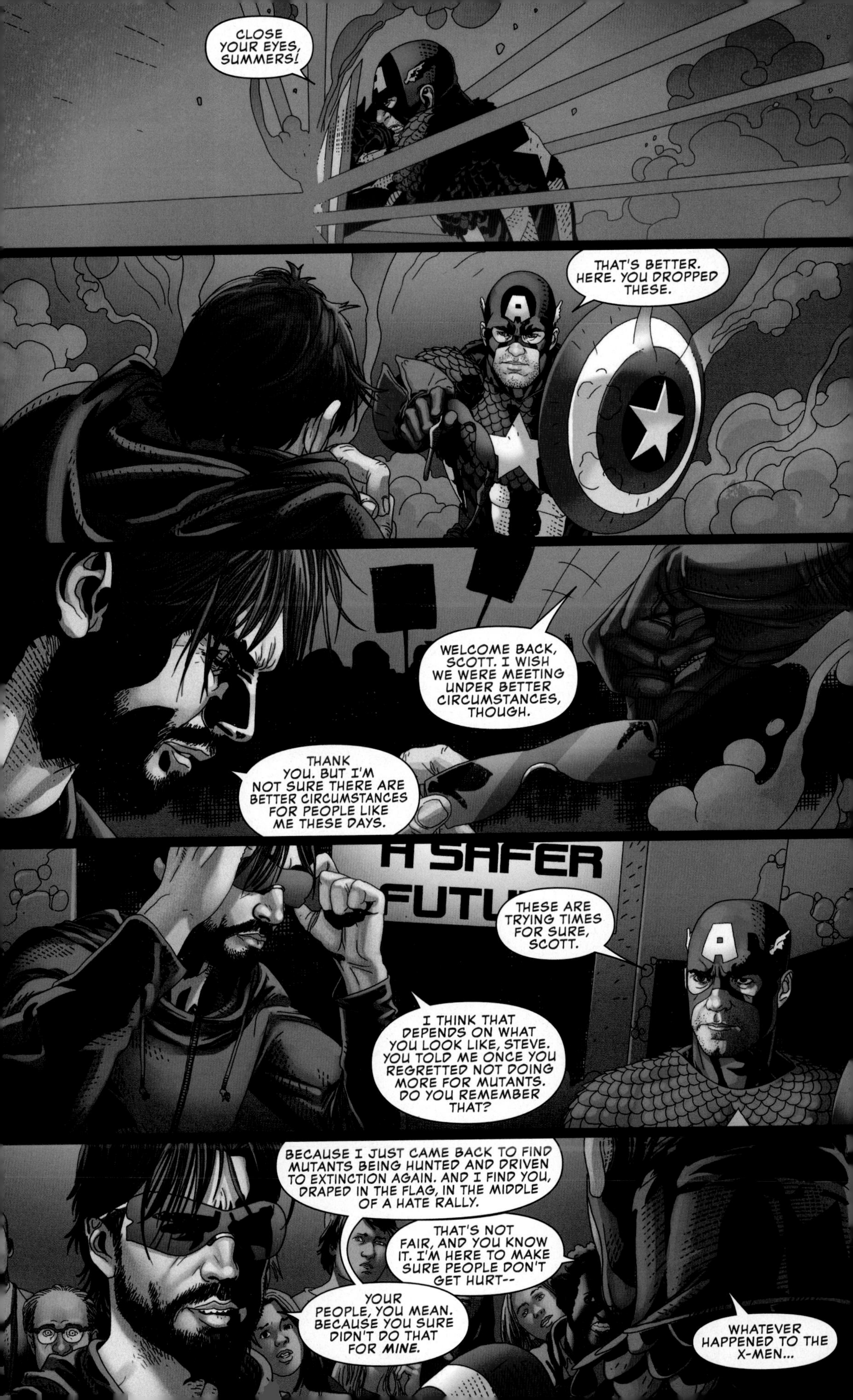
CLOSE YOUR EYES, SUMMERS!
THAT'S BETTER. HERE. YOU DROPPED THESE.
WELCOME BACK, SCOTT. I WISH WE WERE MEETING UNDER BETTER CIRCUMSTANCES, THOUGH.
THANK YOU. BUT I'M NOT SURE THERE ARE BETTER CIRCUMSTANCES FOR PEOPLE LIKE ME THESE DAYS.
A SAFER FUTU
THESE ARE TRYING TIMES FOR SURE, SCOTT.
I THINK THAT DEPENDS ON WHAT YOU LOOK LIKE, STEVE. YOU TOLD ME ONCE YOU REGRETTED NOT DOING MORE FOR MUTANTS. DO YOU REMEMBER THAT?
BECAUSE I JUST CAME BACK TO FIND MUTANTS BEING HUNTED AND DRIVEN TO EXTINCTION AGAIN. AND I FIND YOU, DRAPED IN THE FLAG, IN THE MIDDLE OF A HATE RALLY.
THAT'S NOT FAIR, AND YOU KNOW IT. I'M HERE TO MAKE SURE PEOPLE DON'T GET HURT--
YOUR PEOPLE, YOU MEAN. BECAUSE YOU SURE DIDN'T DO THAT FOR MINE.
WHATEVER HAPPENED TO THE X-MEN...

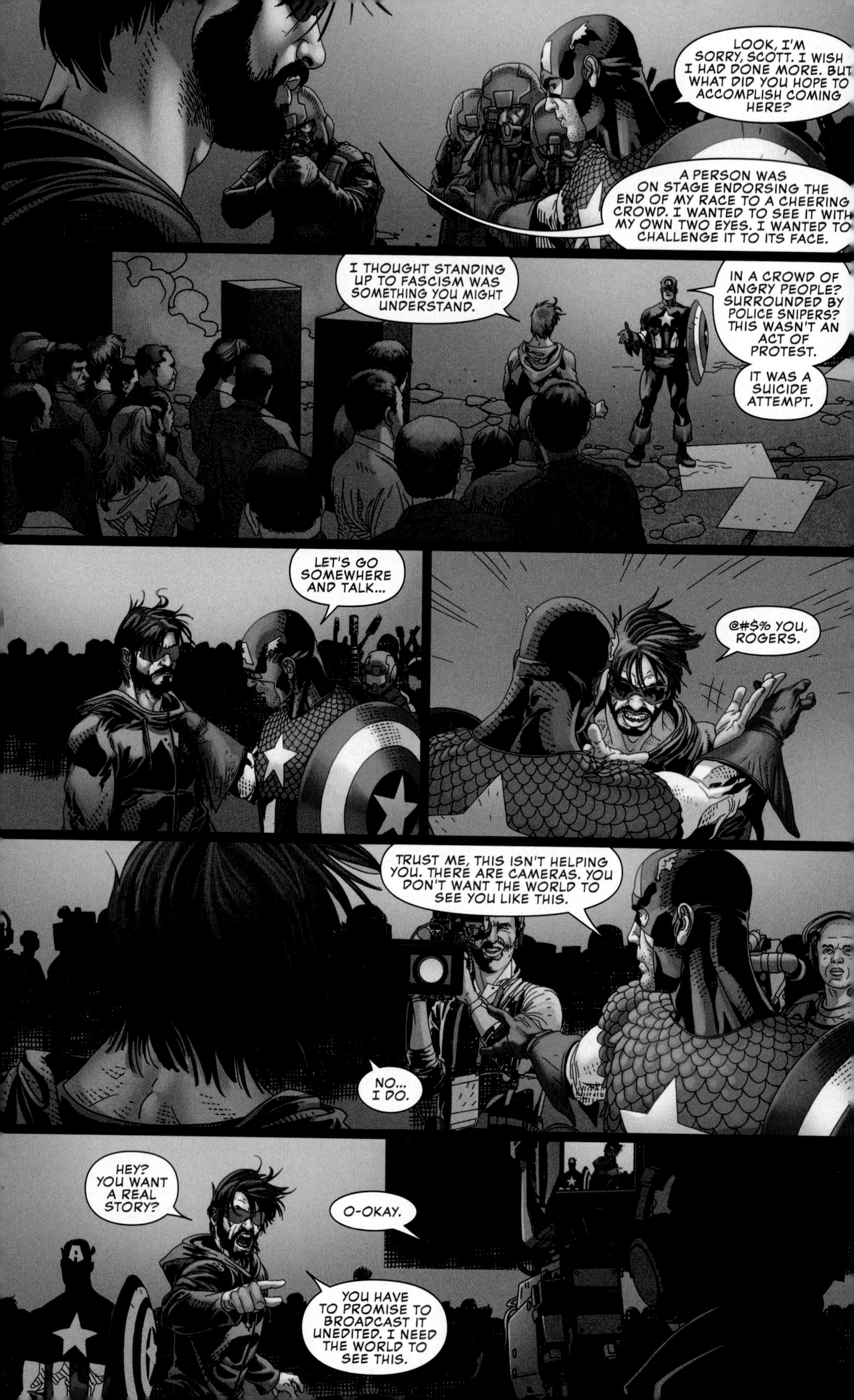
LOOK, I'M SORRY, SCOTT. I WISH I HAD DONE MORE. BUT WHAT DID YOU HOPE TO ACCOMPLISH COMING HERE?
A PERSON WAS ON STAGE ENDORSING THE END OF MY RACE TO A CHEERING CROWD. I WANTED TO SEE IT WITH MY OWN TWO EYES. I WANTED TO CHALLENGE IT TO ITS FACE.
I THOUGHT STANDING UP TO FASCISM WAS SOMETHING YOU MIGHT UNDERSTAND.
IN A CROWD OF ANGRY PEOPLE? SURROUNDED BY POLICE SNIPERS? THIS WASN'T AN ACT OF PROTEST.
IT WAS A SUICIDE ATTEMPT.
LET'S GO SOMEWHERE AND TALK...
@#$% YOU, ROGERS.
TRUST ME, THIS ISN'T HELPING YOU. THERE ARE CAMERAS. YOU DON'T WANT THE WORLD TO SEE YOU LIKE THIS.
NO... I DO.
HEY? YOU WANT A REAL STORY?
O-OKAY.
YOU HAVE TO PROMISE TO BROADCAST IT UNEDITED. I NEED THE WORLD TO SEE THIS.

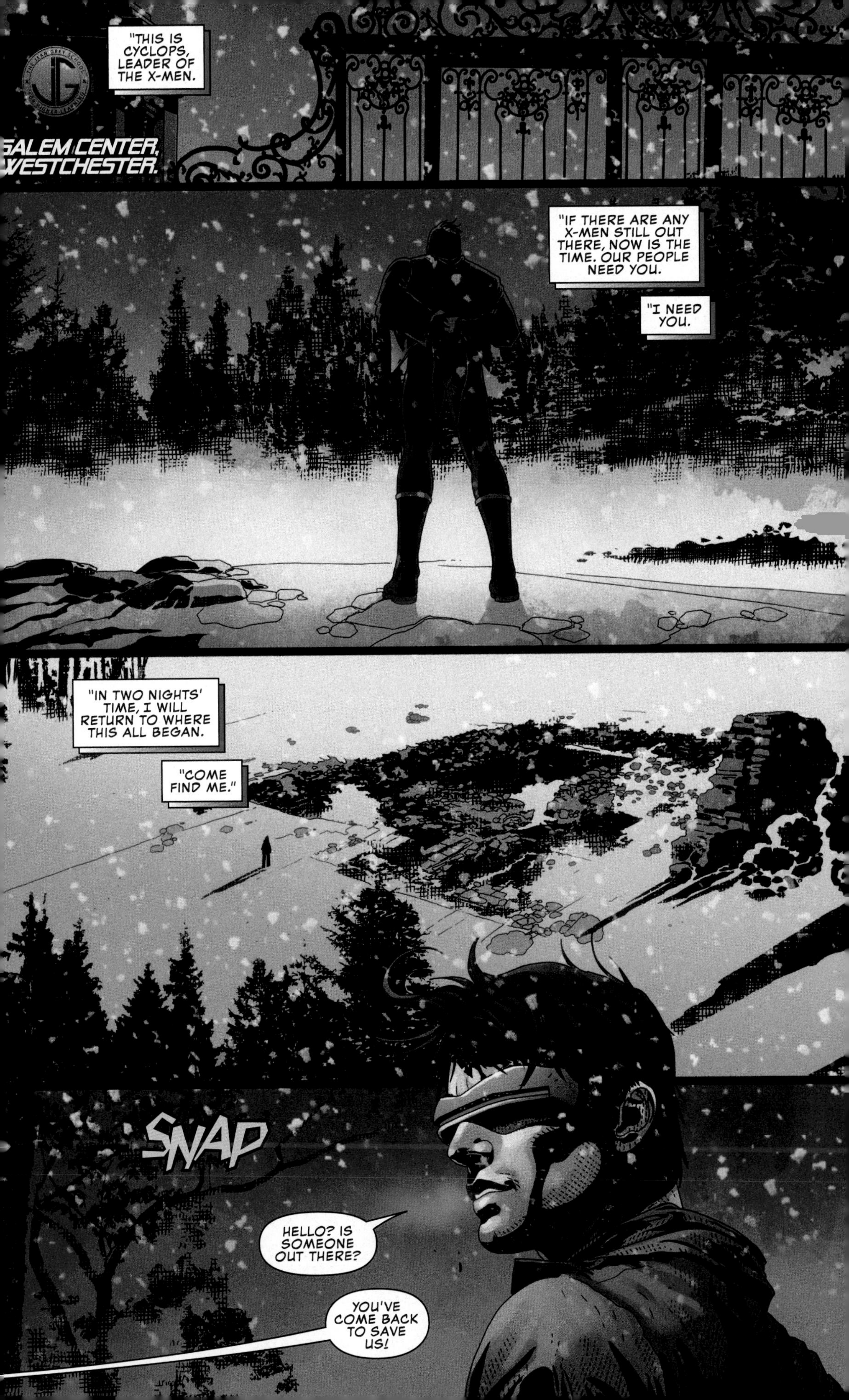
"THIS IS CYCLOPS, LEADER OF THE X-MEN.
SALEM CENTER, WESTCHESTER.
"IF THERE ARE ANY X-MEN STILL OUT THERE, NOW IS THE TIME. OUR PEOPLE NEED YOU.
"I NEED YOU.
"IN TWO NIGHTS' TIME, I WILL RETURN TO WHERE THIS ALL BEGAN.
"COME FIND ME."
SNAP
HELLO? IS SOMEONE OUT THERE?
YOU'VE COME BACK TO SAVE US!

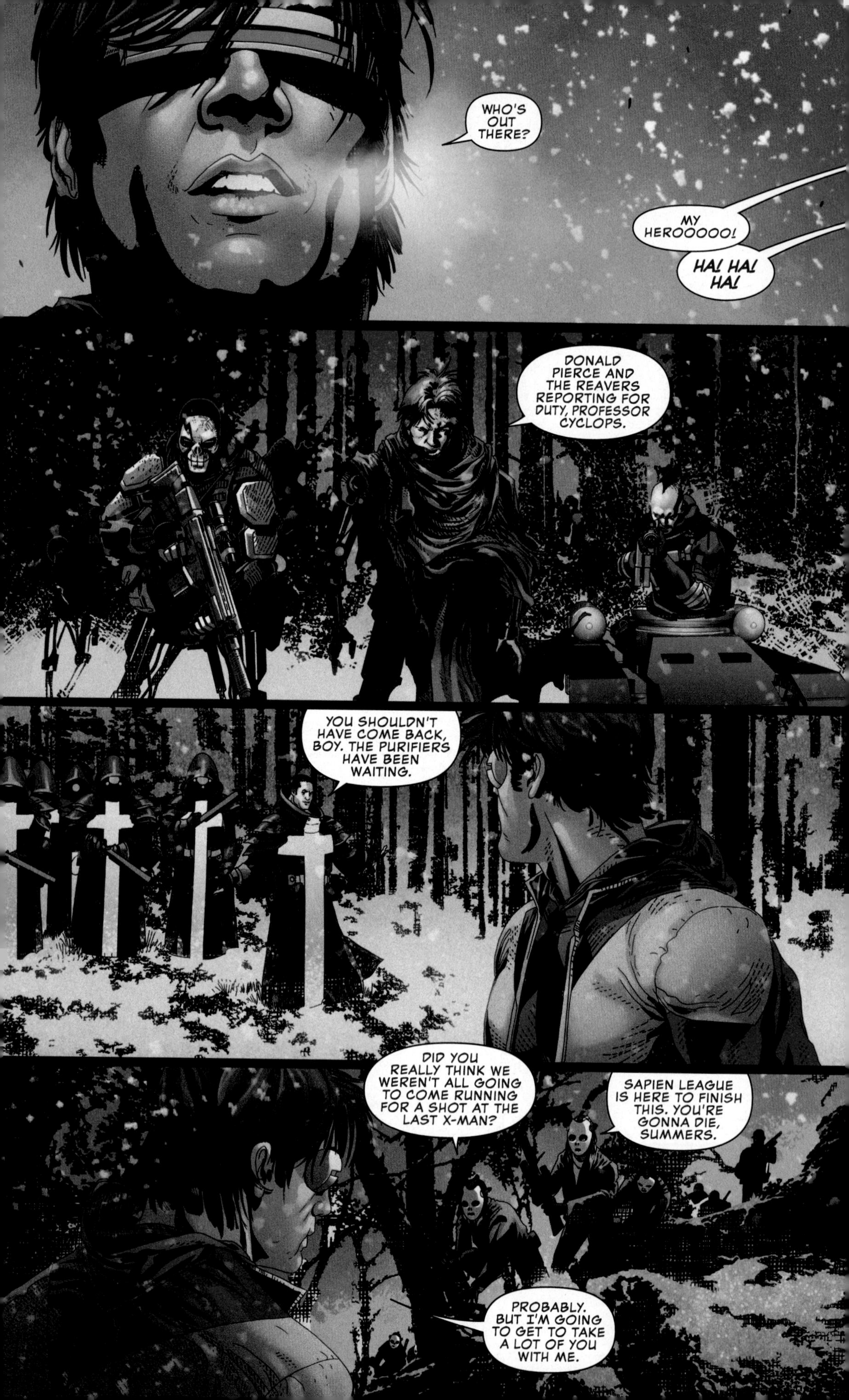
WHO'S OUT THERE?
MY HEROOOOOO!
HA! HA! HA!
DONALD PIERCE AND THE REAVERS REPORTING FOR DUTY, PROFESSOR CYCLOPS.
YOU SHOULDN'T HAVE COME BACK, BOY. THE PURIFIERS HAVE BEEN WAITING.
DID YOU REALLY THINK WE WEREN'T ALL GOING TO COME RUNNING FOR A SHOT AT THE LAST X-MAN?
SAPIEN LEAGUE IS HERE TO FINISH THIS. YOU'RE GONNA DIE, SUMMERS.
PROBABLY. BUT I'M GOING TO GET TO TAKE A LOT OF YOU WITH ME.

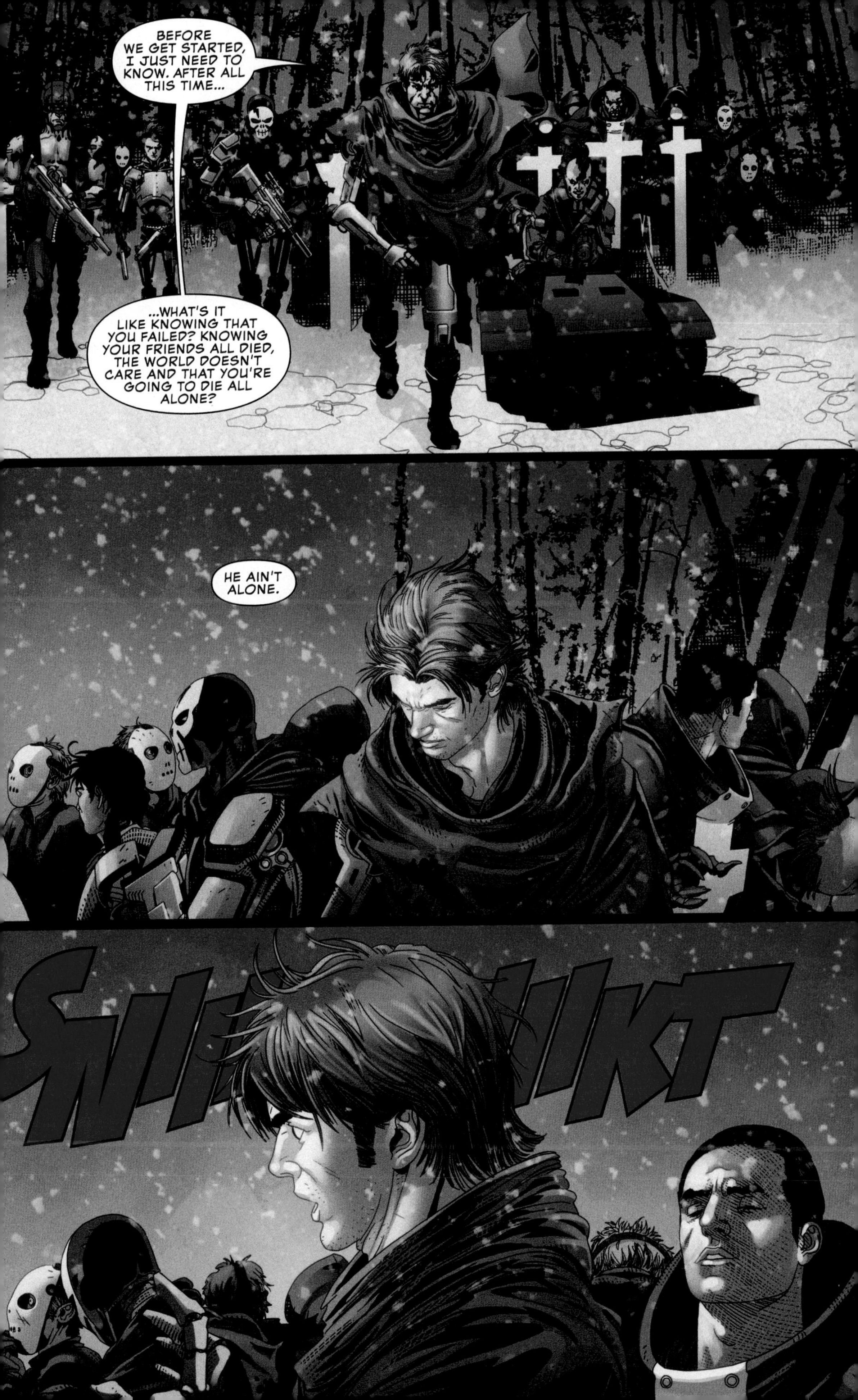
BEFORE WE GET STARTED, I JUST NEED TO KNOW. AFTER ALL THIS TIME...
...WHAT'S IT LIKE KNOWING THAT YOU FAILED? KNOWING YOUR FRIENDS ALL DIED, THE WORLD DOESN'T CARE AND THAT YOU'RE GOING TO DIE ALL ALONE?
HE AIN'T ALONE.

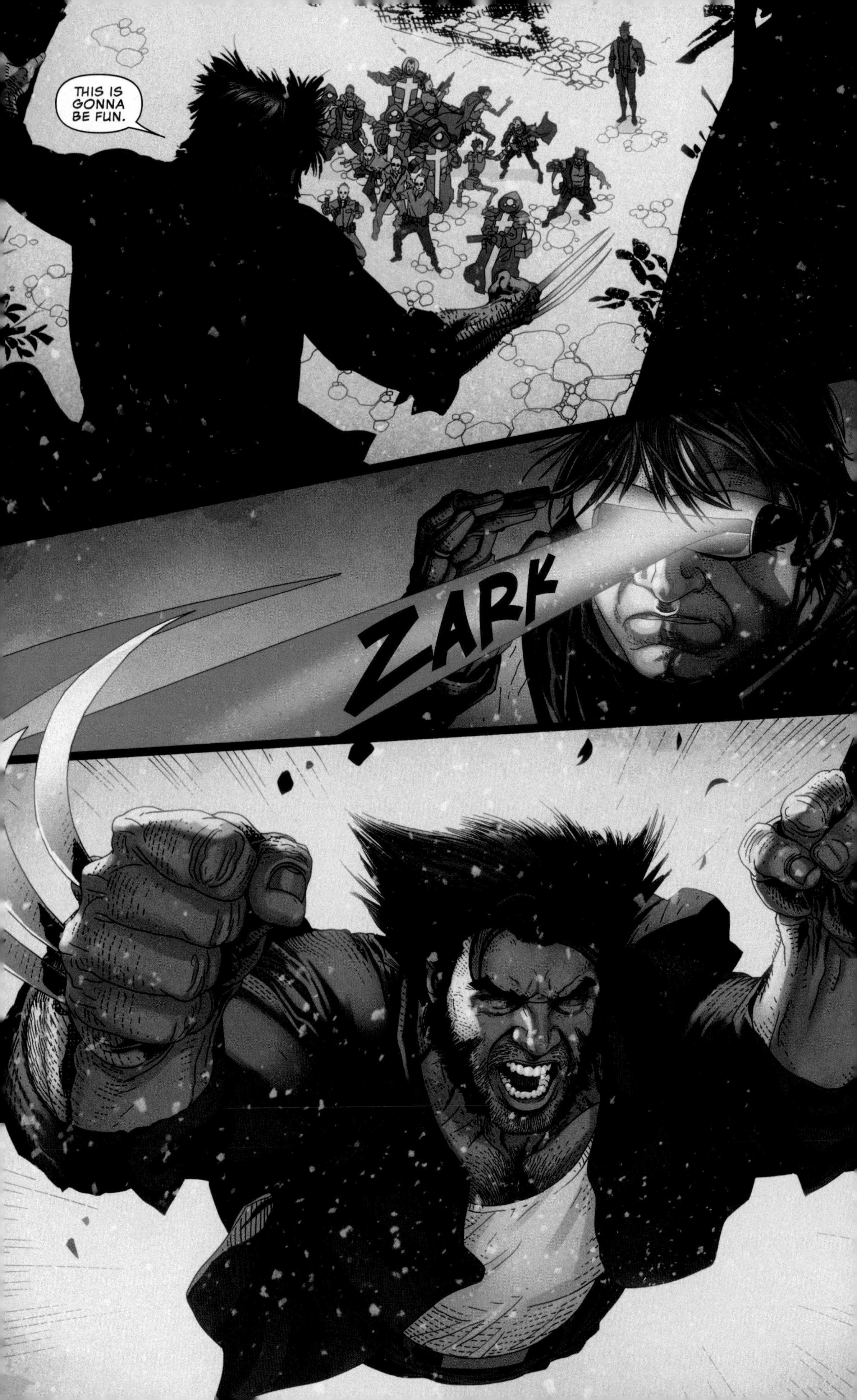
THIS IS GONNA BE FUN.
ZARK

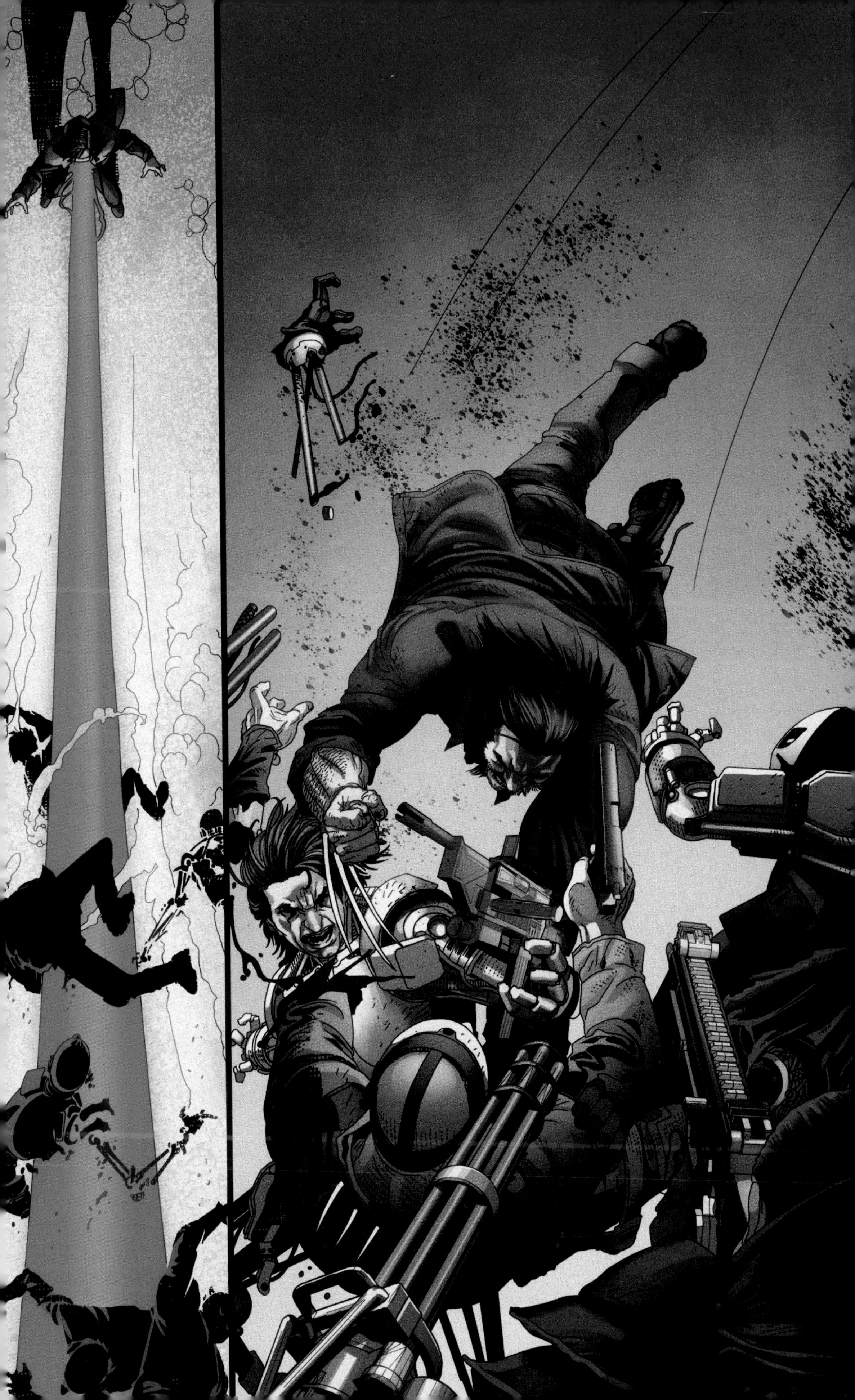

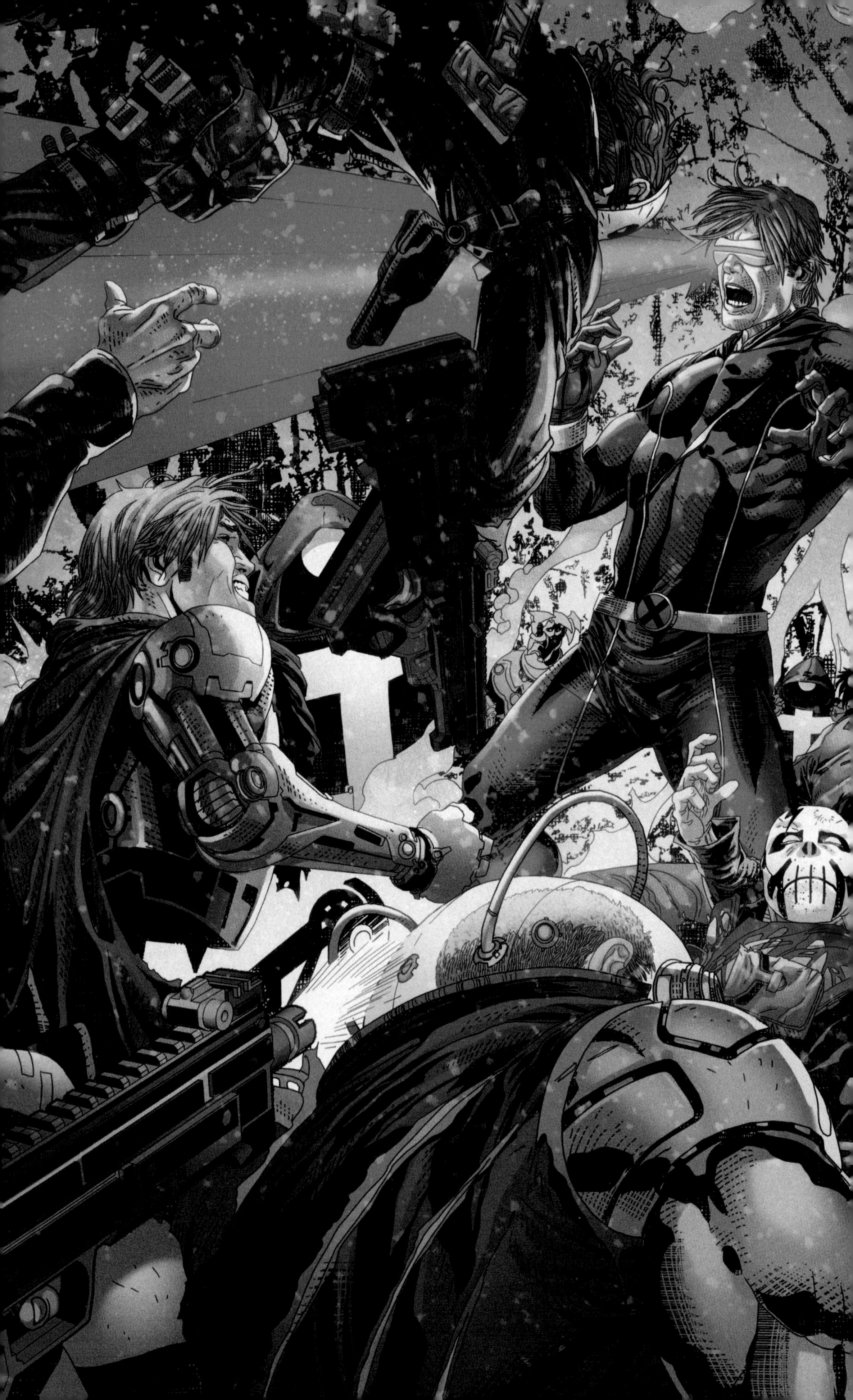

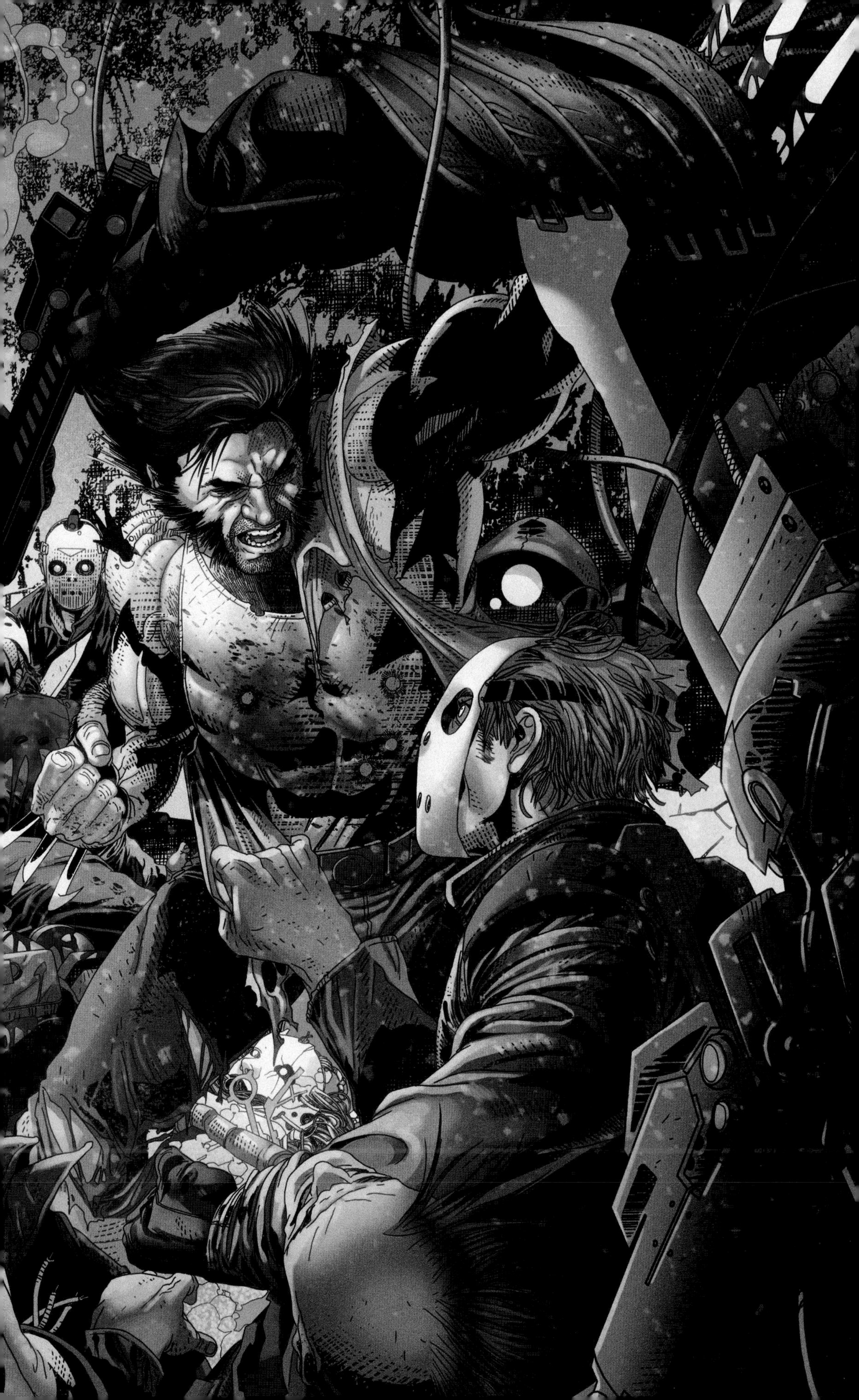

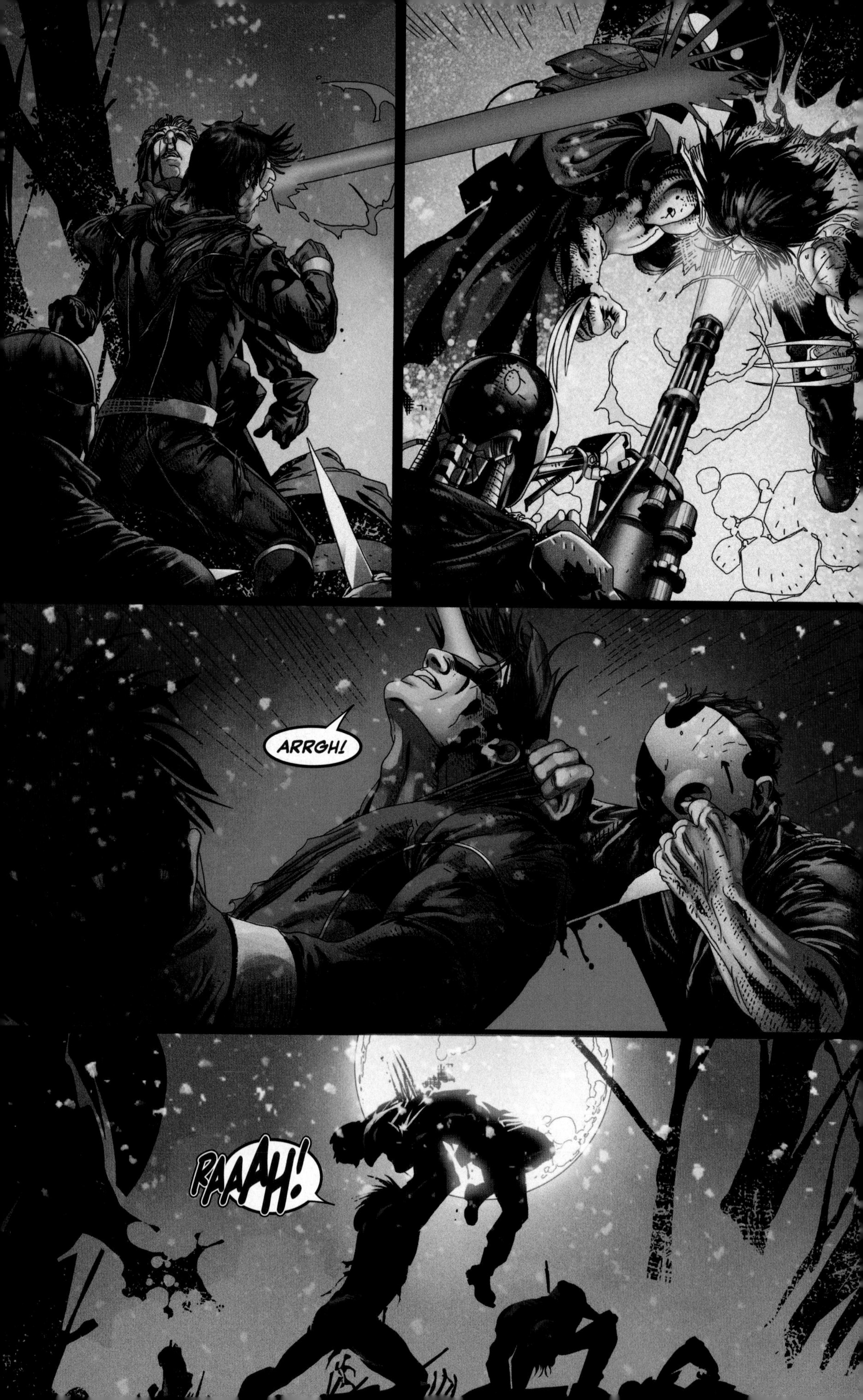
ARRGH!
RAAAH!

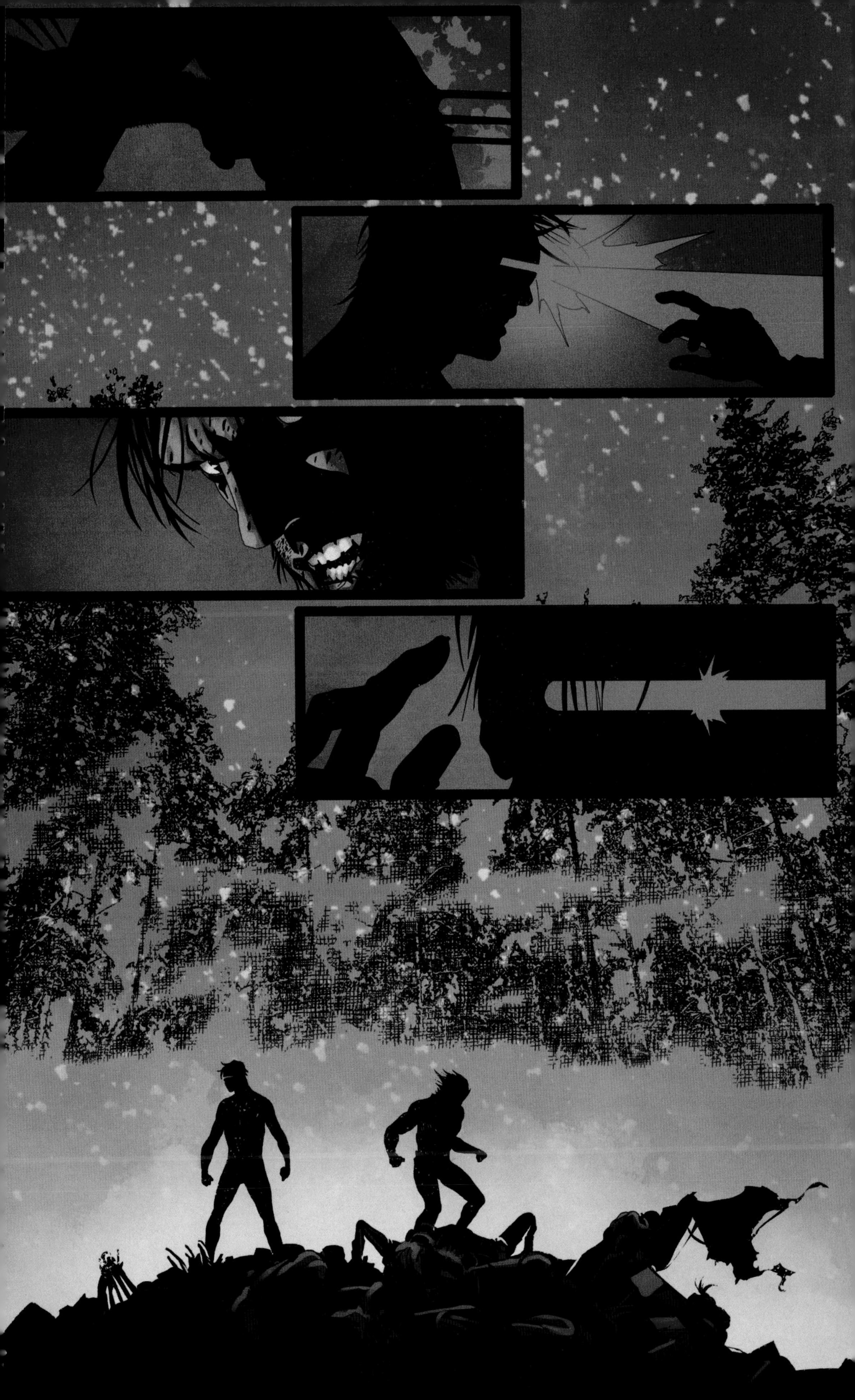

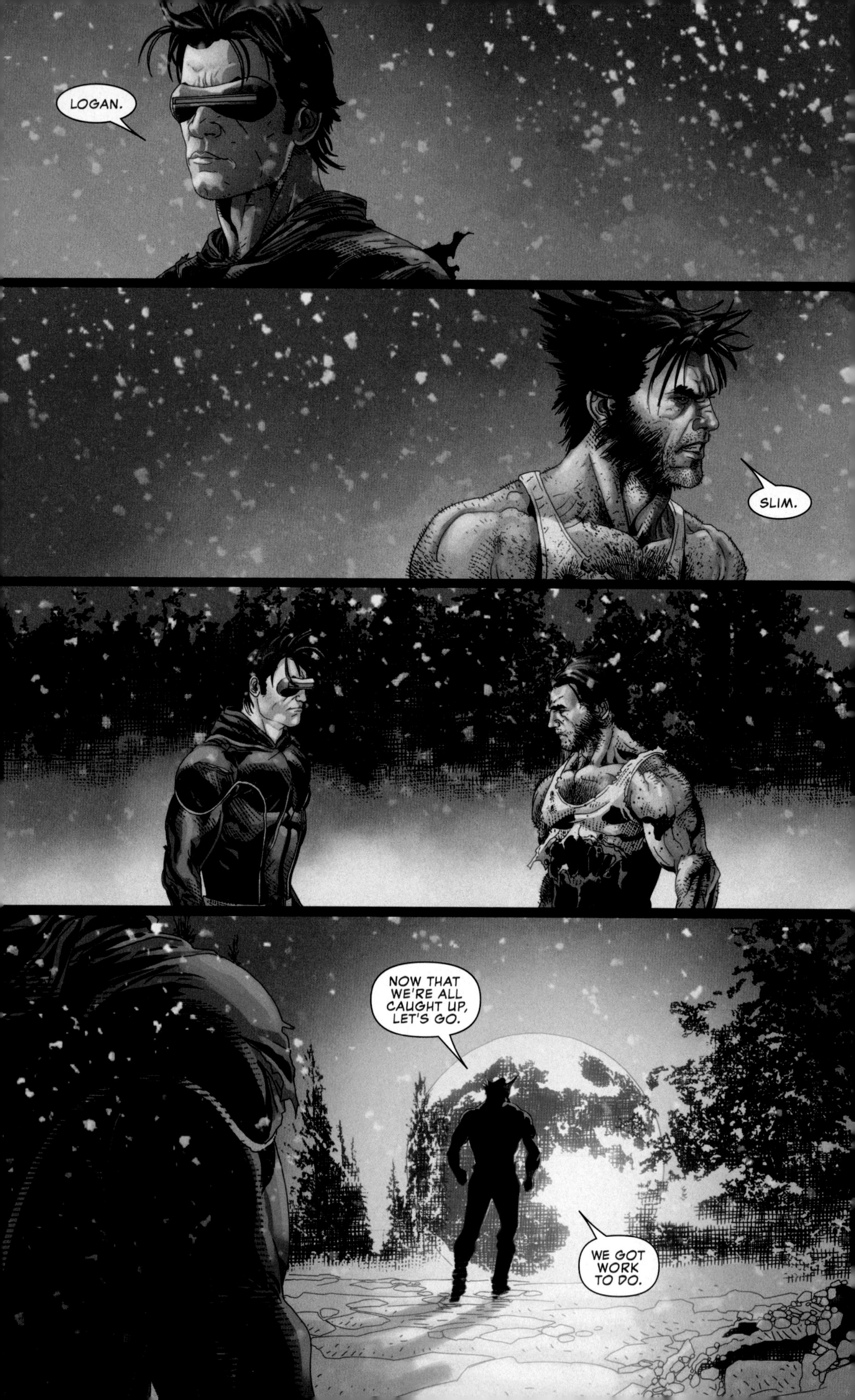
LOGAN.
SLIM.
NOW THAT WE'RE ALL CAUGHT UP, LET'S GO.
WE GOT WORK TO DO.

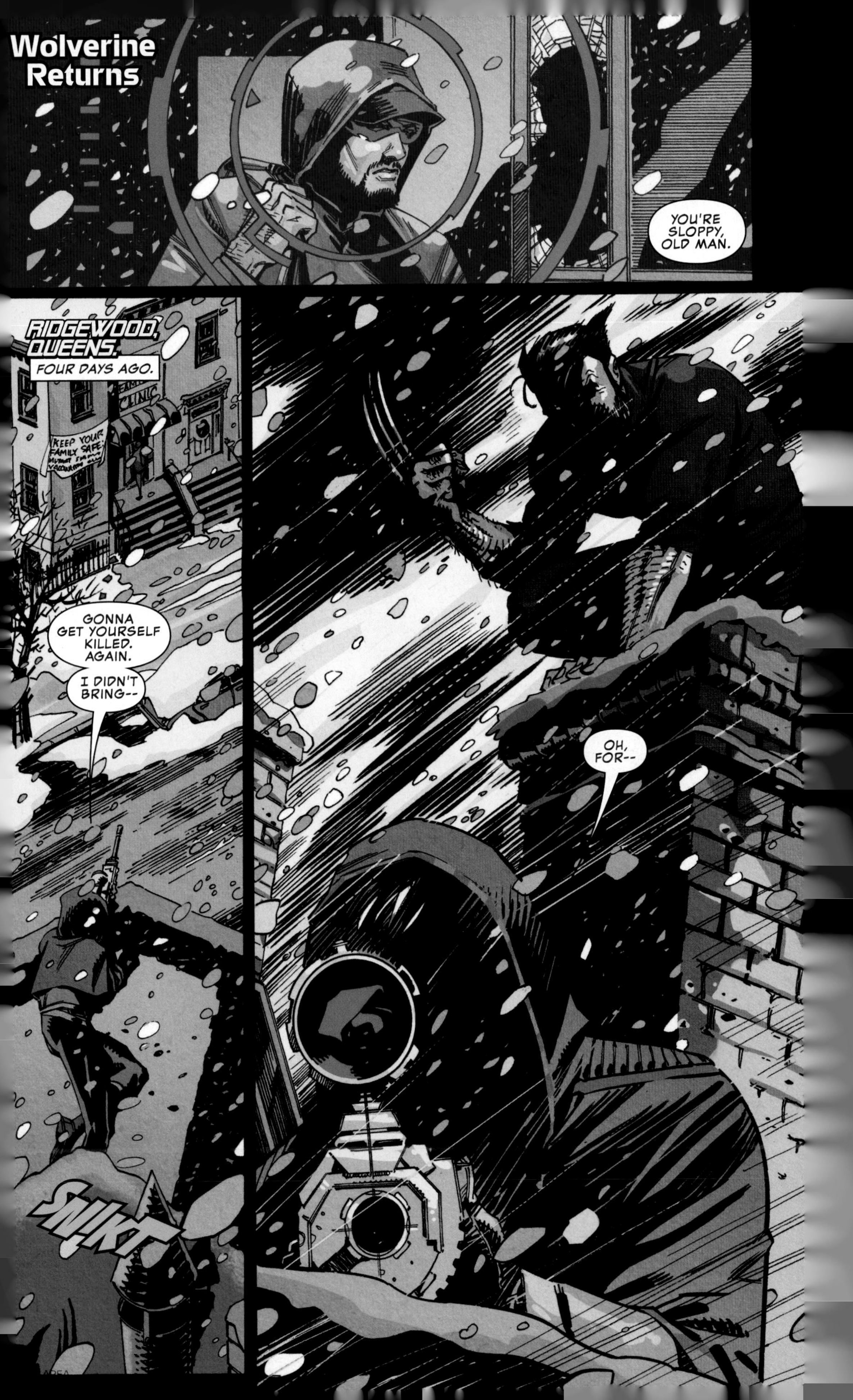
Wolverine Returns
YOU'RE SLOPPY, OLD MAN.
RIDGEWOOD, QUEENS.
FOUR DAYS AGO.
CLINIC
KEEP YOUR FAMILY SAFE!
GONNA GET YOURSELF KILLED. AGAIN.
I DIDN'T BRING--
OH, FOR--
SNIKT

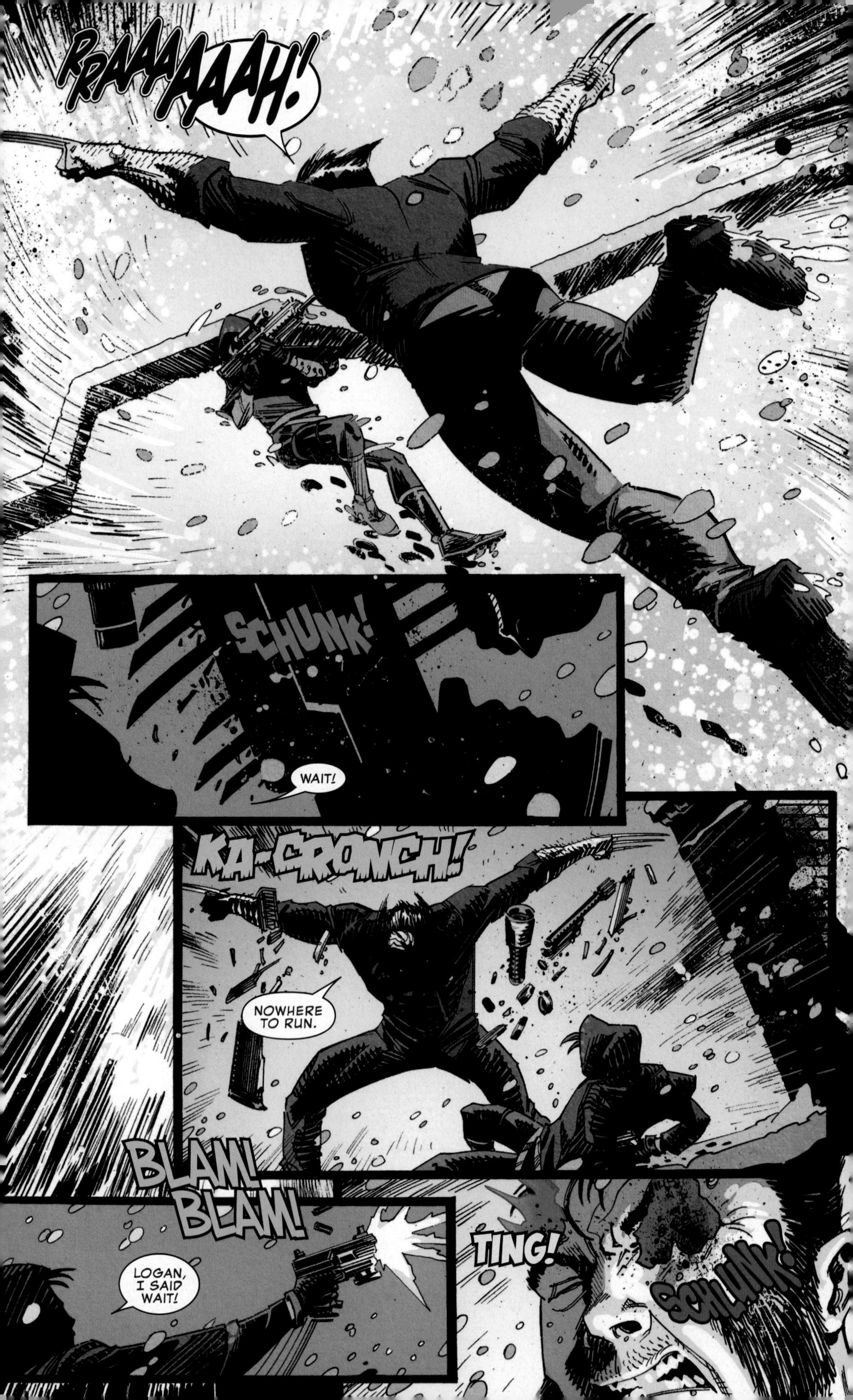
RRAAAAAAAH!
SCHUNK!
WAIT!
KA-CRONCH!
NOWHERE TO RUN.
BLAM! BLAM!
LOGAN, I SAID WAIT!
TING!
SCHLUNK!

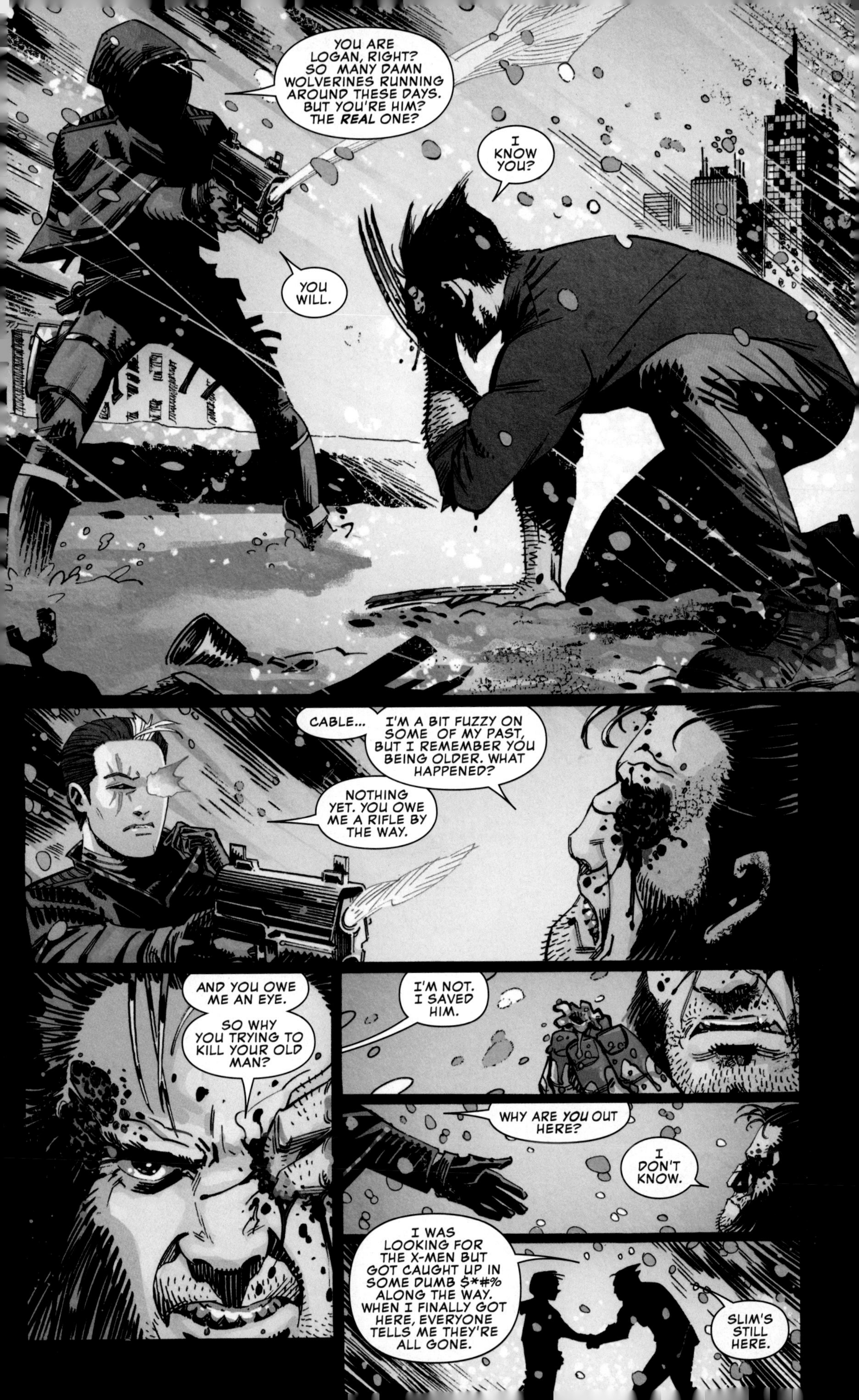
YOU ARE LOGAN, RIGHT? SO MANY DAMN WOLVERINES RUNNING AROUND THESE DAYS. BUT YOU'RE HIM? THE *REAL* ONE?
I KNOW YOU?
YOU WILL.
CABLE...
I'M A BIT FUZZY ON SOME OF MY PAST, BUT I REMEMBER YOU BEING OLDER. WHAT HAPPENED?
NOTHING YET. YOU OWE ME A RIFLE BY THE WAY.
AND YOU OWE ME AN EYE.
SO WHY YOU TRYING TO KILL YOUR OLD MAN?
I'M NOT. I SAVED HIM.
WHY ARE *YOU* OUT HERE?
I DON'T KNOW.
I WAS LOOKING FOR THE X-MEN BUT GOT CAUGHT UP IN SOME DUMB $*#% ALONG THE WAY. WHEN I FINALLY GOT HERE, EVERYONE TELLS ME THEY'RE ALL GONE.
SLIM'S STILL HERE.

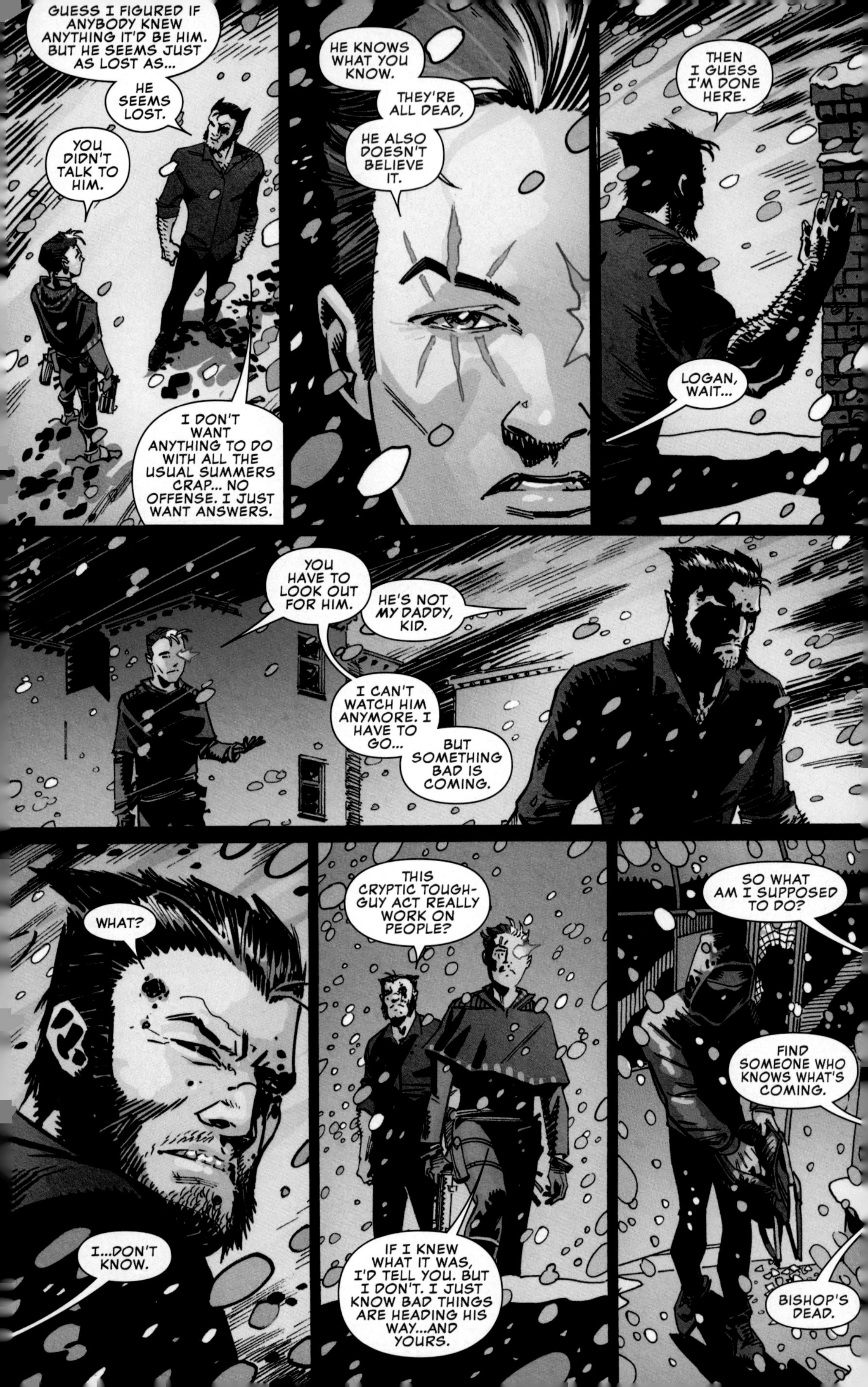
GUESS I FIGURED IF ANYBODY KNEW ANYTHING IT'D BE HIM. BUT HE SEEMS JUST AS LOST AS...
HE SEEMS LOST.
YOU DIDN'T TALK TO HIM.
I DON'T WANT ANYTHING TO DO WITH ALL THE USUAL SUMMERS CRAP... NO OFFENSE. I JUST WANT ANSWERS.
HE KNOWS WHAT YOU KNOW.
THEY'RE ALL DEAD,
HE ALSO DOESN'T BELIEVE IT.
THEN I GUESS I'M DONE HERE.
LOGAN, WAIT...
YOU HAVE TO LOOK OUT FOR HIM.
HE'S NOT MY DADDY, KID.
I CAN'T WATCH HIM ANYMORE. I HAVE TO GO...
BUT SOMETHING BAD IS COMING.
WHAT?
I...DON'T KNOW.
THIS CRYPTIC TOUGH-GUY ACT REALLY WORK ON PEOPLE?
IF I KNEW WHAT IT WAS, I'D TELL YOU. BUT I DON'T. I JUST KNOW BAD THINGS ARE HEADING HIS WAY...AND YOURS.
SO WHAT AM I SUPPOSED TO DO?
FIND SOMEONE WHO KNOWS WHAT'S COMING.
BISHOP'S DEAD.

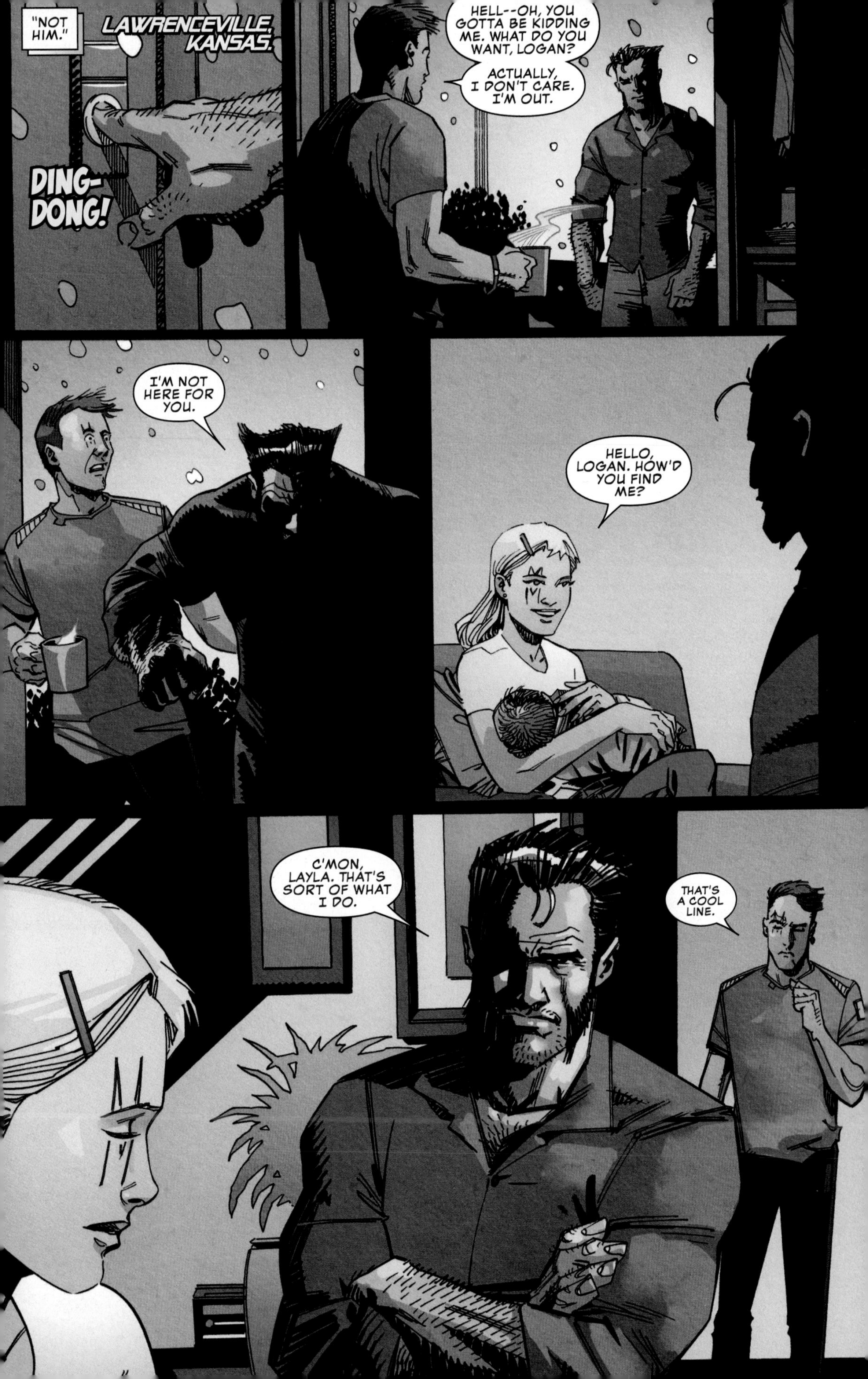
"NOT HIM."
LAWRENCEVILLE, KANSAS.
DING-DONG!
HELL--OH, YOU GOTTA BE KIDDING ME. WHAT DO YOU WANT, LOGAN?
ACTUALLY, I DON'T CARE. I'M OUT.
I'M NOT HERE FOR YOU.
HELLO, LOGAN. HOW'D YOU FIND ME?
C'MON, LAYLA. THAT'S SORT OF WHAT I DO.
THAT'S A COOL LINE.

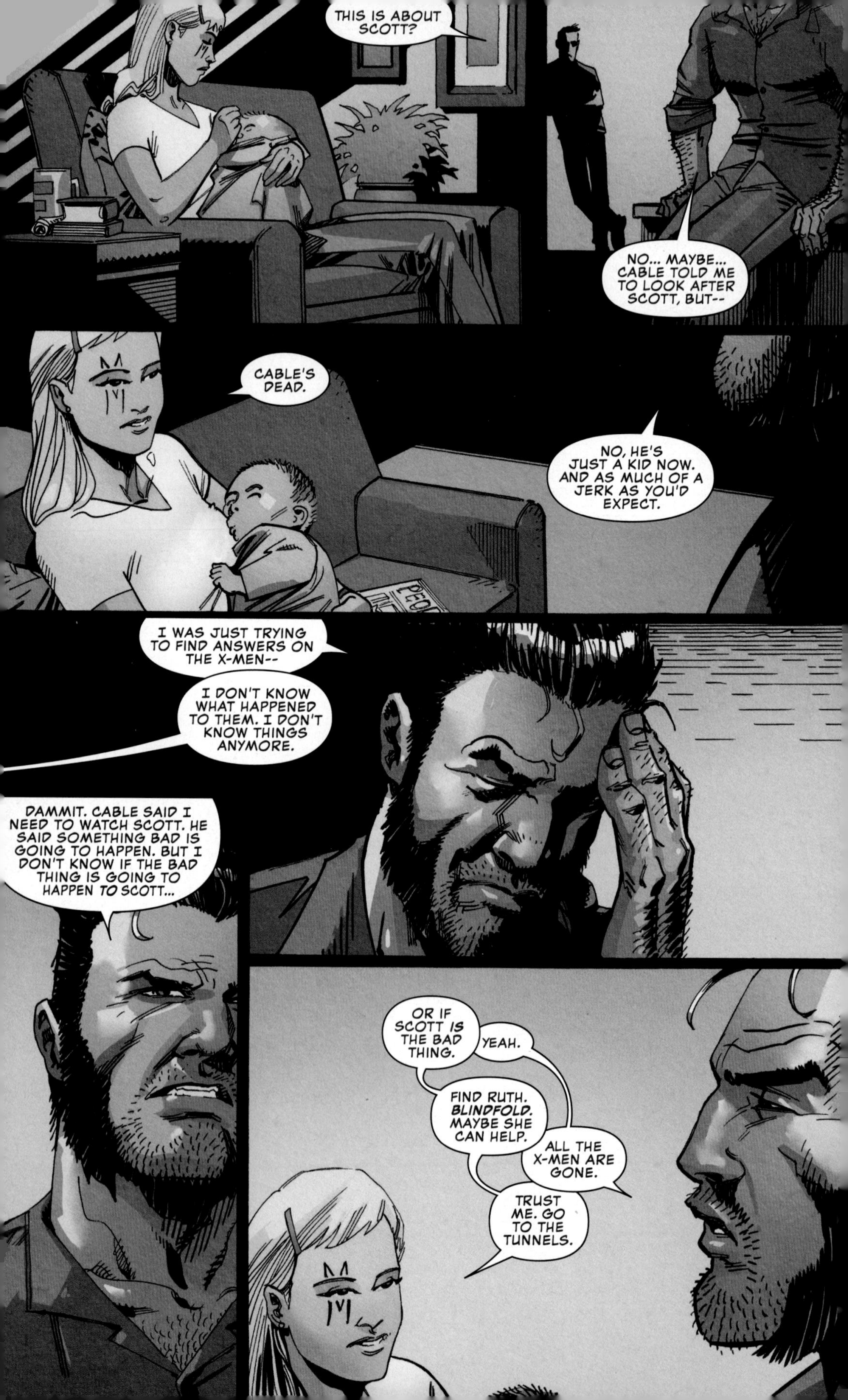
THIS IS ABOUT SCOTT?
NO... MAYBE... CABLE TOLD ME TO LOOK AFTER SCOTT, BUT--
CABLE'S DEAD.
NO, HE'S JUST A KID NOW. AND AS MUCH OF A JERK AS YOU'D EXPECT.
I WAS JUST TRYING TO FIND ANSWERS ON THE X-MEN--
I DON'T KNOW WHAT HAPPENED TO THEM. I DON'T KNOW THINGS ANYMORE.
DAMMIT. CABLE SAID I NEED TO WATCH SCOTT. HE SAID SOMETHING BAD IS GOING TO HAPPEN. BUT I DON'T KNOW IF THE BAD THING IS GOING TO HAPPEN *TO* SCOTT...
OR IF SCOTT *IS* THE BAD THING.
YEAH.
FIND RUTH. ***BLINDFOLD.*** MAYBE SHE CAN HELP.
ALL THE X-MEN ARE GONE.
TRUST ME. GO TO THE TUNNELS.

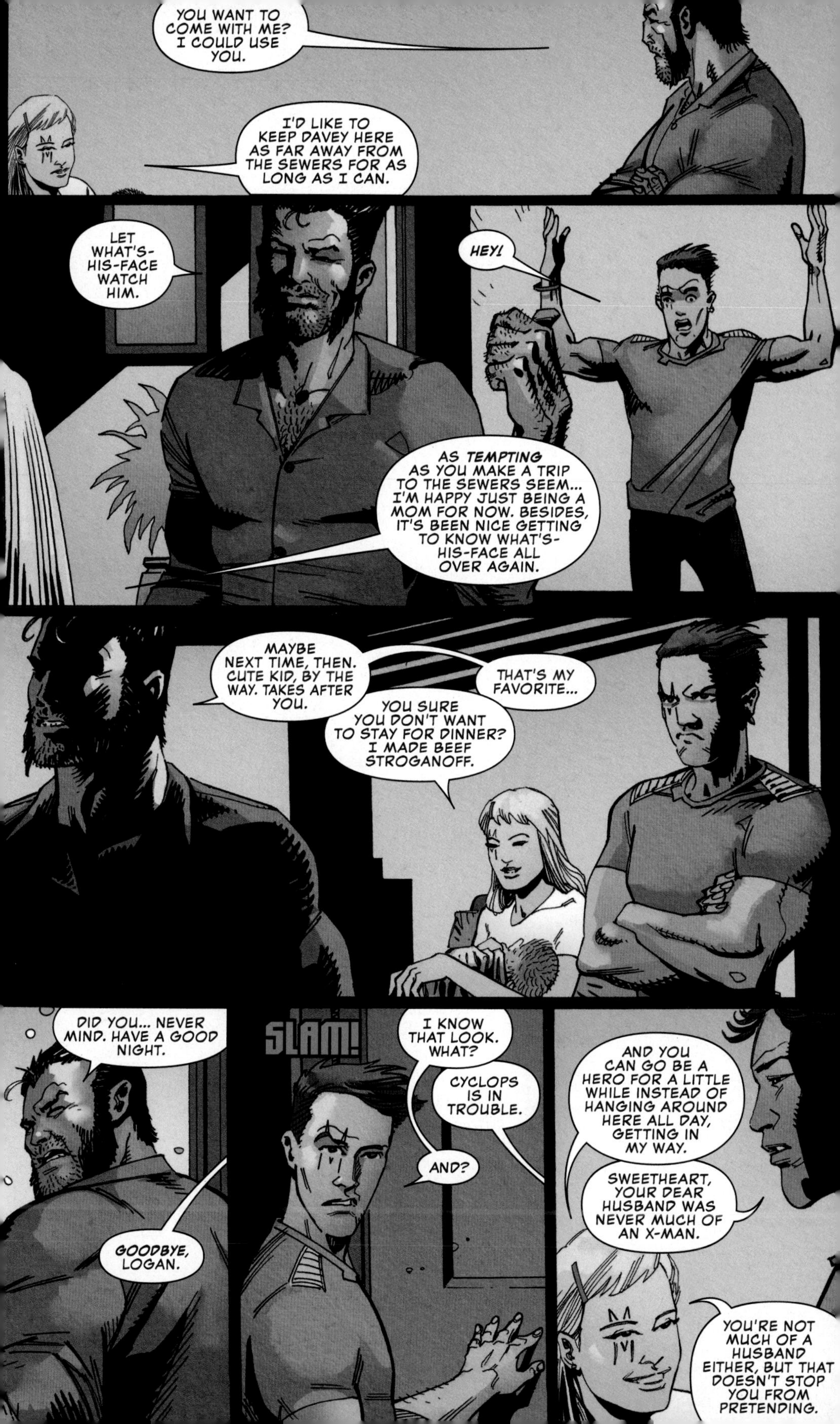
YOU WANT TO COME WITH ME? I COULD USE YOU.
I'D LIKE TO KEEP DAVEY HERE AS FAR AWAY FROM THE SEWERS FOR AS LONG AS I CAN.
LET WHAT'S-HIS-FACE WATCH HIM.
HEY!
AS TEMPTING AS YOU MAKE A TRIP TO THE SEWERS SEEM... I'M HAPPY JUST BEING A MOM FOR NOW. BESIDES, IT'S BEEN NICE GETTING TO KNOW WHAT'S-HIS-FACE ALL OVER AGAIN.
MAYBE NEXT TIME, THEN. CUTE KID, BY THE WAY. TAKES AFTER YOU.
THAT'S MY FAVORITE...
YOU SURE YOU DON'T WANT TO STAY FOR DINNER? I MADE BEEF STROGANOFF.
DID YOU... NEVER MIND. HAVE A GOOD NIGHT.
GOODBYE, LOGAN.
SLAM!
I KNOW THAT LOOK. WHAT?
CYCLOPS IS IN TROUBLE.
AND?
AND YOU CAN GO BE A HERO FOR A LITTLE WHILE INSTEAD OF HANGING AROUND HERE ALL DAY, GETTING IN MY WAY.
SWEETHEART, YOUR DEAR HUSBAND WAS NEVER MUCH OF AN X-MAN.
YOU'RE NOT MUCH OF A HUSBAND EITHER, BUT THAT DOESN'T STOP YOU FROM PRETENDING.

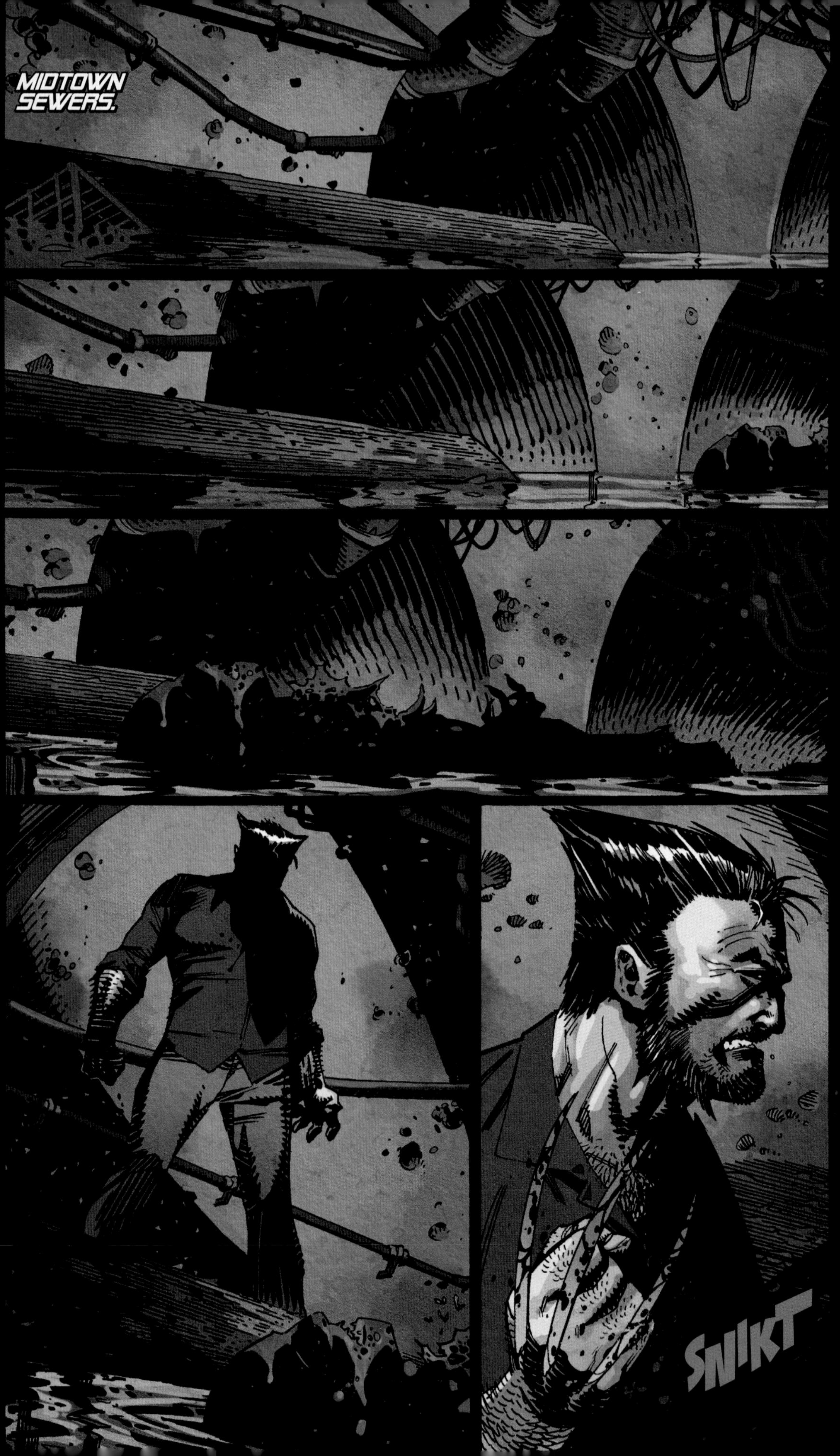
MIDTOWN SEWERS.
SNIKT

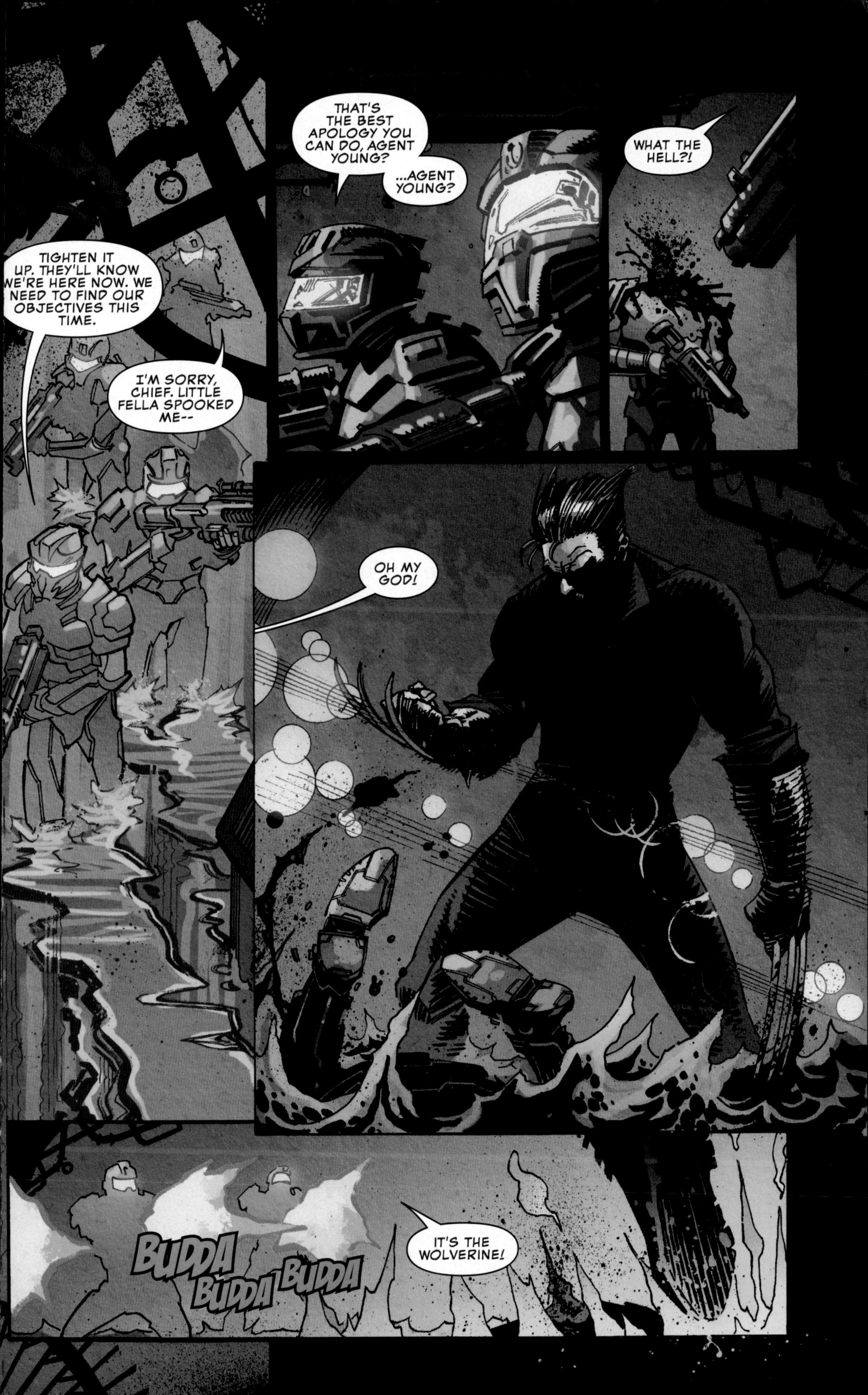
TIGHTEN IT UP. THEY'LL KNOW WE'RE HERE NOW. WE NEED TO FIND OUR OBJECTIVES THIS TIME.
I'M SORRY, CHIEF. LITTLE FELLA SPOOKED ME--
THAT'S THE BEST APOLOGY YOU CAN DO, AGENT YOUNG?
...AGENT YOUNG?
WHAT THE HELL?!
OH MY GOD!
BUDDA BUDDA BUDDA
IT'S THE WOLVERINE!

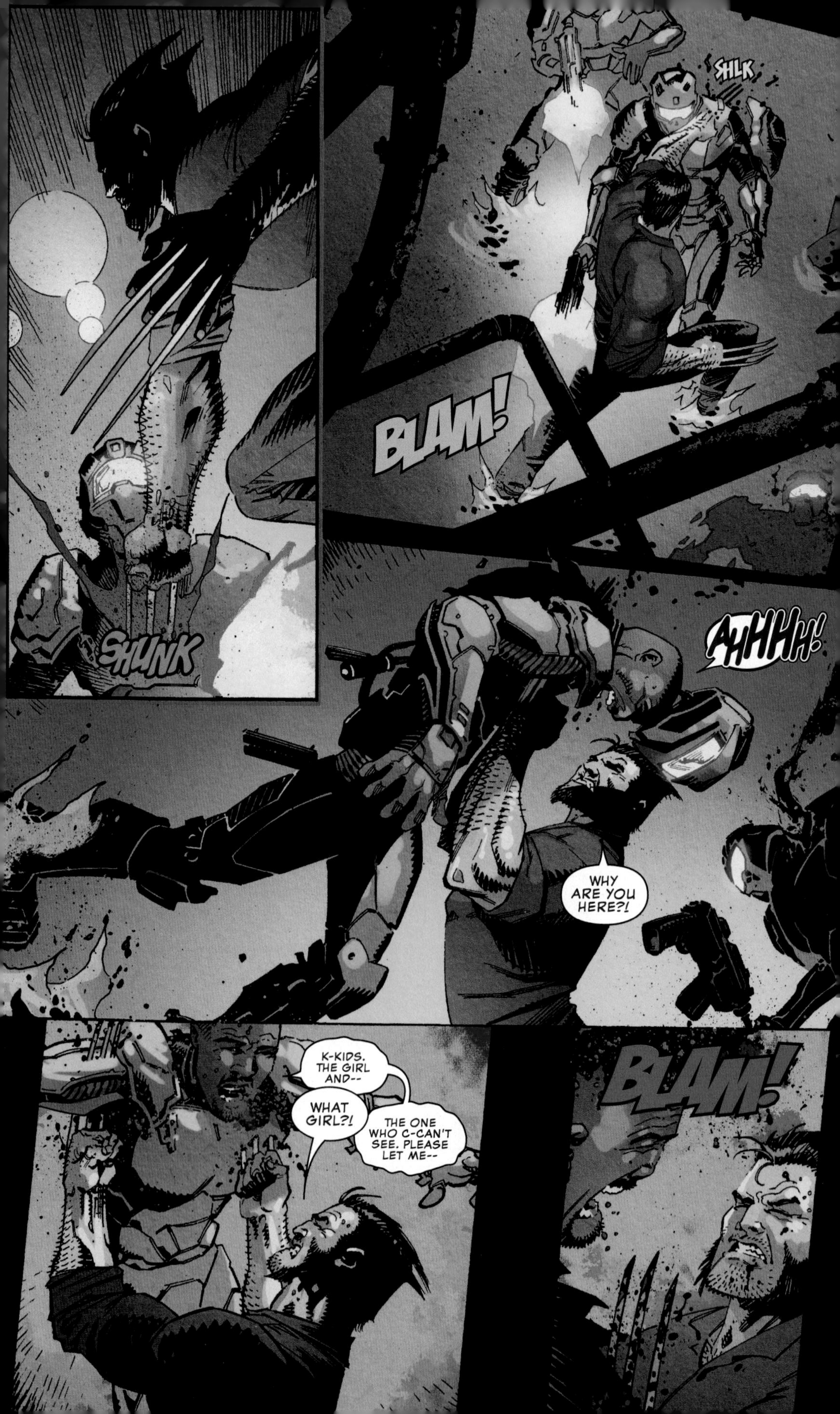
SHUNK
SHLK
BLAM!
AHHHH!
WHY ARE YOU HERE?!
K-KIDS. THE GIRL AND--
WHAT GIRL?!
THE ONE WHO C-CAN'T SEE. PLEASE LET ME--
BLAM!

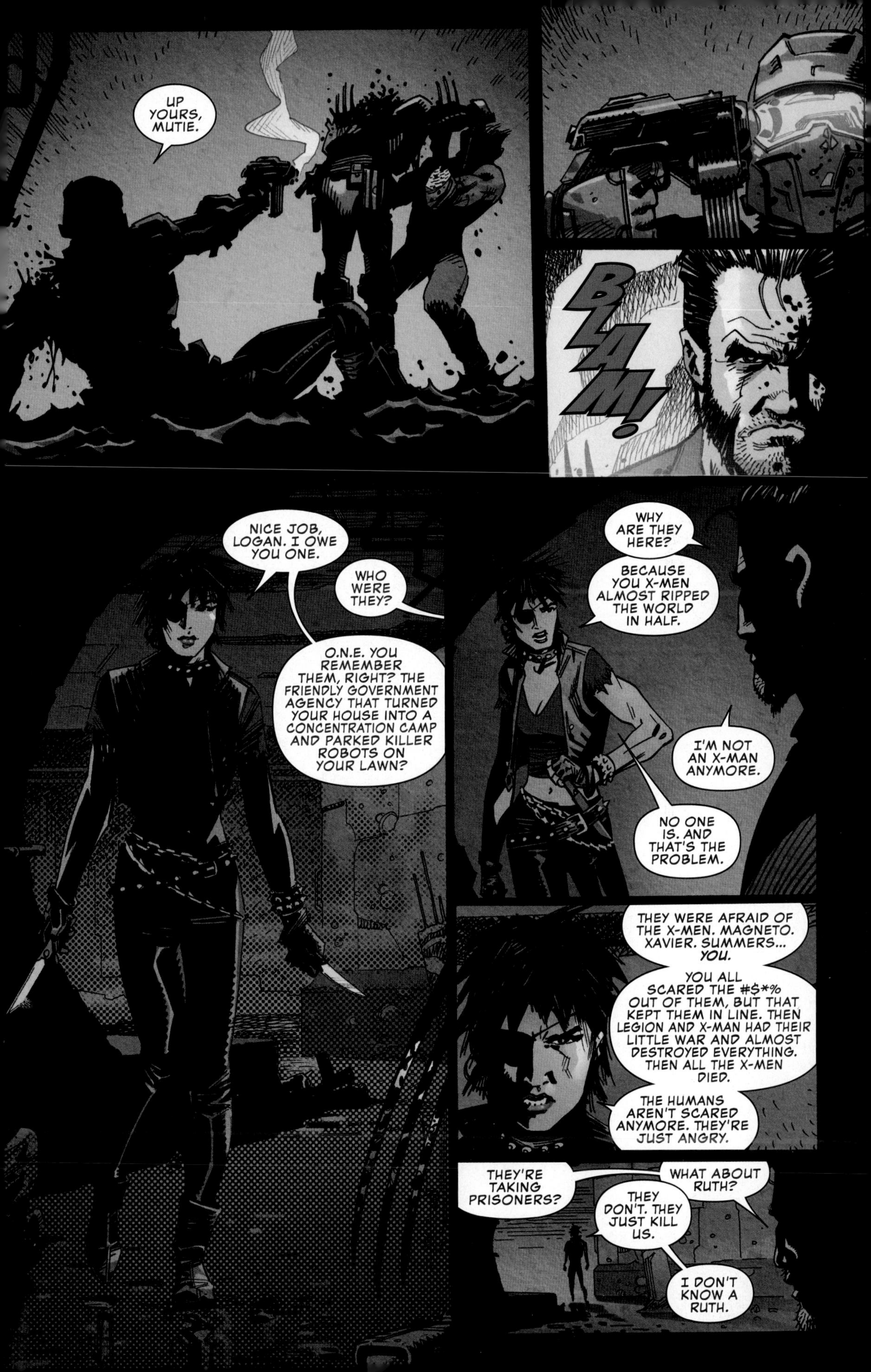
UP YOURS, MUTIE.
BLAM!
NICE JOB, LOGAN. I OWE YOU ONE.
WHO WERE THEY?
O.N.E. YOU REMEMBER THEM, RIGHT? THE FRIENDLY GOVERNMENT AGENCY THAT TURNED YOUR HOUSE INTO A CONCENTRATION CAMP AND PARKED KILLER ROBOTS ON YOUR LAWN?
WHY ARE THEY HERE?
BECAUSE YOU X-MEN ALMOST RIPPED THE WORLD IN HALF.
I'M NOT AN X-MAN ANYMORE.
NO ONE IS. AND THAT'S THE PROBLEM.
THEY WERE AFRAID OF THE X-MEN. MAGNETO. XAVIER. SUMMERS... YOU.
YOU ALL SCARED THE #$*% OUT OF THEM, BUT THAT KEPT THEM IN LINE. THEN LEGION AND X-MAN HAD THEIR LITTLE WAR AND ALMOST DESTROYED EVERYTHING. THEN ALL THE X-MEN DIED.
THE HUMANS AREN'T SCARED ANYMORE. THEY'RE JUST ANGRY.
THEY'RE TAKING PRISONERS?
WHAT ABOUT RUTH?
THEY DON'T. THEY JUST KILL US.
I DON'T KNOW A RUTH.

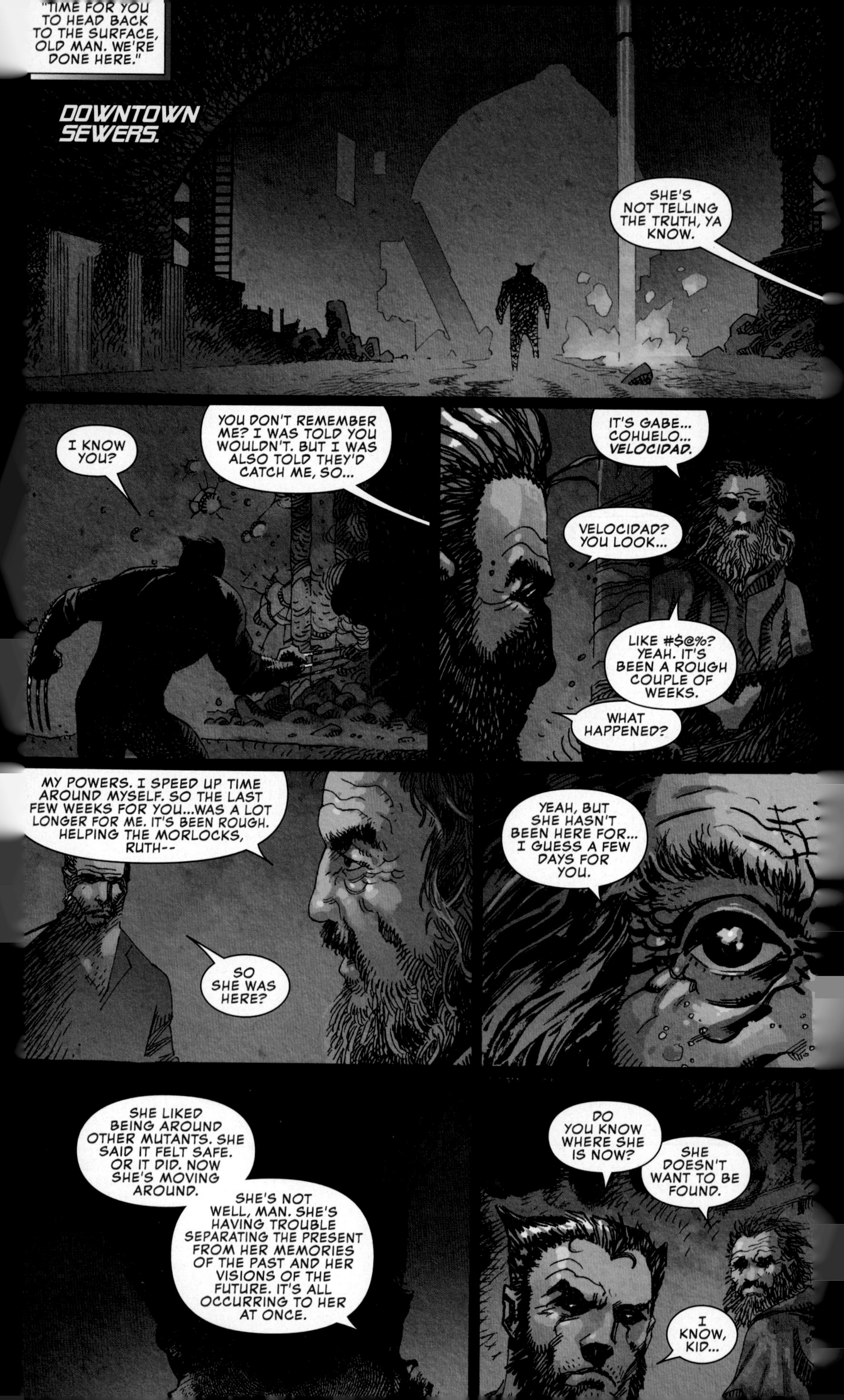
"TIME FOR YOU TO HEAD BACK TO THE SURFACE, OLD MAN. WE'RE DONE HERE."
DOWNTOWN SEWERS.
SHE'S NOT TELLING THE TRUTH, YA KNOW.
I KNOW YOU?
YOU DON'T REMEMBER ME? I WAS TOLD YOU WOULDN'T. BUT I WAS ALSO TOLD THEY'D CATCH ME, SO...
IT'S GABE... COHUELO... VELOCIDAD.
VELOCIDAD? YOU LOOK...
LIKE #$@%? YEAH. IT'S BEEN A ROUGH COUPLE OF WEEKS.
WHAT HAPPENED?
MY POWERS. I SPEED UP TIME AROUND MYSELF. SO THE LAST FEW WEEKS FOR YOU...WAS A LOT LONGER FOR ME. IT'S BEEN ROUGH. HELPING THE MORLOCKS, RUTH--
SO SHE WAS HERE?
YEAH, BUT SHE HASN'T BEEN HERE FOR... I GUESS A FEW DAYS FOR YOU.
SHE LIKED BEING AROUND OTHER MUTANTS. SHE SAID IT FELT SAFE. OR IT DID. NOW SHE'S MOVING AROUND.
SHE'S NOT WELL, MAN. SHE'S HAVING TROUBLE SEPARATING THE PRESENT FROM HER MEMORIES OF THE PAST AND HER VISIONS OF THE FUTURE. IT'S ALL OCCURRING TO HER AT ONCE.
DO YOU KNOW WHERE SHE IS NOW?
SHE DOESN'T WANT TO BE FOUND.
I KNOW, KID...

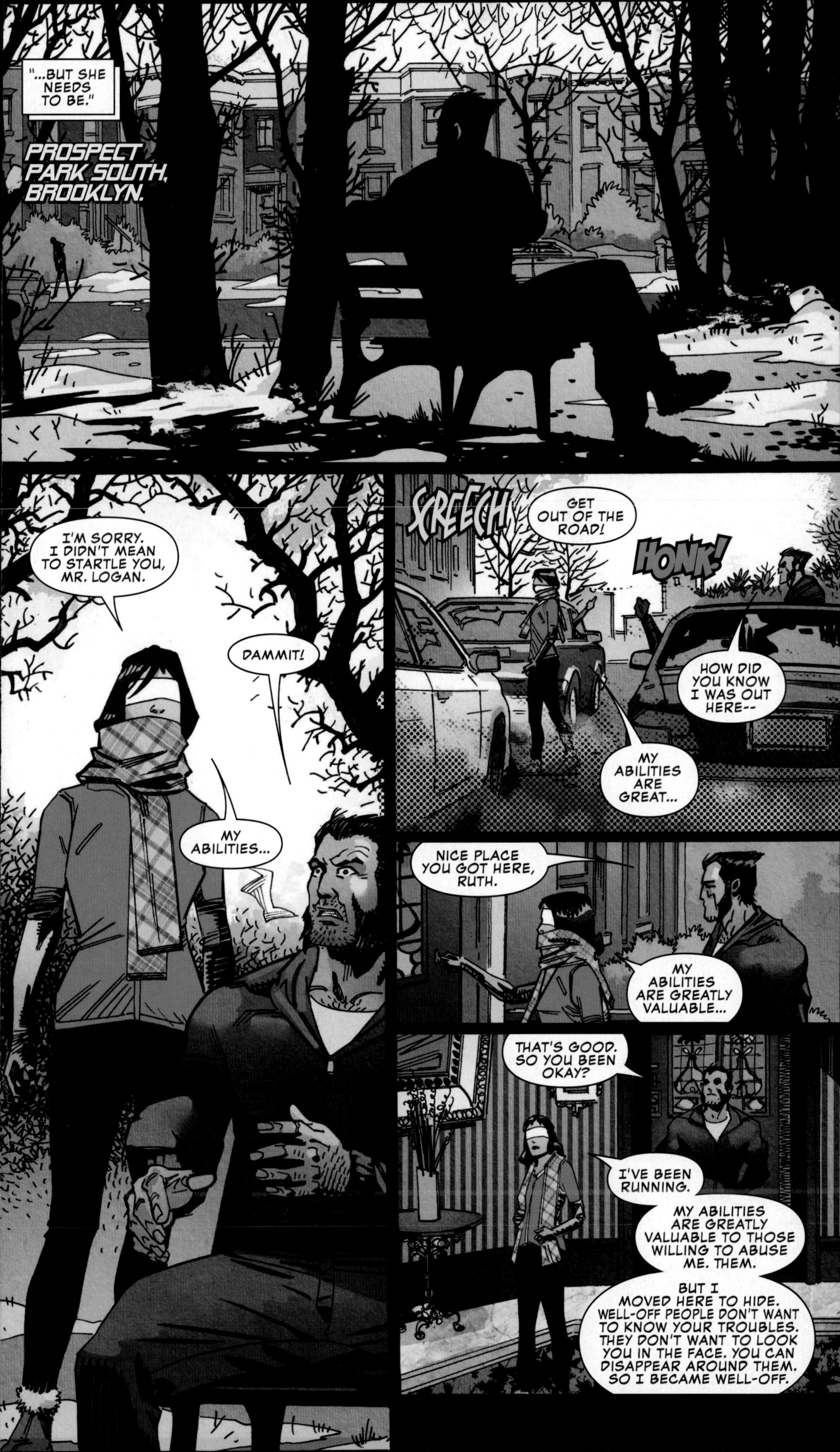
"...BUT SHE NEEDS TO BE."
PROSPECT PARK SOUTH, BROOKLYN.
I'M SORRY. I DIDN'T MEAN TO STARTLE YOU, MR. LOGAN.
DAMMIT!
MY ABILITIES...
SCREECH
GET OUT OF THE ROAD!
HONK!
HOW DID YOU KNOW I WAS OUT HERE--
MY ABILITIES ARE GREAT...
NICE PLACE YOU GOT HERE, RUTH.
MY ABILITIES ARE GREATLY VALUABLE...
THAT'S GOOD. SO YOU BEEN OKAY?
I'VE BEEN RUNNING.
MY ABILITIES ARE GREATLY VALUABLE TO THOSE WILLING TO ABUSE ME. THEM.
BUT I MOVED HERE TO HIDE. WELL-OFF PEOPLE DON'T WANT TO KNOW YOUR TROUBLES. THEY DON'T WANT TO LOOK YOU IN THE FACE. YOU CAN DISAPPEAR AROUND THEM. SO I BECAME WELL-OFF.

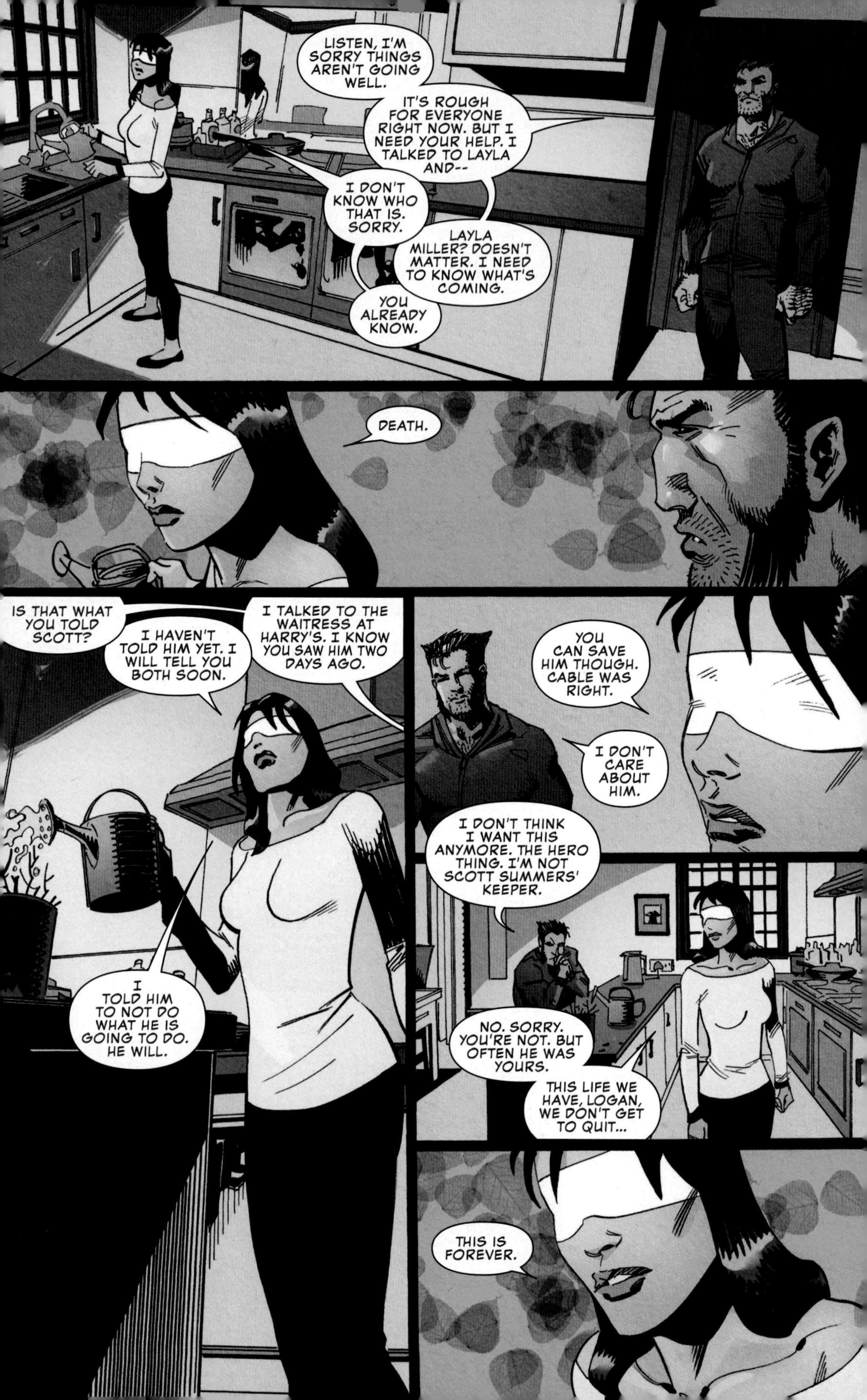
LISTEN, I'M SORRY THINGS AREN'T GOING WELL.
IT'S ROUGH FOR EVERYONE RIGHT NOW. BUT I NEED YOUR HELP. I TALKED TO LAYLA AND--
I DON'T KNOW WHO THAT IS. SORRY.
LAYLA MILLER? DOESN'T MATTER. I NEED TO KNOW WHAT'S COMING.
YOU ALREADY KNOW.
DEATH.
IS THAT WHAT YOU TOLD SCOTT?
I HAVEN'T TOLD HIM YET. I WILL TELL YOU BOTH SOON.
I TALKED TO THE WAITRESS AT HARRY'S. I KNOW YOU SAW HIM TWO DAYS AGO.
I TOLD HIM TO NOT DO WHAT HE IS GOING TO DO. HE WILL.
YOU CAN SAVE HIM THOUGH. CABLE WAS RIGHT.
I DON'T CARE ABOUT HIM.
I DON'T THINK I WANT THIS ANYMORE. THE HERO THING. I'M NOT SCOTT SUMMERS' KEEPER.
NO. SORRY. YOU'RE NOT. BUT OFTEN HE WAS YOURS.
THIS LIFE WE HAVE, LOGAN, WE DON'T GET TO QUIT...
THIS IS FOREVER.

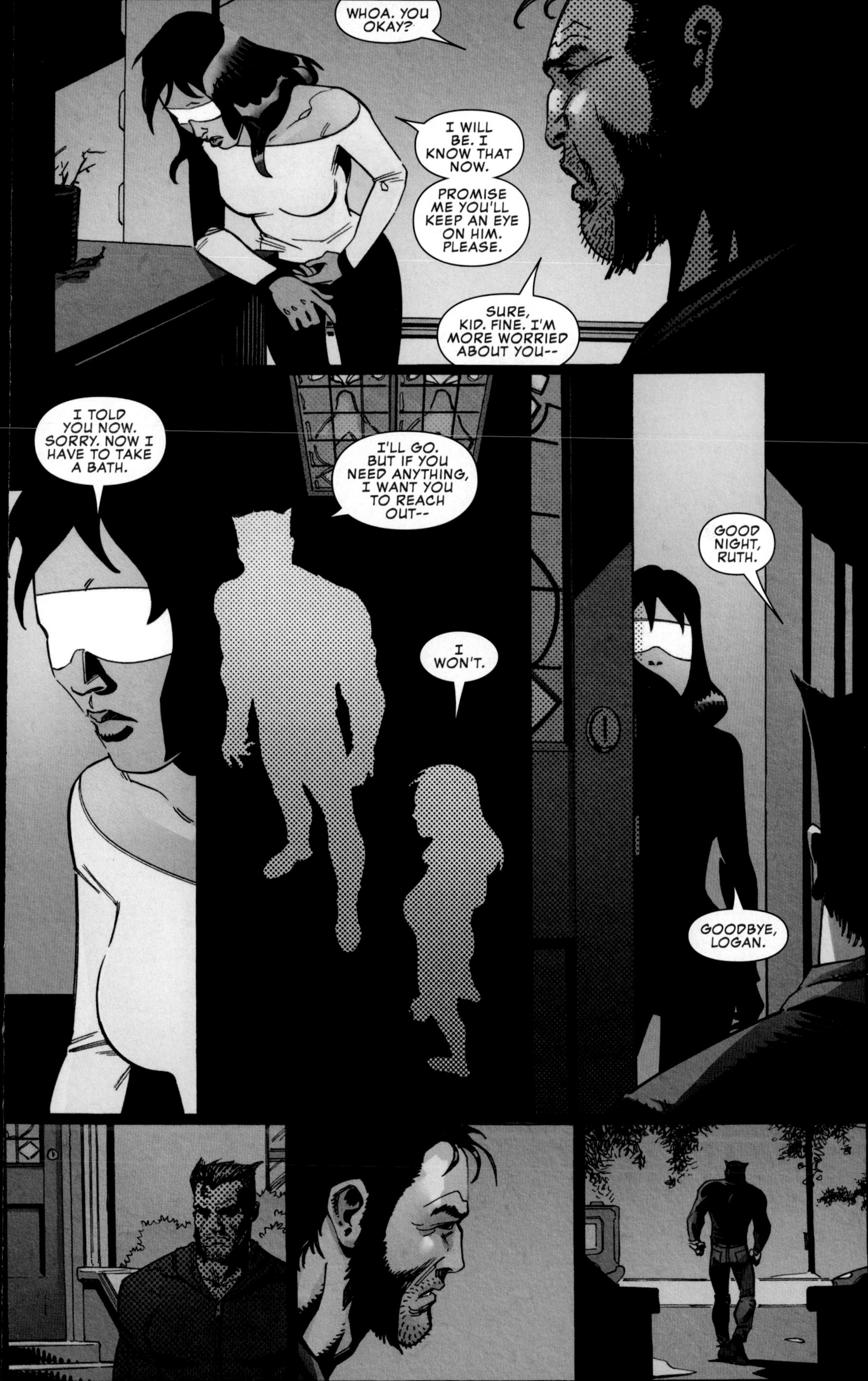
WHOA. YOU OKAY?
I WILL BE. I KNOW THAT NOW.
PROMISE ME YOU'LL KEEP AN EYE ON HIM. PLEASE.
SURE, KID. FINE. I'M MORE WORRIED ABOUT YOU--
I TOLD YOU NOW. SORRY. NOW I HAVE TO TAKE A BATH.
I'LL GO. BUT IF YOU NEED ANYTHING, I WANT YOU TO REACH OUT--
I WON'T.
GOOD NIGHT, RUTH.
GOODBYE, LOGAN.

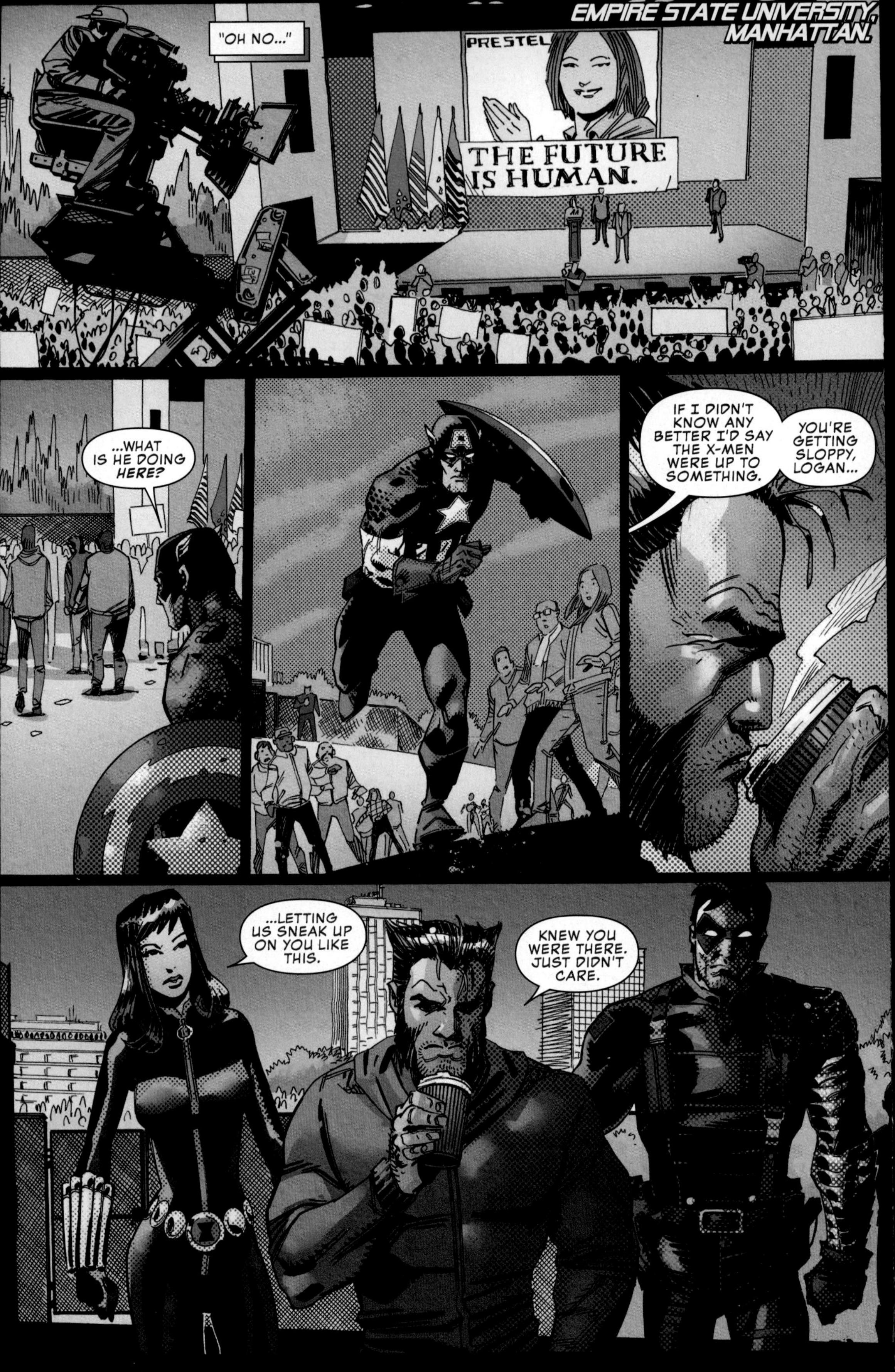
EMPIRE STATE UNIVERSITY, MANHATTAN.
"OH NO..."
PRESTEL
THE FUTURE IS HUMAN.
...WHAT IS HE DOING HERE?
IF I DIDN'T KNOW ANY BETTER I'D SAY THE X-MEN WERE UP TO SOMETHING.
YOU'RE GETTING SLOPPY, LOGAN...
...LETTING US SNEAK UP ON YOU LIKE THIS.
KNEW YOU WERE THERE. JUST DIDN'T CARE.

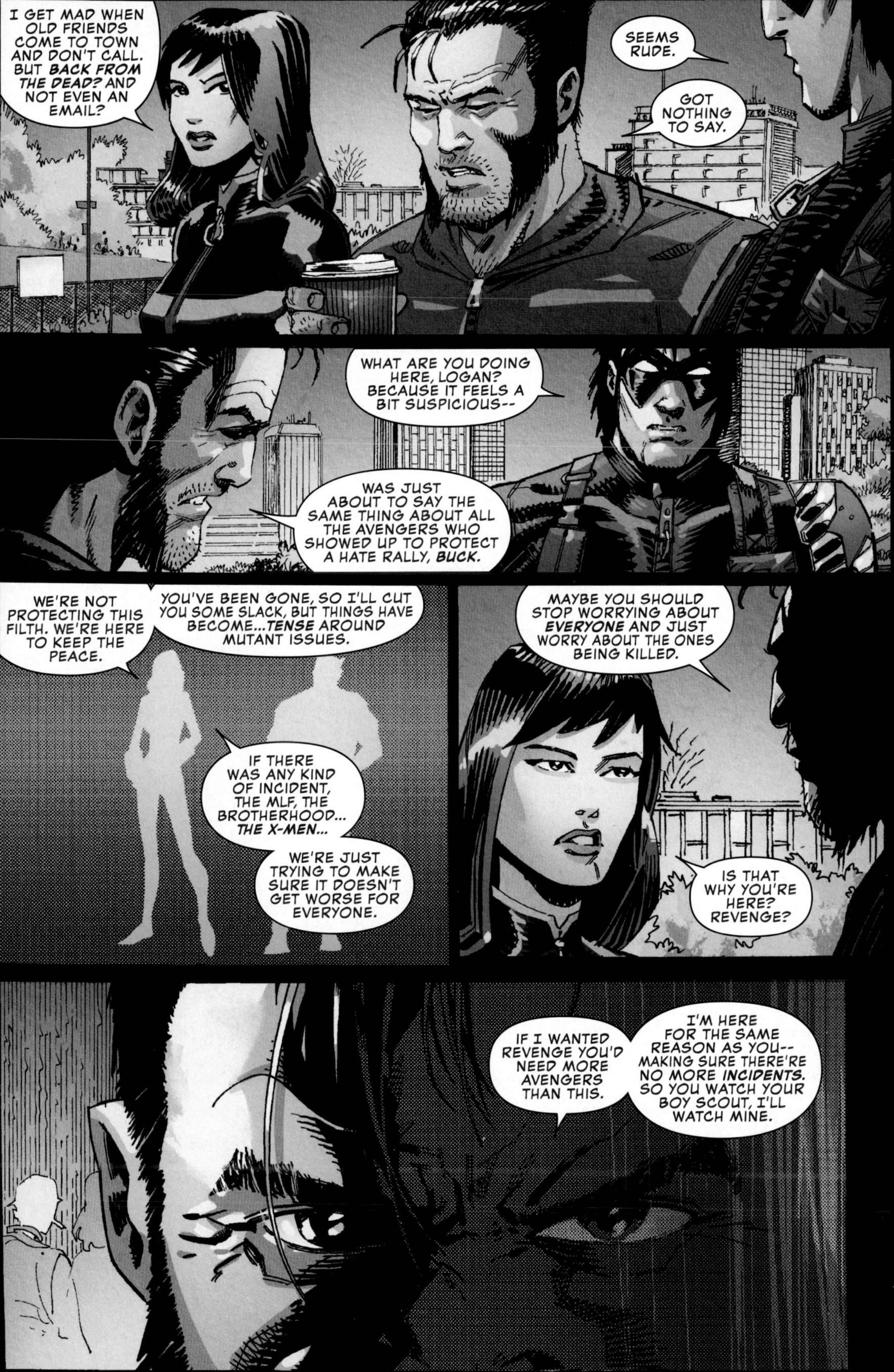
I GET MAD WHEN OLD FRIENDS COME TO TOWN AND DON'T CALL. BUT BACK FROM THE DEAD? AND NOT EVEN AN EMAIL?
SEEMS RUDE.
GOT NOTHING TO SAY.
WHAT ARE YOU DOING HERE, LOGAN? BECAUSE IT FEELS A BIT SUSPICIOUS--
WAS JUST ABOUT TO SAY THE SAME THING ABOUT ALL THE AVENGERS WHO SHOWED UP TO PROTECT A HATE RALLY, BUCK.
WE'RE NOT PROTECTING THIS FILTH. WE'RE HERE TO KEEP THE PEACE.
YOU'VE BEEN GONE, SO I'LL CUT YOU SOME SLACK, BUT THINGS HAVE BECOME...TENSE AROUND MUTANT ISSUES.
IF THERE WAS ANY KIND OF INCIDENT, THE MLF, THE BROTHERHOOD... THE X-MEN...
WE'RE JUST TRYING TO MAKE SURE IT DOESN'T GET WORSE FOR EVERYONE.
MAYBE YOU SHOULD STOP WORRYING ABOUT EVERYONE AND JUST WORRY ABOUT THE ONES BEING KILLED.
IS THAT WHY YOU'RE HERE? REVENGE?
IF I WANTED REVENGE YOU'D NEED MORE AVENGERS THAN THIS.
I'M HERE FOR THE SAME REASON AS YOU-- MAKING SURE THERE'RE NO MORE INCIDENTS. SO YOU WATCH YOUR BOY SCOUT, I'LL WATCH MINE.

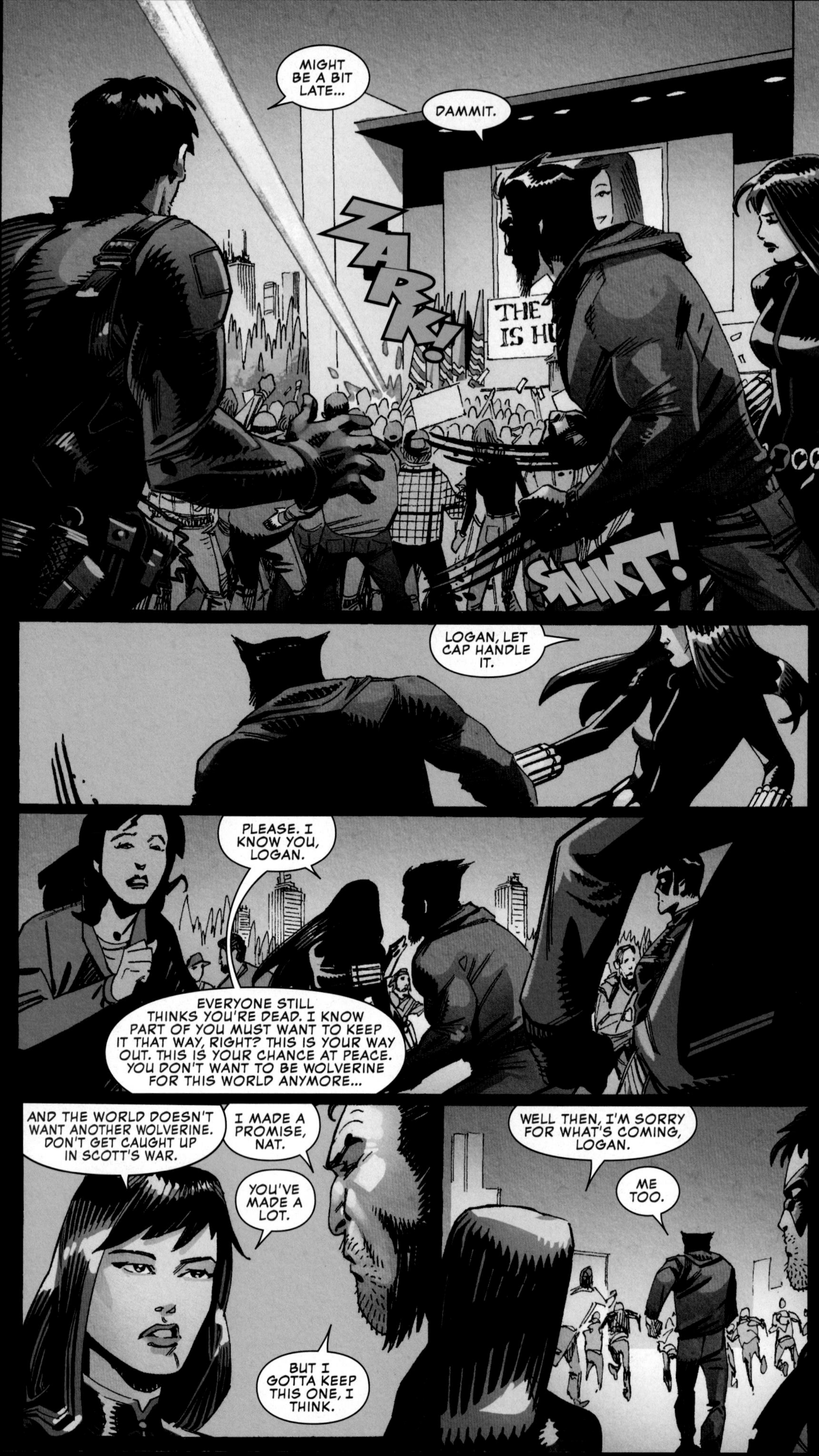
MIGHT BE A BIT LATE...
DAMMIT.
ZARK!
THE IS HU
SNIKT!
LOGAN, LET CAP HANDLE IT.
PLEASE. I KNOW YOU, LOGAN.
EVERYONE STILL THINKS YOU'RE DEAD. I KNOW PART OF YOU MUST WANT TO KEEP IT THAT WAY, RIGHT? THIS IS YOUR WAY OUT. THIS IS YOUR CHANCE AT PEACE. YOU DON'T WANT TO BE WOLVERINE FOR THIS WORLD ANYMORE...
AND THE WORLD DOESN'T WANT ANOTHER WOLVERINE. DON'T GET CAUGHT UP IN SCOTT'S WAR.
I MADE A PROMISE, NAT.
YOU'VE MADE A LOT.
BUT I GOTTA KEEP THIS ONE, I THINK.
WELL THEN, I'M SORRY FOR WHAT'S COMING, LOGAN.
ME TOO.

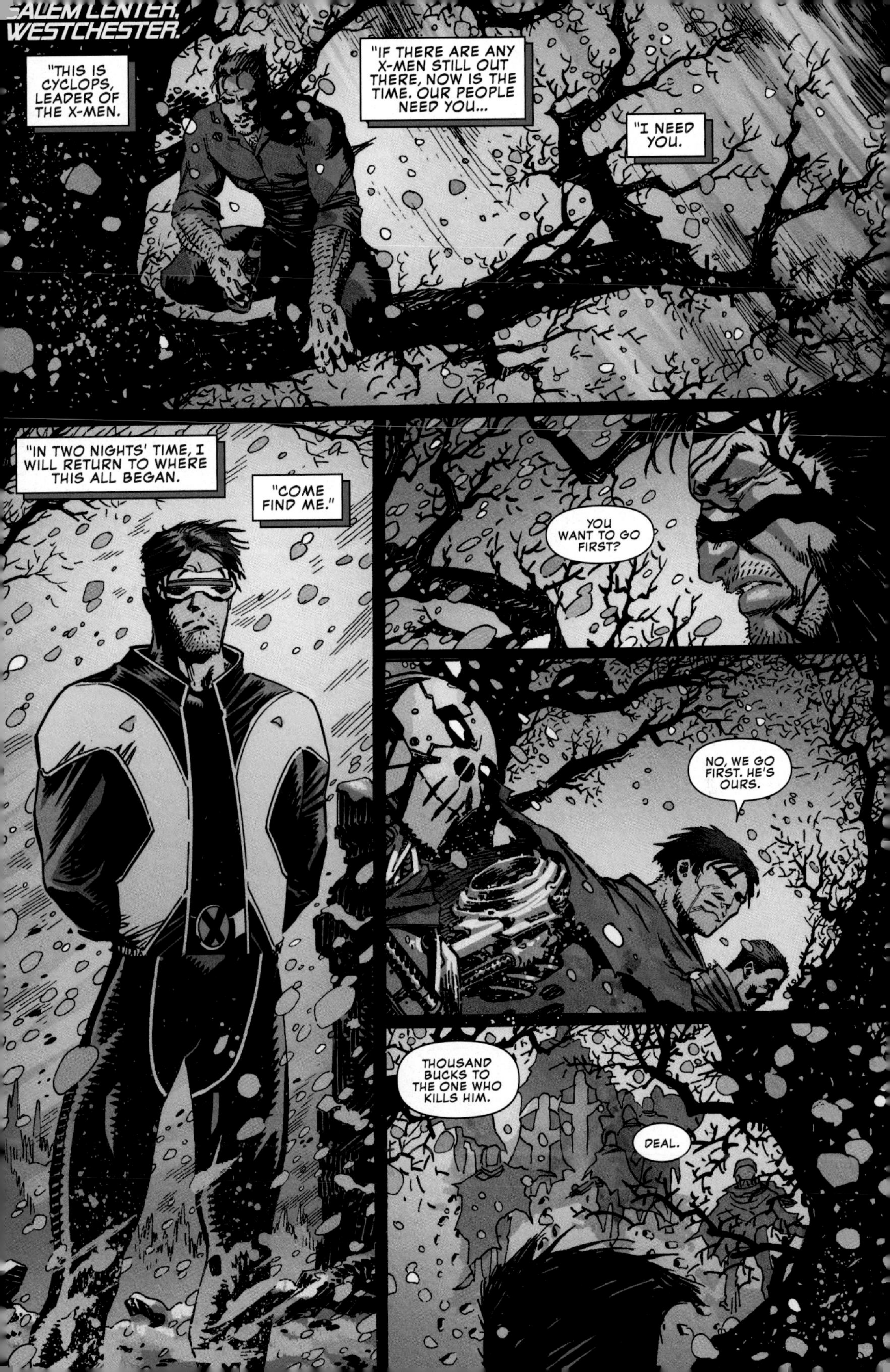
SALEM CENTER, WESTCHESTER.
"THIS IS CYCLOPS, LEADER OF THE X-MEN.
"IF THERE ARE ANY X-MEN STILL OUT THERE, NOW IS THE TIME. OUR PEOPLE NEED YOU...
"I NEED YOU.
"IN TWO NIGHTS' TIME, I WILL RETURN TO WHERE THIS ALL BEGAN.
"COME FIND ME."
YOU WANT TO GO FIRST?
NO, WE GO FIRST. HE'S OURS.
THOUSAND BUCKS TO THE ONE WHO KILLS HIM.
DEAL.

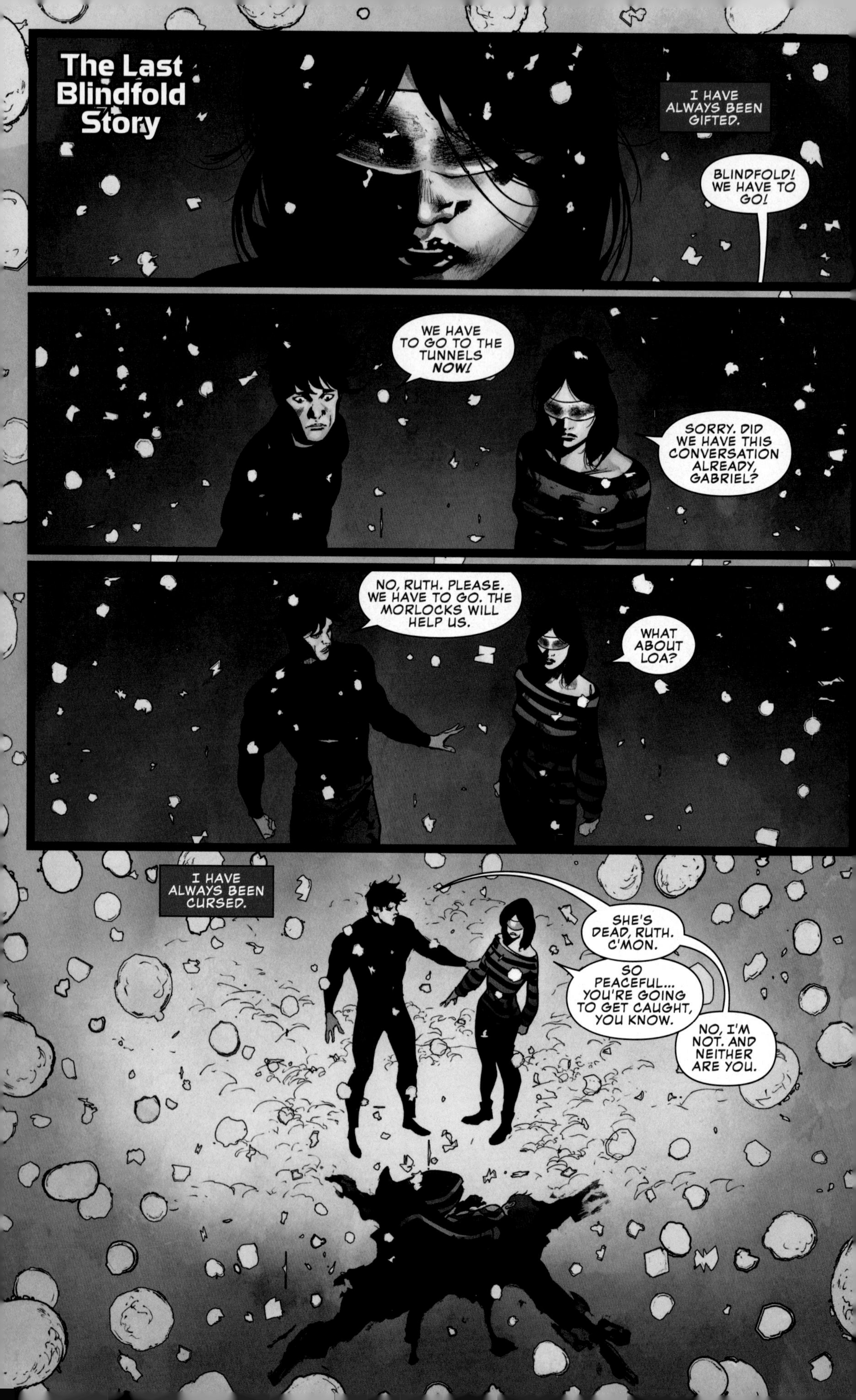
The Last Blindfold Story
I HAVE ALWAYS BEEN GIFTED.
BLINDFOLD! WE HAVE TO GO!
WE HAVE TO GO TO THE TUNNELS NOW!
SORRY. DID WE HAVE THIS CONVERSATION ALREADY, GABRIEL?
NO, RUTH. PLEASE. WE HAVE TO GO. THE MORLOCKS WILL HELP US.
WHAT ABOUT LOA?
I HAVE ALWAYS BEEN CURSED.
SHE'S DEAD, RUTH. C'MON.
SO PEACEFUL... YOU'RE GOING TO GET CAUGHT, YOU KNOW.
NO, I'M NOT. AND NEITHER ARE YOU.

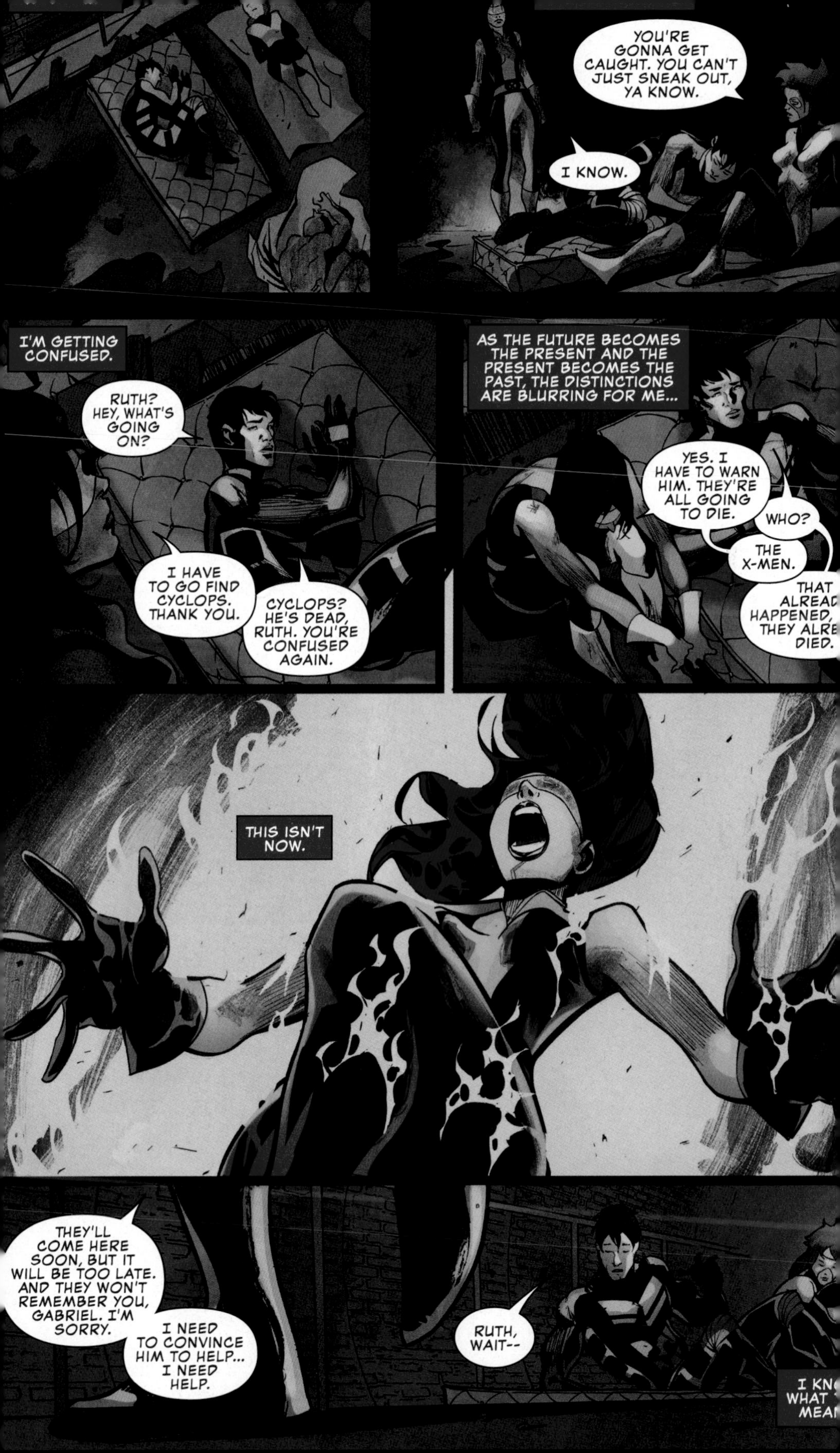

YOU'RE GONNA GET CAUGHT. YOU CAN'T JUST SNEAK OUT, YA KNOW.
I KNOW.
I'M GETTING CONFUSED.
RUTH? HEY, WHAT'S GOING ON?
I HAVE TO GO FIND CYCLOPS. THANK YOU.
CYCLOPS? HE'S DEAD, RUTH. YOU'RE CONFUSED AGAIN.
AS THE FUTURE BECOMES THE PRESENT AND THE PRESENT BECOMES THE PAST, THE DISTINCTIONS ARE BLURRING FOR ME...
YES. I HAVE TO WARN HIM. THEY'RE ALL GOING TO DIE.
WHO?
THE X-MEN.
THIS ISN'T NOW.
THEY'LL COME HERE SOON, BUT IT WILL BE TOO LATE. AND THEY WON'T REMEMBER YOU, GABRIEL. I'M SORRY.
I NEED TO CONVINCE HIM TO HELP... I NEED HELP.
RUTH, WAIT--

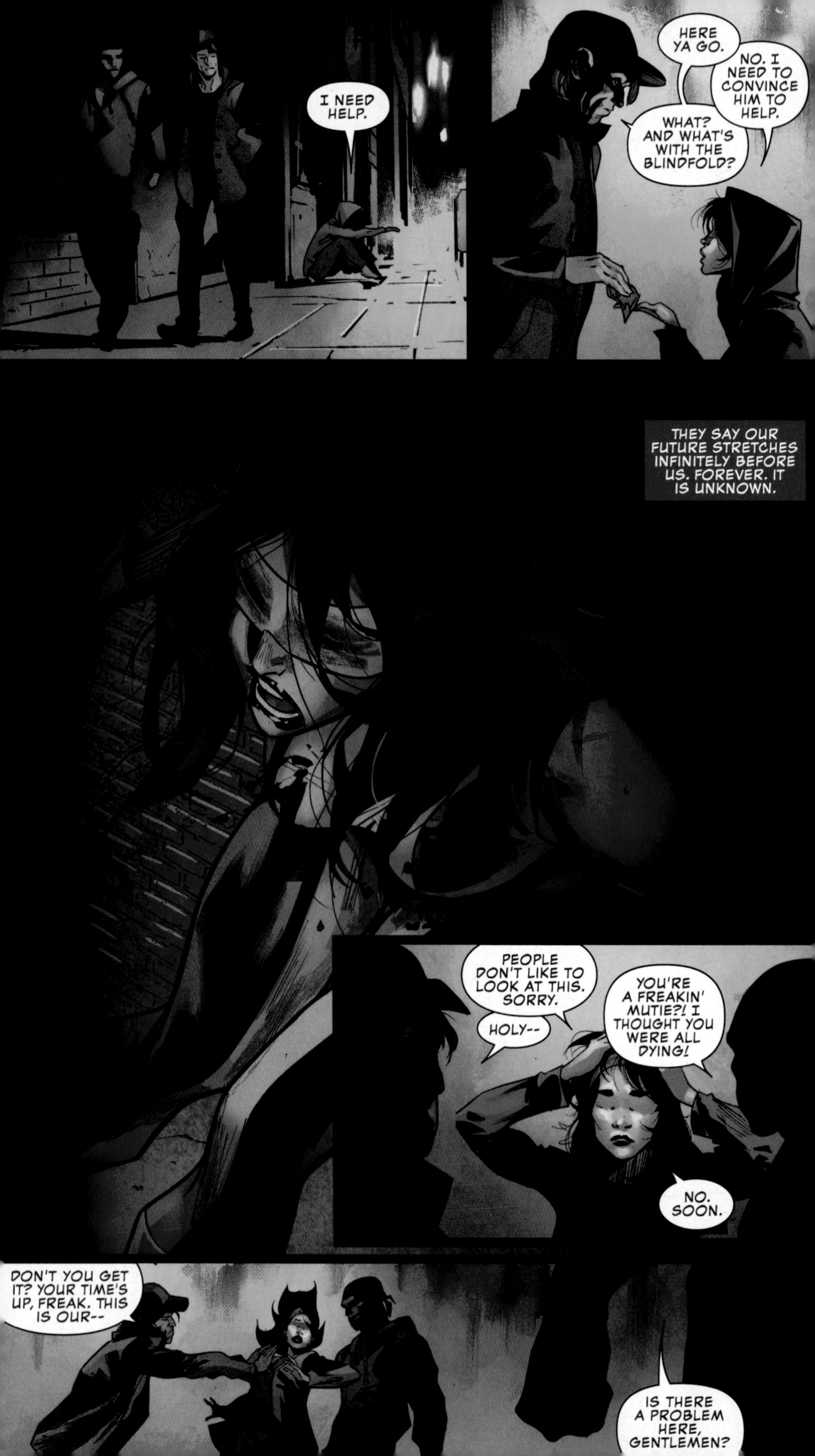

I NEED HELP.
HERE YA GO.
NO. I NEED TO CONVINCE HIM TO HELP.
WHAT? AND WHAT'S WITH THE BLINDFOLD?
THEY SAY OUR FUTURE STRETCHES INFINITELY BEFORE US. FOREVER. IT IS UNKNOWN.
PEOPLE DON'T LIKE TO LOOK AT THIS. SORRY.
HOLY--
YOU'RE A FREAKIN' MUTIE?! I THOUGHT YOU WERE ALL DYING!
NO. SOON.
DON'T YOU GET IT? YOUR TIME'S UP, FREAK. THIS IS OUR--
IS THERE A PROBLEM HERE, GENTLEMEN?

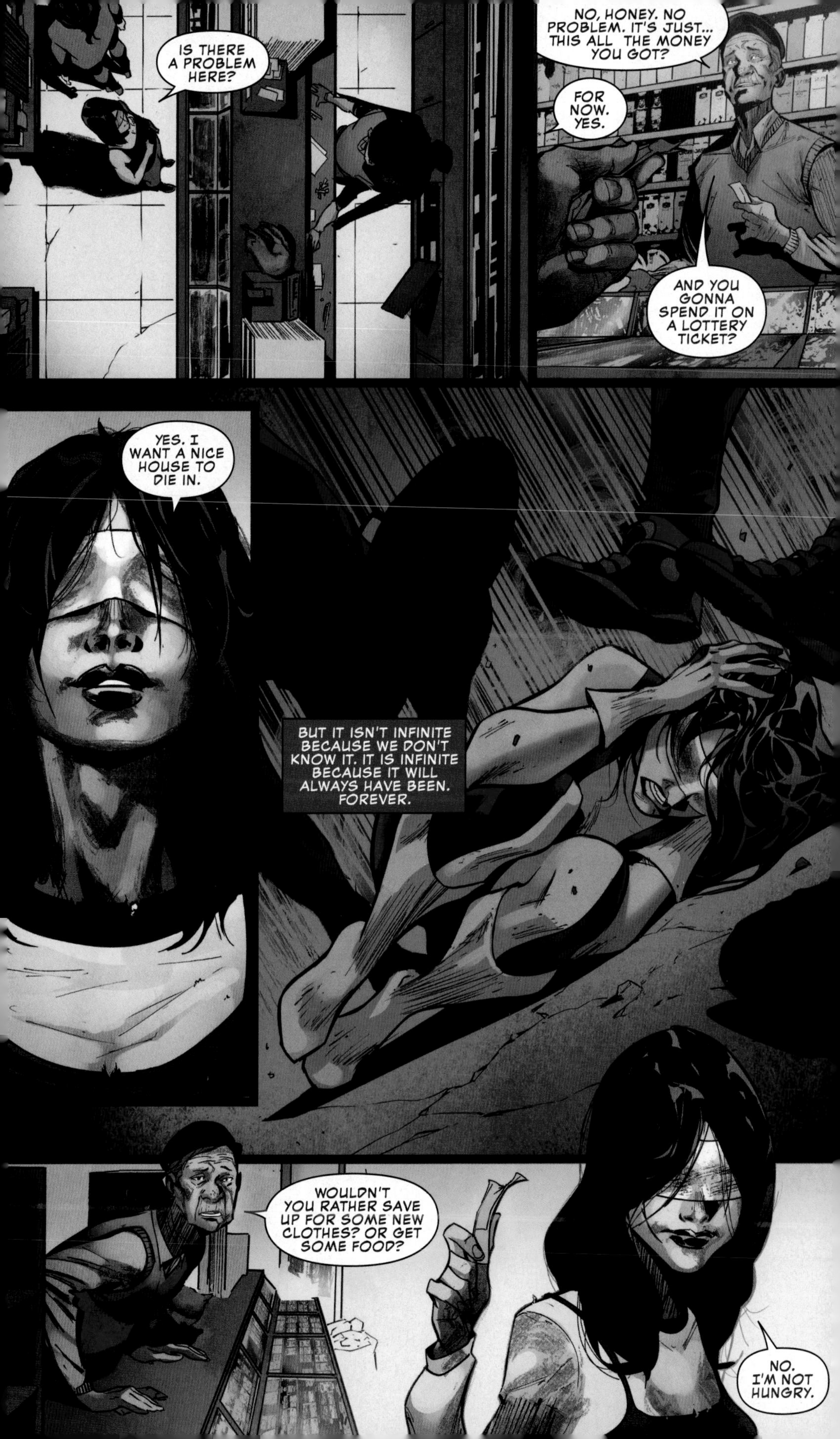
IS THERE A PROBLEM HERE?
NO, HONEY. NO PROBLEM. IT'S JUST... THIS ALL THE MONEY YOU GOT?
FOR NOW. YES.
AND YOU GONNA SPEND IT ON A LOTTERY TICKET?
YES. I WANT A NICE HOUSE TO DIE IN.
BUT IT ISN'T INFINITE BECAUSE WE DON'T KNOW IT. IT IS INFINITE BECAUSE IT WILL ALWAYS HAVE BEEN. FOREVER.
WOULDN'T YOU RATHER SAVE UP FOR SOME NEW CLOTHES? OR GET SOME FOOD?
NO. I'M NOT HUNGRY.

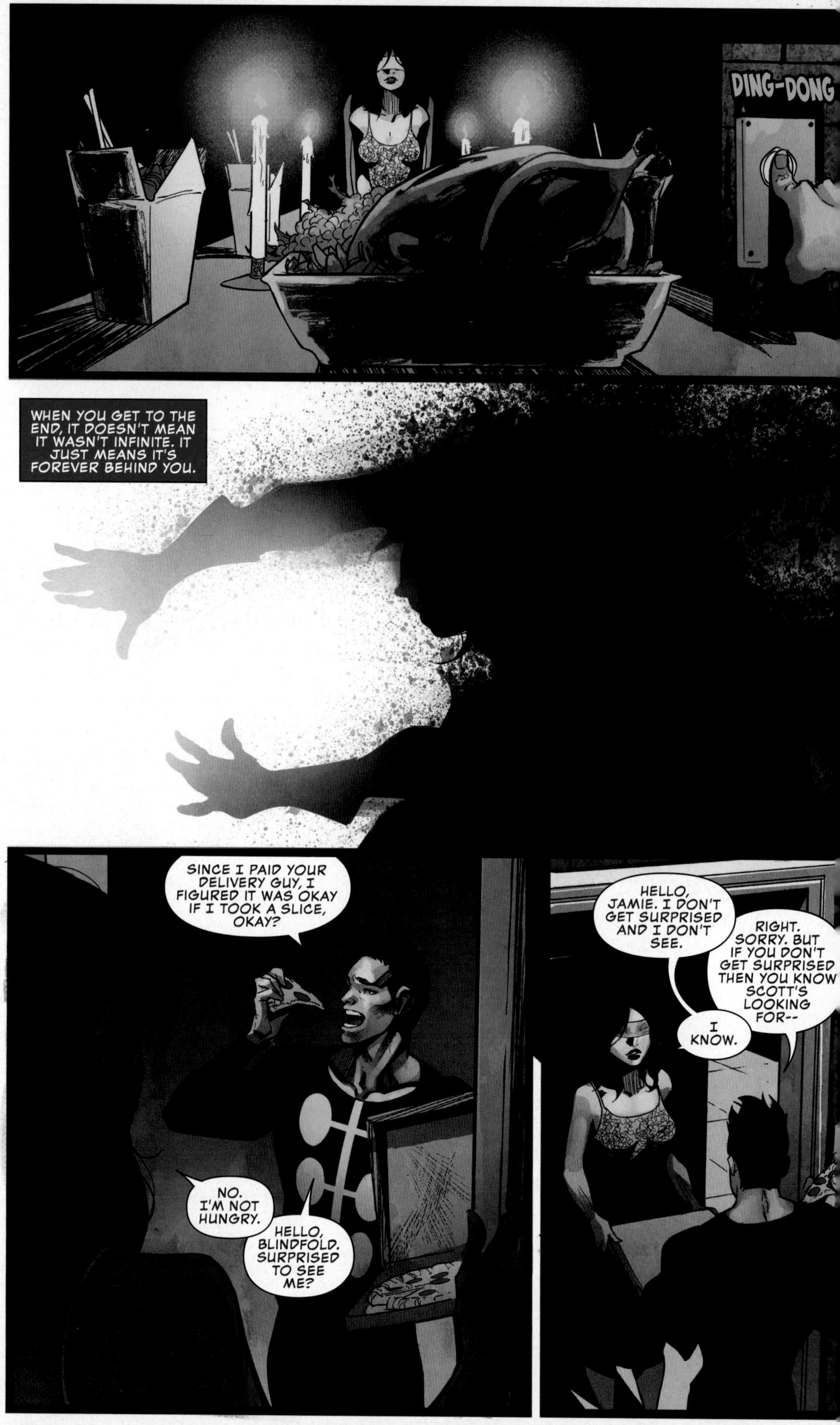
DING-DONG
WHEN YOU GET TO THE END, IT DOESN'T MEAN IT WASN'T INFINITE. IT JUST MEANS IT'S FOREVER BEHIND YOU.
SINCE I PAID YOUR DELIVERY GUY, I FIGURED IT WAS OKAY IF I TOOK A SLICE, OKAY?
NO. I'M NOT HUNGRY.
HELLO, BLINDFOLD. SURPRISED TO SEE ME?
HELLO, JAMIE. I DON'T GET SURPRISED AND I DON'T SEE.
RIGHT. SORRY. BUT IF YOU DON'T GET SURPRISED THEN YOU KNOW SCOTT'S LOOKING FOR--
I KNOW.

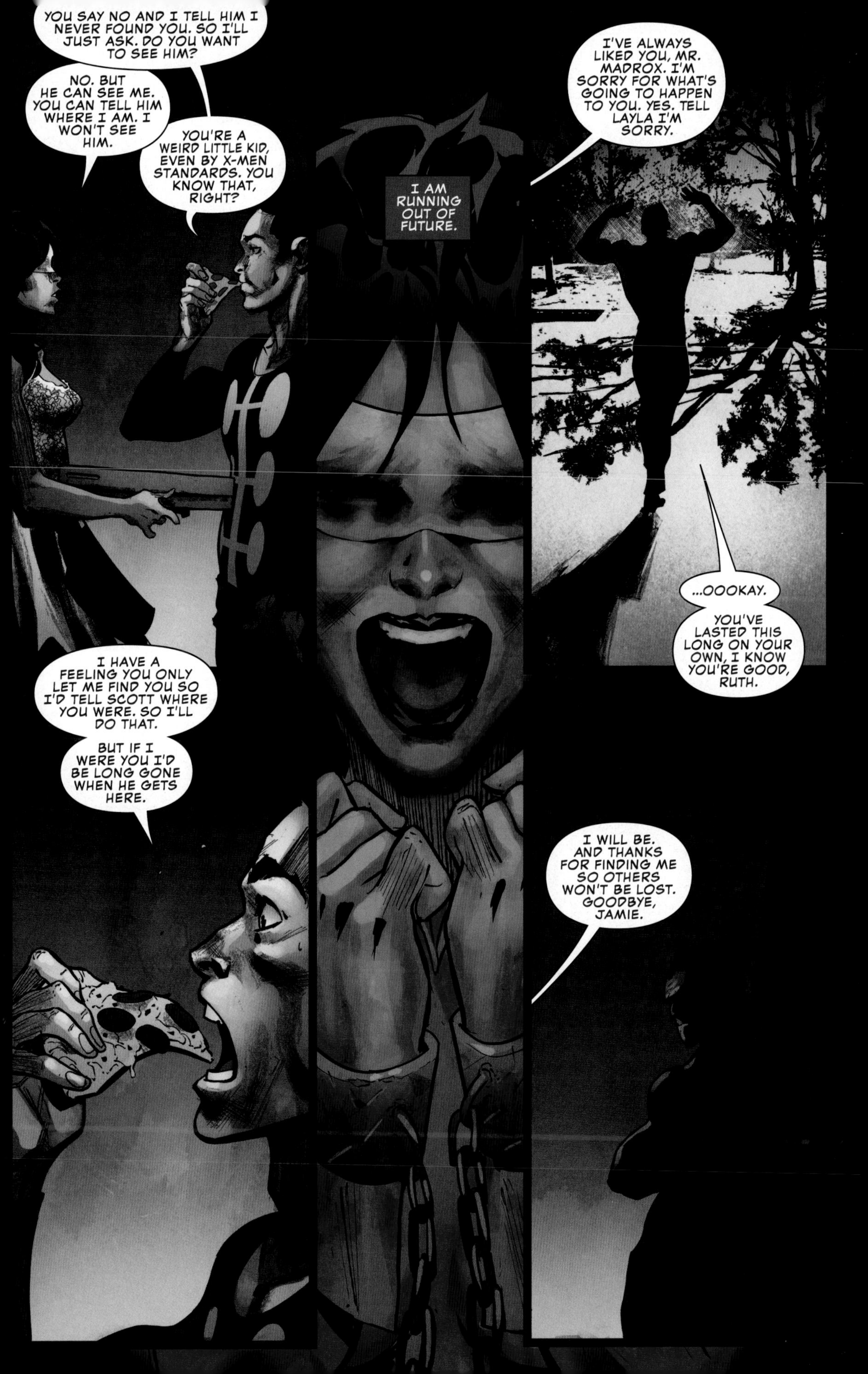
YOU SAY NO AND I TELL HIM I NEVER FOUND YOU. SO I'LL JUST ASK. DO YOU WANT TO SEE HIM?
NO. BUT HE CAN SEE ME. YOU CAN TELL HIM WHERE I AM. I WON'T SEE HIM.
YOU'RE A WEIRD LITTLE KID, EVEN BY X-MEN STANDARDS. YOU KNOW THAT, RIGHT?
I AM RUNNING OUT OF FUTURE.
I'VE ALWAYS LIKED YOU, MR. MADROX. I'M SORRY FOR WHAT'S GOING TO HAPPEN TO YOU. YES. TELL LAYLA I'M SORRY.
...OOOKAY.
YOU'VE LASTED THIS LONG ON YOUR OWN, I KNOW YOU'RE GOOD, RUTH.
I HAVE A FEELING YOU ONLY LET ME FIND YOU SO I'D TELL SCOTT WHERE YOU WERE. SO I'LL DO THAT.
BUT IF I WERE YOU I'D BE LONG GONE WHEN HE GETS HERE.
I WILL BE. AND THANKS FOR FINDING ME SO OTHERS WON'T BE LOST. GOODBYE, JAMIE.

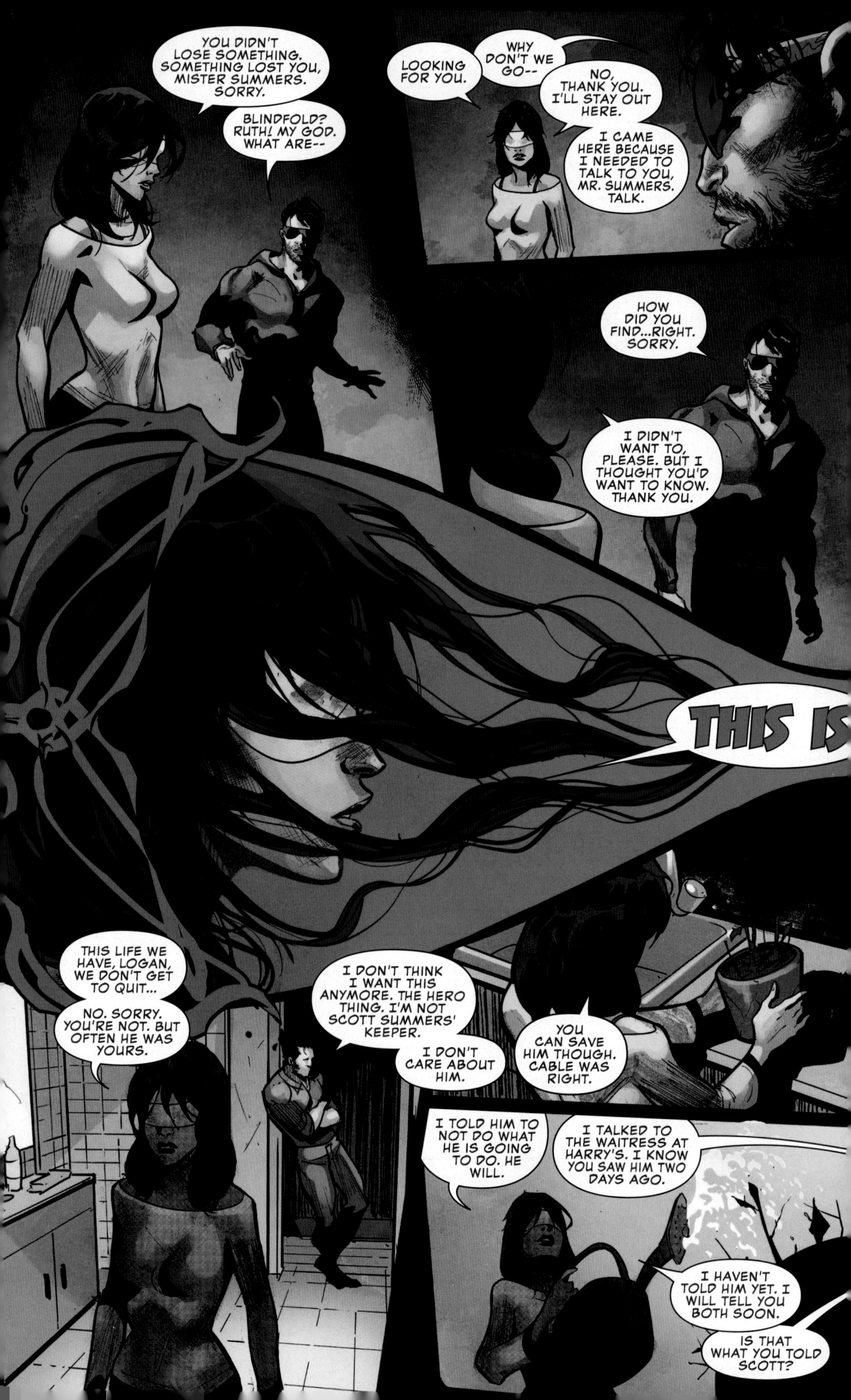
YOU DIDN'T LOSE SOMETHING. SOMETHING LOST YOU, MISTER SUMMERS. SORRY.
BLINDFOLD? RUTH! MY GOD. WHAT ARE--
LOOKING FOR YOU.
WHY DON'T WE GO--
NO, THANK YOU. I'LL STAY OUT HERE.
I CAME HERE BECAUSE I NEEDED TO TALK TO YOU, MR. SUMMERS. TALK.
HOW DID YOU FIND...RIGHT. SORRY.
I DIDN'T WANT TO, PLEASE. BUT I THOUGHT YOU'D WANT TO KNOW. THANK YOU.
THIS IS
THIS LIFE WE HAVE, LOGAN, WE DON'T GET TO QUIT...
NO. SORRY. YOU'RE NOT. BUT OFTEN HE WAS YOURS.
I DON'T THINK I WANT THIS ANYMORE. THE HERO THING. I'M NOT SCOTT SUMMERS' KEEPER.
I DON'T CARE ABOUT HIM.
YOU CAN SAVE HIM THOUGH. CABLE WAS RIGHT.
I TOLD HIM TO NOT DO WHAT HE IS GOING TO DO. HE WILL.
I TALKED TO THE WAITRESS AT HARRY'S. I KNOW YOU SAW HIM TWO DAYS AGO.
I HAVEN'T TOLD HIM YET. I WILL TELL YOU BOTH SOON.
IS THAT WHAT YOU TOLD SCOTT?

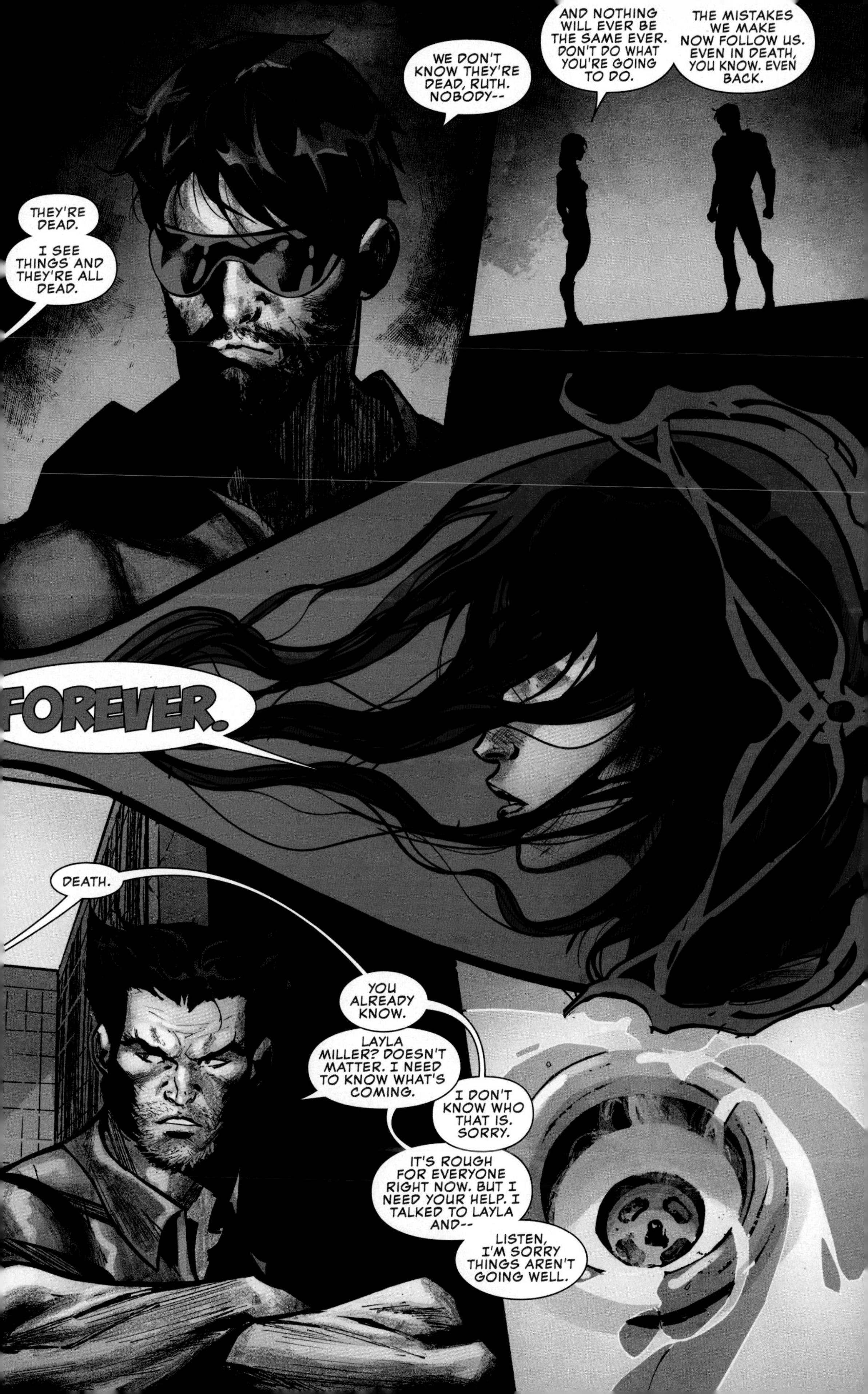
THEY'RE DEAD.
I SEE THINGS AND THEY'RE ALL DEAD.
WE DON'T KNOW THEY'RE DEAD, RUTH. NOBODY--
AND NOTHING WILL EVER BE THE SAME EVER. DON'T DO WHAT YOU'RE GOING TO DO.
THE MISTAKES WE MAKE NOW FOLLOW US. EVEN IN DEATH, YOU KNOW. EVEN BACK.
FOREVER.
DEATH.
YOU ALREADY KNOW.
LAYLA MILLER? DOESN'T MATTER. I NEED TO KNOW WHAT'S COMING.
I DON'T KNOW WHO THAT IS. SORRY.
IT'S ROUGH FOR EVERYONE RIGHT NOW. BUT I NEED YOUR HELP. I TALKED TO LAYLA AND--
LISTEN, I'M SORRY THINGS AREN'T GOING WELL.

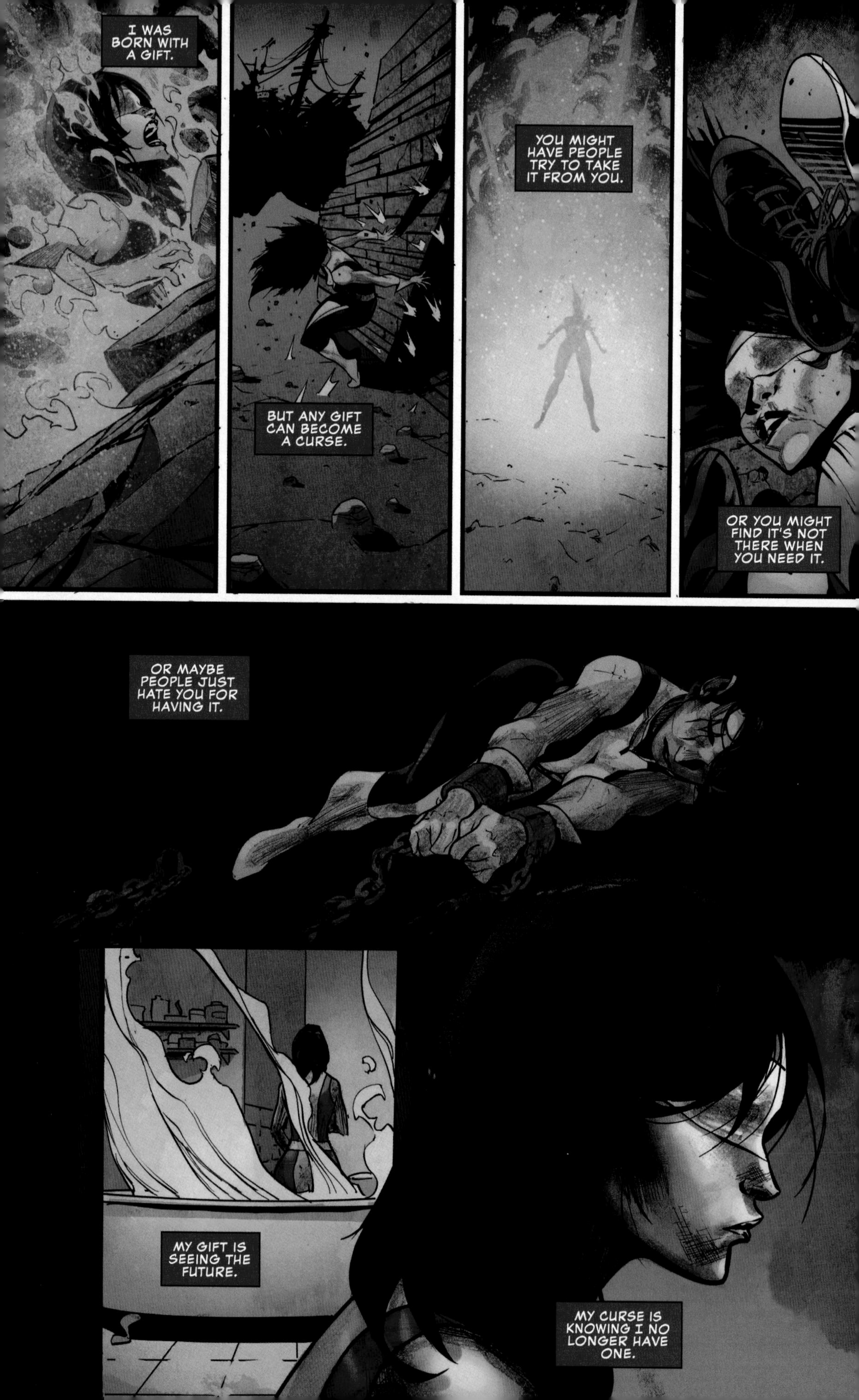
I WAS BORN WITH A GIFT.
BUT ANY GIFT CAN BECOME A CURSE.
YOU MIGHT HAVE PEOPLE TRY TO TAKE IT FROM YOU.
OR YOU MIGHT FIND IT'S NOT THERE WHEN YOU NEED IT.
OR MAYBE PEOPLE JUST HATE YOU FOR HAVING IT.
MY GIFT IS SEEING THE FUTURE.
MY CURSE IS KNOWING I NO LONGER HAVE ONE.

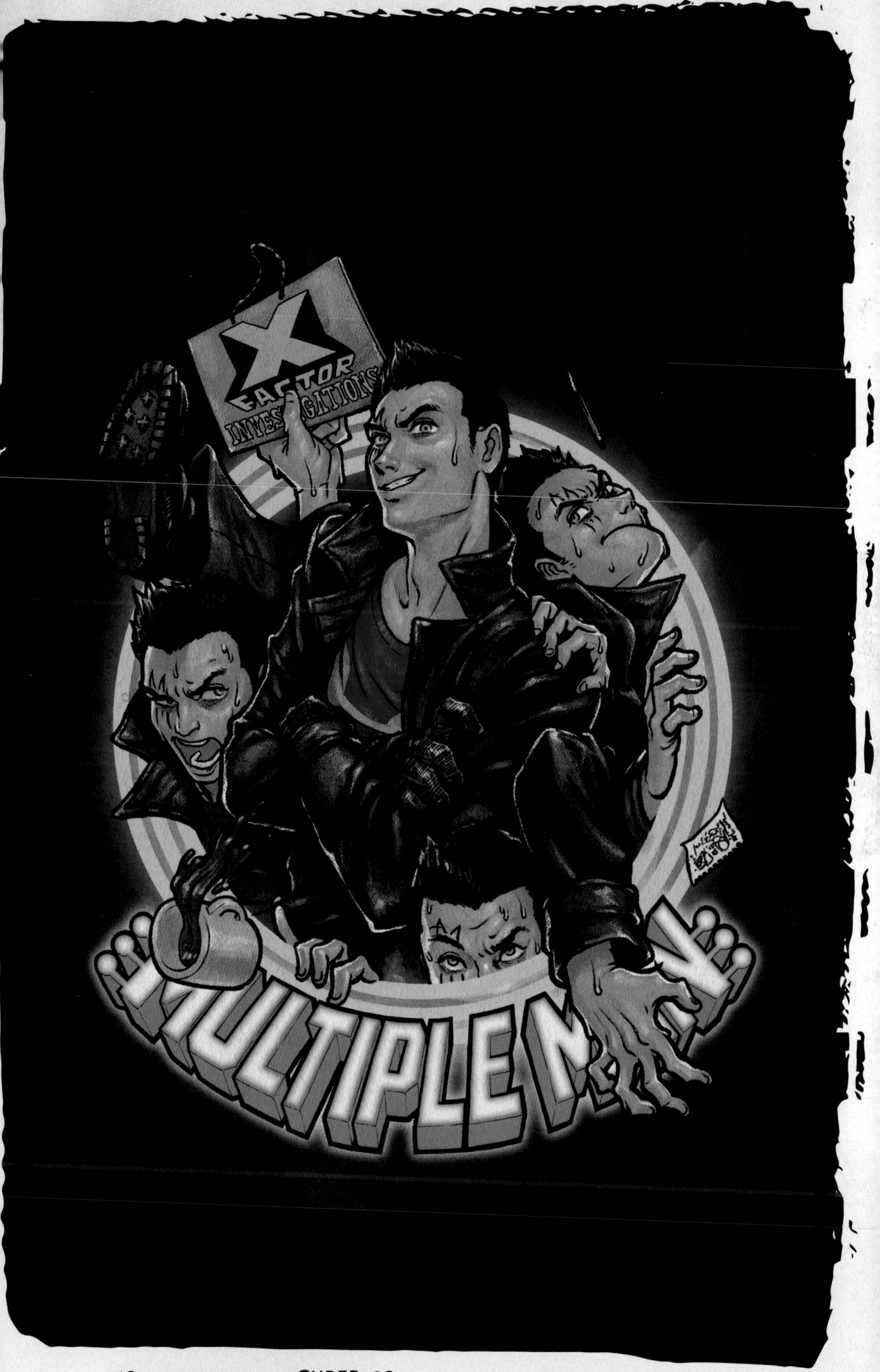
X
FACTOR
MULTIPLE

#12 VARIANT COVER BY SUPERLOG

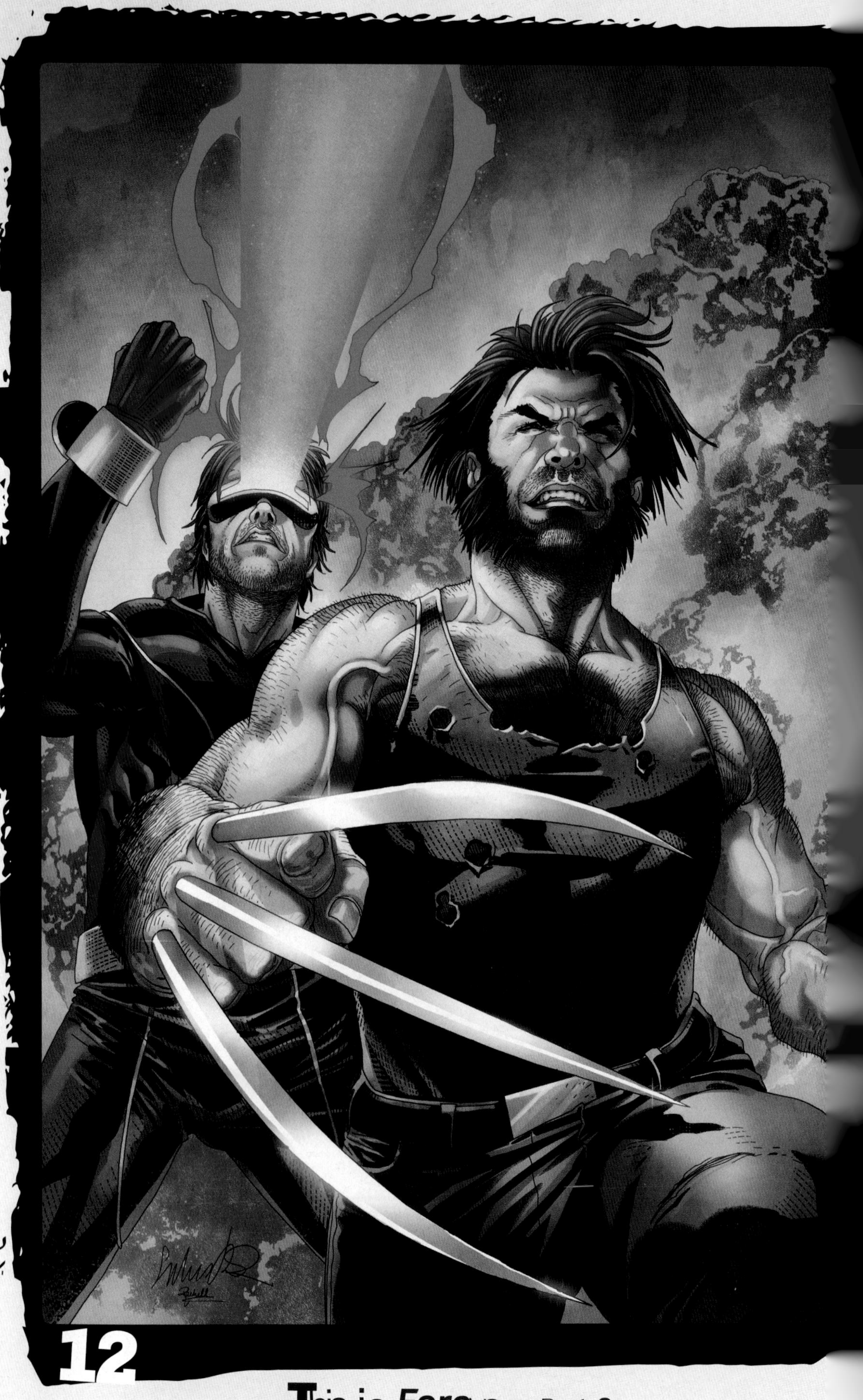
12

This is Forever Part 2

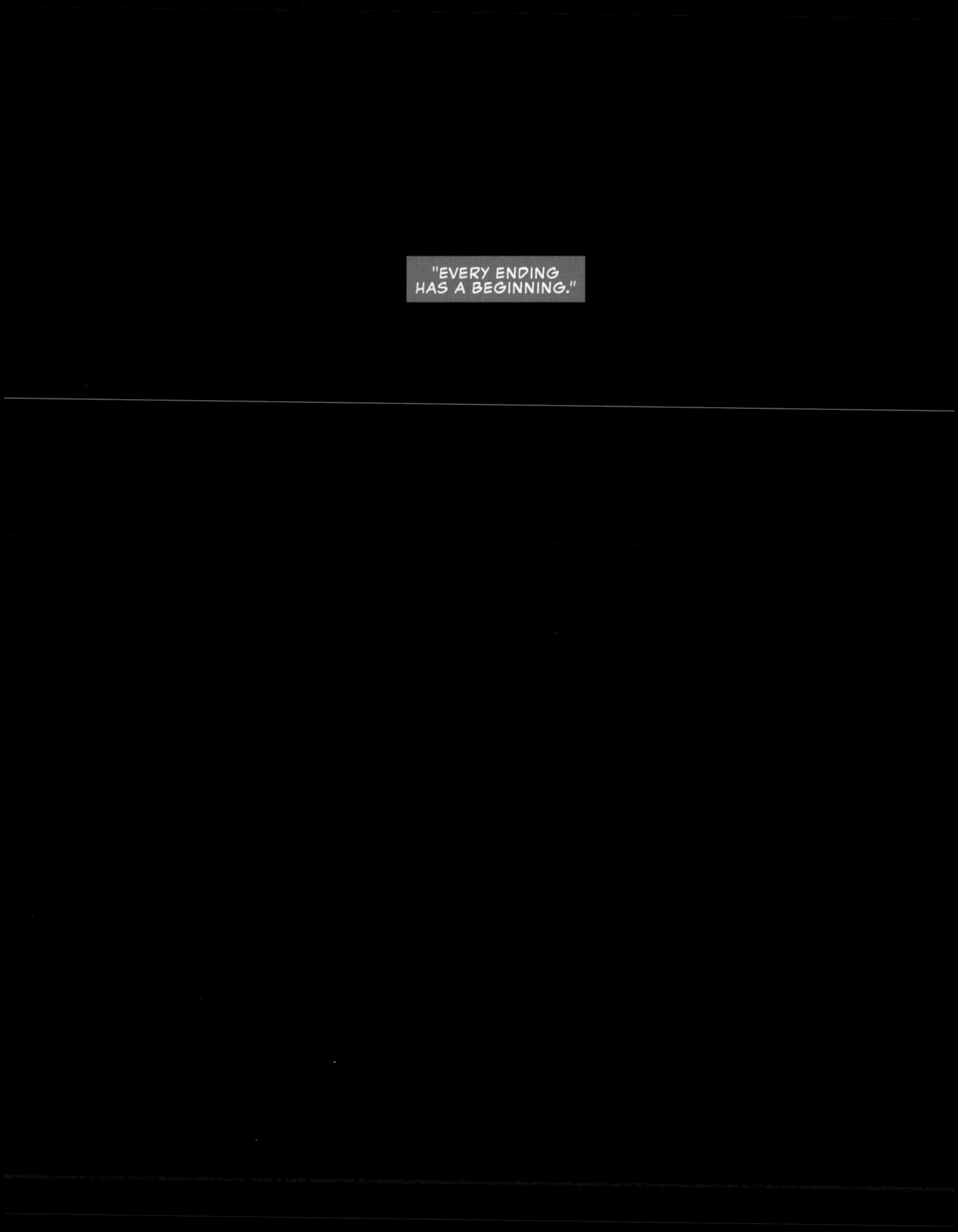
"EVERY ENDING
HAS A BEGINNING."

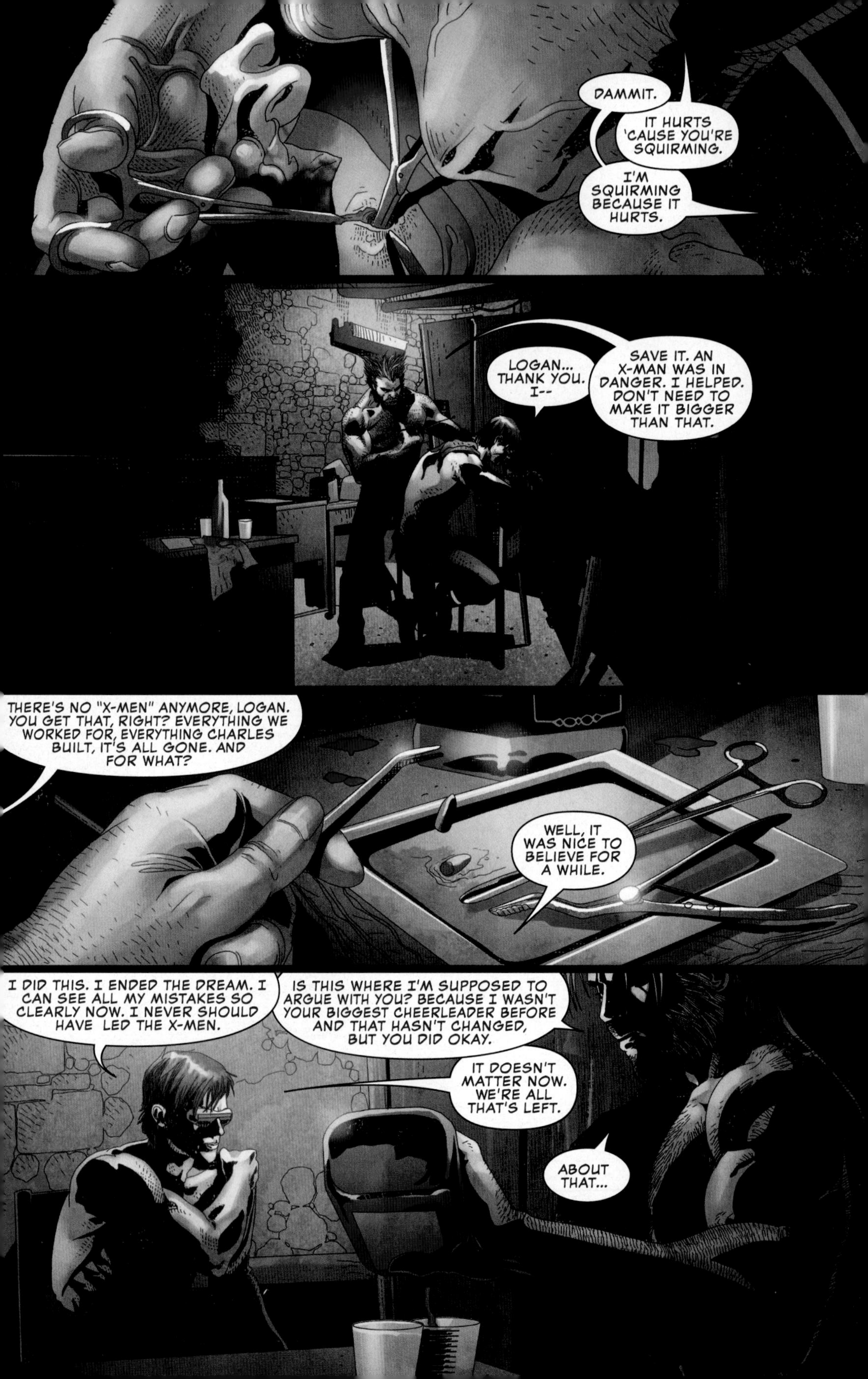
DAMMIT.
IT HURTS 'CAUSE YOU'RE SQUIRMING.
I'M SQUIRMING BECAUSE IT HURTS.
LOGAN... THANK YOU. I--
SAVE IT. AN X-MAN WAS IN DANGER. I HELPED. DON'T NEED TO MAKE IT BIGGER THAN THAT.
THERE'S NO "X-MEN" ANYMORE, LOGAN. YOU GET THAT, RIGHT? EVERYTHING WE WORKED FOR, EVERYTHING CHARLES BUILT, IT'S ALL GONE. AND FOR WHAT?
WELL, IT WAS NICE TO BELIEVE FOR A WHILE.
I DID THIS. I ENDED THE DREAM. I CAN SEE ALL MY MISTAKES SO CLEARLY NOW. I NEVER SHOULD HAVE LED THE X-MEN.
IS THIS WHERE I'M SUPPOSED TO ARGUE WITH YOU? BECAUSE I WASN'T YOUR BIGGEST CHEERLEADER BEFORE AND THAT HASN'T CHANGED, BUT YOU DID OKAY.
IT DOESN'T MATTER NOW. WE'RE ALL THAT'S LEFT.
ABOUT THAT...

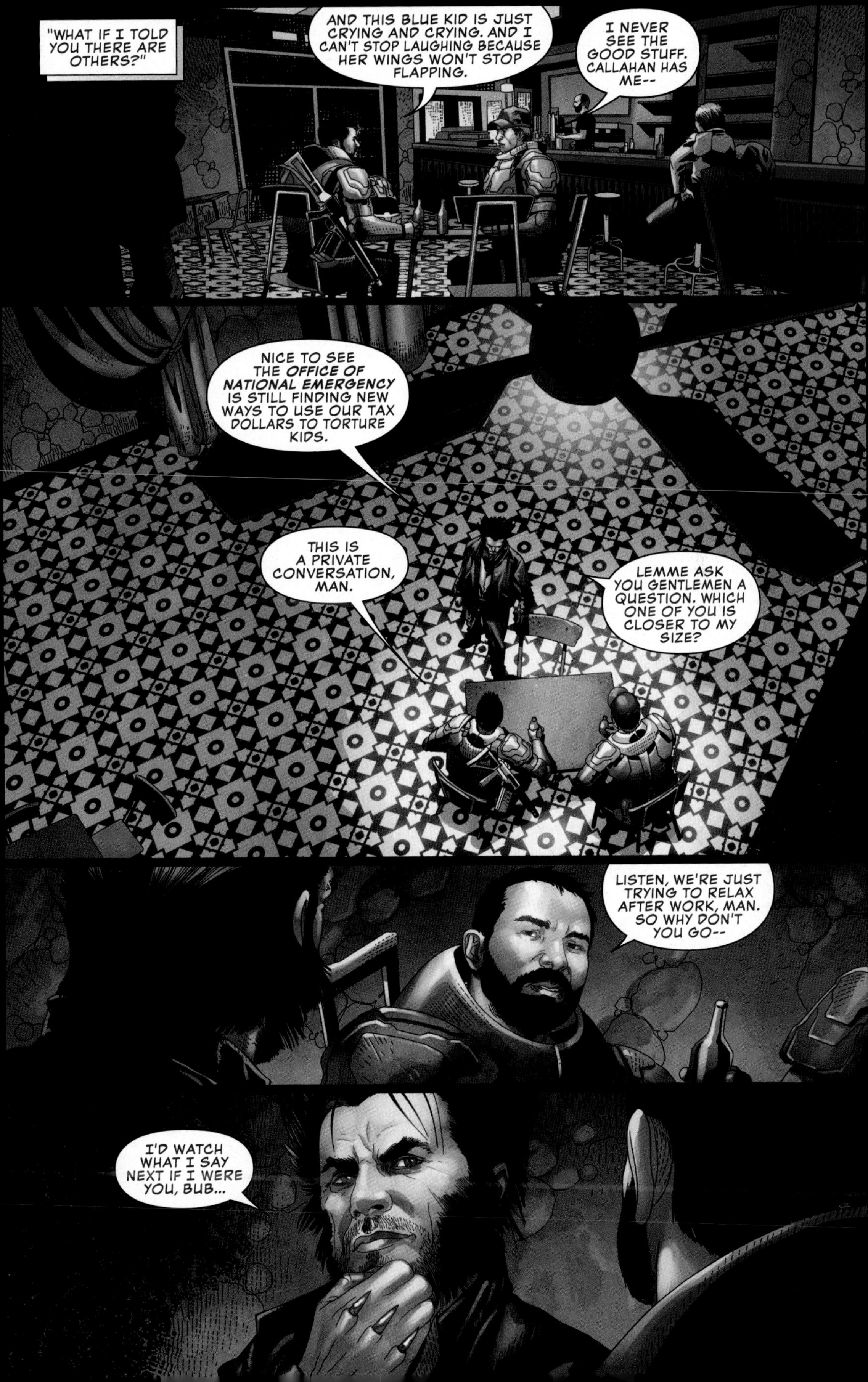
"WHAT IF I TOLD YOU THERE ARE OTHERS?"
AND THIS BLUE KID IS JUST CRYING AND CRYING. AND I CAN'T STOP LAUGHING BECAUSE HER WINGS WON'T STOP FLAPPING.
I NEVER SEE THE GOOD STUFF. CALLAHAN HAS ME--
NICE TO SEE THE OFFICE OF NATIONAL EMERGENCY IS STILL FINDING NEW WAYS TO USE OUR TAX DOLLARS TO TORTURE KIDS.
THIS IS A PRIVATE CONVERSATION, MAN.
LEMME ASK YOU GENTLEMEN A QUESTION. WHICH ONE OF YOU IS CLOSER TO MY SIZE?
LISTEN, WE'RE JUST TRYING TO RELAX AFTER WORK, MAN. SO WHY DON'T YOU GO--
I'D WATCH WHAT I SAY NEXT IF I WERE YOU, BUB...

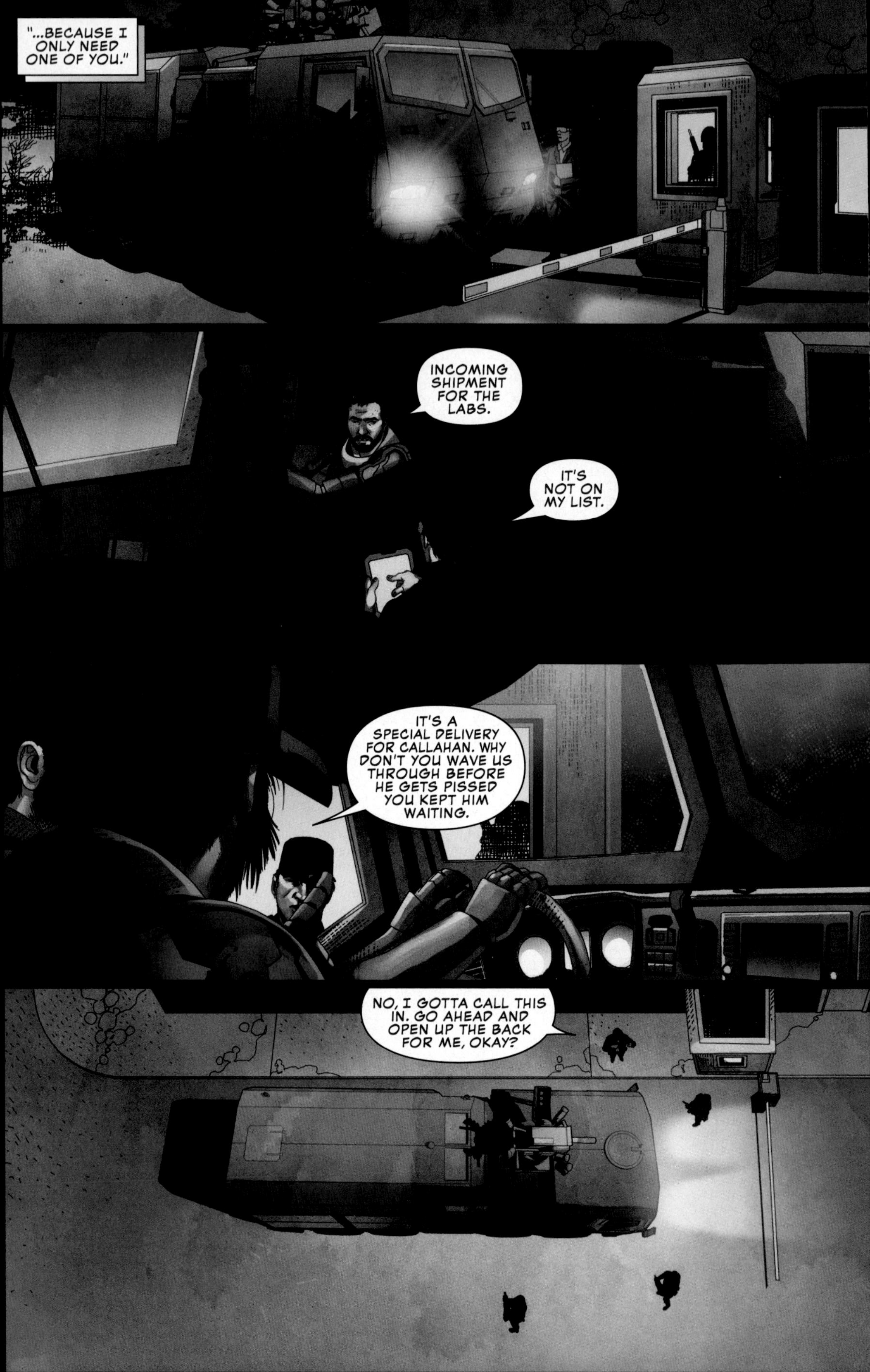
"...BECAUSE I ONLY NEED ONE OF YOU."
INCOMING SHIPMENT FOR THE LABS.
IT'S NOT ON MY LIST.
IT'S A SPECIAL DELIVERY FOR CALLAHAN. WHY DON'T YOU WAVE US THROUGH BEFORE HE GETS PISSED YOU KEPT HIM WAITING.
NO, I GOTTA CALL THIS IN. GO AHEAD AND OPEN UP THE BACK FOR ME, OKAY?

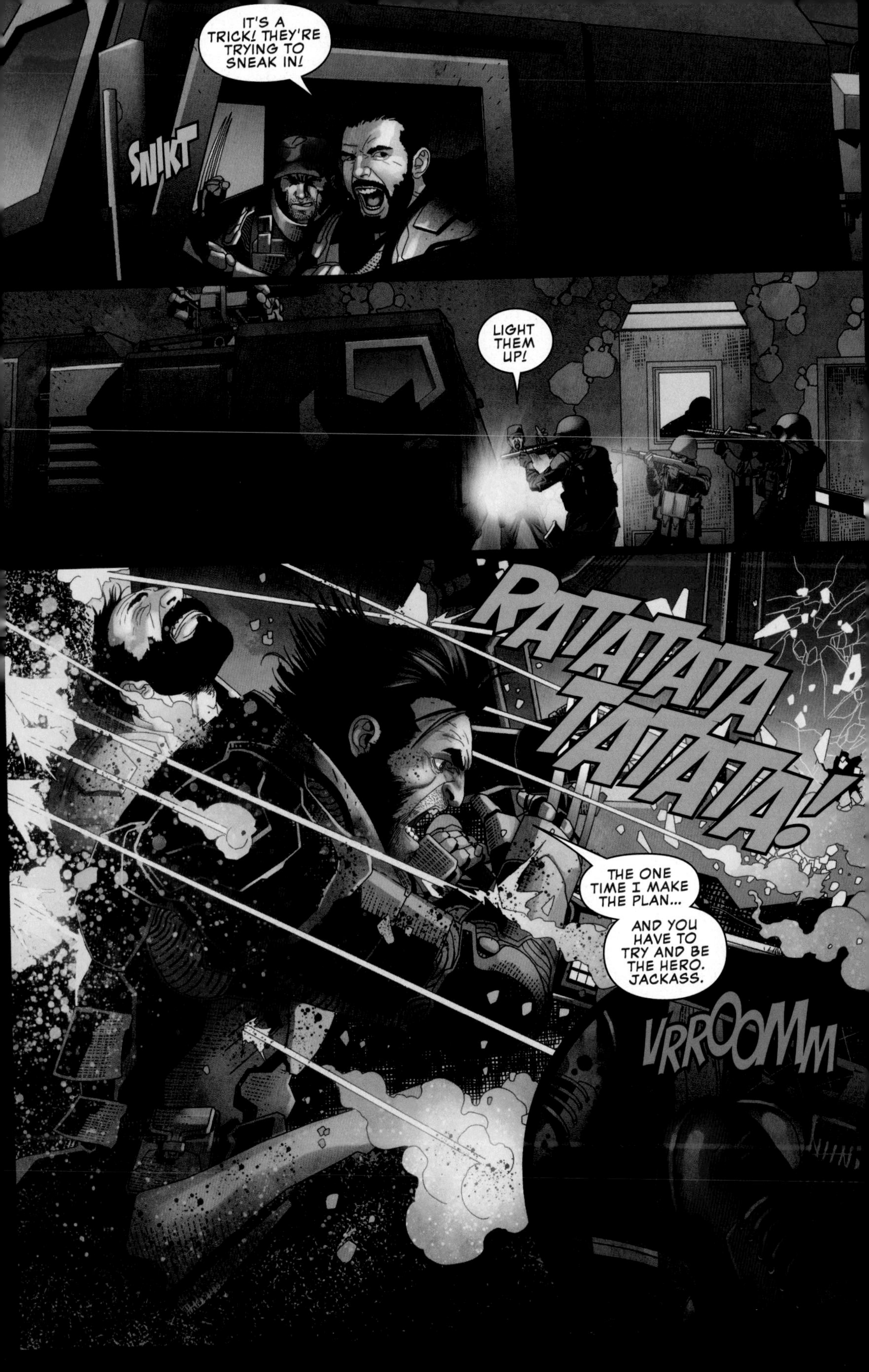
IT'S A TRICK! THEY'RE TRYING TO SNEAK IN!
SNIKT
LIGHT THEM UP!
RATATATATA TATATATA!
THE ONE TIME I MAKE THE PLAN...
AND YOU HAVE TO TRY AND BE THE HERO. JACKASS.
VRROOMM

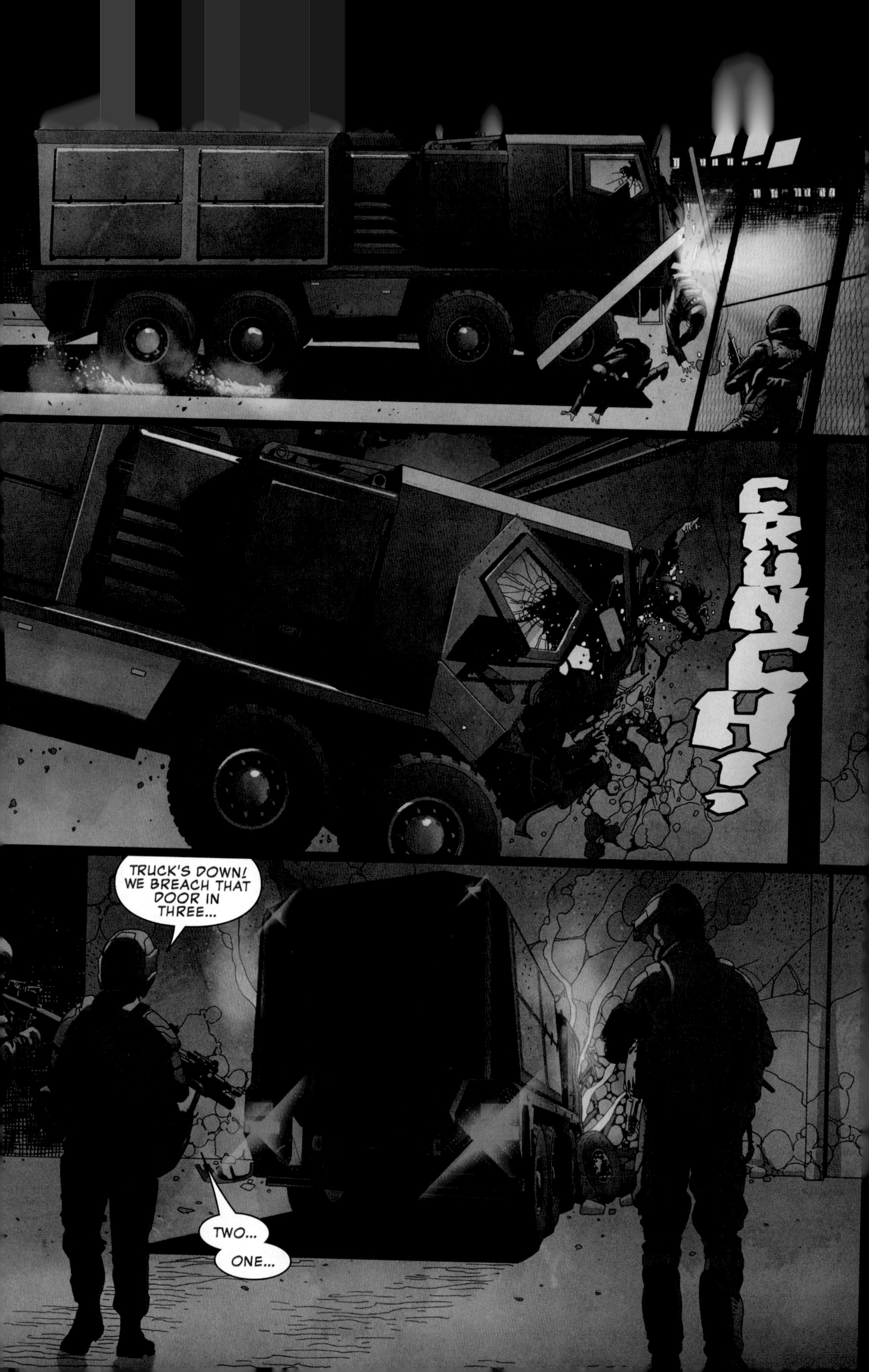
CRUNCH!!
TRUCK'S DOWN! WE BREACH THAT DOOR IN THREE...
TWO...
ONE...

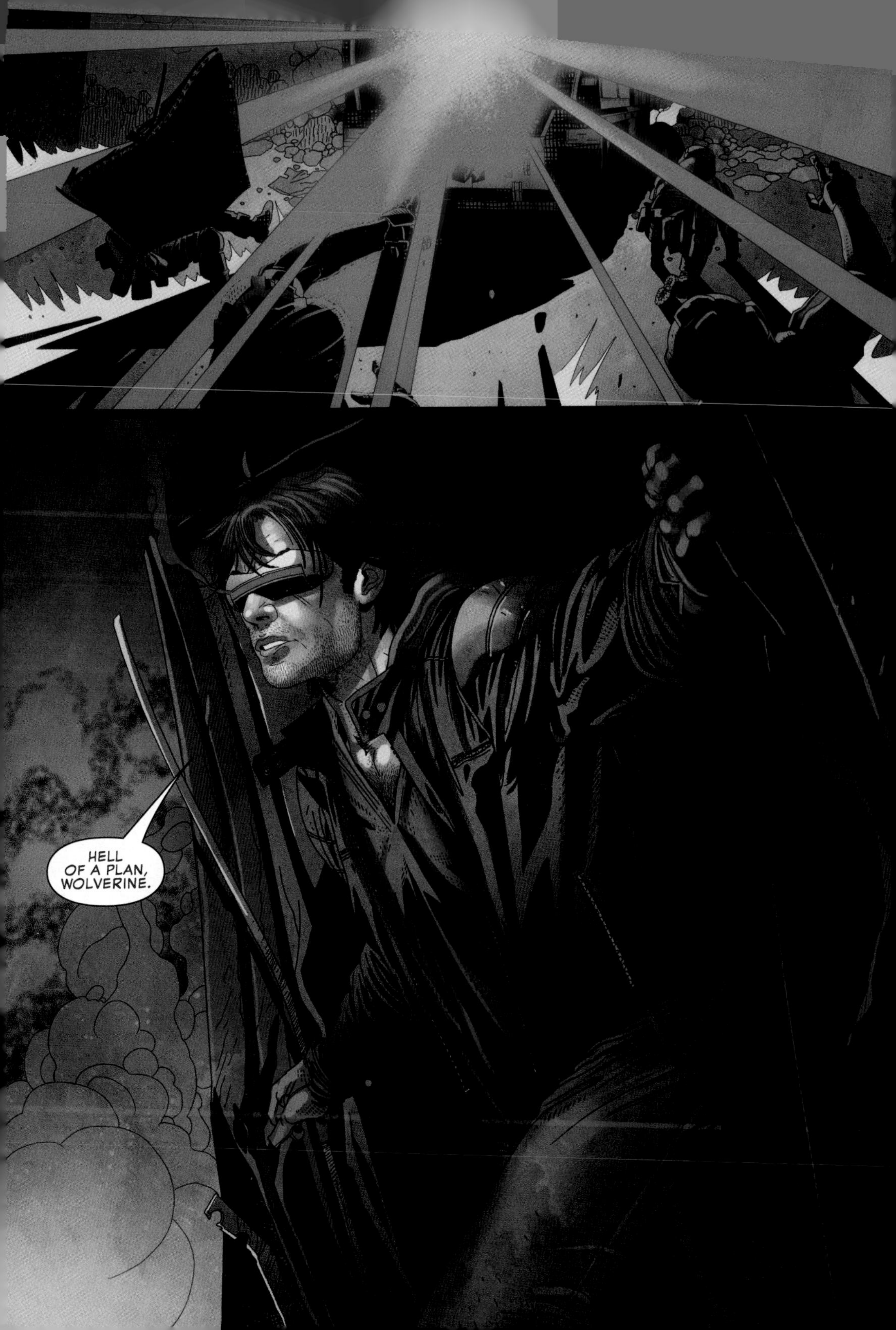
HELL OF A PLAN, WOLVERINE.

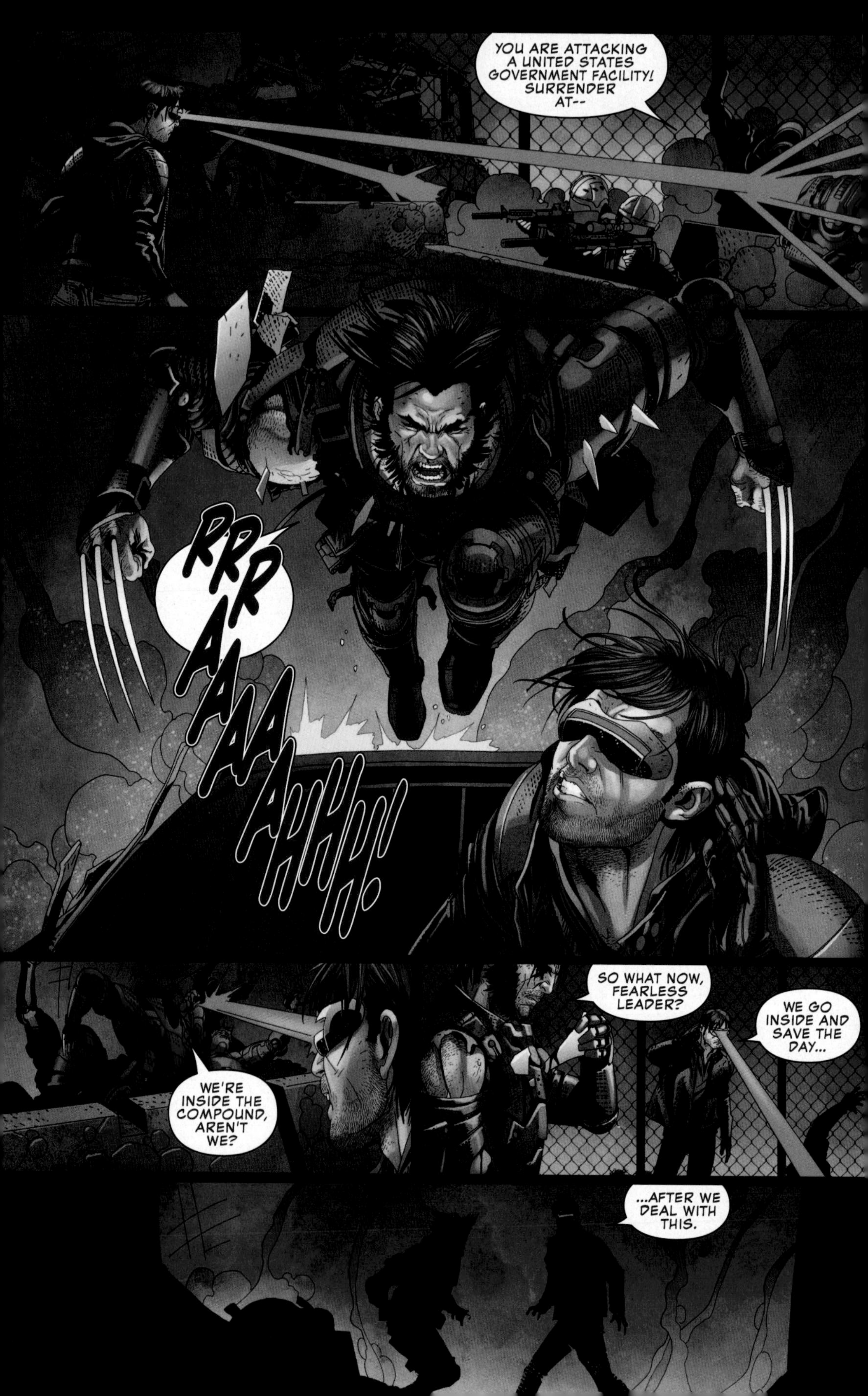
YOU ARE ATTACKING A UNITED STATES GOVERNMENT FACILITY! SURRENDER AT--
RRRAAAAAHHH!
SO WHAT NOW, FEARLESS LEADER?
WE'RE INSIDE THE COMPOUND, AREN'T WE?
WE GO INSIDE AND SAVE THE DAY...
...AFTER WE DEAL WITH THIS.

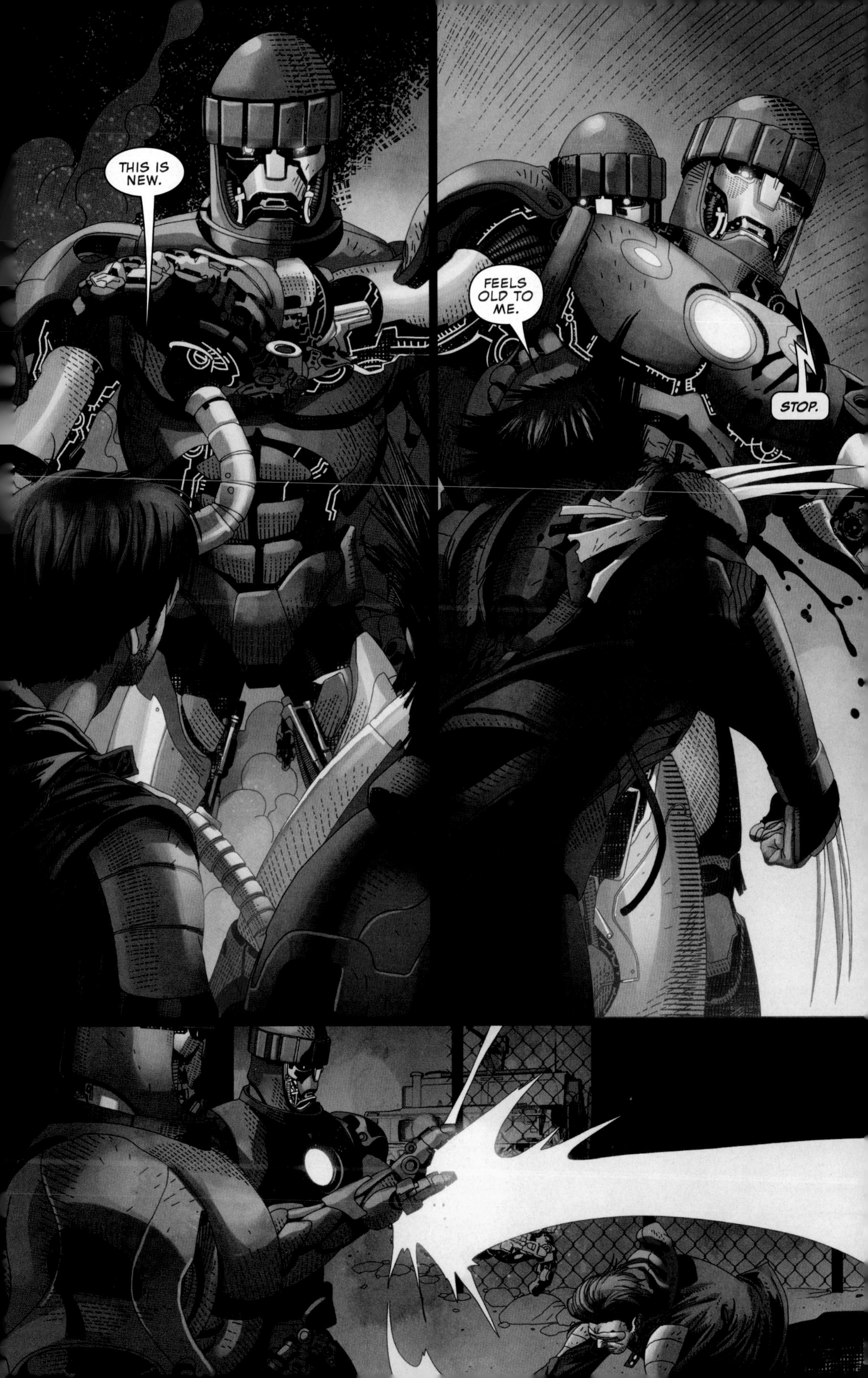
THIS IS NEW.
FEELS OLD TO ME.
STOP.

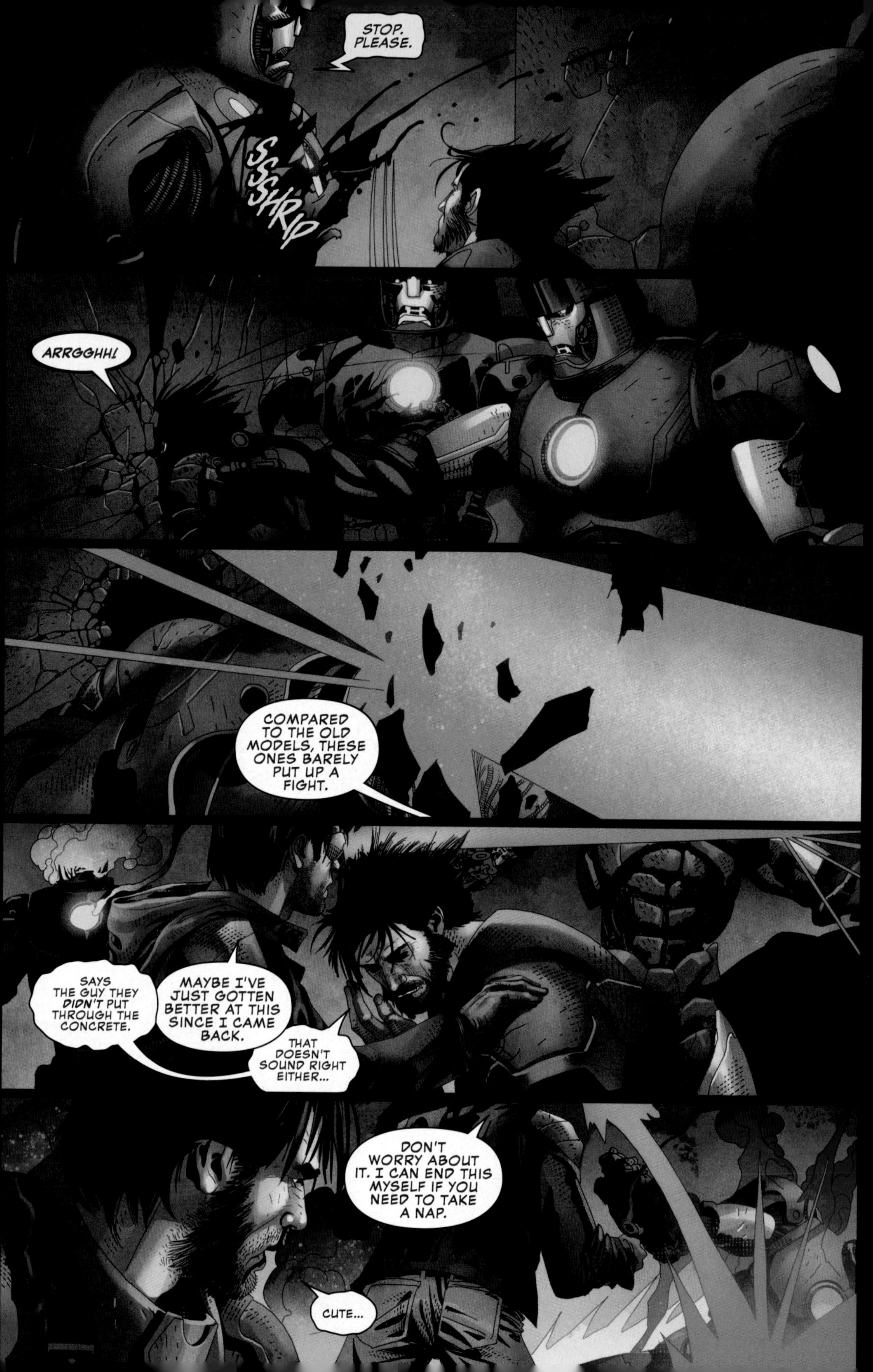
STOP. PLEASE.
SSSHRIP
ARRGGHH!
COMPARED TO THE OLD MODELS, THESE ONES BARELY PUT UP A FIGHT.
SAYS THE GUY THEY DIDN'T PUT THROUGH THE CONCRETE.
MAYBE I'VE JUST GOTTEN BETTER AT THIS SINCE I CAME BACK.
THAT DOESN'T SOUND RIGHT EITHER...
DON'T WORRY ABOUT IT. I CAN END THIS MYSELF IF YOU NEED TO TAKE A NAP.
CUTE...

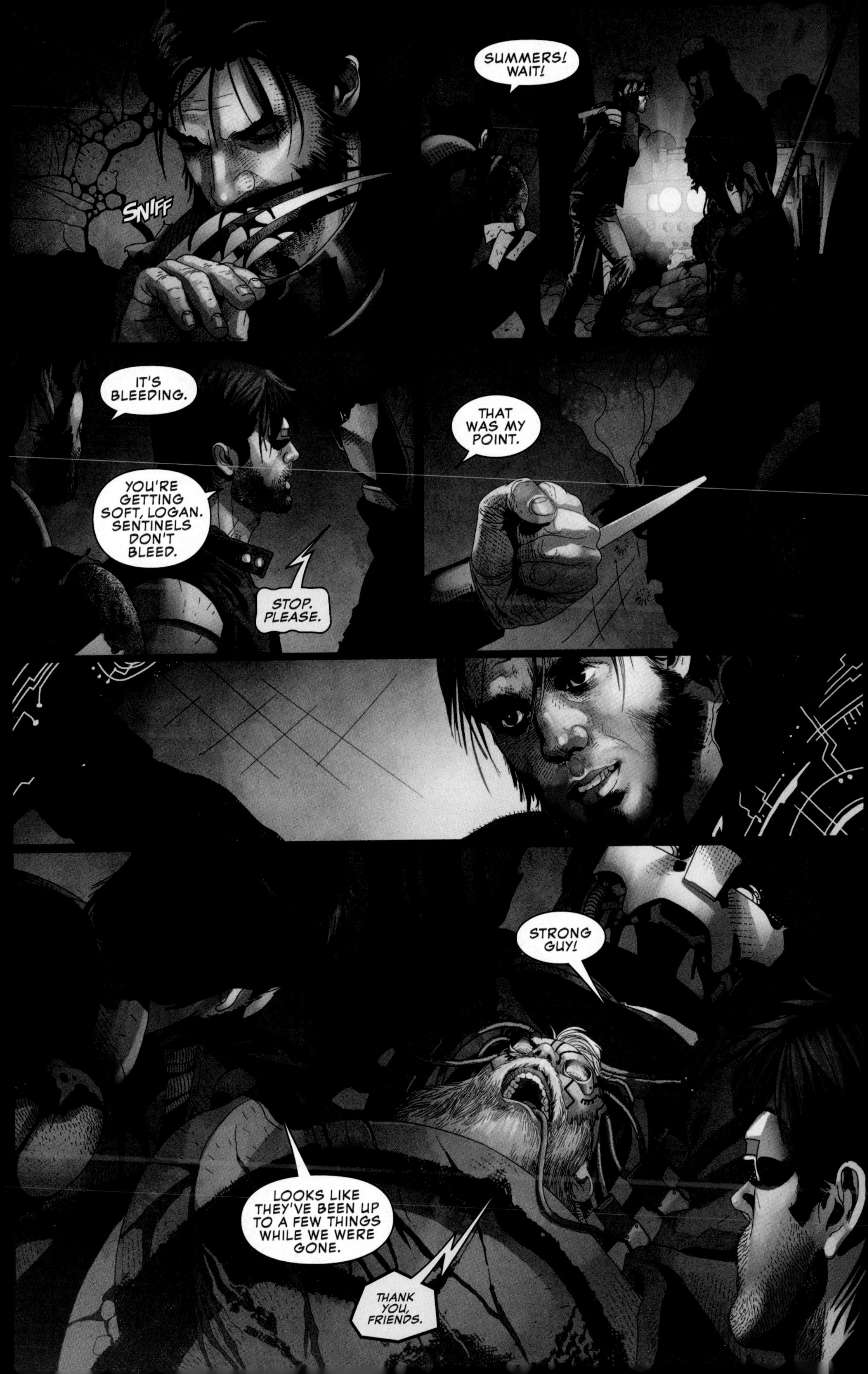
SNIFF
SUMMERS! WAIT!
IT'S BLEEDING.
YOU'RE GETTING SOFT, LOGAN. SENTINELS DON'T BLEED.
STOP. PLEASE.
THAT WAS MY POINT.
STRONG GUY!
LOOKS LIKE THEY'VE BEEN UP TO A FEW THINGS WHILE WE WERE GONE.
THANK YOU, FRIENDS.

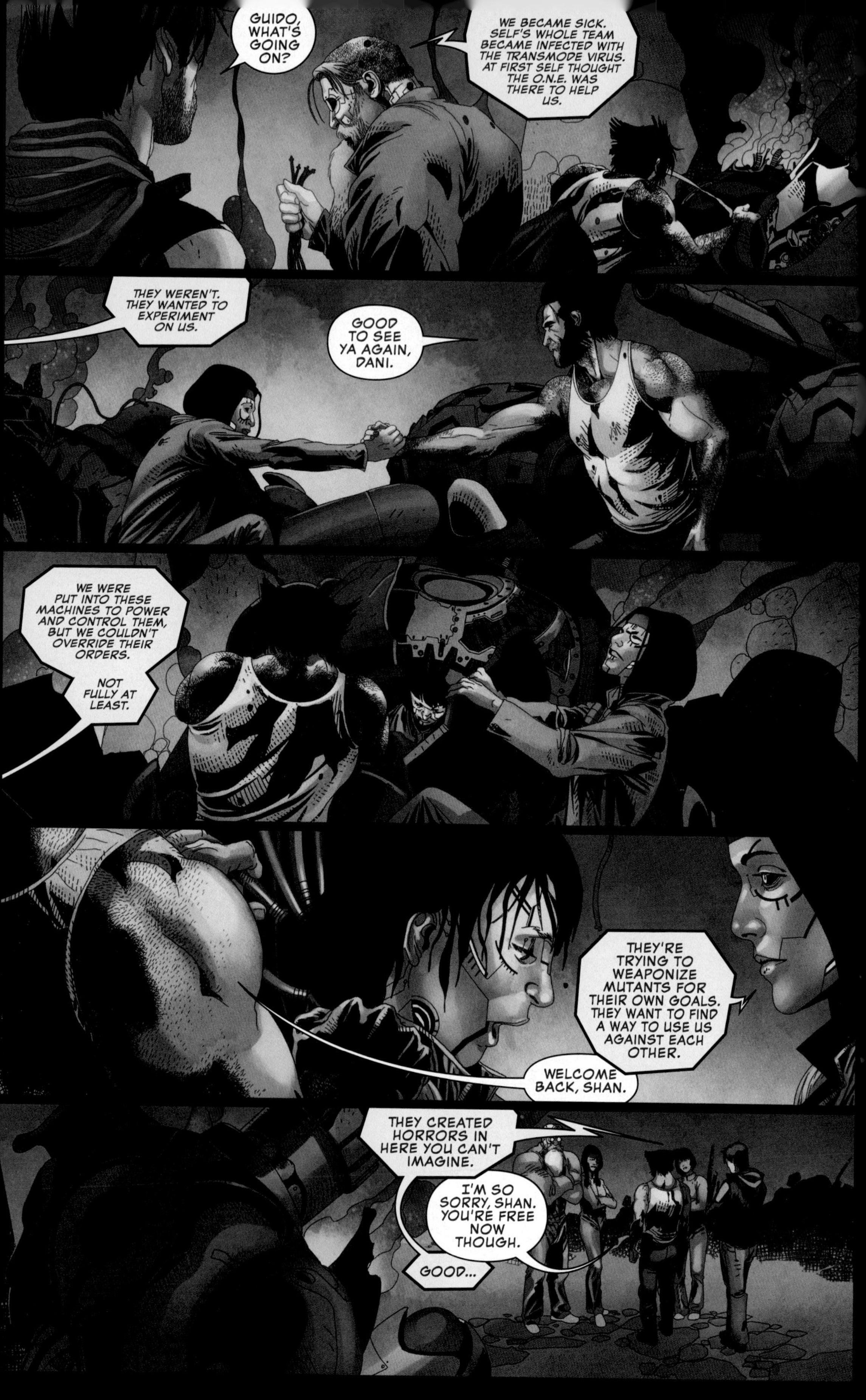
GUIDO, WHAT'S GOING ON?
WE BECAME SICK. SELF'S WHOLE TEAM BECAME INFECTED WITH THE TRANSMODE VIRUS. AT FIRST SELF THOUGHT THE O.N.E. WAS THERE TO HELP US.
THEY WEREN'T. THEY WANTED TO EXPERIMENT ON US.
GOOD TO SEE YA AGAIN, DANI.
WE WERE PUT INTO THESE MACHINES TO POWER AND CONTROL THEM, BUT WE COULDN'T OVERRIDE THEIR ORDERS.
NOT FULLY AT LEAST.
THEY'RE TRYING TO WEAPONIZE MUTANTS FOR THEIR OWN GOALS. THEY WANT TO FIND A WAY TO USE US AGAINST EACH OTHER.
WELCOME BACK, SHAN.
THEY CREATED HORRORS IN HERE YOU CAN'T IMAGINE.
I'M SO SORRY, SHAN. YOU'RE FREE NOW THOUGH.
GOOD...

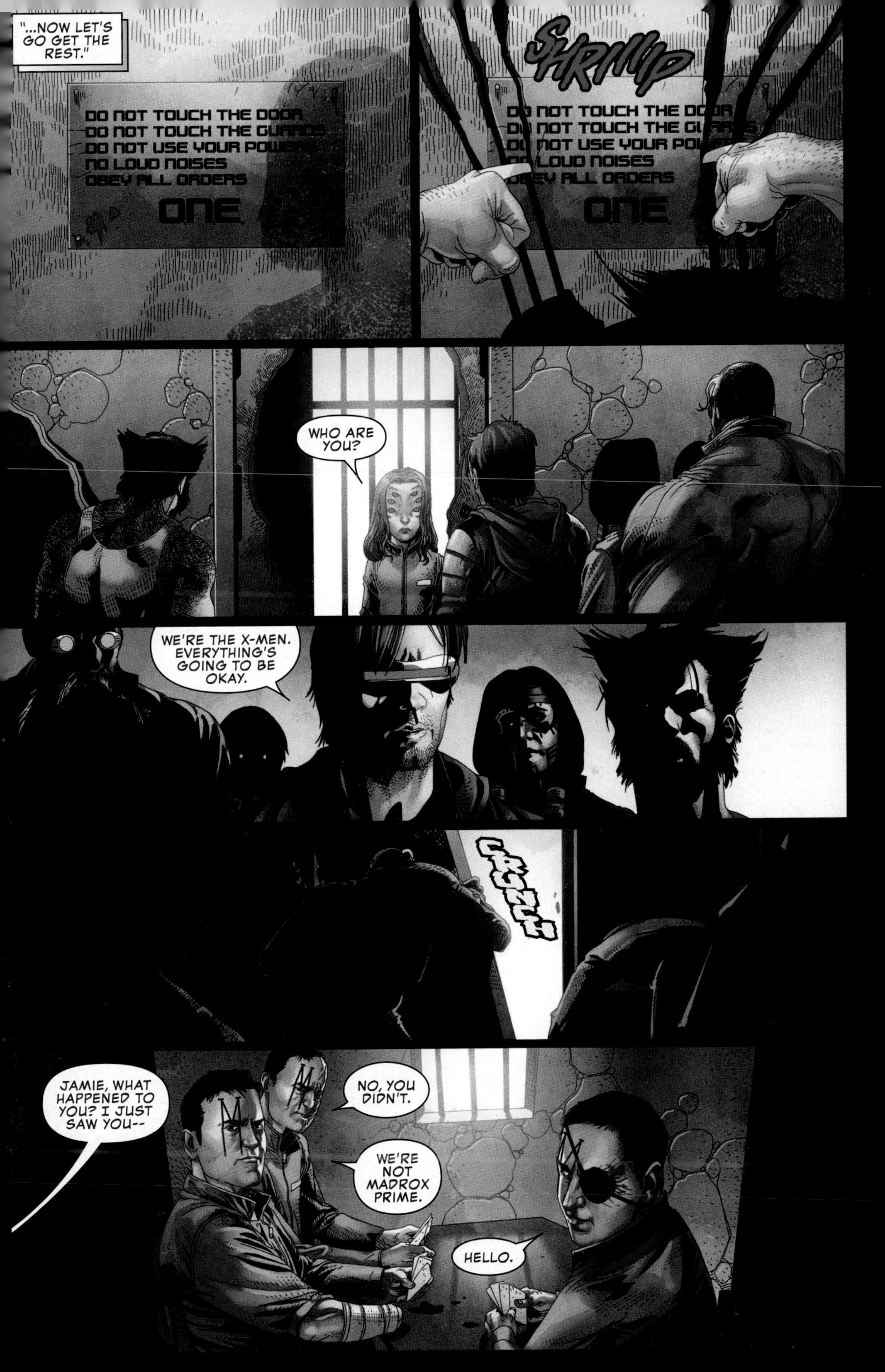
"...NOW LET'S GO GET THE REST."
DO NOT TOUCH THE DOOR
DO NOT TOUCH THE GUARDS
DO NOT USE YOUR POWERS
NO LOUD NOISES
OBEY ALL ORDERS
ONE
SHRIIIP
WHO ARE YOU?
WE'RE THE X-MEN. EVERYTHING'S GOING TO BE OKAY.
CRUNCH
JAMIE, WHAT HAPPENED TO YOU? I JUST SAW YOU--
NO, YOU DIDN'T.
WE'RE NOT MADROX PRIME.
HELLO.

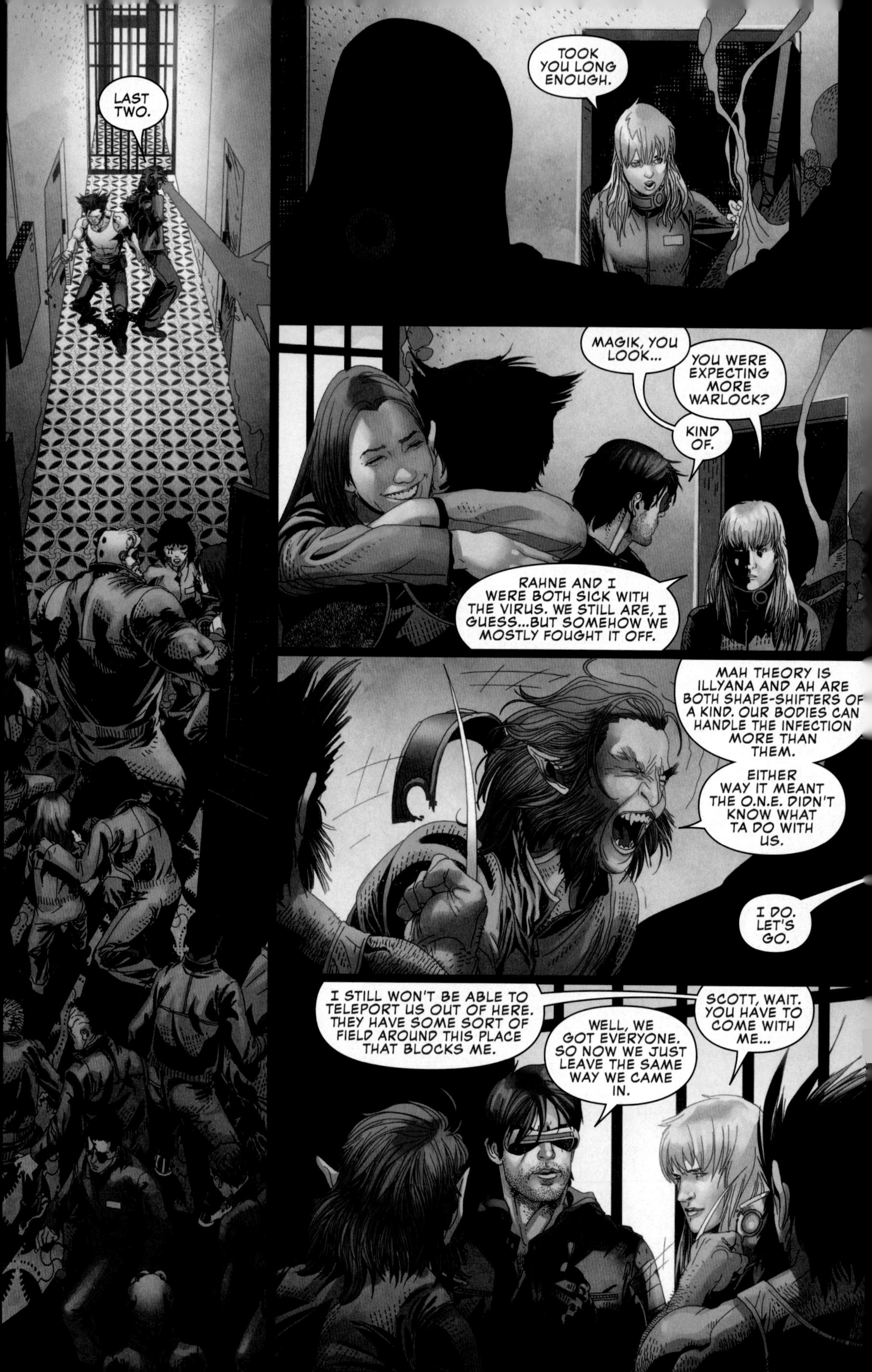
LAST TWO.
TOOK YOU LONG ENOUGH.
MAGIK, YOU LOOK...
YOU WERE EXPECTING MORE WARLOCK?
KIND OF.
RAHNE AND I WERE BOTH SICK WITH THE VIRUS. WE STILL ARE, I GUESS...BUT SOMEHOW WE MOSTLY FOUGHT IT OFF.
MAH THEORY IS ILLYANA AND AH ARE BOTH SHAPE-SHIFTERS OF A KIND. OUR BODIES CAN HANDLE THE INFECTION MORE THAN THEM.
EITHER WAY IT MEANT THE O.N.E. DIDN'T KNOW WHAT TA DO WITH US.
I DO. LET'S GO.
I STILL WON'T BE ABLE TO TELEPORT US OUT OF HERE. THEY HAVE SOME SORT OF FIELD AROUND THIS PLACE THAT BLOCKS ME.
WELL, WE GOT EVERYONE. SO NOW WE JUST LEAVE THE SAME WAY WE CAME IN.
SCOTT, WAIT. YOU HAVE TO COME WITH ME...

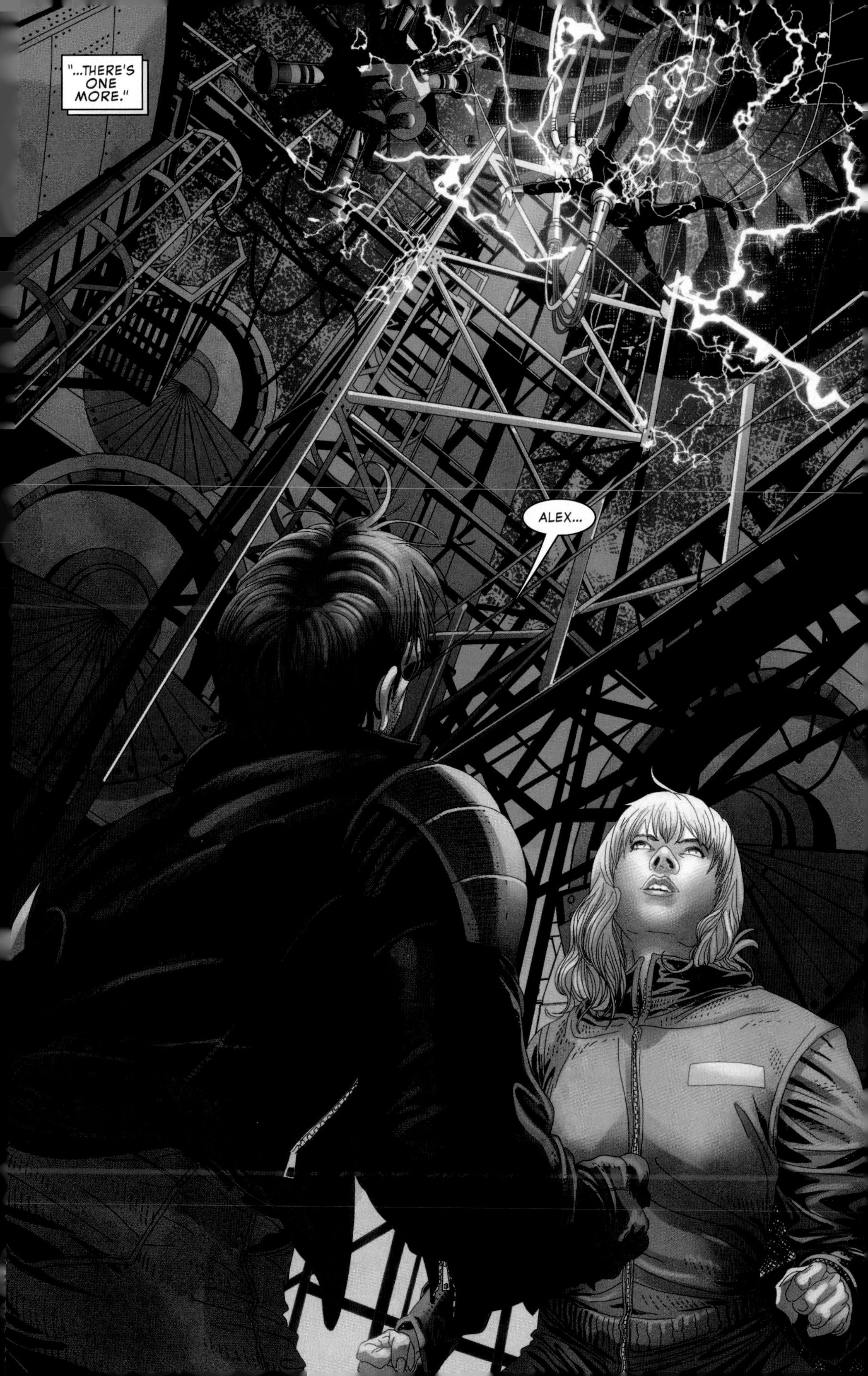
"...THERE'S ONE MORE."
ALEX...

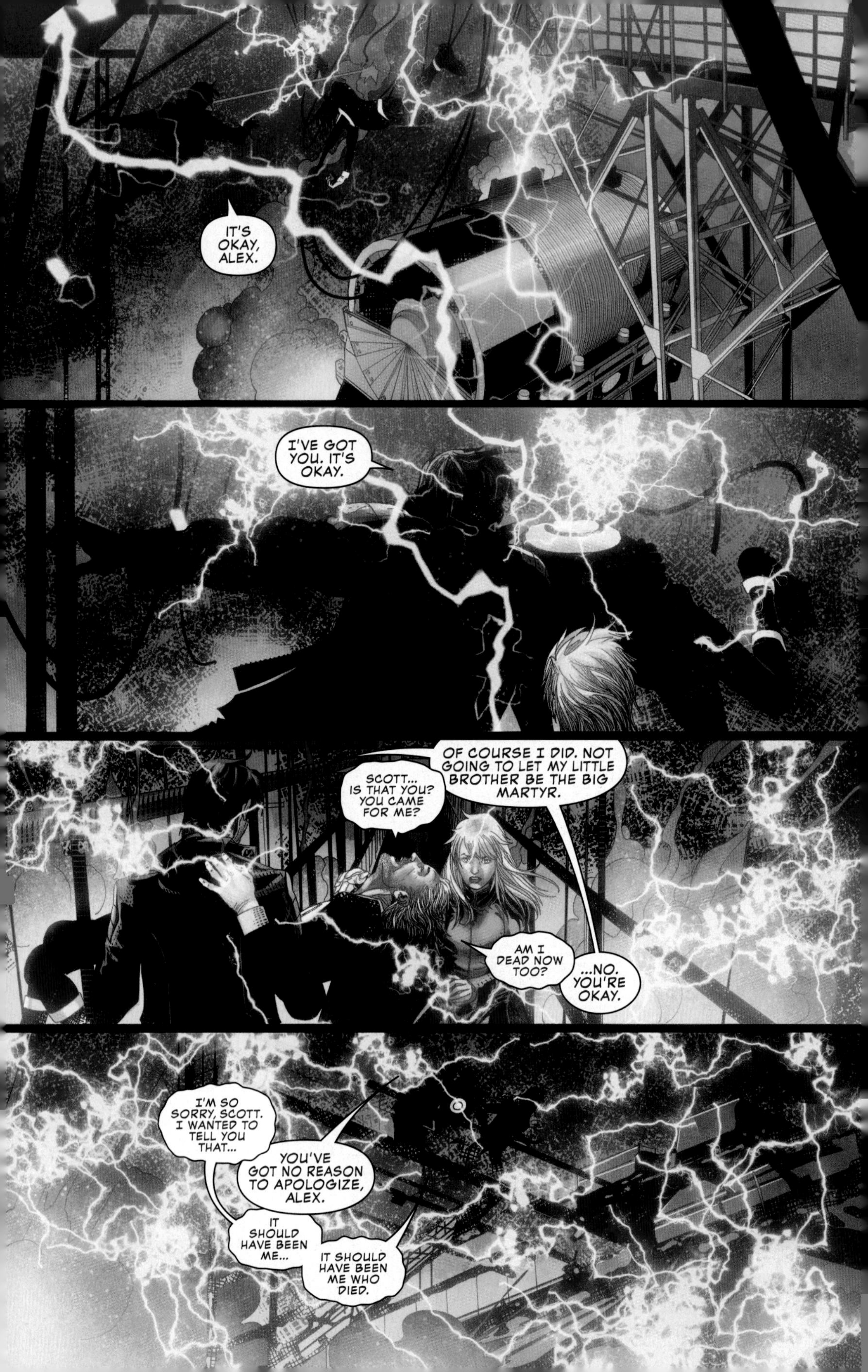
IT'S OKAY, ALEX.
I'VE GOT YOU. IT'S OKAY.
SCOTT... IS THAT YOU? YOU CAME FOR ME?
OF COURSE I DID. NOT GOING TO LET MY LITTLE BROTHER BE THE BIG MARTYR.
AM I DEAD NOW TOO?
...NO. YOU'RE OKAY.
I'M SO SORRY, SCOTT. I WANTED TO TELL YOU THAT...
YOU'VE GOT NO REASON TO APOLOGIZE, ALEX.
IT SHOULD HAVE BEEN ME...
IT SHOULD HAVE BEEN ME WHO DIED.

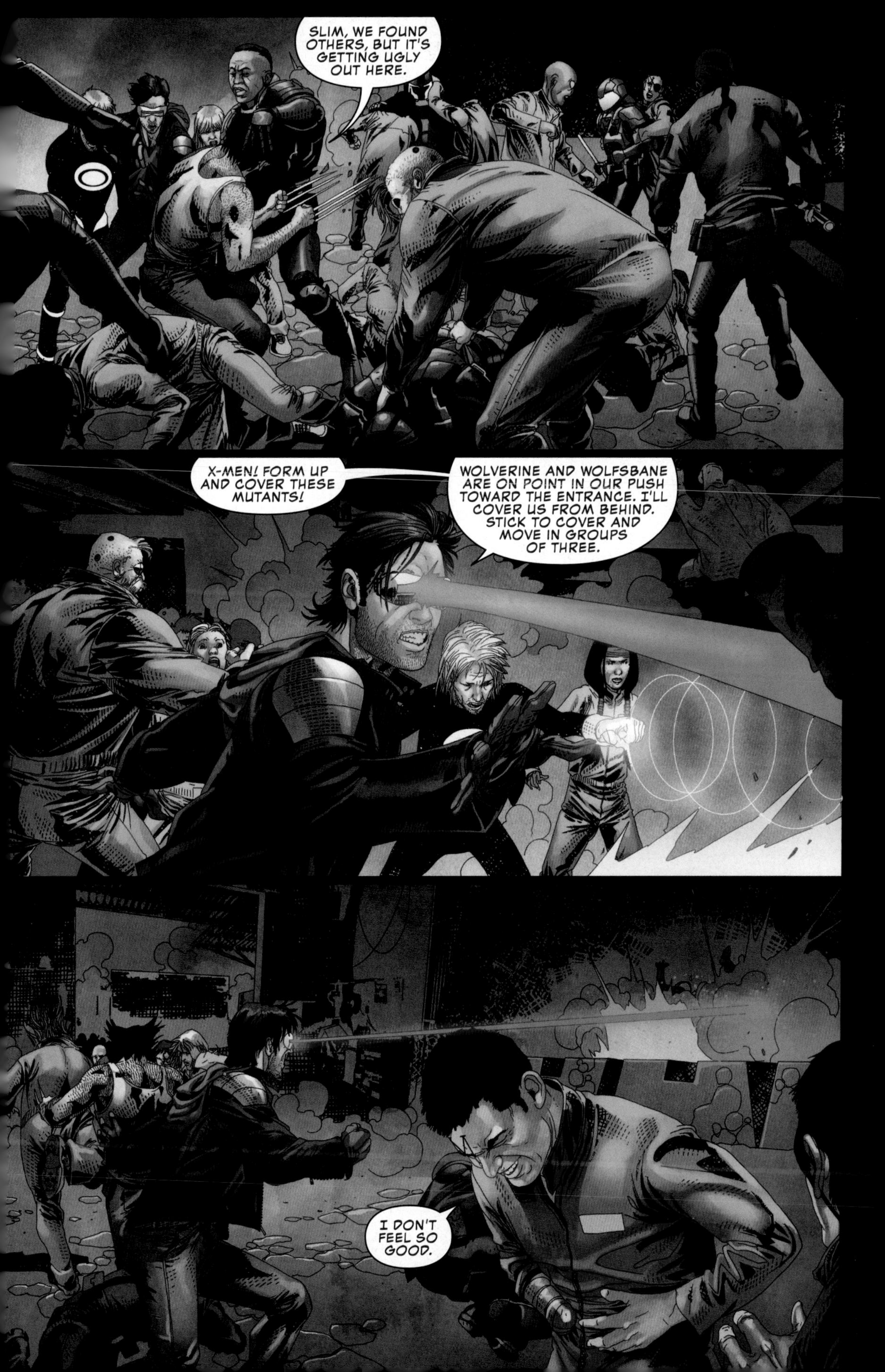
SLIM, WE FOUND OTHERS, BUT IT'S GETTING UGLY OUT HERE.
X-MEN! FORM UP AND COVER THESE MUTANTS!
WOLVERINE AND WOLFSBANE ARE ON POINT IN OUR PUSH TOWARD THE ENTRANCE. I'LL COVER US FROM BEHIND. STICK TO COVER AND MOVE IN GROUPS OF THREE.
I DON'T FEEL SO GOOD.

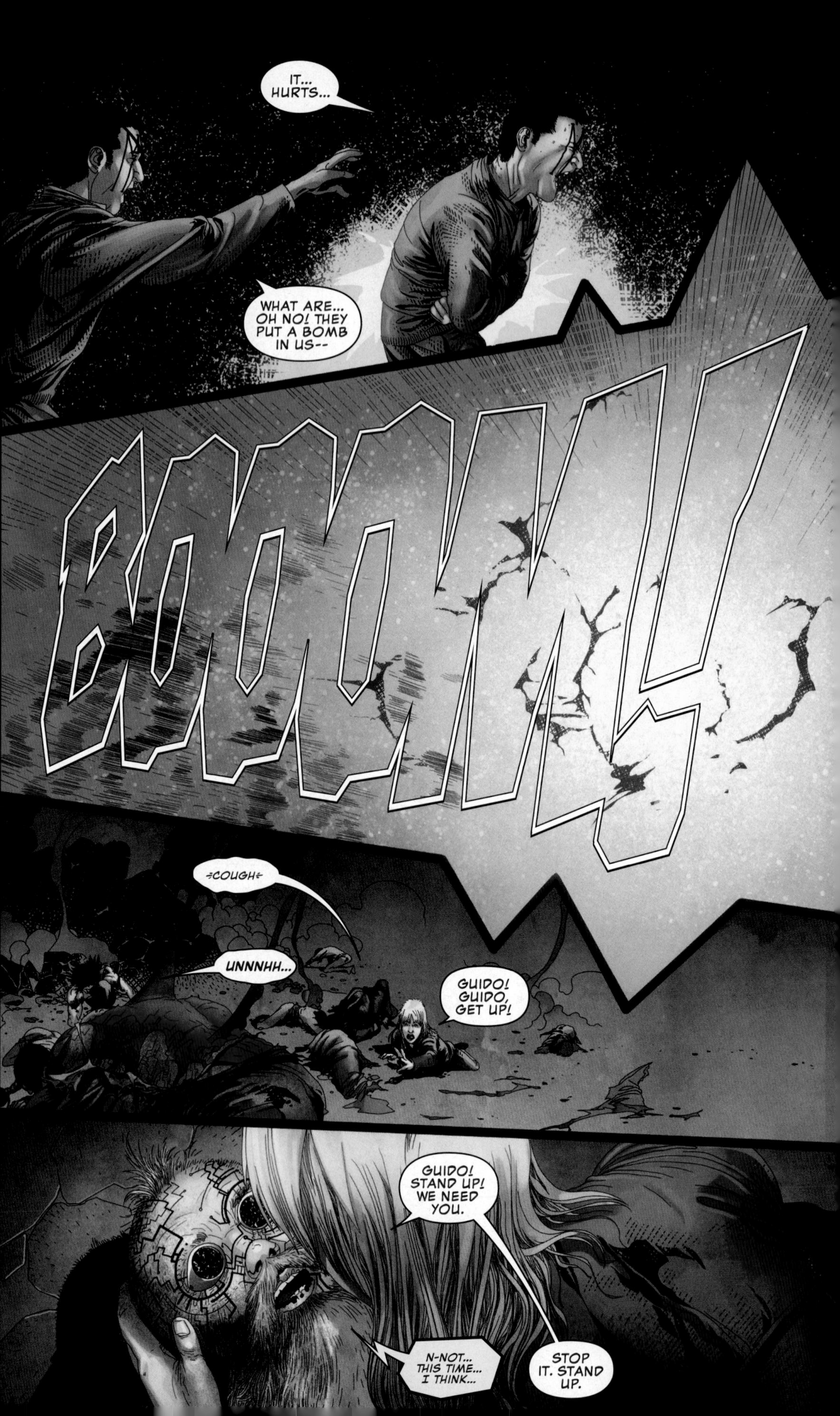
IT... HURTS...
WHAT ARE... OH NO! THEY PUT A BOMB IN US--
=COUGH=
UNNNHH...
GUIDO! GUIDO, GET UP!
GUIDO! STAND UP! WE NEED YOU.
N-NOT... THIS TIME... I THINK...
STOP IT. STAND UP.

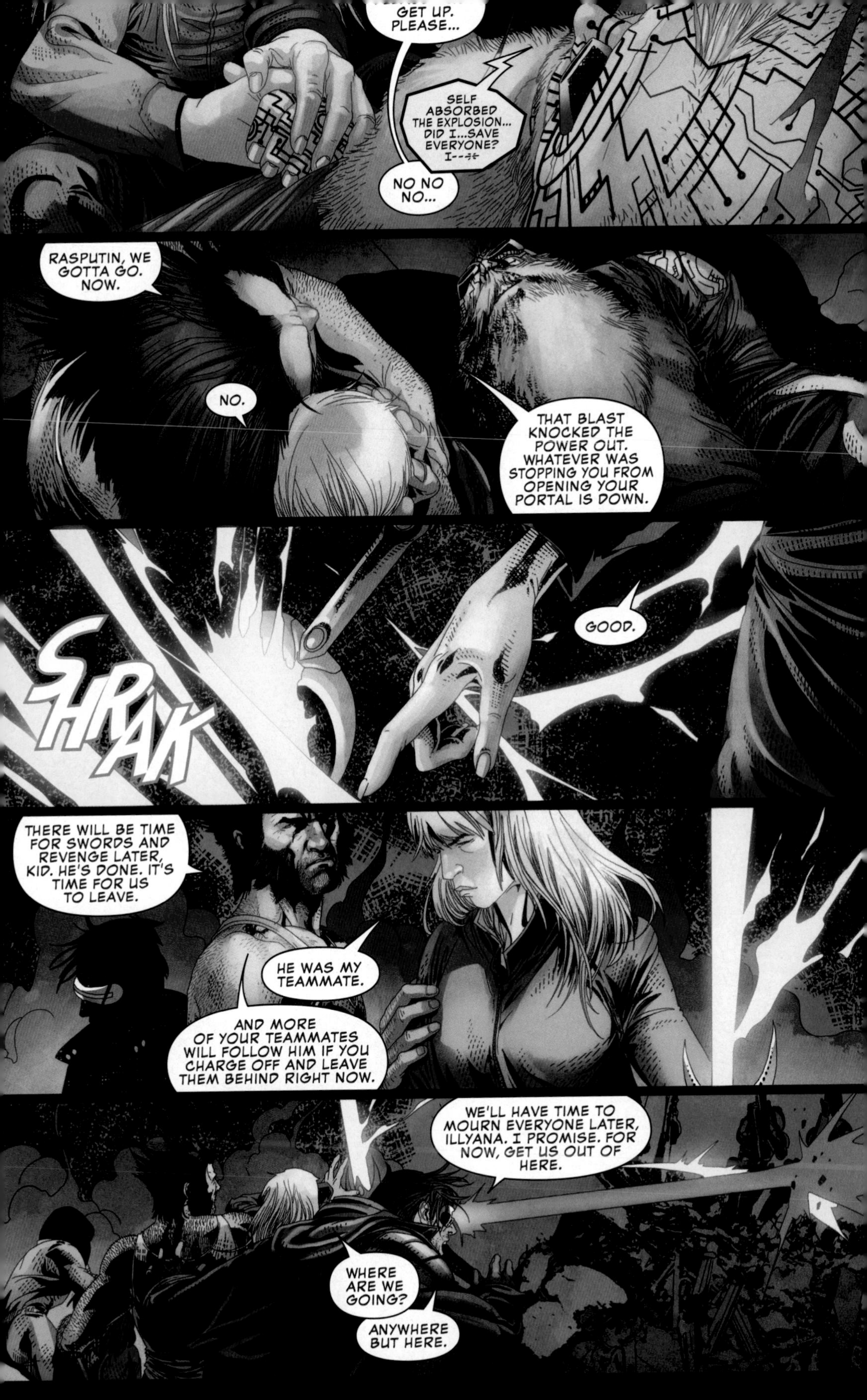
GET UP. PLEASE...
SELF ABSORBED THE EXPLOSION... DID I...SAVE EVERYONE? I--
NO NO NO...
RASPUTIN, WE GOTTA GO. NOW.
NO.
THAT BLAST KNOCKED THE POWER OUT. WHATEVER WAS STOPPING YOU FROM OPENING YOUR PORTAL IS DOWN.
SHRAK
GOOD.
THERE WILL BE TIME FOR SWORDS AND REVENGE LATER, KID. HE'S DONE. IT'S TIME FOR US TO LEAVE.
HE WAS MY TEAMMATE.
AND MORE OF YOUR TEAMMATES WILL FOLLOW HIM IF YOU CHARGE OFF AND LEAVE THEM BEHIND RIGHT NOW.
WE'LL HAVE TIME TO MOURN EVERYONE LATER, ILLYANA. I PROMISE. FOR NOW, GET US OUT OF HERE.
WHERE ARE WE GOING?
ANYWHERE BUT HERE.

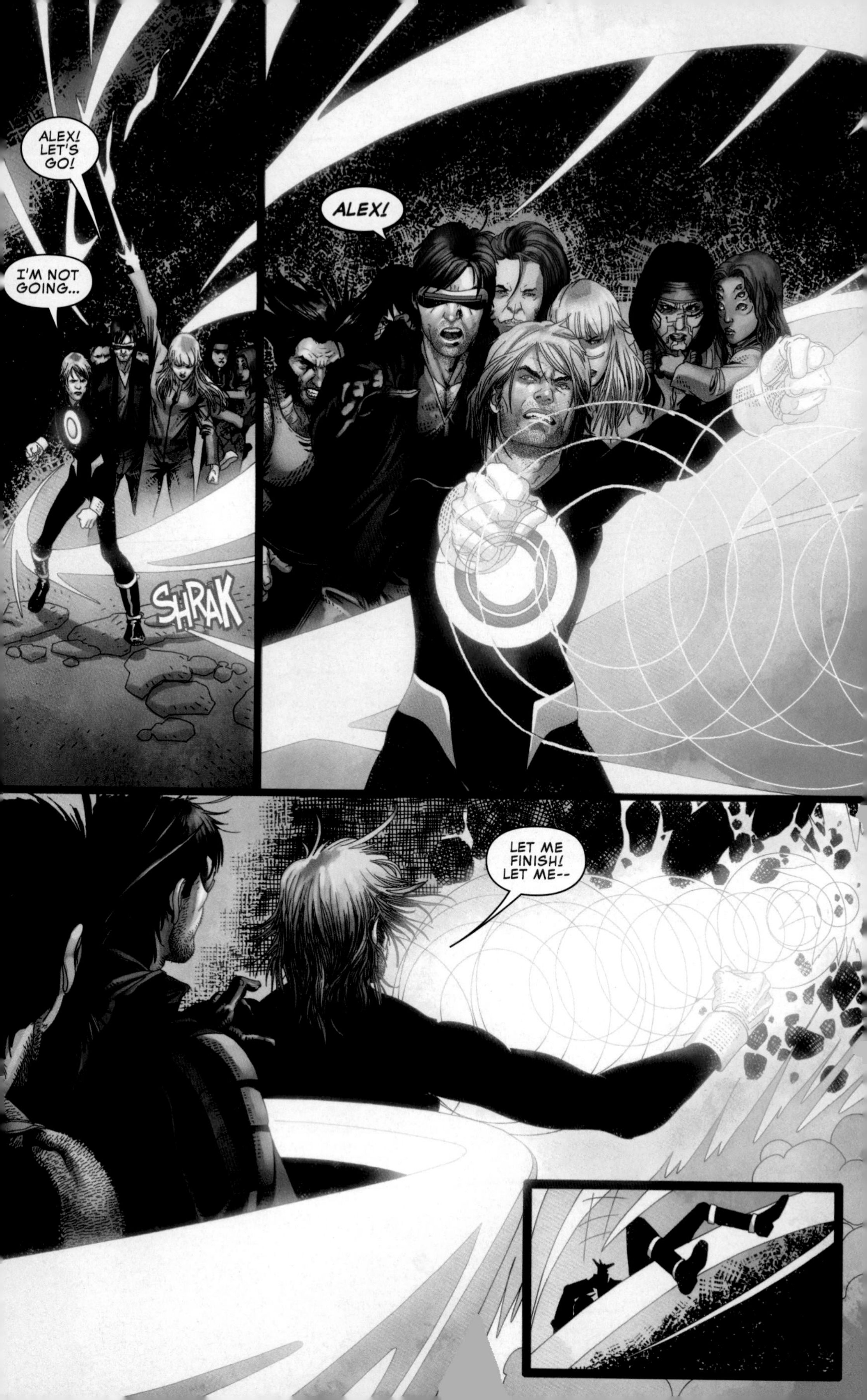
ALEX! LET'S GO!
I'M NOT GOING...
SHRAK
ALEX!
LET ME FINISH! LET ME--

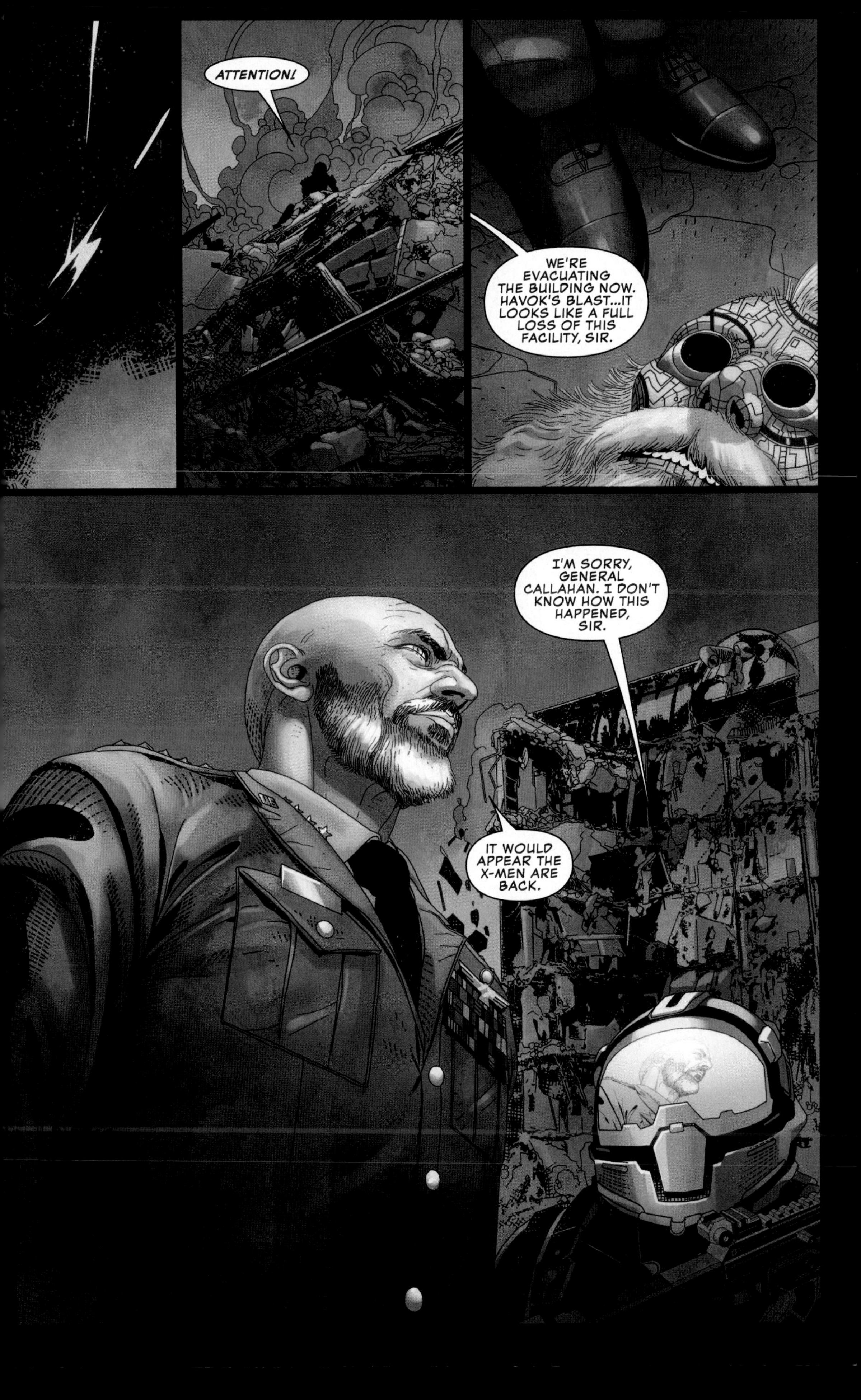
ATTENTION!
WE'RE EVACUATING THE BUILDING NOW. HAVOK'S BLAST...IT LOOKS LIKE A FULL LOSS OF THIS FACILITY, SIR.
I'M SORRY, GENERAL CALLAHAN. I DON'T KNOW HOW THIS HAPPENED, SIR.
IT WOULD APPEAR THE X-MEN ARE BACK.

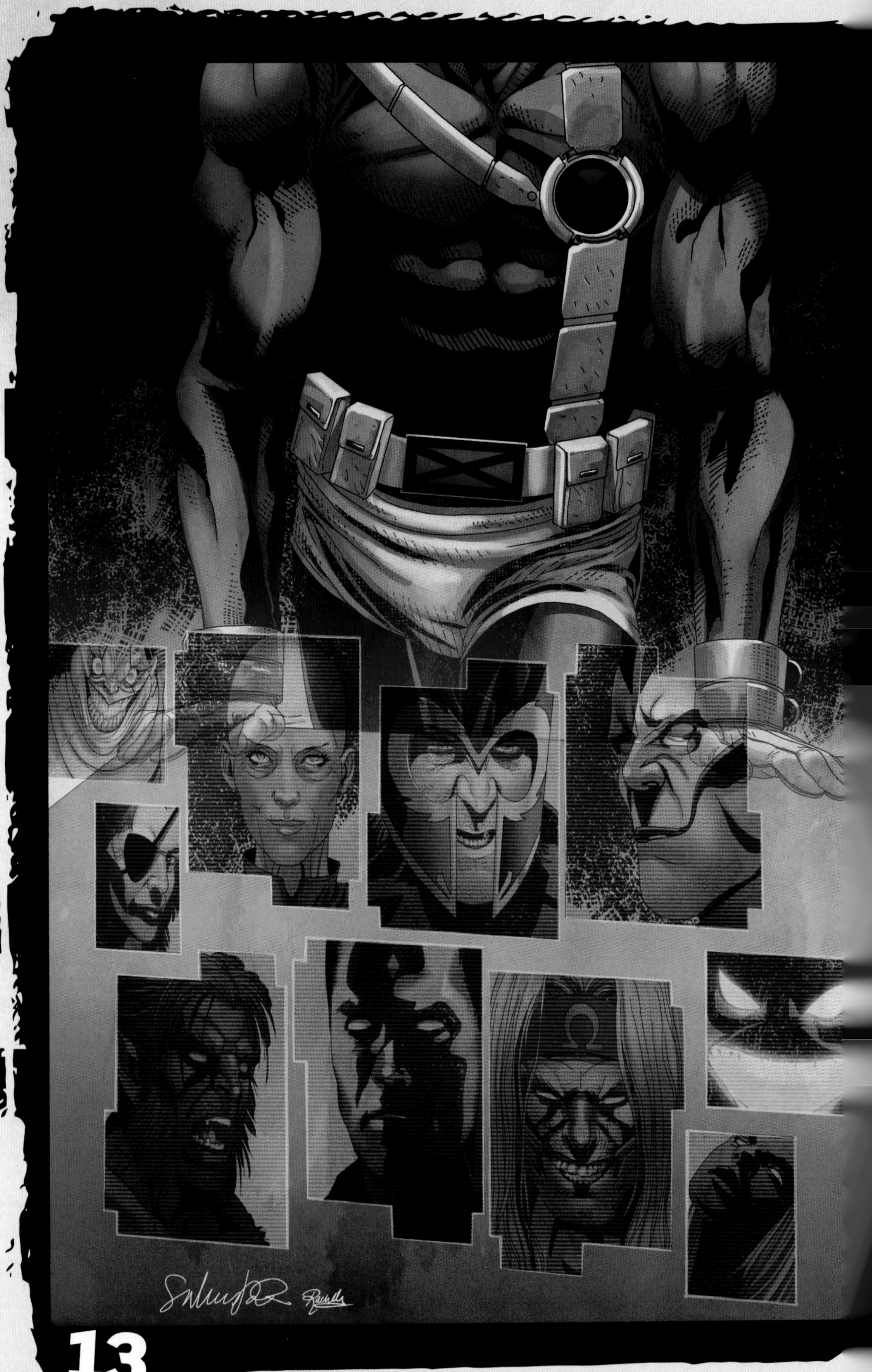

13

This is Forever Part 3

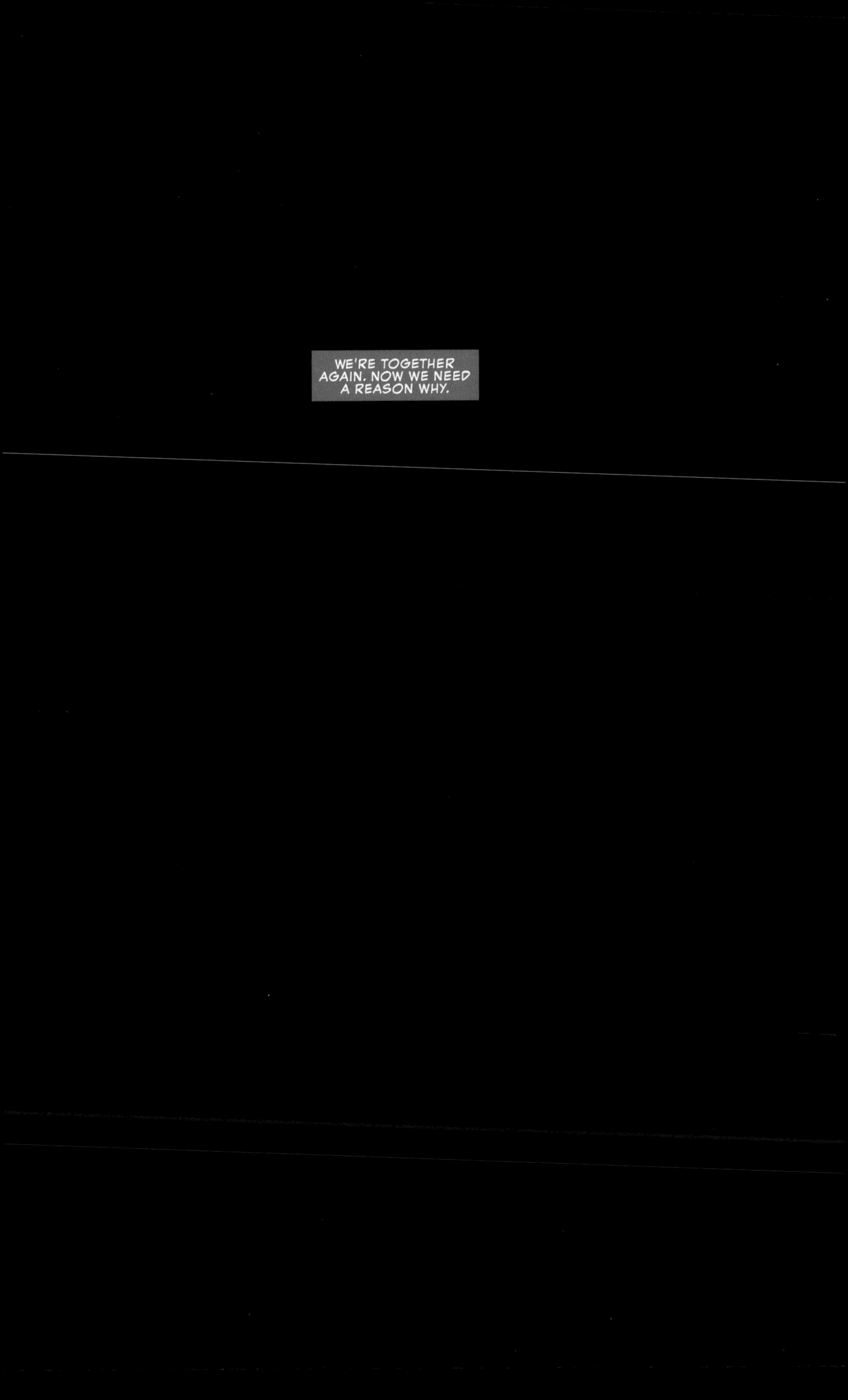
WE'RE TOGETHER AGAIN. NOW WE NEED A REASON WHY.

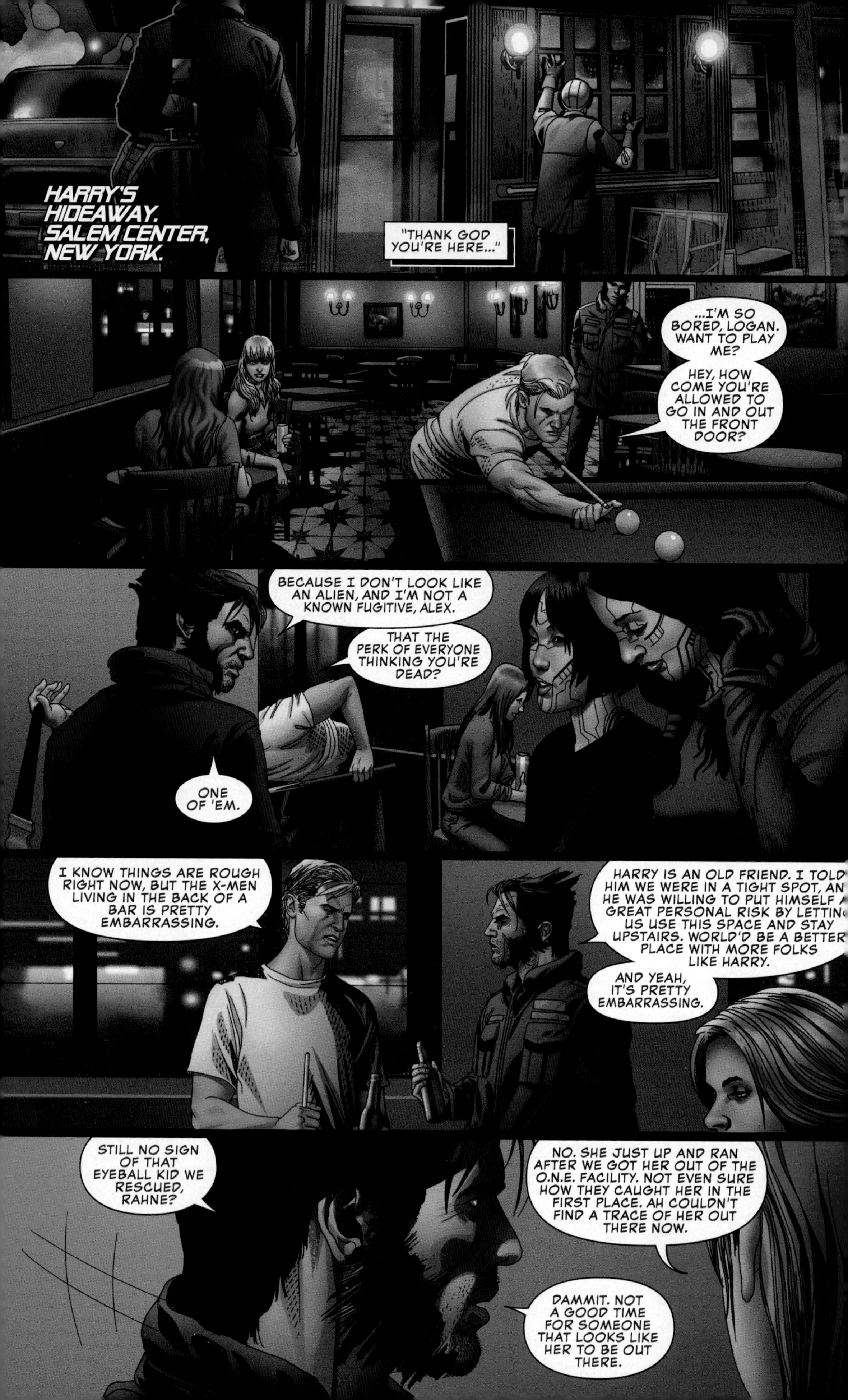
HARRY'S HIDEAWAY. SALEM CENTER, NEW YORK.
"THANK GOD YOU'RE HERE..."
...I'M SO BORED, LOGAN. WANT TO PLAY ME?
HEY, HOW COME YOU'RE ALLOWED TO GO IN AND OUT THE FRONT DOOR?
BECAUSE I DON'T LOOK LIKE AN ALIEN, AND I'M NOT A KNOWN FUGITIVE, ALEX.
THAT THE PERK OF EVERYONE THINKING YOU'RE DEAD?
ONE OF 'EM.
I KNOW THINGS ARE ROUGH RIGHT NOW, BUT THE X-MEN LIVING IN THE BACK OF A BAR IS PRETTY EMBARRASSING.
HARRY IS AN OLD FRIEND. I TOLD HIM WE WERE IN A TIGHT SPOT, AN HE WAS WILLING TO PUT HIMSELF GREAT PERSONAL RISK BY LETTIN US USE THIS SPACE AND STAY UPSTAIRS. WORLD'D BE A BETTER PLACE WITH MORE FOLKS LIKE HARRY.
AND YEAH, IT'S PRETTY EMBARRASSING.
STILL NO SIGN OF THAT EYEBALL KID WE RESCUED, RAHNE?
NO. SHE JUST UP AND RAN AFTER WE GOT HER OUT OF THE O.N.E. FACILITY. NOT EVEN SURE HOW THEY CAUGHT HER IN THE FIRST PLACE. AH COULDN'T FIND A TRACE OF HER OUT THERE NOW.
DAMMIT. NOT A GOOD TIME FOR SOMEONE THAT LOOKS LIKE HER TO BE OUT THERE.

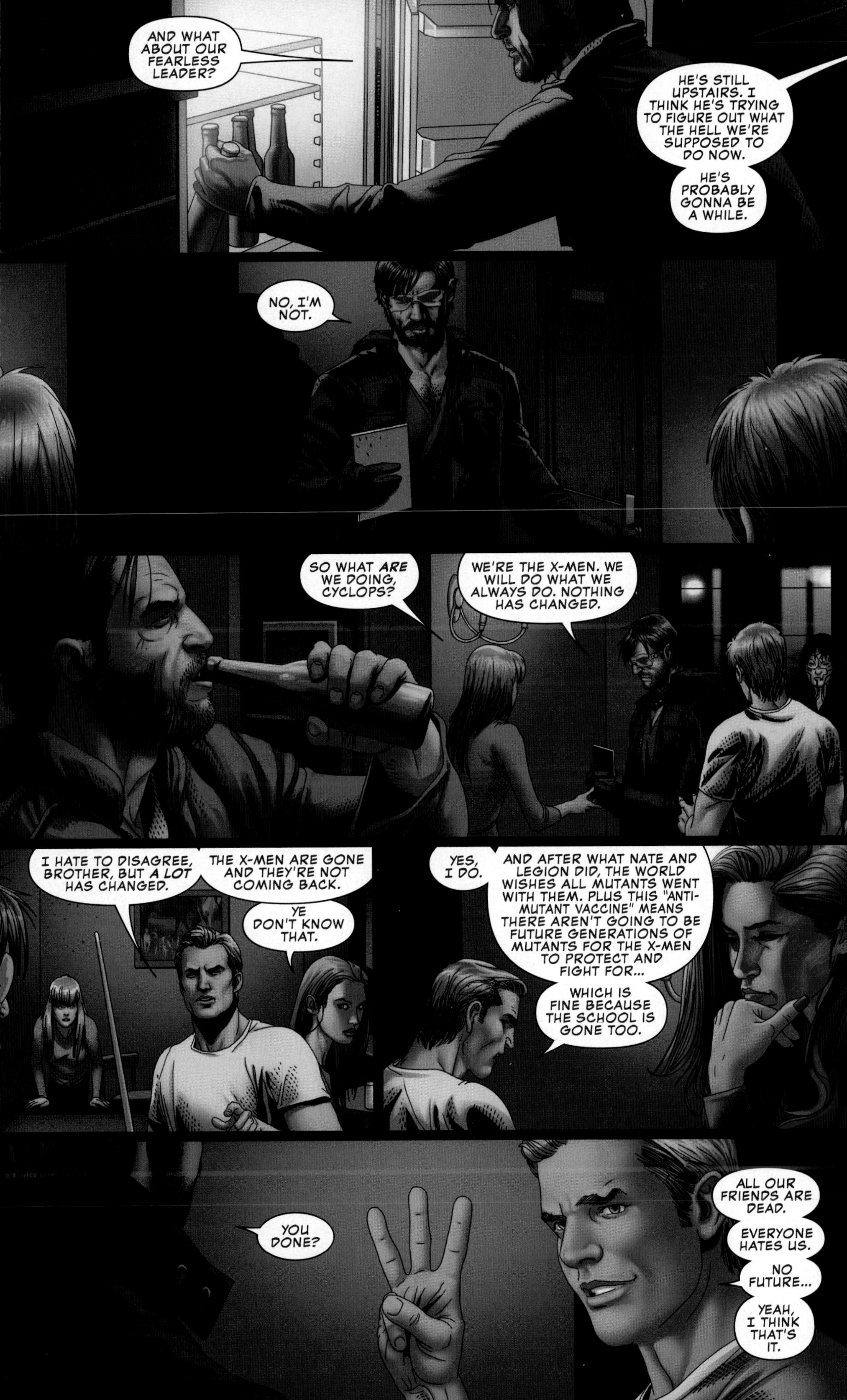
AND WHAT ABOUT OUR FEARLESS LEADER?
HE'S STILL UPSTAIRS. I THINK HE'S TRYING TO FIGURE OUT WHAT THE HELL WE'RE SUPPOSED TO DO NOW.
HE'S PROBABLY GONNA BE A WHILE.
NO, I'M NOT.
SO WHAT ARE WE DOING, CYCLOPS?
WE'RE THE X-MEN. WE WILL DO WHAT WE ALWAYS DO. NOTHING HAS CHANGED.
I HATE TO DISAGREE, BROTHER, BUT A LOT HAS CHANGED.
THE X-MEN ARE GONE AND THEY'RE NOT COMING BACK.
YE DON'T KNOW THAT.
YES, I DO.
AND AFTER WHAT NATE AND LEGION DID, THE WORLD WISHES ALL MUTANTS WENT WITH THEM. PLUS THIS "ANTI-MUTANT VACCINE" MEANS THERE AREN'T GOING TO BE FUTURE GENERATIONS OF MUTANTS FOR THE X-MEN TO PROTECT AND FIGHT FOR...
WHICH IS FINE BECAUSE THE SCHOOL IS GONE TOO.
ALL OUR FRIENDS ARE DEAD.
EVERYONE HATES US.
NO FUTURE...
YEAH, I THINK THAT'S IT.
YOU DONE?

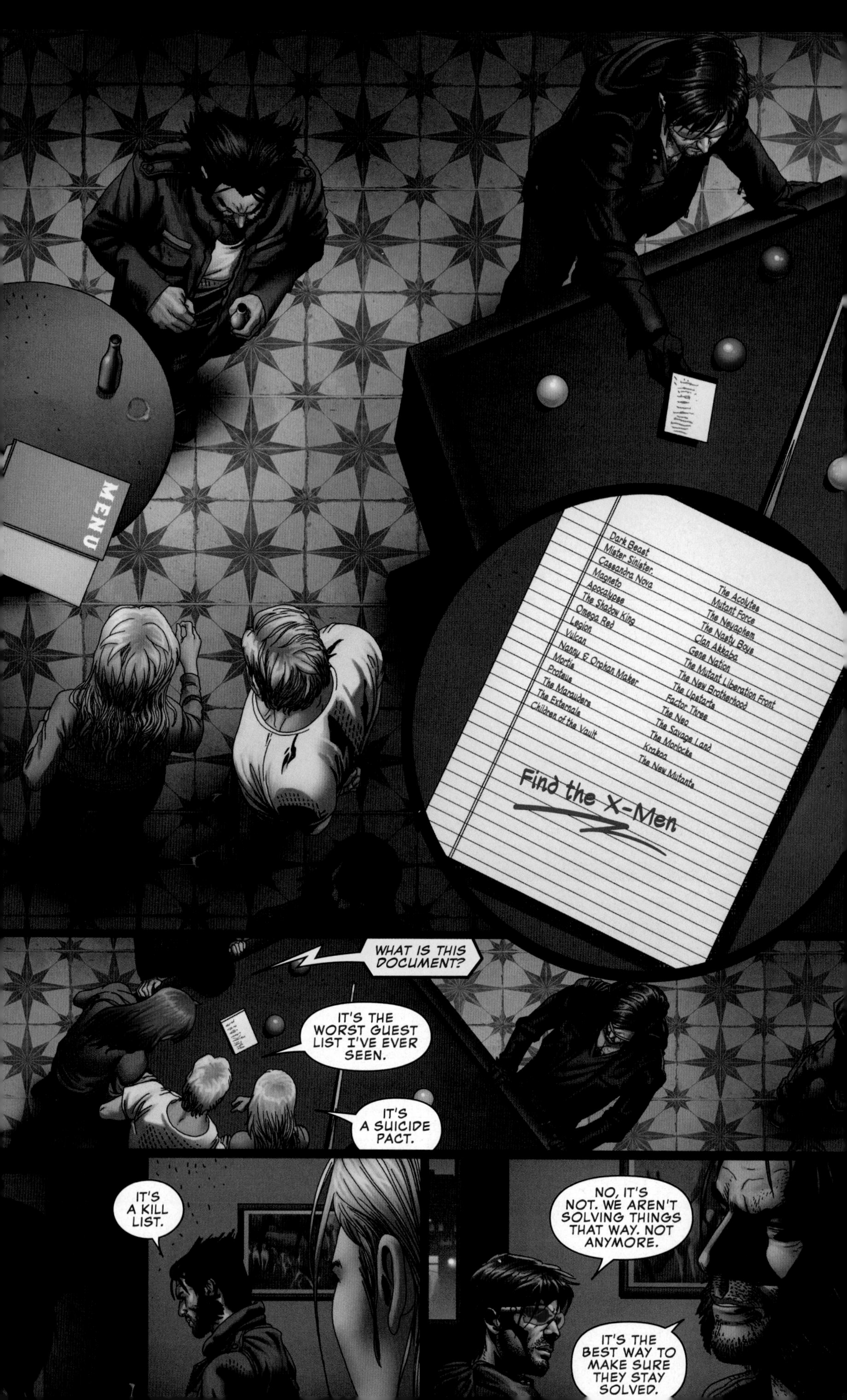
MENU
Dark Beast
Mister Sinister
Cassandra Nova
Magneto
Apocalypse
The Shadow King
Omega Red
Legion
Vulcan
Nanny & Orphan Maker
Mortis
Proteus
The Marauders
The Externals
Children of the Vault
The Acolytes
Mutant Force
The Neyaphem
The Nasty Boys
Clan Akkaba
Gene Nation
The Mutant Liberation Front
The New Brotherhood
The Upstarts
Factor Three
The Neo
The Savage Land
The Morlocks
Krakoa
The New Mutants
Find the X-Men
WHAT IS THIS DOCUMENT?
IT'S THE WORST GUEST LIST I'VE EVER SEEN.
IT'S A SUICIDE PACT.
IT'S A KILL LIST.
NO, IT'S NOT. WE AREN'T SOLVING THINGS THAT WAY. NOT ANYMORE.
IT'S THE BEST WAY TO MAKE SURE THEY STAY SOLVED.

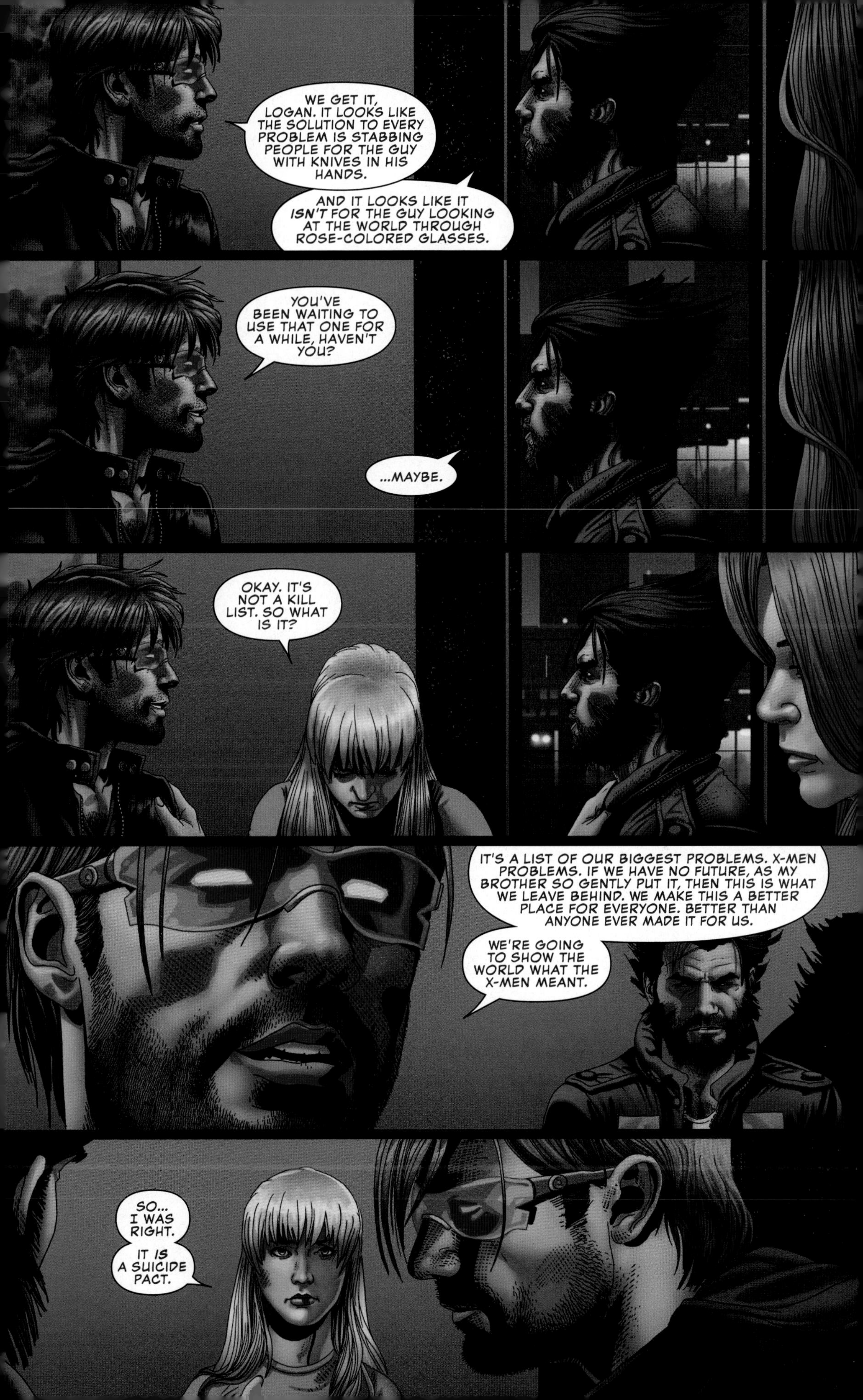
WE GET IT, LOGAN. IT LOOKS LIKE THE SOLUTION TO EVERY PROBLEM IS STABBING PEOPLE FOR THE GUY WITH KNIVES IN HIS HANDS.
AND IT LOOKS LIKE IT *ISN'T* FOR THE GUY LOOKING AT THE WORLD THROUGH ROSE-COLORED GLASSES.
YOU'VE BEEN WAITING TO USE THAT ONE FOR A WHILE, HAVEN'T YOU?
...MAYBE.
OKAY. IT'S NOT A KILL LIST. SO WHAT IS IT?
IT'S A LIST OF OUR BIGGEST PROBLEMS. X-MEN PROBLEMS. IF WE HAVE NO FUTURE, AS MY BROTHER SO GENTLY PUT IT, THEN THIS IS WHAT WE LEAVE BEHIND. WE MAKE THIS A BETTER PLACE FOR EVERYONE. BETTER THAN ANYONE EVER MADE IT FOR US.
WE'RE GOING TO SHOW THE WORLD WHAT THE X-MEN MEANT.
SO... I WAS RIGHT.
IT *IS* A SUICIDE PACT.

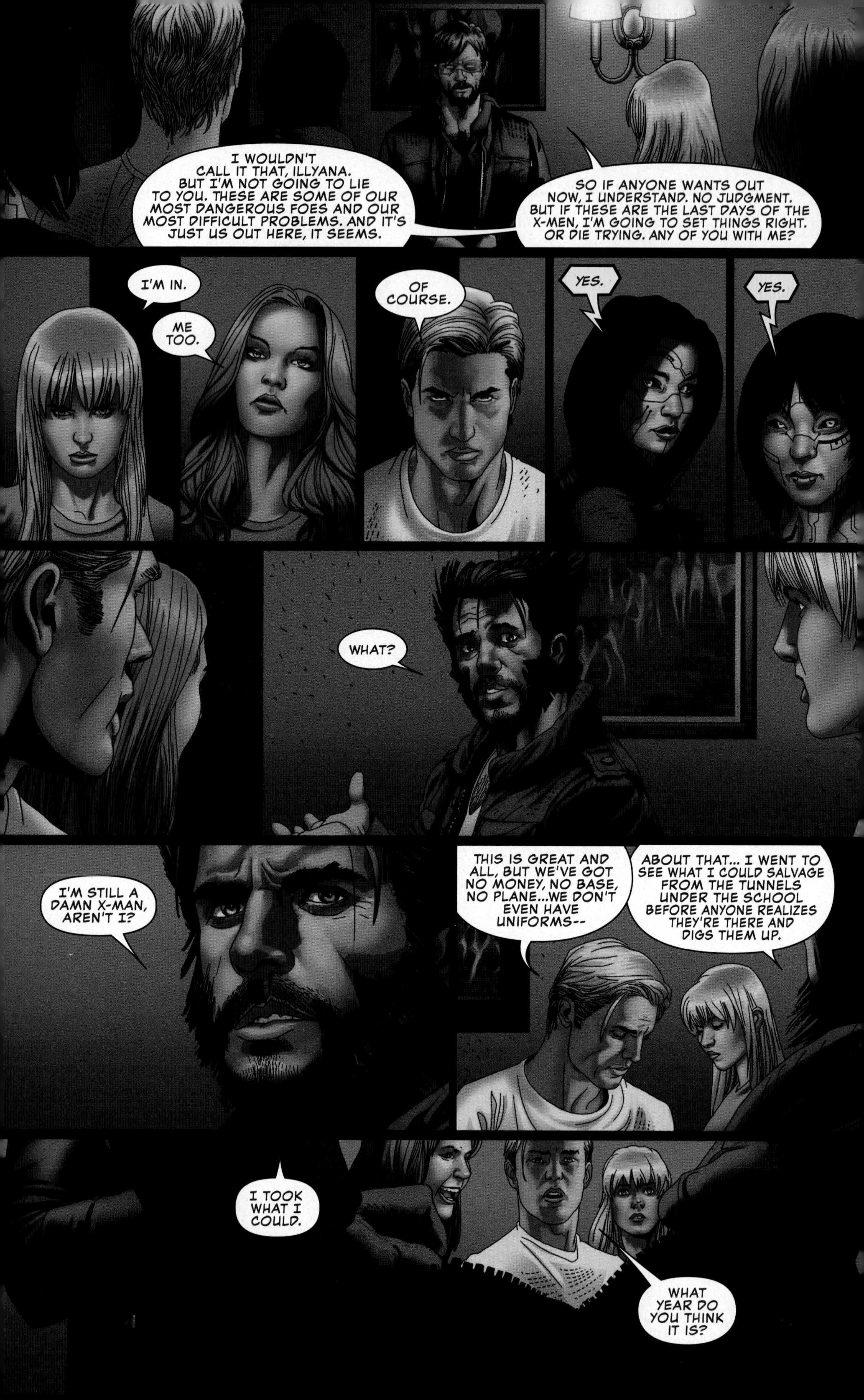
I WOULDN'T CALL IT THAT, ILLYANA. BUT I'M NOT GOING TO LIE TO YOU. THESE ARE SOME OF OUR MOST DANGEROUS FOES AND OUR MOST DIFFICULT PROBLEMS. AND IT'S JUST US OUT HERE, IT SEEMS.
SO IF ANYONE WANTS OUT NOW, I UNDERSTAND. NO JUDGMENT. BUT IF THESE ARE THE LAST DAYS OF THE X-MEN, I'M GOING TO SET THINGS RIGHT. OR DIE TRYING. ANY OF YOU WITH ME?
I'M IN.
ME TOO.
OF COURSE.
YES.
YES.
WHAT?
I'M STILL A DAMN X-MAN, AREN'T I?
THIS IS GREAT AND ALL, BUT WE'VE GOT NO MONEY, NO BASE, NO PLANE...WE DON'T EVEN HAVE UNIFORMS--
ABOUT THAT... I WENT TO SEE WHAT I COULD SALVAGE FROM THE TUNNELS UNDER THE SCHOOL BEFORE ANYONE REALIZES THEY'RE THERE AND DIGS THEM UP.
I TOOK WHAT I COULD.
WHAT YEAR DO YOU THINK IT IS?

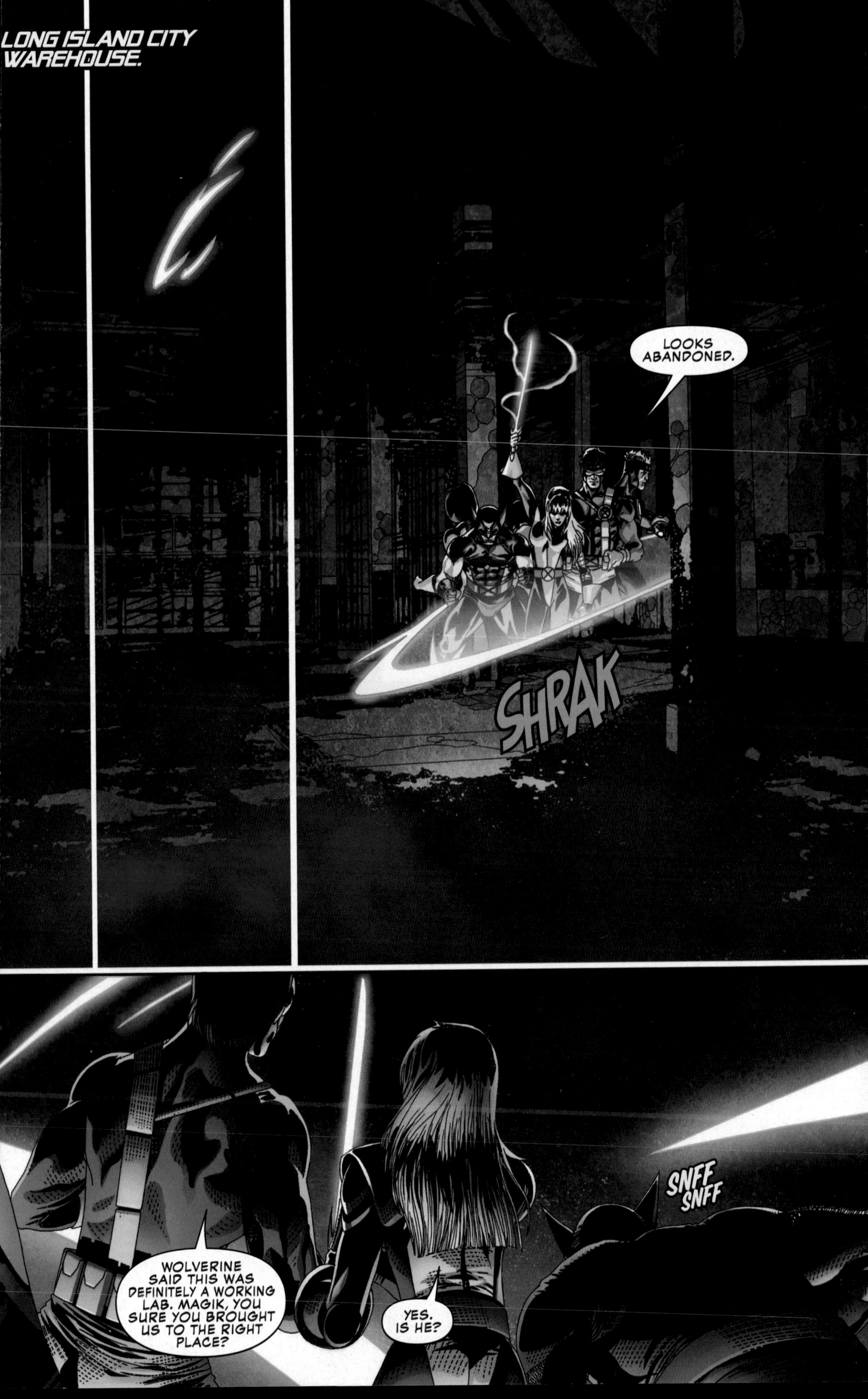
LONG ISLAND CITY WAREHOUSE.
LOOKS ABANDONED.
SHRAK
SNFF SNFF
WOLVERINE SAID THIS WAS DEFINITELY A WORKING LAB. MAGIK, YOU SURE YOU BROUGHT US TO THE RIGHT PLACE?
YES. IS HE?

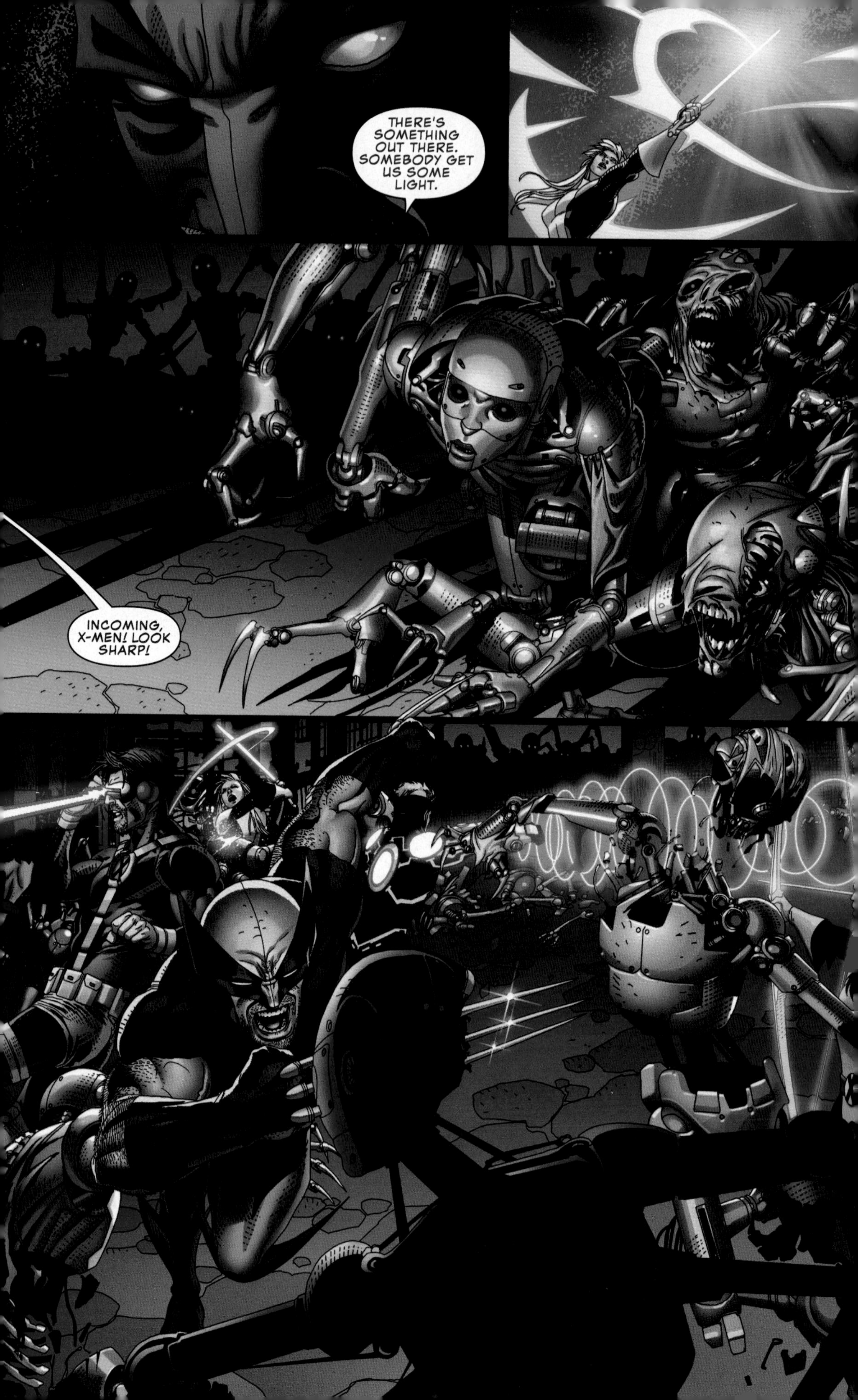

THERE'S SOMETHING OUT THERE. SOMEBODY GET US SOME LIGHT.
INCOMING, X-MEN! LOOK SHARP!

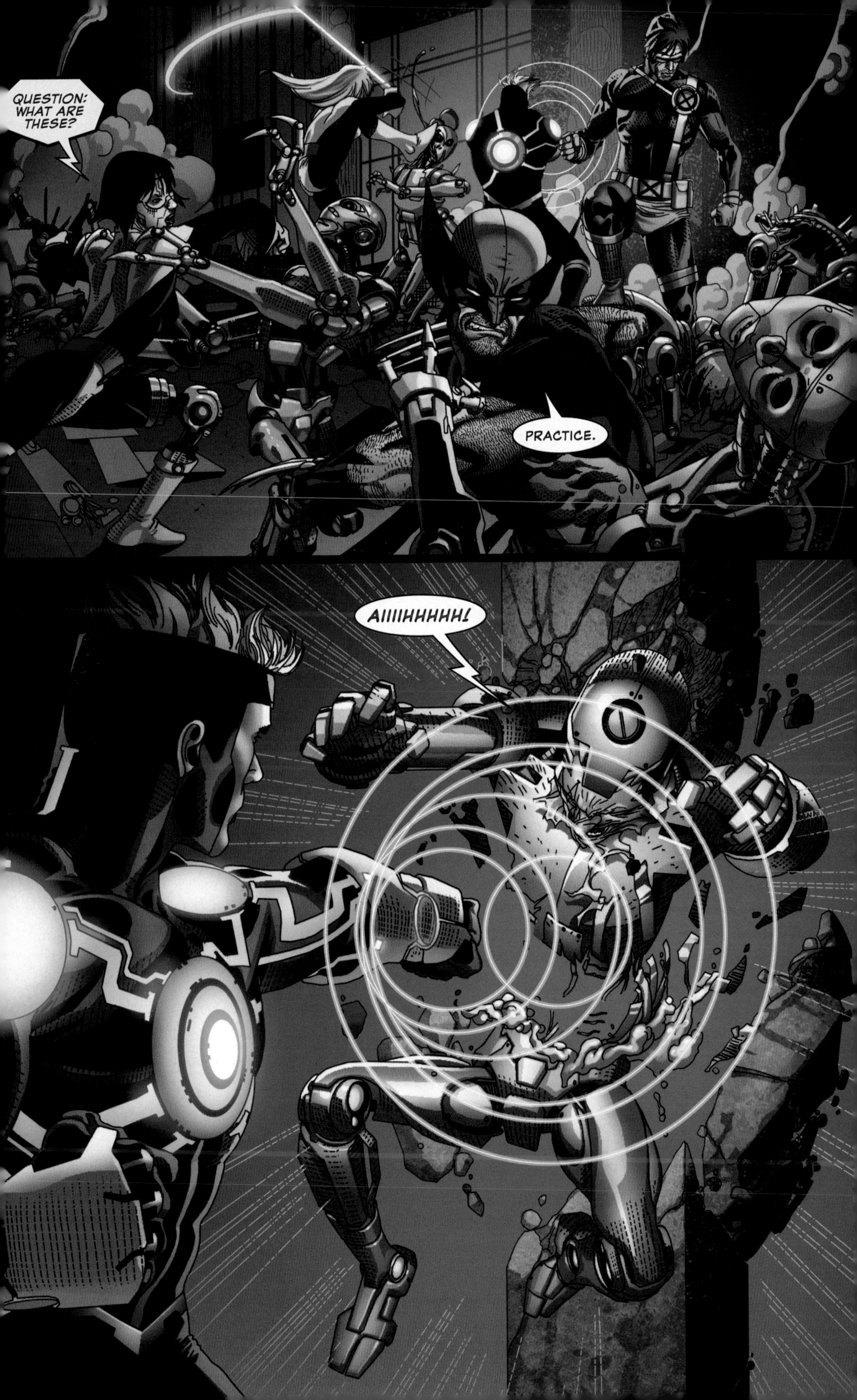
QUESTION: WHAT ARE THESE?
PRACTICE.
AIIIHHHHH!

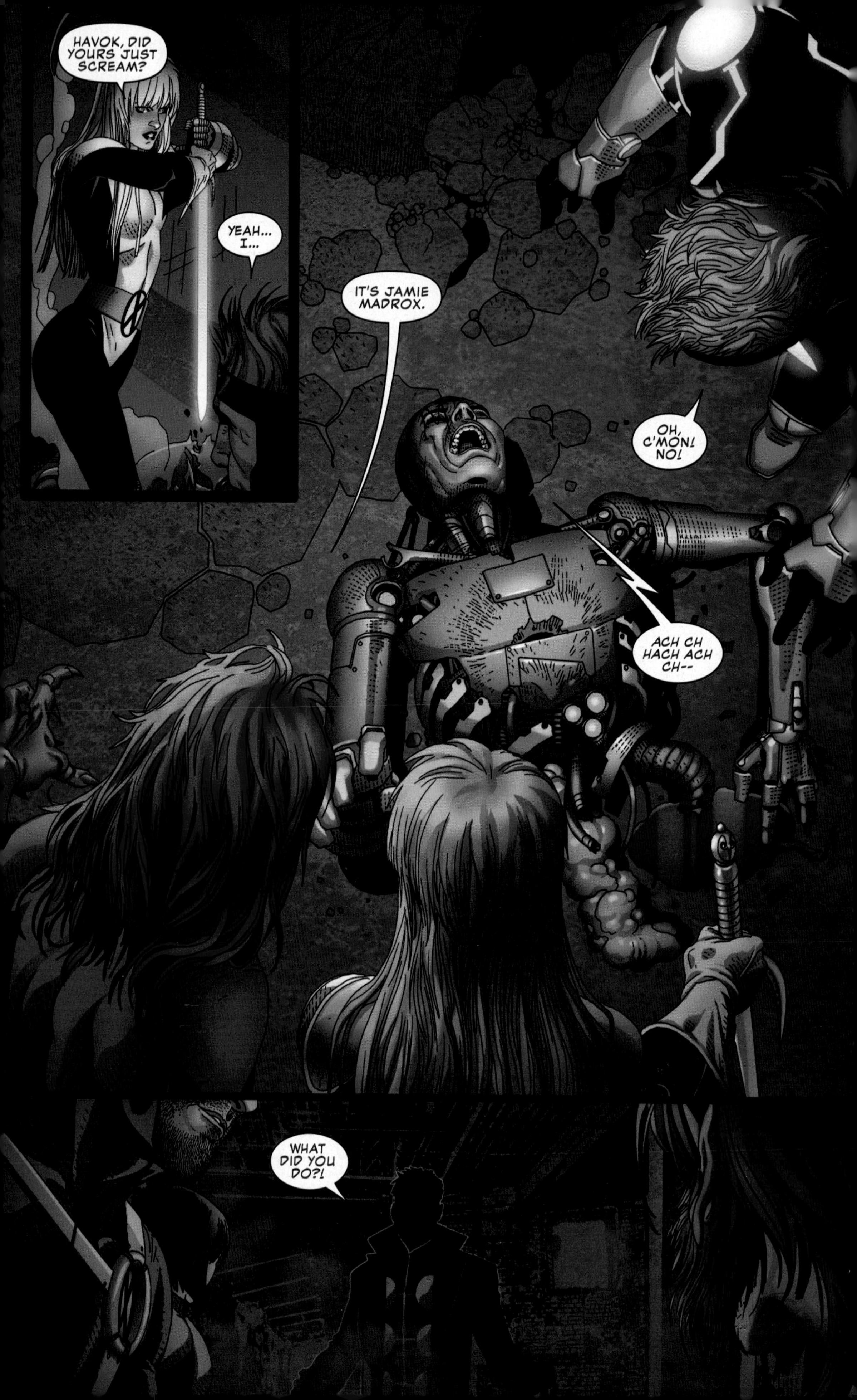

HAVOK, DID YOURS JUST SCREAM?
YEAH... I...
IT'S JAMIE MADROX.
OH, C'MON! NO!
ACH CH HACH ACH CH--
WHAT DID YOU DO?!

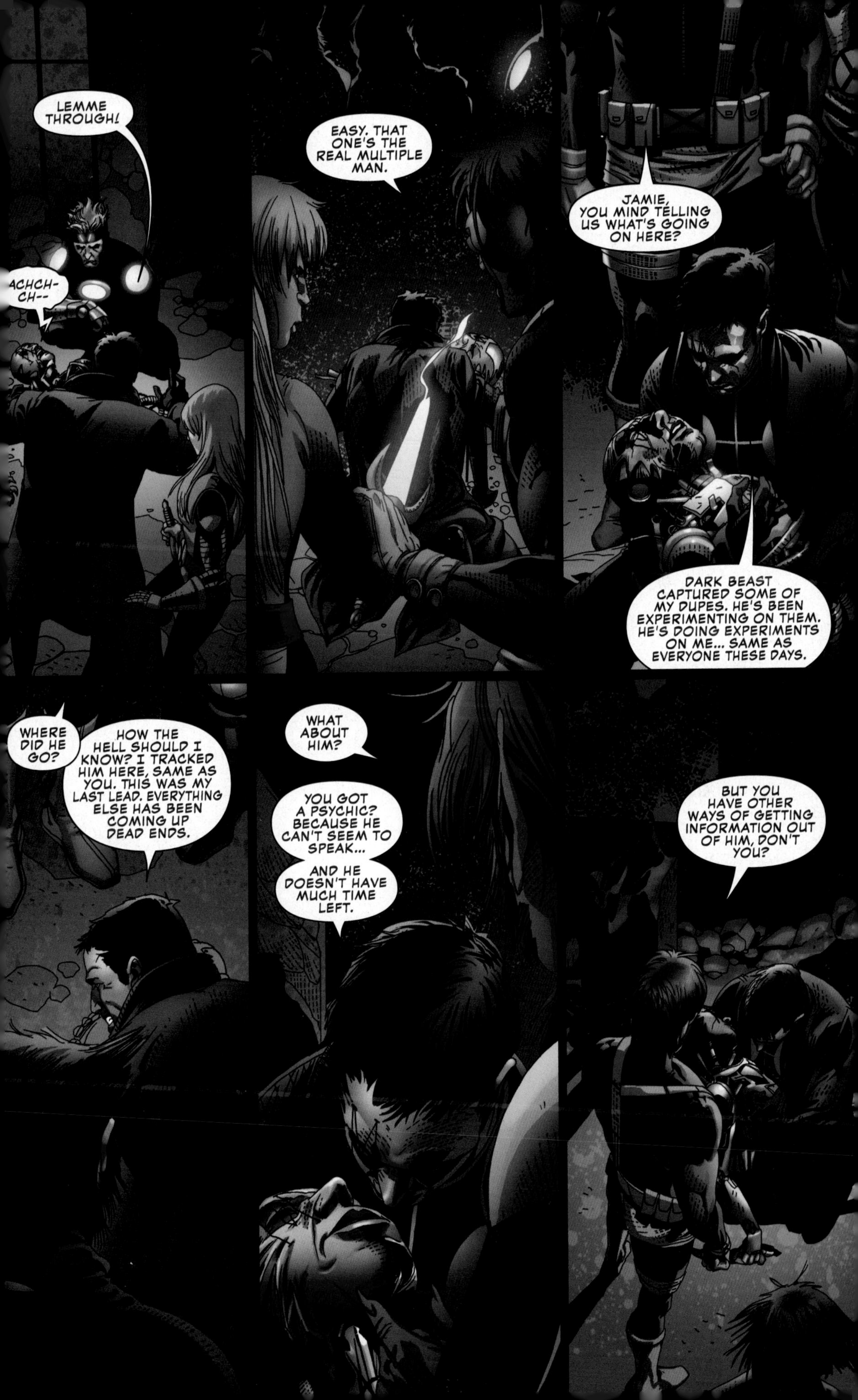
LEMME THROUGH!
ACHCH-CH--
EASY. THAT ONE'S THE REAL MULTIPLE MAN.
JAMIE, YOU MIND TELLING US WHAT'S GOING ON HERE?
DARK BEAST CAPTURED SOME OF MY DUPES. HE'S BEEN EXPERIMENTING ON THEM. HE'S DOING EXPERIMENTS ON ME... SAME AS EVERYONE THESE DAYS.
WHERE DID HE GO?
HOW THE HELL SHOULD I KNOW? I TRACKED HIM HERE, SAME AS YOU. THIS WAS MY LAST LEAD. EVERYTHING ELSE HAS BEEN COMING UP DEAD ENDS.
WHAT ABOUT HIM?
YOU GOT A PSYCHIC? BECAUSE HE CAN'T SEEM TO SPEAK...
AND HE DOESN'T HAVE MUCH TIME LEFT.
BUT YOU HAVE OTHER WAYS OF GETTING INFORMATION OUT OF HIM, DON'T YOU?

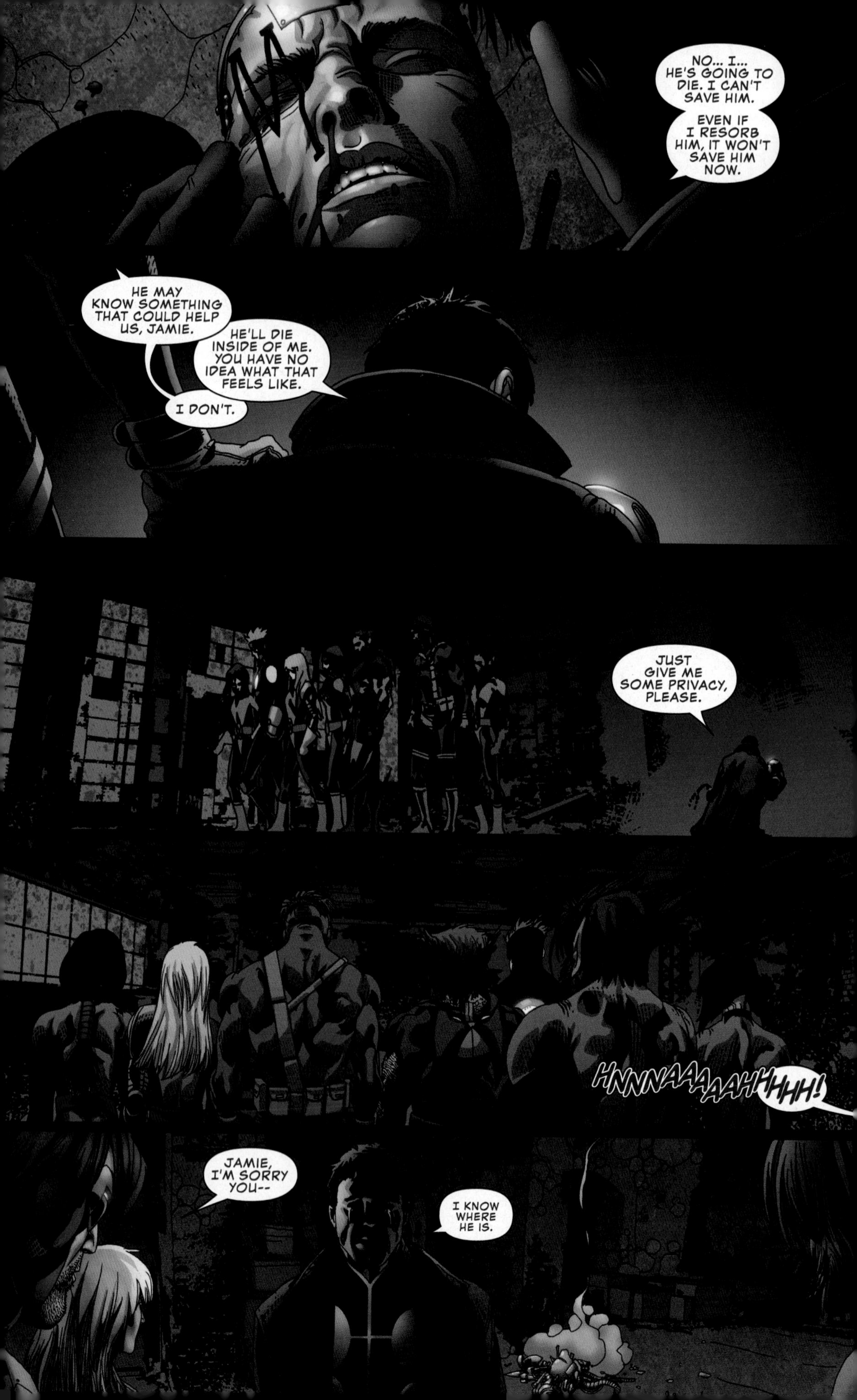
NO... I... HE'S GOING TO DIE. I CAN'T SAVE HIM.
EVEN IF I RESORB HIM, IT WON'T SAVE HIM NOW.
HE MAY KNOW SOMETHING THAT COULD HELP US, JAMIE.
HE'LL DIE INSIDE OF ME. YOU HAVE NO IDEA WHAT THAT FEELS LIKE.
I DON'T.
JUST GIVE ME SOME PRIVACY, PLEASE.
HNNNAAAAAHHHHH!
JAMIE, I'M SORRY YOU--
I KNOW WHERE HE IS.

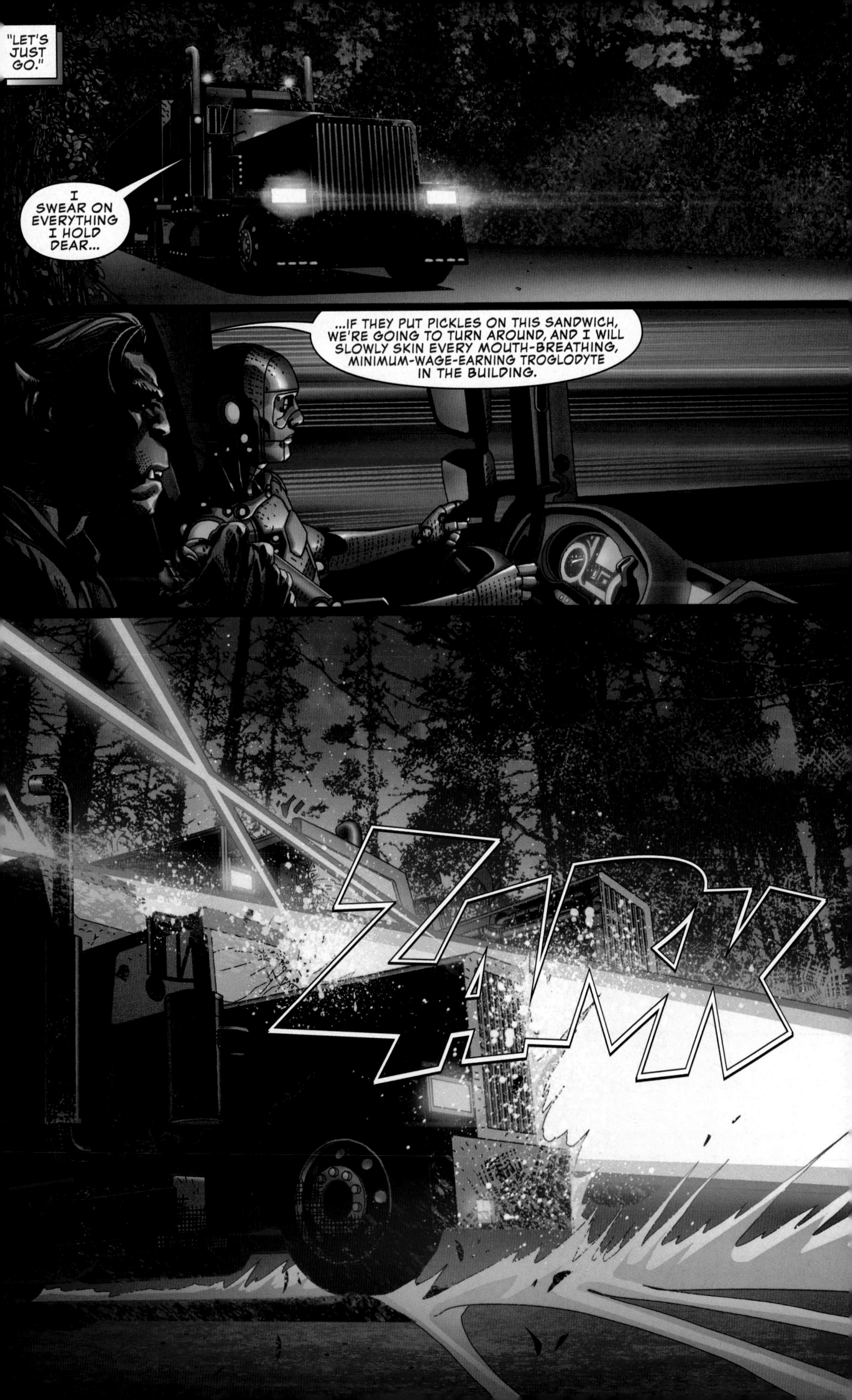
"LET'S JUST GO."
I SWEAR ON EVERYTHING I HOLD DEAR...
...IF THEY PUT PICKLES ON THIS SANDWICH, WE'RE GOING TO TURN AROUND, AND I WILL SLOWLY SKIN EVERY MOUTH-BREATHING, MINIMUM-WAGE-EARNING TROGLODYTE IN THE BUILDING.
ZARK

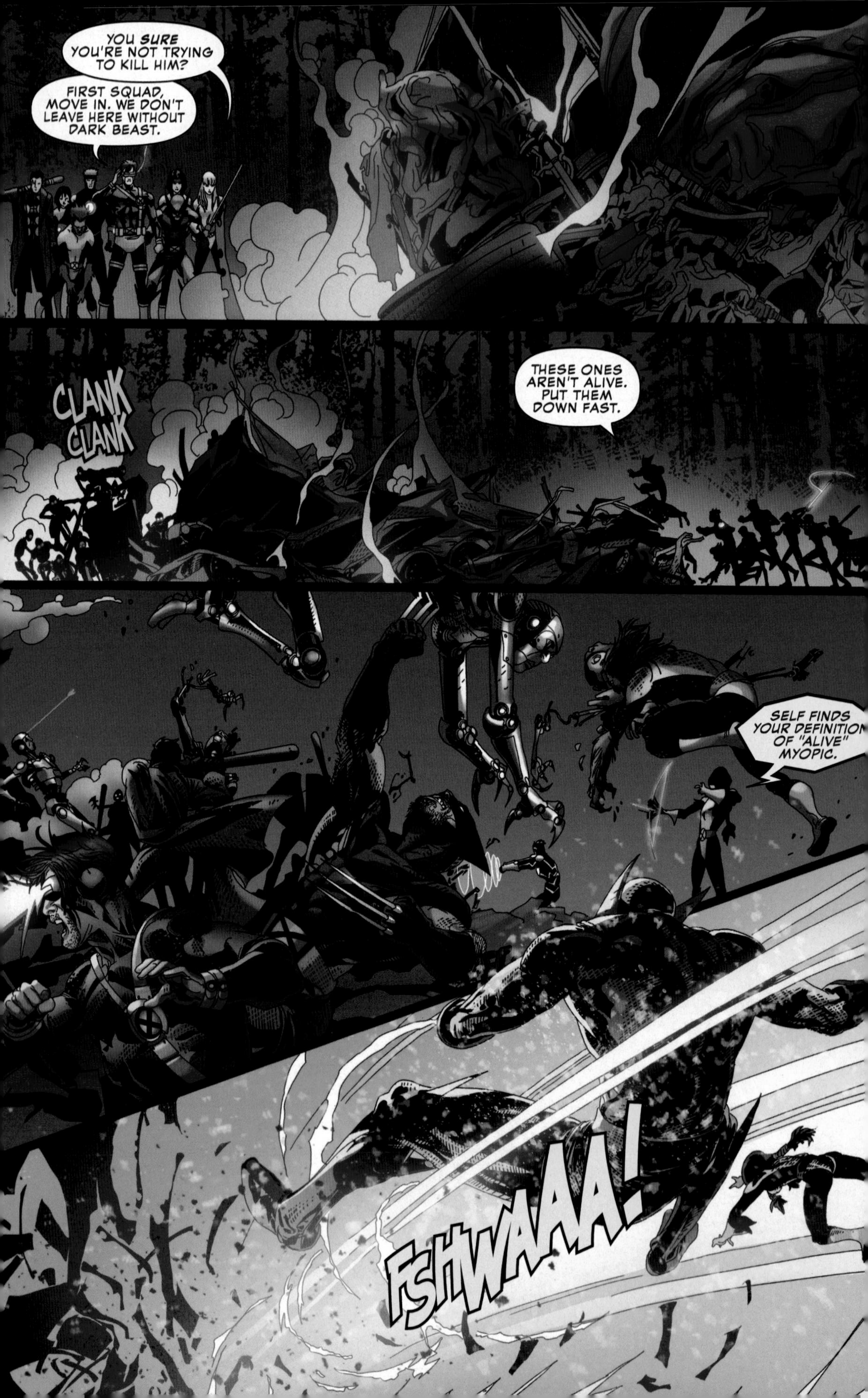
YOU SURE YOU'RE NOT TRYING TO KILL HIM?
FIRST SQUAD, MOVE IN. WE DON'T LEAVE HERE WITHOUT DARK BEAST.
CLANK CLANK
THESE ONES AREN'T ALIVE. PUT THEM DOWN FAST.
SELF FINDS YOUR DEFINITIO OF "ALIVE" MYOPIC.
FSHWAAA!

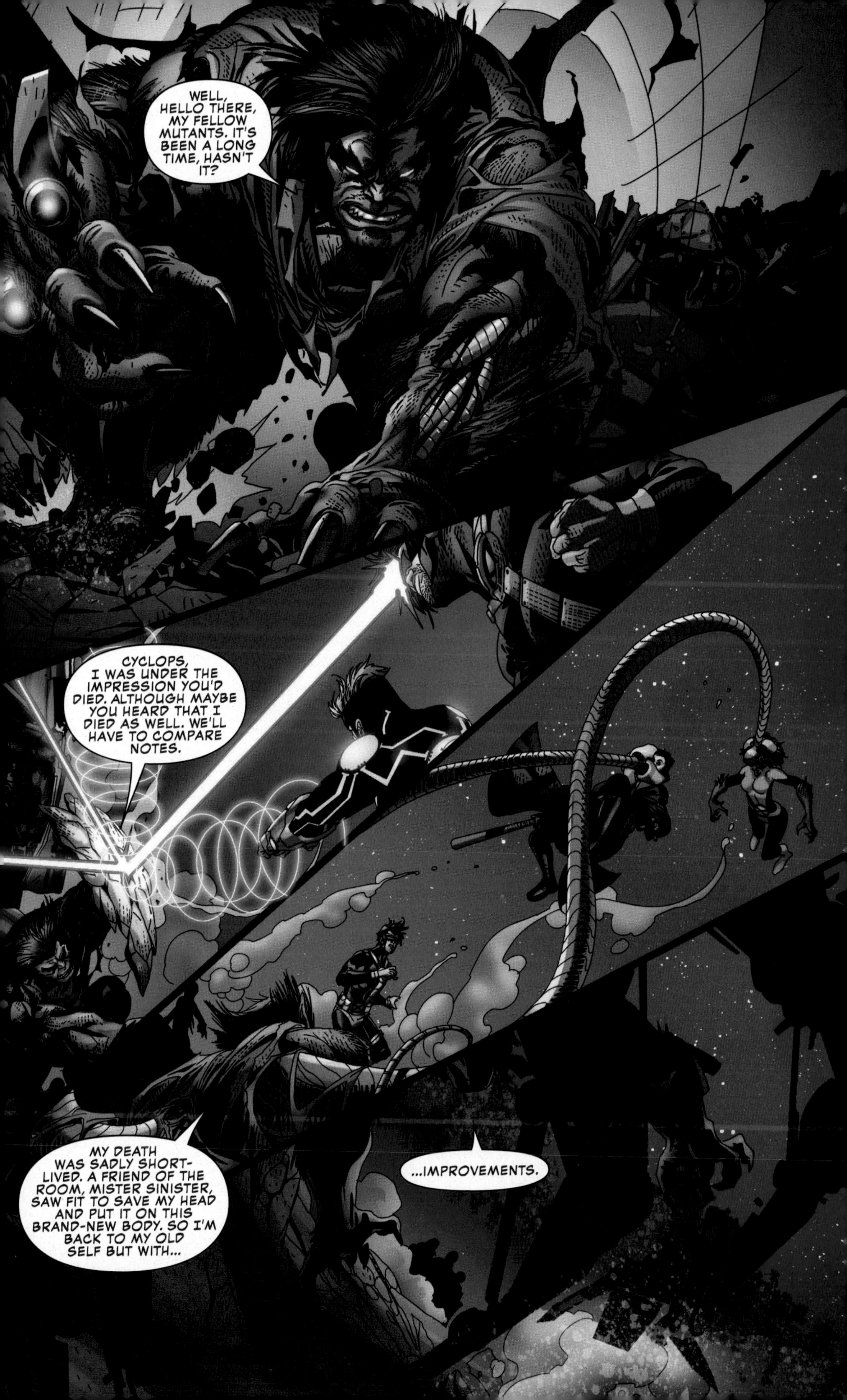
WELL, HELLO THERE, MY FELLOW MUTANTS. IT'S BEEN A LONG TIME, HASN'T IT?
CYCLOPS, I WAS UNDER THE IMPRESSION YOU'D DIED. ALTHOUGH MAYBE YOU HEARD THAT I DIED AS WELL. WE'LL HAVE TO COMPARE NOTES.
MY DEATH WAS SADLY SHORT-LIVED. A FRIEND OF THE ROOM, MISTER SINISTER, SAW FIT TO SAVE MY HEAD AND PUT IT ON THIS BRAND-NEW BODY. SO I'M BACK TO MY OLD SELF BUT WITH...
...IMPROVEMENTS.

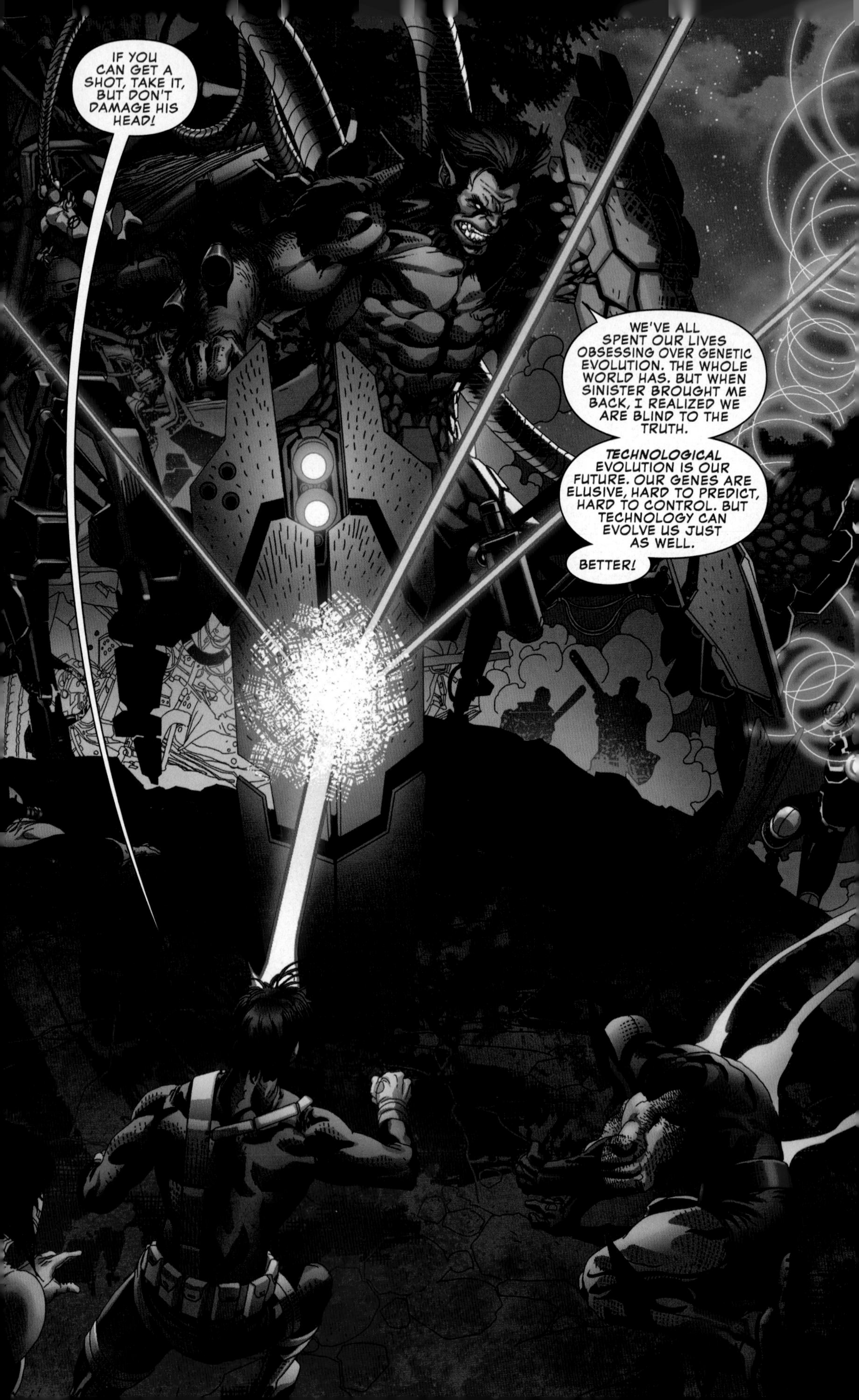
IF YOU CAN GET A SHOT, TAKE IT, BUT DON'T DAMAGE HIS HEAD!
WE'VE ALL SPENT OUR LIVES OBSESSING OVER GENETIC EVOLUTION. THE WHOLE WORLD HAS. BUT WHEN SINISTER BROUGHT ME BACK, I REALIZED WE ARE BLIND TO THE TRUTH.
TECHNOLOGICAL EVOLUTION IS OUR FUTURE. OUR GENES ARE ELUSIVE, HARD TO PREDICT, HARD TO CONTROL. BUT TECHNOLOGY CAN EVOLVE US JUST AS WELL.
BETTER!

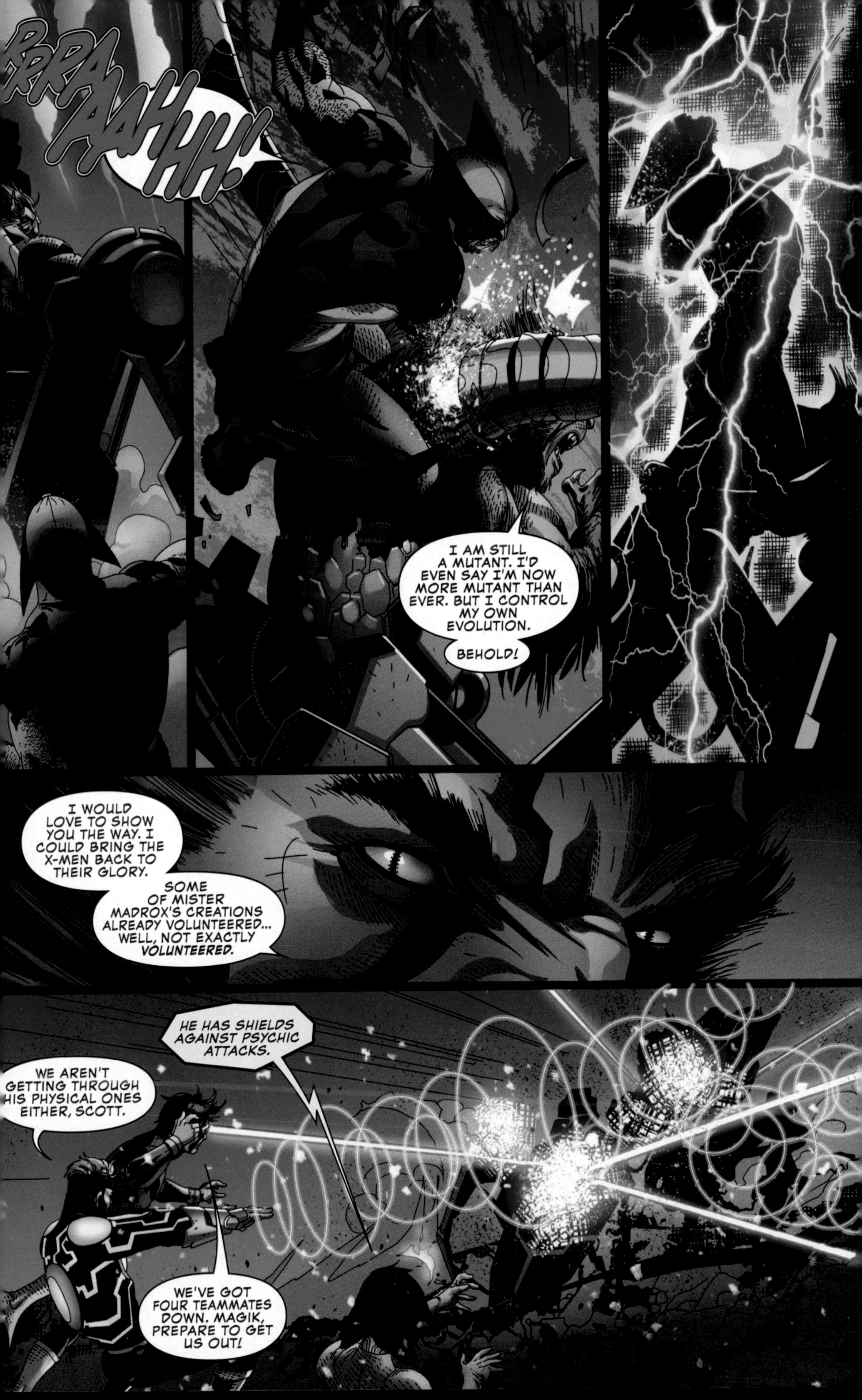
RRRAAAHHH!
I AM STILL A MUTANT. I'D EVEN SAY I'M NOW MORE MUTANT THAN EVER. BUT I CONTROL MY OWN EVOLUTION.
BEHOLD!
I WOULD LOVE TO SHOW YOU THE WAY. I COULD BRING THE X-MEN BACK TO THEIR GLORY.
SOME OF MISTER MADROX'S CREATIONS ALREADY VOLUNTEERED... WELL, NOT EXACTLY *VOLUNTEERED*.
HE HAS SHIELDS AGAINST PSYCHIC ATTACKS.
WE AREN'T GETTING THROUGH HIS PHYSICAL ONES EITHER, SCOTT.
WE'VE GOT FOUR TEAMMATES DOWN. MAGIK, PREPARE TO GET US OUT!

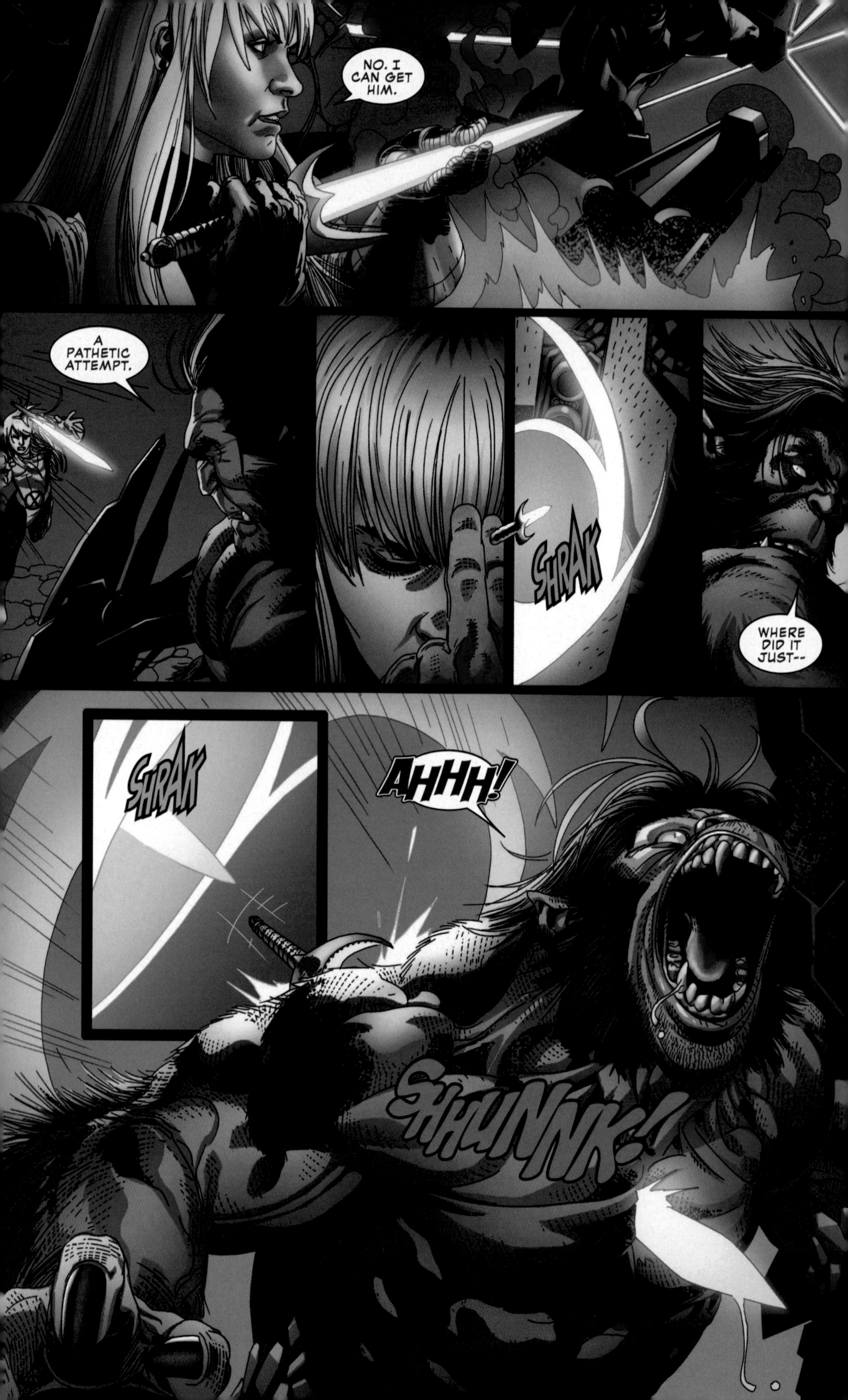
NO. I CAN GET HIM.
A PATHETIC ATTEMPT.
SHRAK
WHERE DID IT JUST--
SHRAK
AHHH!
SHHUNNK!!

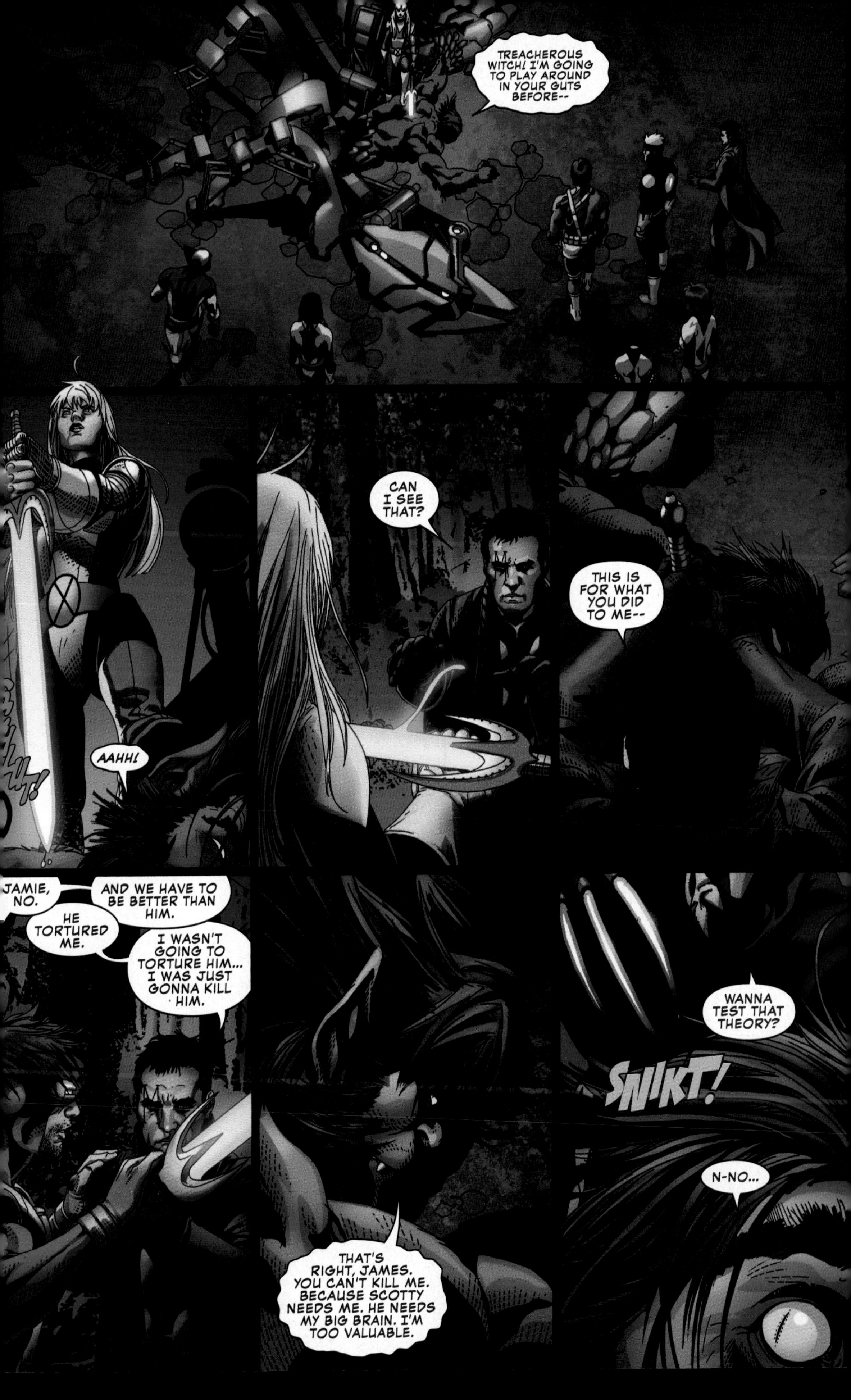
TREACHEROUS WITCH! I'M GOING TO PLAY AROUND IN YOUR GUTS BEFORE--
AAHH!
CAN I SEE THAT?
THIS IS FOR WHAT YOU DID TO ME--
JAMIE, NO.
HE TORTURED ME.
AND WE HAVE TO BE BETTER THAN HIM.
I WASN'T GOING TO TORTURE HIM... I WAS JUST GONNA KILL HIM.
THAT'S RIGHT, JAMES. YOU CAN'T KILL ME. BECAUSE SCOTTY NEEDS ME. HE NEEDS MY BIG BRAIN. I'M TOO VALUABLE.
WANNA TEST THAT THEORY?
SNIKT!
N-NO...

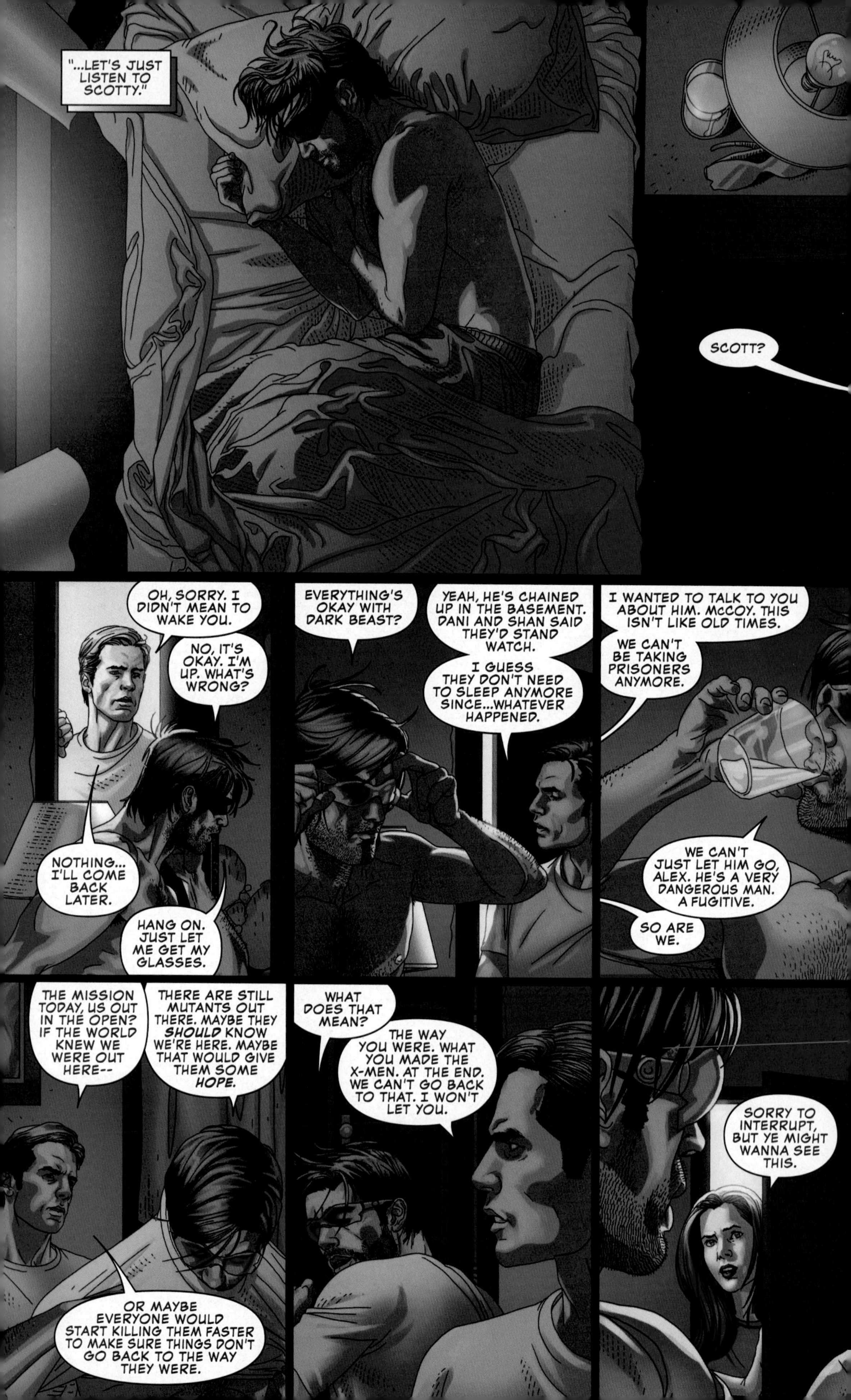
"...LET'S JUST LISTEN TO SCOTTY."
SCOTT?
OH, SORRY. I DIDN'T MEAN TO WAKE YOU.
NO, IT'S OKAY. I'M UP. WHAT'S WRONG?
NOTHING... I'LL COME BACK LATER.
HANG ON. JUST LET ME GET MY GLASSES.
EVERYTHING'S OKAY WITH DARK BEAST?
YEAH, HE'S CHAINED UP IN THE BASEMENT. DANI AND SHAN SAID THEY'D STAND WATCH.
I GUESS THEY DON'T NEED TO SLEEP ANYMORE SINCE...WHATEVER HAPPENED.
I WANTED TO TALK TO YOU ABOUT HIM. McCOY. THIS ISN'T LIKE OLD TIMES.
WE CAN'T BE TAKING PRISONERS ANYMORE.
WE CAN'T JUST LET HIM GO, ALEX. HE'S A VERY DANGEROUS MAN. A FUGITIVE.
SO ARE WE.
THE MISSION TODAY, US OUT IN THE OPEN? IF THE WORLD KNEW WE WERE OUT HERE--
THERE ARE STILL MUTANTS OUT THERE. MAYBE THEY SHOULD KNOW WE'RE HERE. MAYBE THAT WOULD GIVE THEM SOME HOPE.
OR MAYBE EVERYONE WOULD START KILLING THEM FASTER TO MAKE SURE THINGS DON'T GO BACK TO THE WAY THEY WERE.
WHAT DOES THAT MEAN?
THE WAY YOU WERE. WHAT YOU MADE THE X-MEN. AT THE END. WE CAN'T GO BACK TO THAT. I WON'T LET YOU.
SORRY TO INTERRUPT, BUT YE MIGHT WANNA SEE THIS.

FOLLOWING THE REAPPEARANCE OF SCOTT SUMMERS, A.K.A. CYCLOPS, LAST WEEK, NEW EVIDENCE EMERGES TONIGHT POINTING TO THE RETURN OF THE RADICAL MUTANT GROUP THE X-MEN.

SECURITY CAMERAS CAUGHT THEM ATTACKING THE MIDDLE RIVER HEALTH CLINIC IN DANBURY TONIGHT.

WELL, #$%&.

THIS IS THE FIFTH ATTACK IN AS MANY DAYS ON FACILITIES THAT ARE HANDLING THE NOW-MANDATORY VAXX INJECTIONS, MORE COMMONLY REFERRED TO AS THE "ANTI-MUTANT VACCINE."

THOSE AREN'T X-MEN! THAT'S THE MUTANT LIBERATION FRONT. THEY CAN'T EVEN TELL US APART ANYMORE?!

THE MLF WAS ON OUR LIST. LOOKS LIKE THEY JUST JUMPED UP A FEW...WAIT... PAUSE IT.

MUTANT TERRORISTS ATTACK VAXX PLANTS

WELL, BROTHER, YOU SAID THE WORLD NEEDED HOPE--THERE SHE IS.

AND BANSHEE.

X-MEN ATTACK!

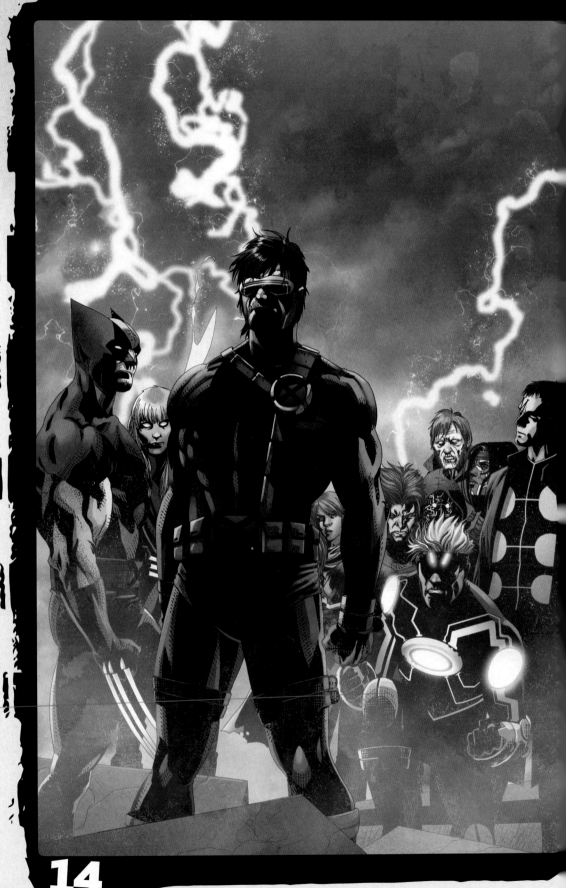

This is Forever Part 4

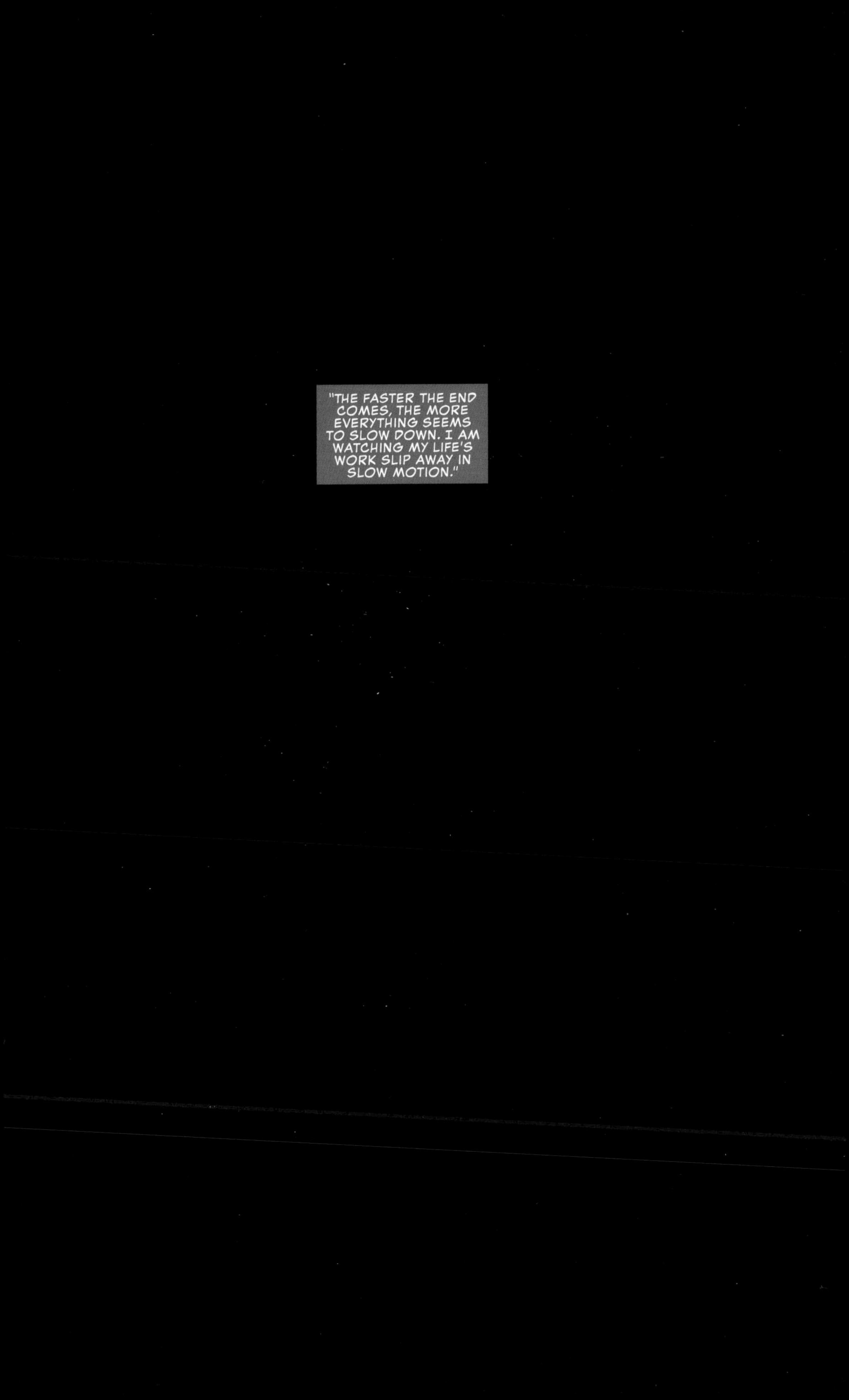
"THE FASTER THE END COMES, THE MORE EVERYTHING SEEMS TO SLOW DOWN. I AM WATCHING MY LIFE'S WORK SLIP AWAY IN SLOW MOTION."

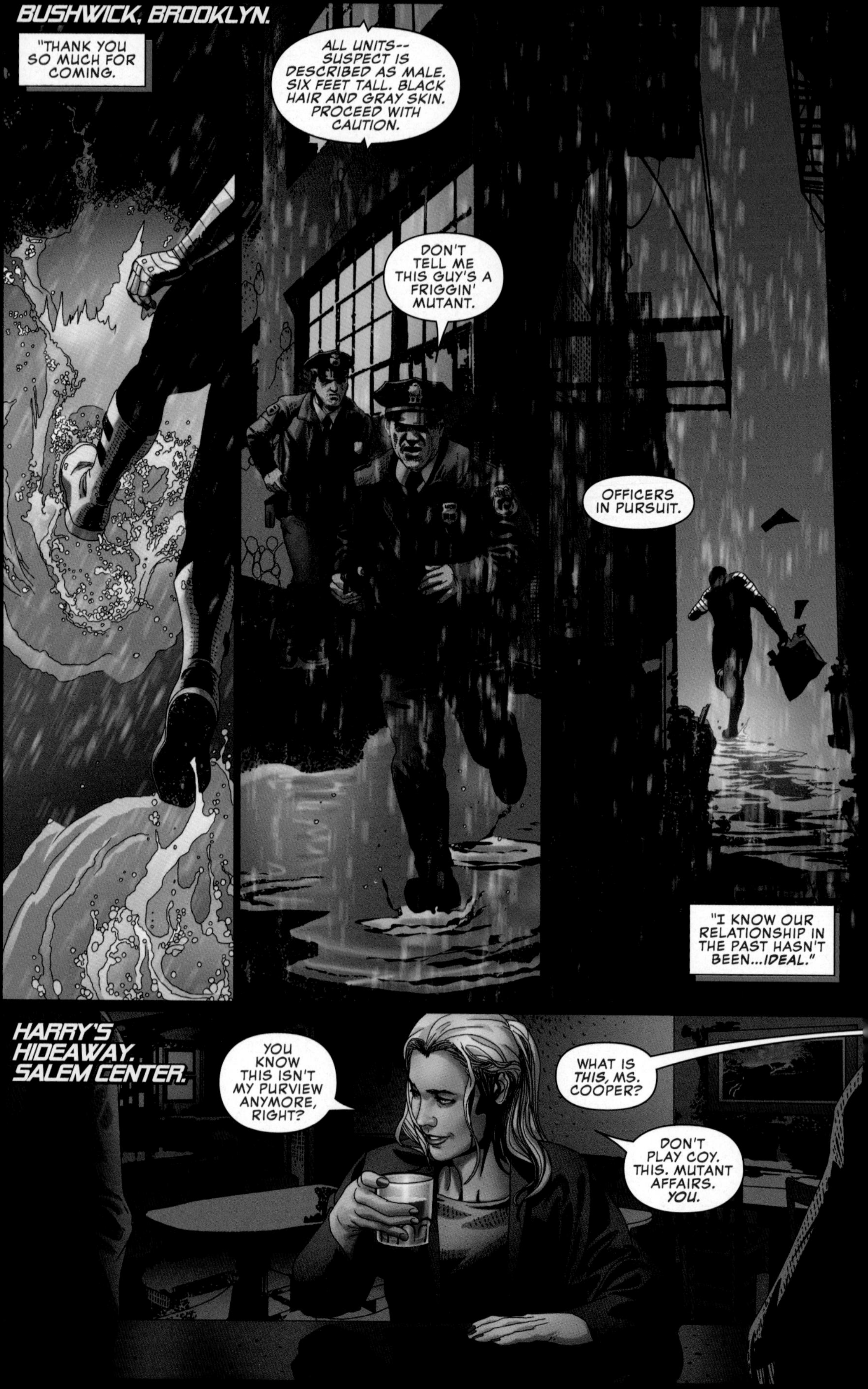
BUSHWICK, BROOKLYN.
"THANK YOU SO MUCH FOR COMING.
ALL UNITS-- SUSPECT IS DESCRIBED AS MALE. SIX FEET TALL. BLACK HAIR AND GRAY SKIN. PROCEED WITH CAUTION.
DON'T TELL ME THIS GUY'S A FRIGGIN' MUTANT.
OFFICERS IN PURSUIT.
"I KNOW OUR RELATIONSHIP IN THE PAST HASN'T BEEN...IDEAL."
HARRY'S HIDEAWAY. SALEM CENTER.
YOU KNOW THIS ISN'T MY PURVIEW ANYMORE, RIGHT?
WHAT IS THIS, MS. COOPER?
DON'T PLAY COY. THIS. MUTANT AFFAIRS. YOU.

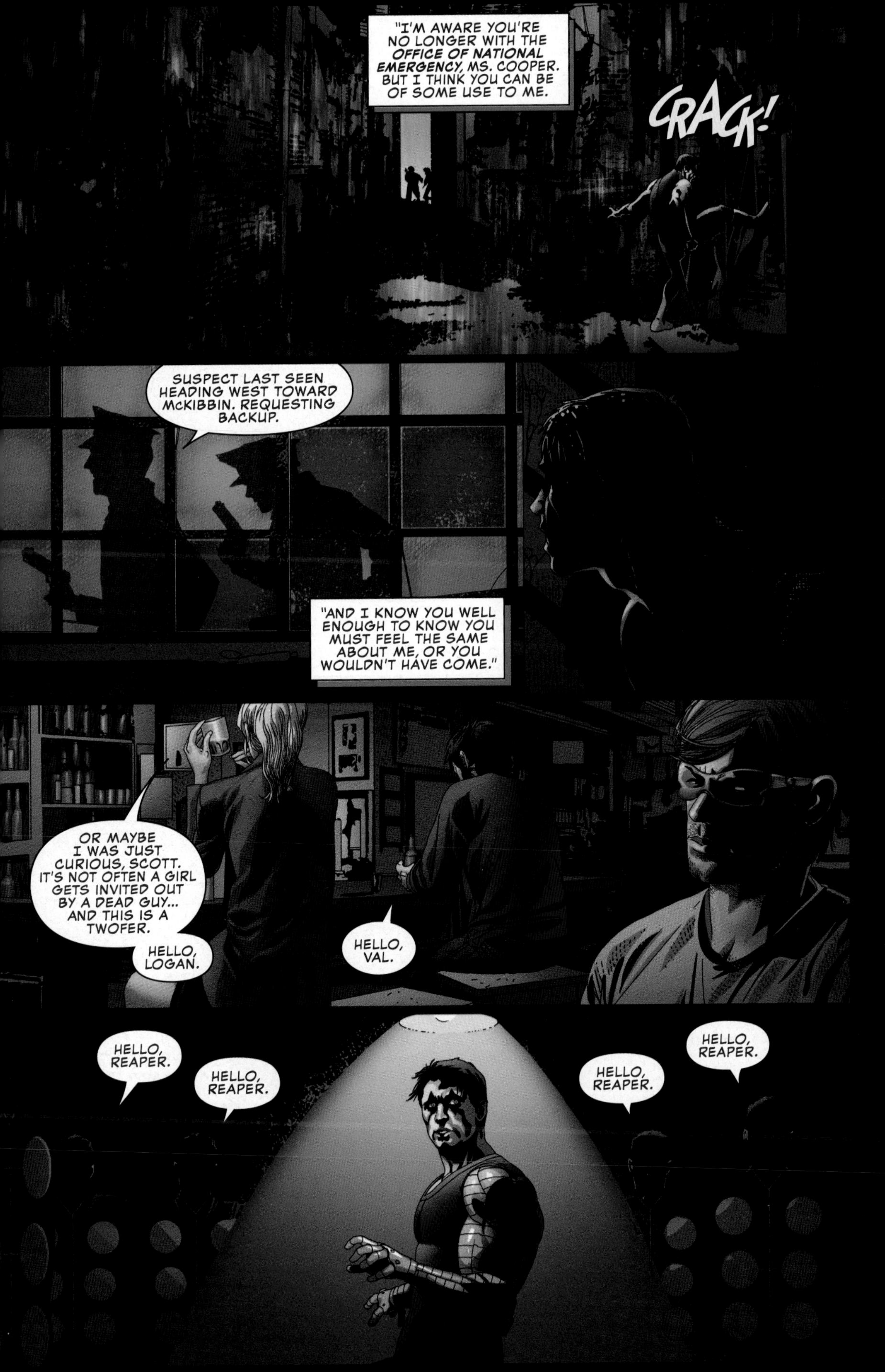
"I'M AWARE YOU'RE NO LONGER WITH THE *OFFICE OF NATIONAL EMERGENCY*, MS. COOPER. BUT I THINK YOU CAN BE OF SOME USE TO ME.
CRACK!
SUSPECT LAST SEEN HEADING WEST TOWARD McKIBBIN. REQUESTING BACKUP.
"AND I KNOW YOU WELL ENOUGH TO KNOW YOU MUST FEEL THE SAME ABOUT ME, OR YOU WOULDN'T HAVE COME."
OR MAYBE I WAS JUST CURIOUS, SCOTT. IT'S NOT OFTEN A GIRL GETS INVITED OUT BY A DEAD GUY... AND THIS IS A TWOFER.
HELLO, LOGAN.
HELLO, VAL.
HELLO, REAPER.
HELLO, REAPER.
HELLO, REAPER.
HELLO, REAPER.

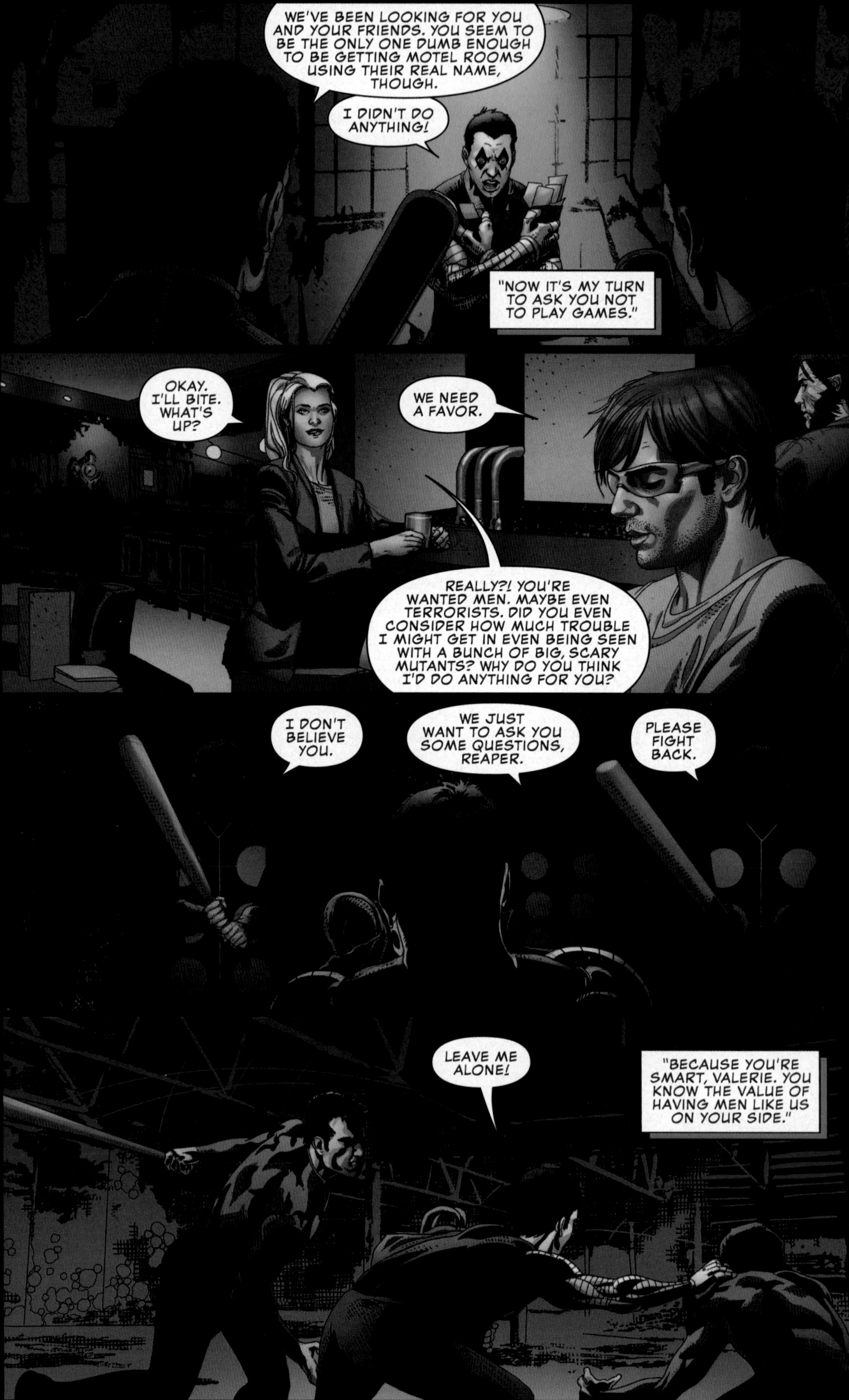
WE'VE BEEN LOOKING FOR YOU AND YOUR FRIENDS. YOU SEEM TO BE THE ONLY ONE DUMB ENOUGH TO BE GETTING MOTEL ROOMS USING THEIR REAL NAME, THOUGH.
I DIDN'T DO ANYTHING!
"NOW IT'S MY TURN TO ASK YOU NOT TO PLAY GAMES."
OKAY. I'LL BITE. WHAT'S UP?
WE NEED A FAVOR.
REALLY?! YOU'RE WANTED MEN. MAYBE EVEN TERRORISTS. DID YOU EVEN CONSIDER HOW MUCH TROUBLE I MIGHT GET IN EVEN BEING SEEN WITH A BUNCH OF BIG, SCARY MUTANTS? WHY DO YOU THINK I'D DO ANYTHING FOR YOU?
I DON'T BELIEVE YOU.
WE JUST WANT TO ASK YOU SOME QUESTIONS, REAPER.
PLEASE FIGHT BACK.
LEAVE ME ALONE!
"BECAUSE YOU'RE SMART, VALERIE. YOU KNOW THE VALUE OF HAVING MEN LIKE US ON YOUR SIDE."

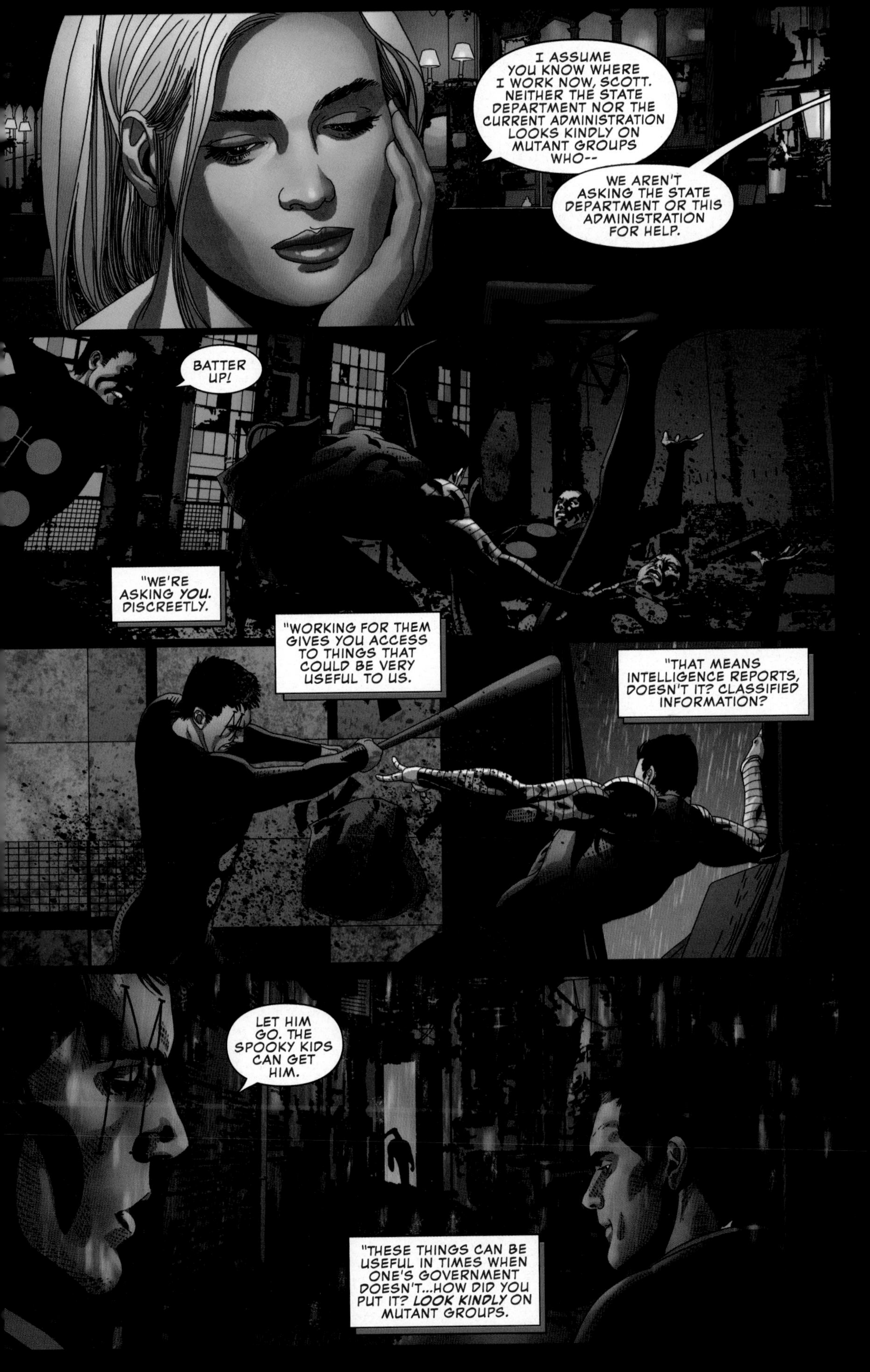
I ASSUME YOU KNOW WHERE I WORK NOW, SCOTT. NEITHER THE STATE DEPARTMENT NOR THE CURRENT ADMINISTRATION LOOKS KINDLY ON MUTANT GROUPS WHO--
WE AREN'T ASKING THE STATE DEPARTMENT OR THIS ADMINISTRATION FOR HELP.
BATTER UP!
"WE'RE ASKING *YOU*. DISCREETLY.
"WORKING FOR THEM GIVES YOU ACCESS TO THINGS THAT COULD BE VERY USEFUL TO US.
"THAT MEANS INTELLIGENCE REPORTS, DOESN'T IT? CLASSIFIED INFORMATION?
LET HIM GO. THE SPOOKY KIDS CAN GET HIM.
"THESE THINGS CAN BE USEFUL IN TIMES WHEN ONE'S GOVERNMENT DOESN'T...HOW DID YOU PUT IT? *LOOK KINDLY* ON MUTANT GROUPS.

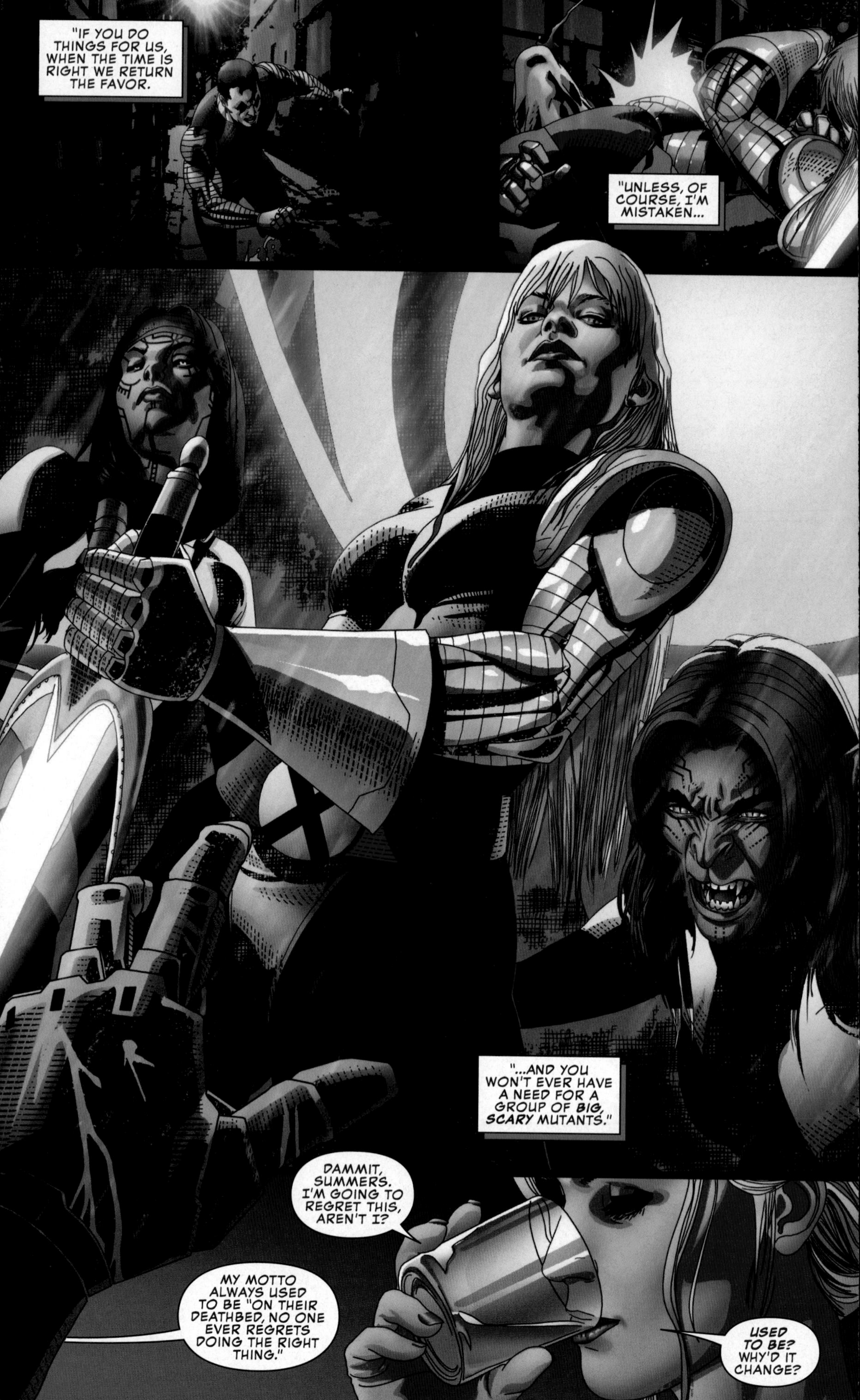
"IF YOU DO THINGS FOR US, WHEN THE TIME IS RIGHT WE RETURN THE FAVOR.
"UNLESS, OF COURSE, I'M MISTAKEN...
"...AND YOU WON'T EVER HAVE A NEED FOR A GROUP OF *BIG, SCARY* MUTANTS."
DAMMIT, SUMMERS. I'M GOING TO REGRET THIS, AREN'T I?
MY MOTTO ALWAYS USED TO BE "ON THEIR DEATHBED, NO ONE EVER REGRETS DOING THE RIGHT THING."
USED TO BE? WHY'D IT CHANGE?

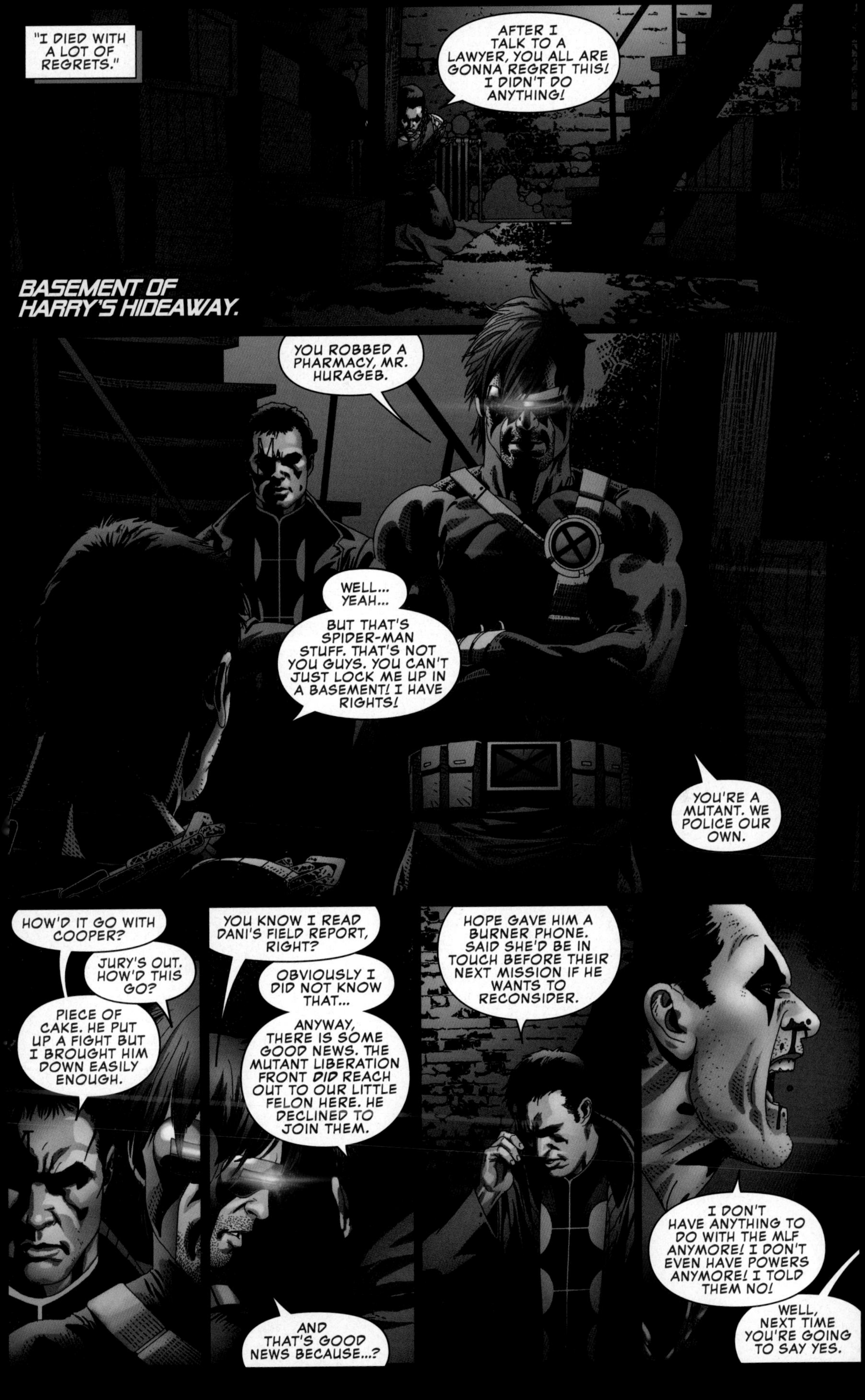
"I DIED WITH A LOT OF REGRETS."
AFTER I TALK TO A LAWYER, YOU ALL ARE GONNA REGRET THIS! I DIDN'T DO ANYTHING!
BASEMENT OF HARRY'S HIDEAWAY.
YOU ROBBED A PHARMACY, MR. HURAGEB.
WELL... YEAH...
BUT THAT'S SPIDER-MAN STUFF. THAT'S NOT YOU GUYS. YOU CAN'T JUST LOCK ME UP IN A BASEMENT! I HAVE RIGHTS!
YOU'RE A MUTANT. WE POLICE OUR OWN.
HOW'D IT GO WITH COOPER?
JURY'S OUT. HOW'D THIS GO?
PIECE OF CAKE. HE PUT UP A FIGHT BUT I BROUGHT HIM DOWN EASILY ENOUGH.
YOU KNOW I READ DANI'S FIELD REPORT, RIGHT?
OBVIOUSLY I DID NOT KNOW THAT...
ANYWAY, THERE IS SOME GOOD NEWS. THE MUTANT LIBERATION FRONT DID REACH OUT TO OUR LITTLE FELON HERE. HE DECLINED TO JOIN THEM.
AND THAT'S GOOD NEWS BECAUSE...?
HOPE GAVE HIM A BURNER PHONE. SAID SHE'D BE IN TOUCH BEFORE THEIR NEXT MISSION IF HE WANTS TO RECONSIDER.
I DON'T HAVE ANYTHING TO DO WITH THE MLF ANYMORE! I DON'T EVEN HAVE POWERS ANYMORE! I TOLD THEM NO!
WELL, NEXT TIME YOU'RE GOING TO SAY YES.

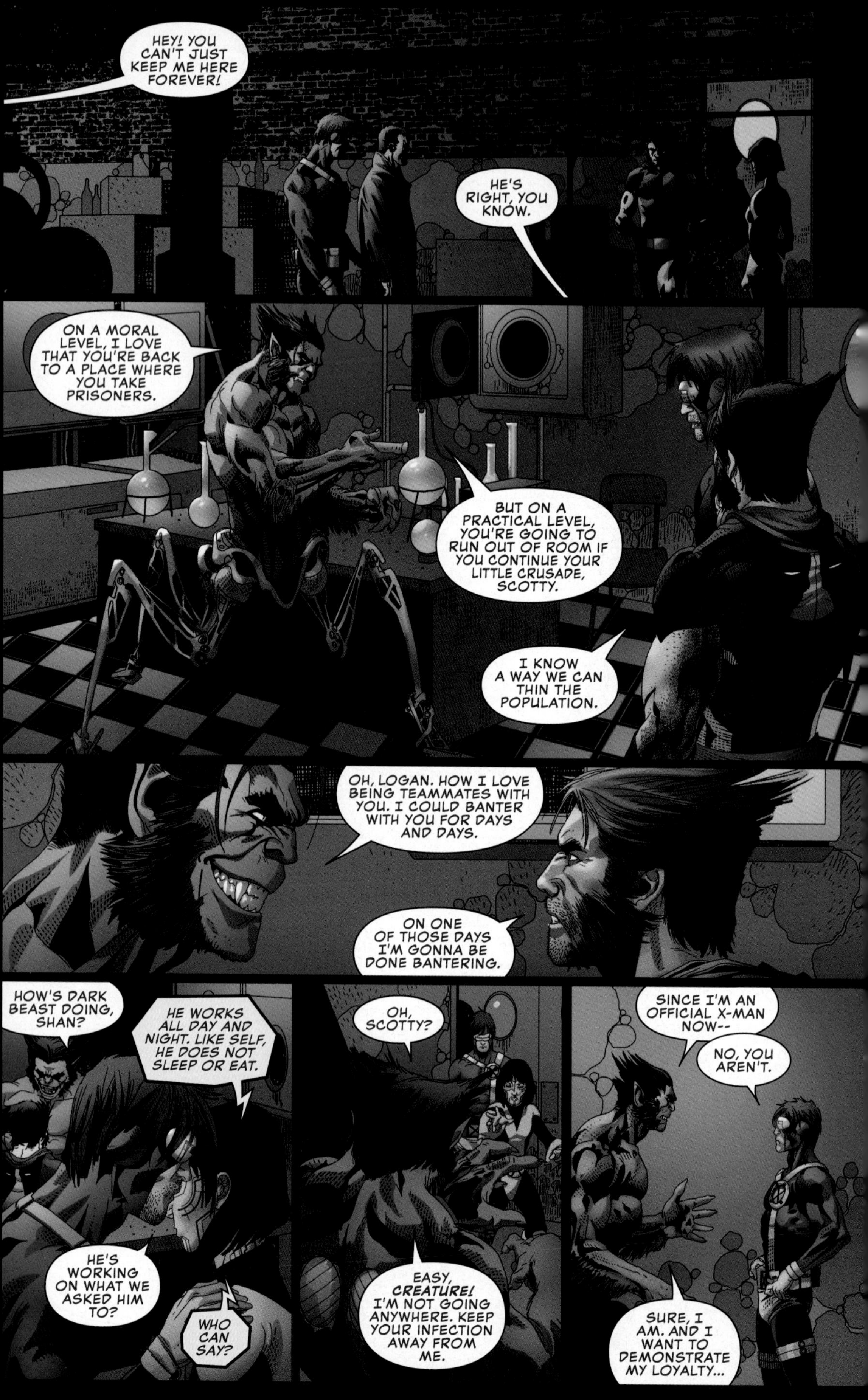
HEY! YOU CAN'T JUST KEEP ME HERE FOREVER!
HE'S RIGHT, YOU KNOW.
ON A MORAL LEVEL, I LOVE THAT YOU'RE BACK TO A PLACE WHERE YOU TAKE PRISONERS.
BUT ON A PRACTICAL LEVEL, YOU'RE GOING TO RUN OUT OF ROOM IF YOU CONTINUE YOUR LITTLE CRUSADE, SCOTTY.
I KNOW A WAY WE CAN THIN THE POPULATION.
OH, LOGAN. HOW I LOVE BEING TEAMMATES WITH YOU. I COULD BANTER WITH YOU FOR DAYS AND DAYS.
ON ONE OF THOSE DAYS I'M GONNA BE DONE BANTERING.
HOW'S DARK BEAST DOING, SHAN?
HE WORKS ALL DAY AND NIGHT. LIKE SELF, HE DOES NOT SLEEP OR EAT.
HE'S WORKING ON WHAT WE ASKED HIM TO?
WHO CAN SAY?
OH, SCOTTY?
EASY, CREATURE! I'M NOT GOING ANYWHERE. KEEP YOUR INFECTION AWAY FROM ME.
SINCE I'M AN OFFICIAL X-MAN NOW--
NO, YOU AREN'T.
SURE, I AM. AND I WANT TO DEMONSTRATE MY LOYALTY...

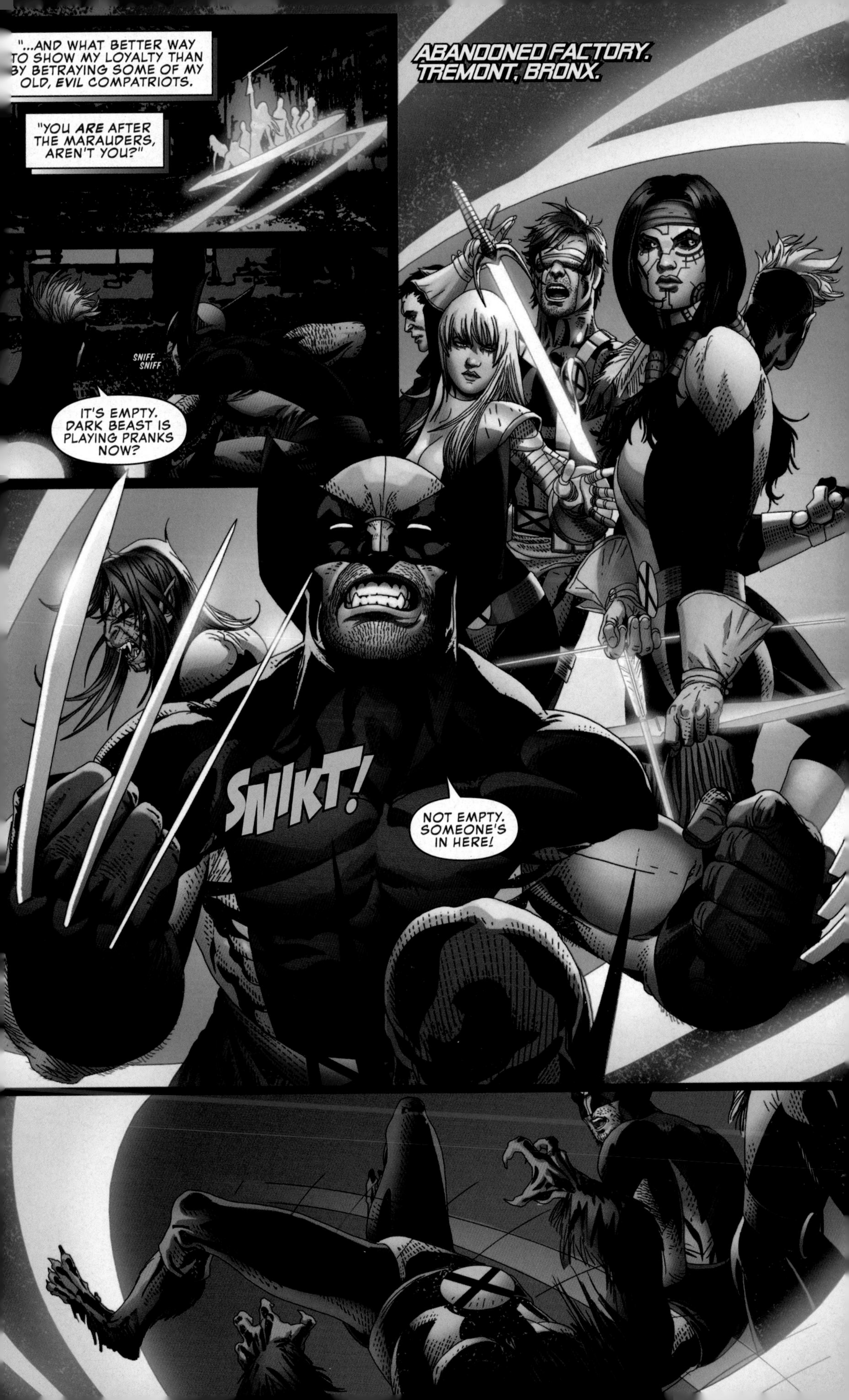
"...AND WHAT BETTER WAY TO SHOW MY LOYALTY THAN BY BETRAYING SOME OF MY OLD, EVIL COMPATRIOTS.
"YOU ARE AFTER THE MARAUDERS, AREN'T YOU?"
ABANDONED FACTORY. TREMONT, BRONX.
SNIFF SNIFF
IT'S EMPTY. DARK BEAST IS PLAYING PRANKS NOW?
SNIKT!
NOT EMPTY. SOMEONE'S IN HERE!

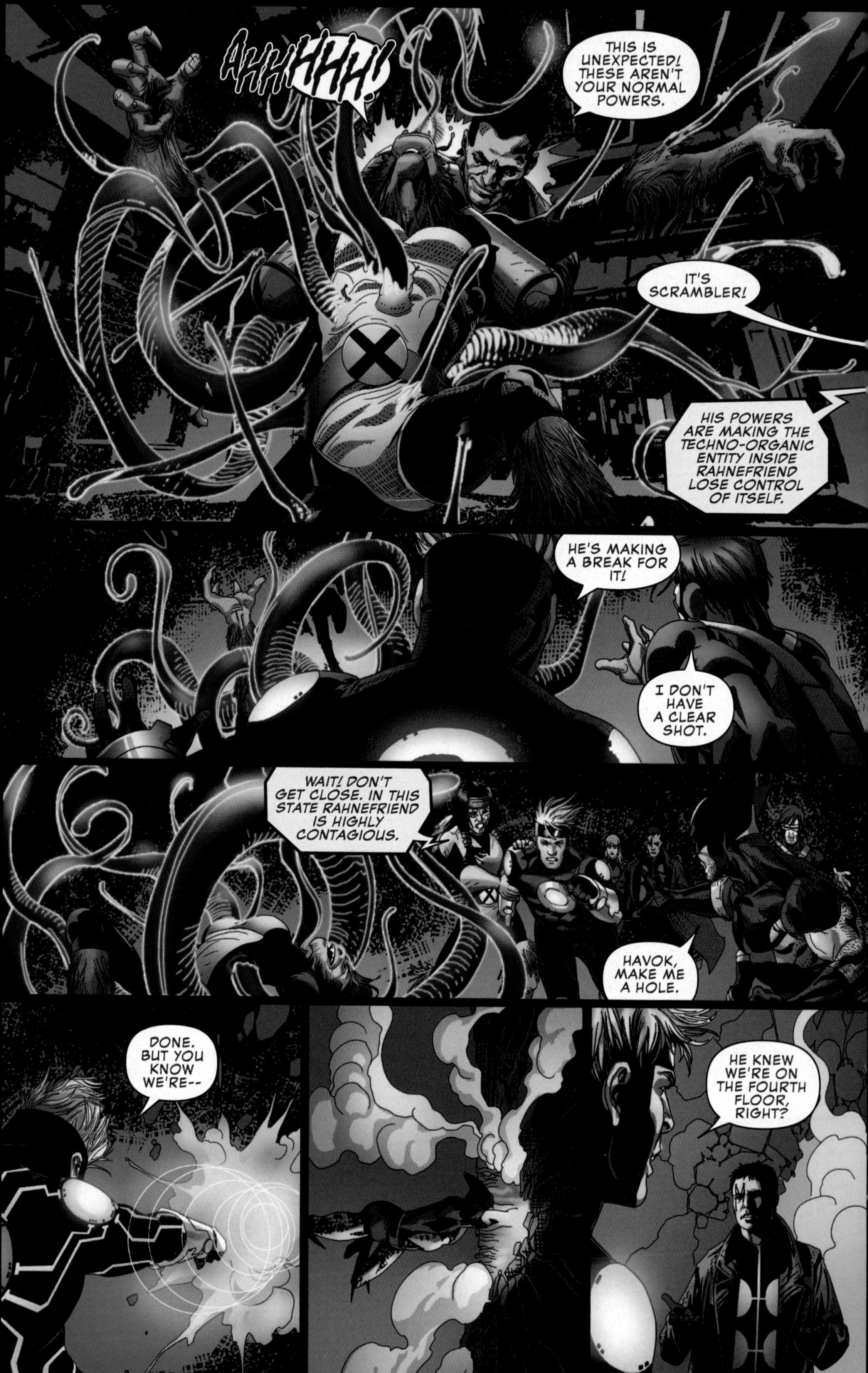
AHHHHH!
THIS IS UNEXPECTED! THESE AREN'T YOUR NORMAL POWERS.
IT'S SCRAMBLER!
HIS POWERS ARE MAKING THE TECHNO-ORGANIC ENTITY INSIDE RAHNEFRIEND LOSE CONTROL OF ITSELF.
HE'S MAKING A BREAK FOR IT!
I DON'T HAVE A CLEAR SHOT.
WAIT! DON'T GET CLOSE. IN THIS STATE RAHNEFRIEND IS HIGHLY CONTAGIOUS.
HAVOK, MAKE ME A HOLE.
DONE. BUT YOU KNOW WE'RE--
HE KNEW WE'RE ON THE FOURTH FLOOR, RIGHT?

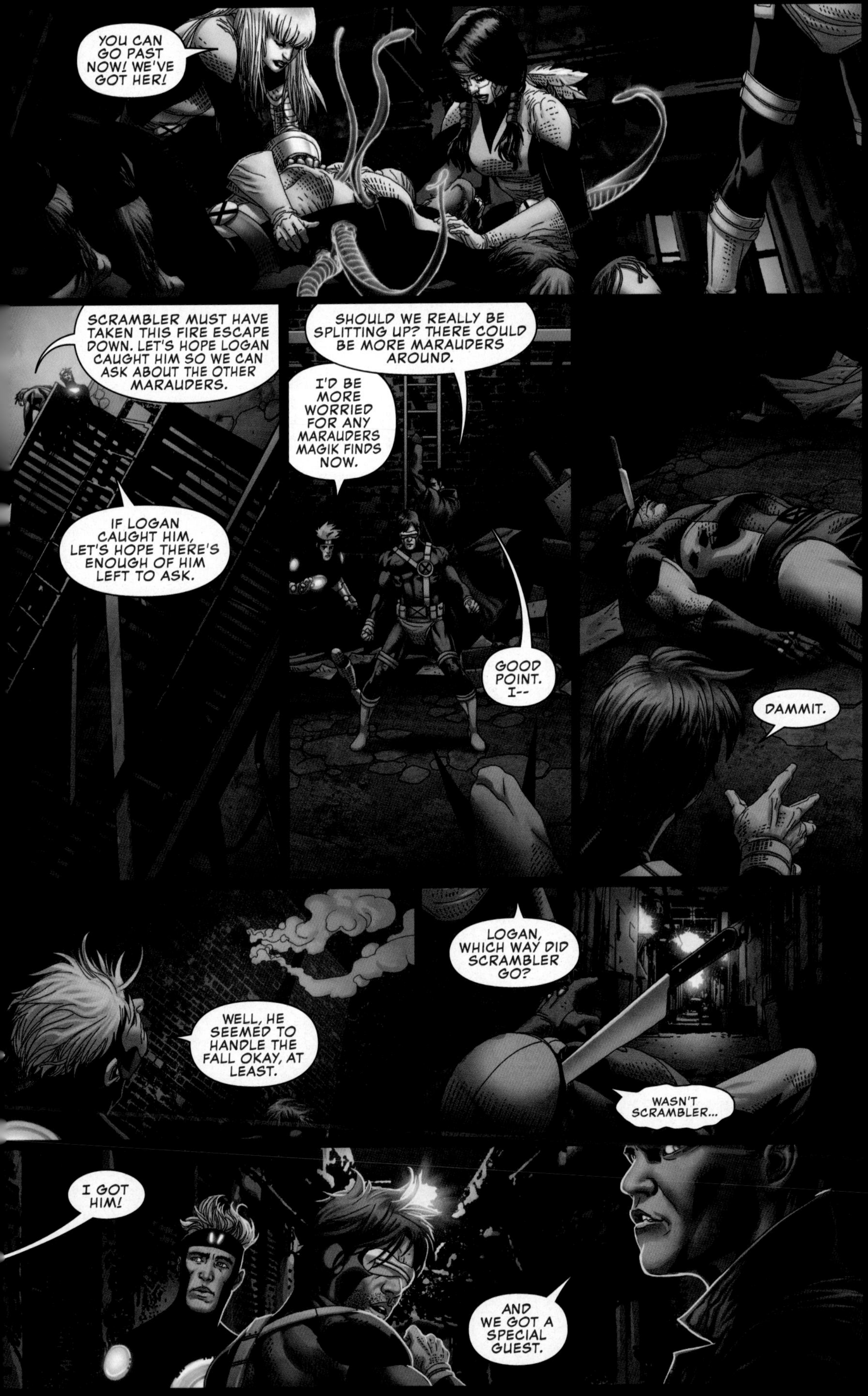
YOU CAN GO PAST NOW! WE'VE GOT HER!
SCRAMBLER MUST HAVE TAKEN THIS FIRE ESCAPE DOWN. LET'S HOPE LOGAN CAUGHT HIM SO WE CAN ASK ABOUT THE OTHER MARAUDERS.
IF LOGAN CAUGHT HIM, LET'S HOPE THERE'S ENOUGH OF HIM LEFT TO ASK.
SHOULD WE REALLY BE SPLITTING UP? THERE COULD BE MORE MARAUDERS AROUND.
I'D BE MORE WORRIED FOR ANY MARAUDERS MAGIK FINDS NOW.
GOOD POINT. I--
DAMMIT.
WELL, HE SEEMED TO HANDLE THE FALL OKAY, AT LEAST.
LOGAN, WHICH WAY DID SCRAMBLER GO?
WASN'T SCRAMBLER...
I GOT HIM!
AND WE GOT A SPECIAL GUEST.

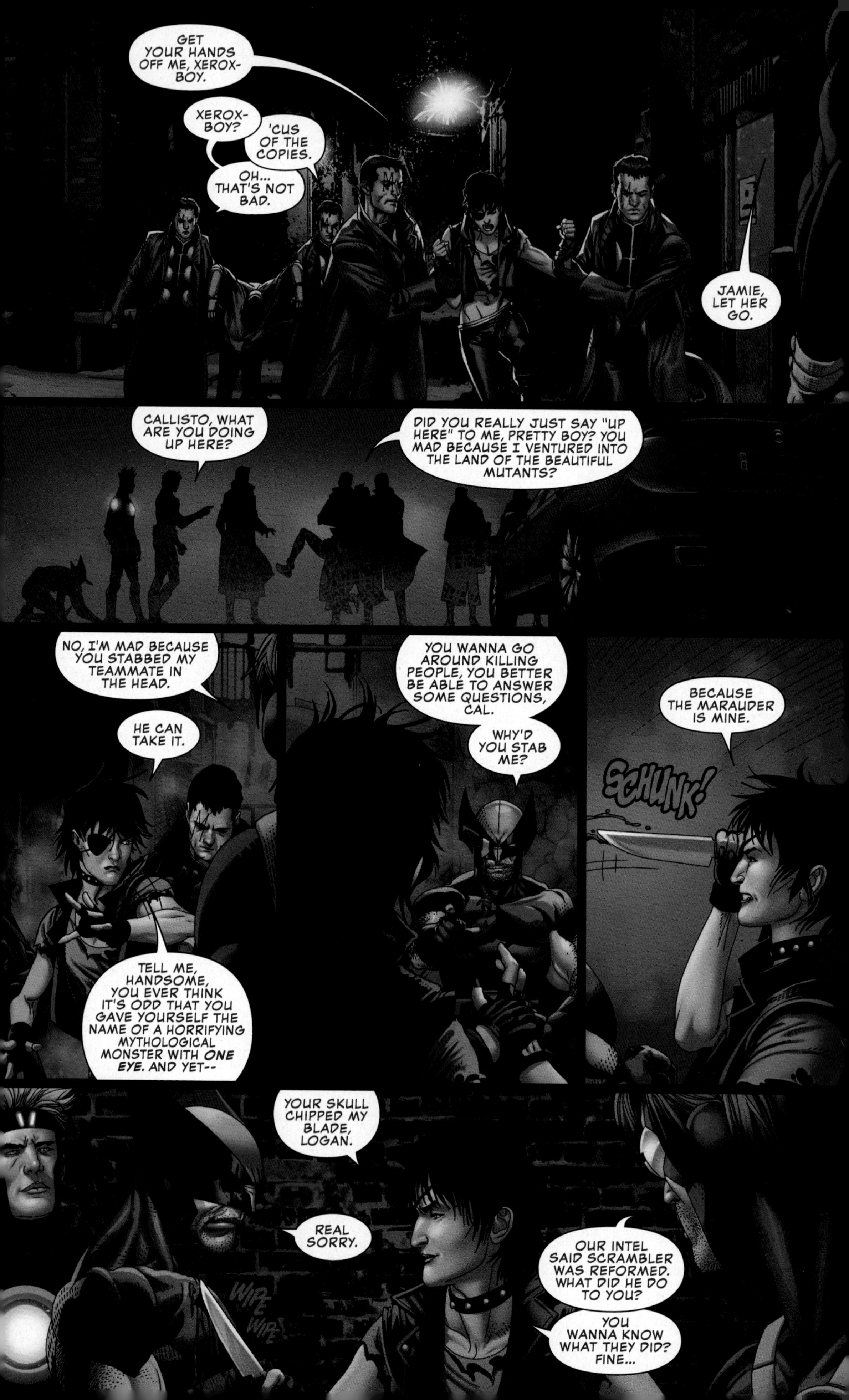
GET YOUR HANDS OFF ME, XEROX-BOY.
XEROX-BOY?
'CUS OF THE COPIES.
OH... THAT'S NOT BAD.
JAMIE, LET HER GO.
CALLISTO, WHAT ARE YOU DOING UP HERE?
DID YOU REALLY JUST SAY "UP HERE" TO ME, PRETTY BOY? YOU MAD BECAUSE I VENTURED INTO THE LAND OF THE BEAUTIFUL MUTANTS?
NO, I'M MAD BECAUSE YOU STABBED MY TEAMMATE IN THE HEAD.
HE CAN TAKE IT.
TELL ME, HANDSOME, YOU EVER THINK IT'S ODD THAT YOU GAVE YOURSELF THE NAME OF A HORRIFYING MYTHOLOGICAL MONSTER WITH ONE EYE. AND YET--
YOU WANNA GO AROUND KILLING PEOPLE, YOU BETTER BE ABLE TO ANSWER SOME QUESTIONS, CAL.
WHY'D YOU STAB ME?
BECAUSE THE MARAUDER IS MINE.
SCHUNK!
YOUR SKULL CHIPPED MY BLADE, LOGAN.
REAL SORRY.
WIPE WIPE
OUR INTEL SAID SCRAMBLER WAS REFORMED. WHAT DID HE DO TO YOU?
YOU WANNA KNOW WHAT THEY DID? FINE...

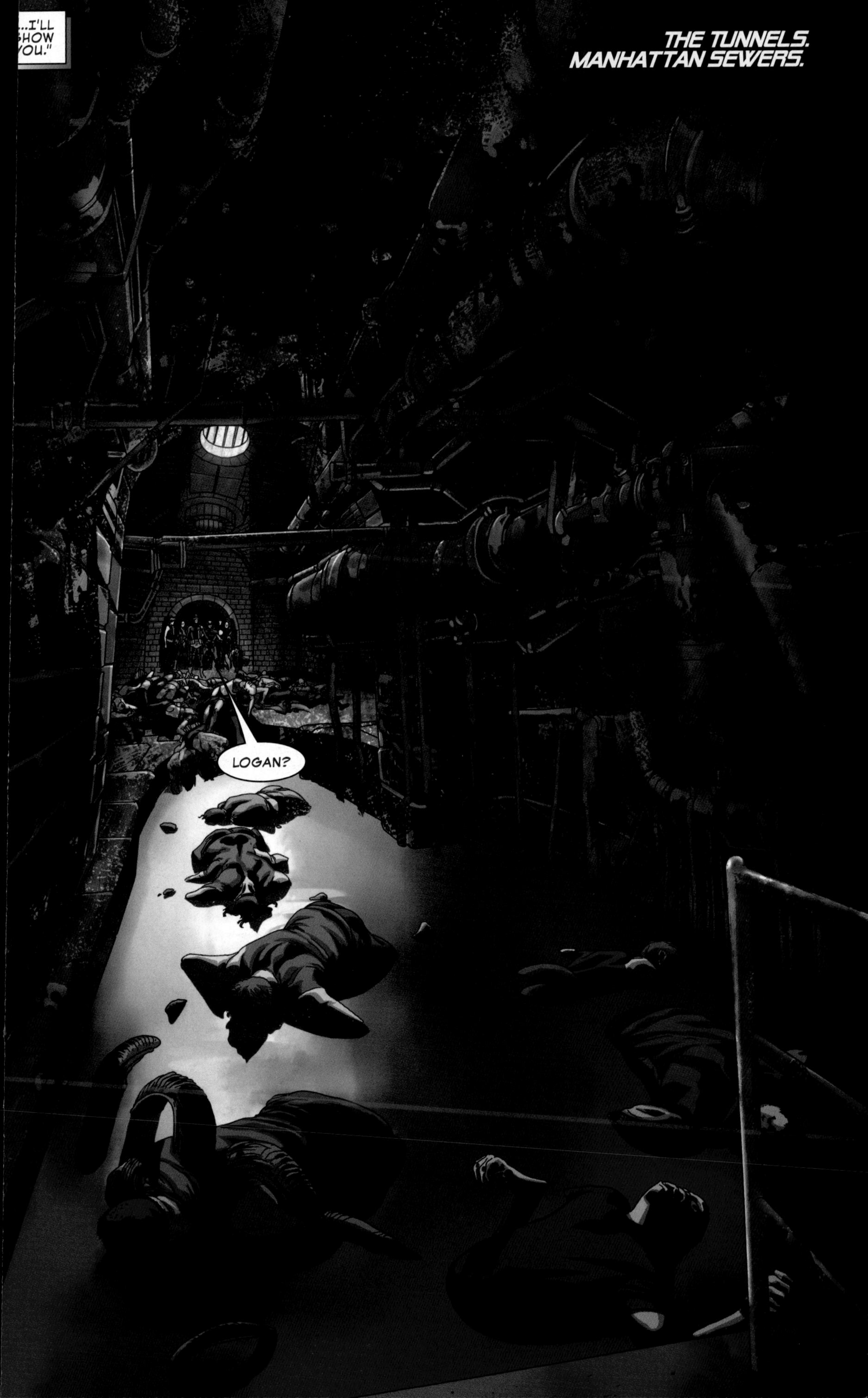

...I'LL SHOW YOU."
THE TUNNELS. MANHATTAN SEWERS.
LOGAN?

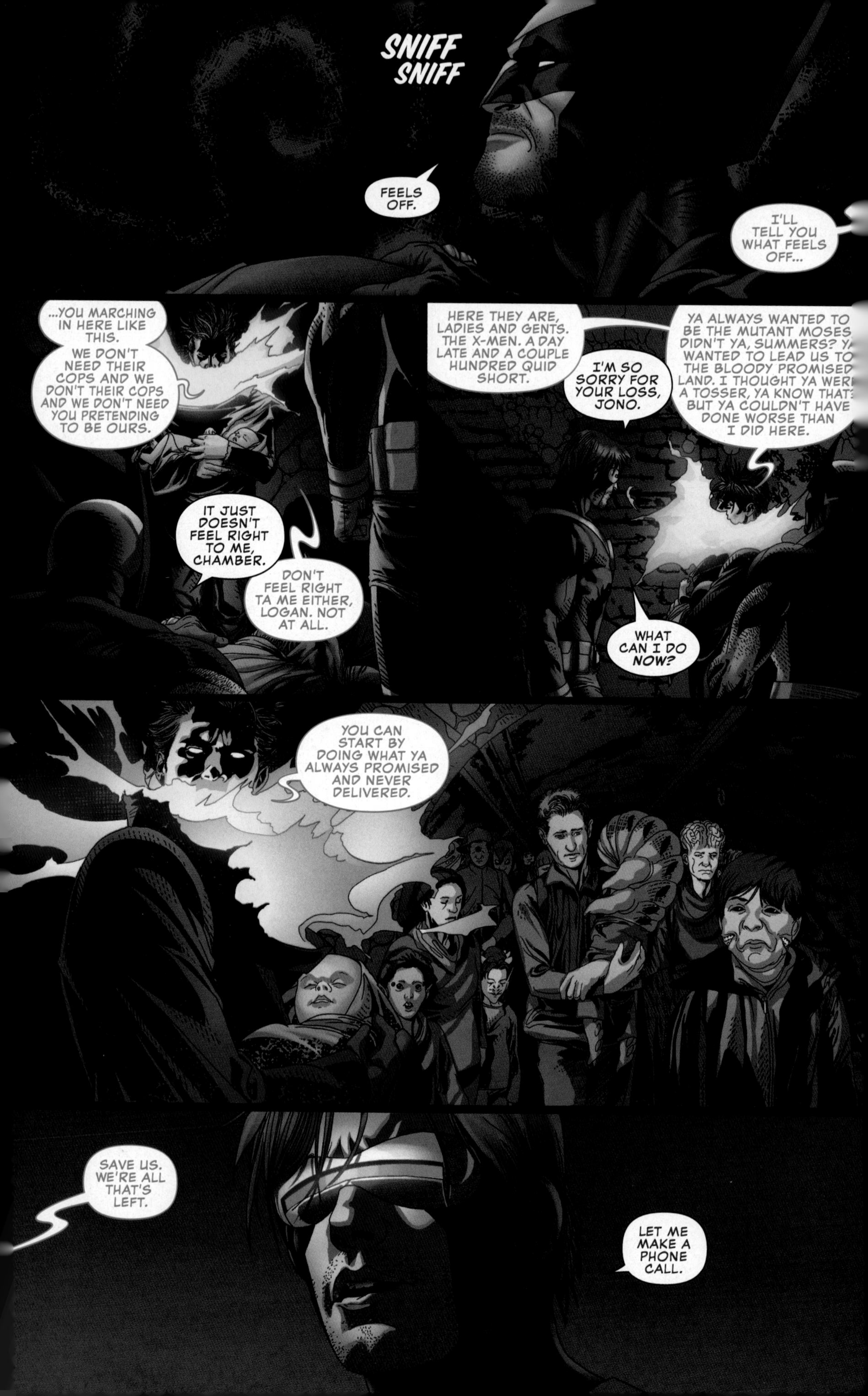
SNIFF SNIFF
FEELS OFF.
I'LL TELL YOU WHAT FEELS OFF...
...YOU MARCHING IN HERE LIKE THIS.
WE DON'T NEED THEIR COPS AND WE DON'T THEIR COPS AND WE DON'T NEED YOU PRETENDING TO BE OURS.
IT JUST DOESN'T FEEL RIGHT TO ME, CHAMBER.
DON'T FEEL RIGHT TA ME EITHER, LOGAN. NOT AT ALL.
HERE THEY ARE, LADIES AND GENTS. THE X-MEN. A DAY LATE AND A COUPLE HUNDRED QUID SHORT.
I'M SO SORRY FOR YOUR LOSS, JONO.
YA ALWAYS WANTED TO BE THE MUTANT MOSES DIDN'T YA, SUMMERS? YA WANTED TO LEAD US TO THE BLOODY PROMISED LAND. I THOUGHT YA WERE A TOSSER, YA KNOW THAT? BUT YA COULDN'T HAVE DONE WORSE THAN I DID HERE.
WHAT CAN I DO NOW?
YOU CAN START BY DOING WHAT YA ALWAYS PROMISED AND NEVER DELIVERED.
SAVE US. WE'RE ALL THAT'S LEFT.
LET ME MAKE A PHONE CALL.

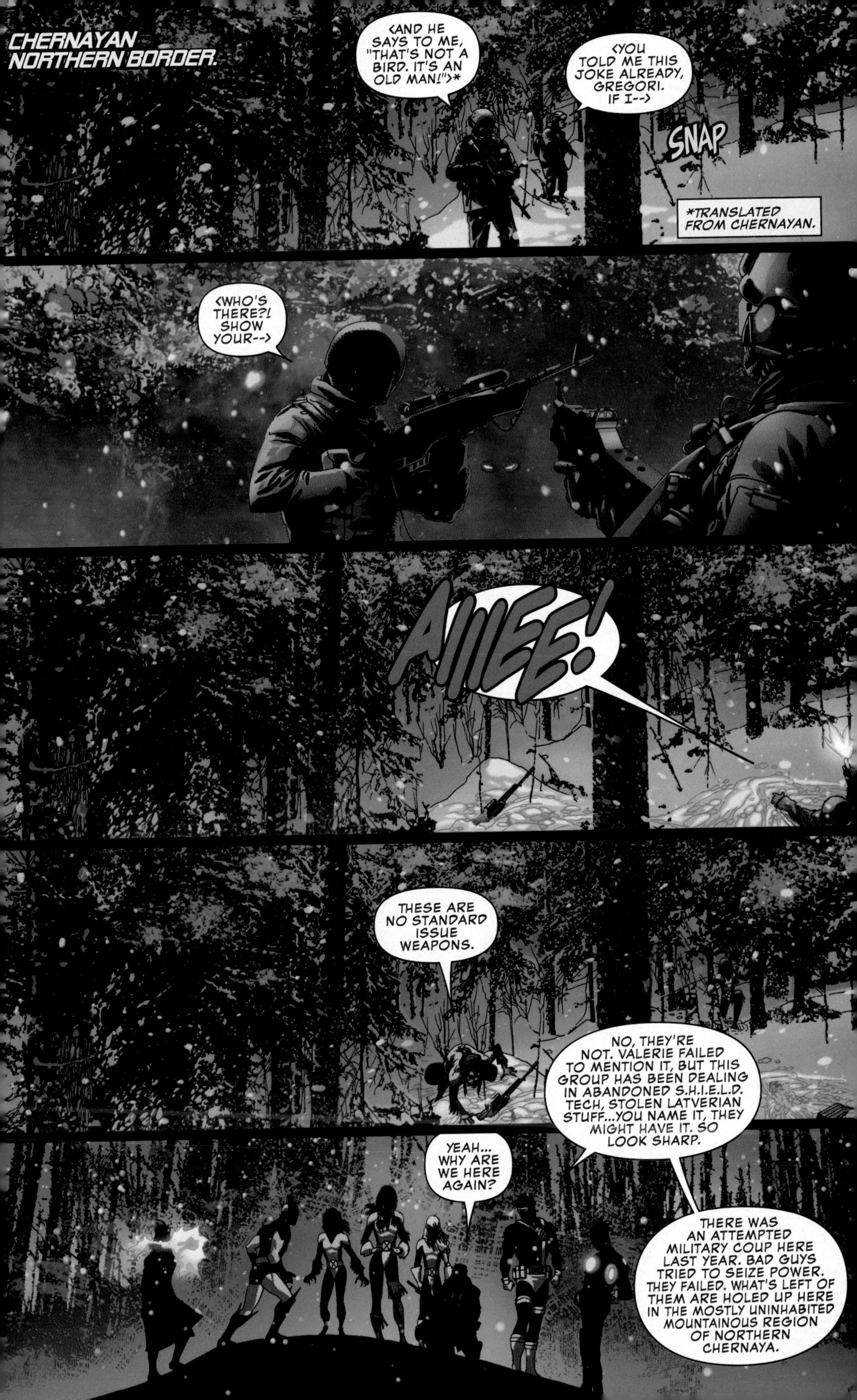

CHERNAYAN NORTHERN BORDER.
<AND HE SAYS TO ME, "THAT'S NOT A BIRD. IT'S AN OLD MAN!">*
<YOU TOLD ME THIS JOKE ALREADY, GREGORI. IF I-->
SNAP
*TRANSLATED FROM CHERNAYAN.
<WHO'S THERE?! SHOW YOUR-->
AIIIEE!
THESE ARE NO STANDARD ISSUE WEAPONS.
NO, THEY'RE NOT. VALERIE FAILED TO MENTION IT, BUT THIS GROUP HAS BEEN DEALING IN ABANDONED S.H.I.E.L.D. TECH, STOLEN LATVERIAN STUFF...YOU NAME IT, THEY MIGHT HAVE IT. SO LOOK SHARP.
YEAH... WHY ARE WE HERE AGAIN?
THERE WAS AN ATTEMPTED MILITARY COUP HERE LAST YEAR. BAD GUYS TRIED TO SEIZE POWER. THEY FAILED. WHAT'S LEFT OF THEM ARE HOLED UP HERE IN THE MOSTLY UNINHABITED MOUNTAINOUS REGION OF NORTHERN CHERNAYA.

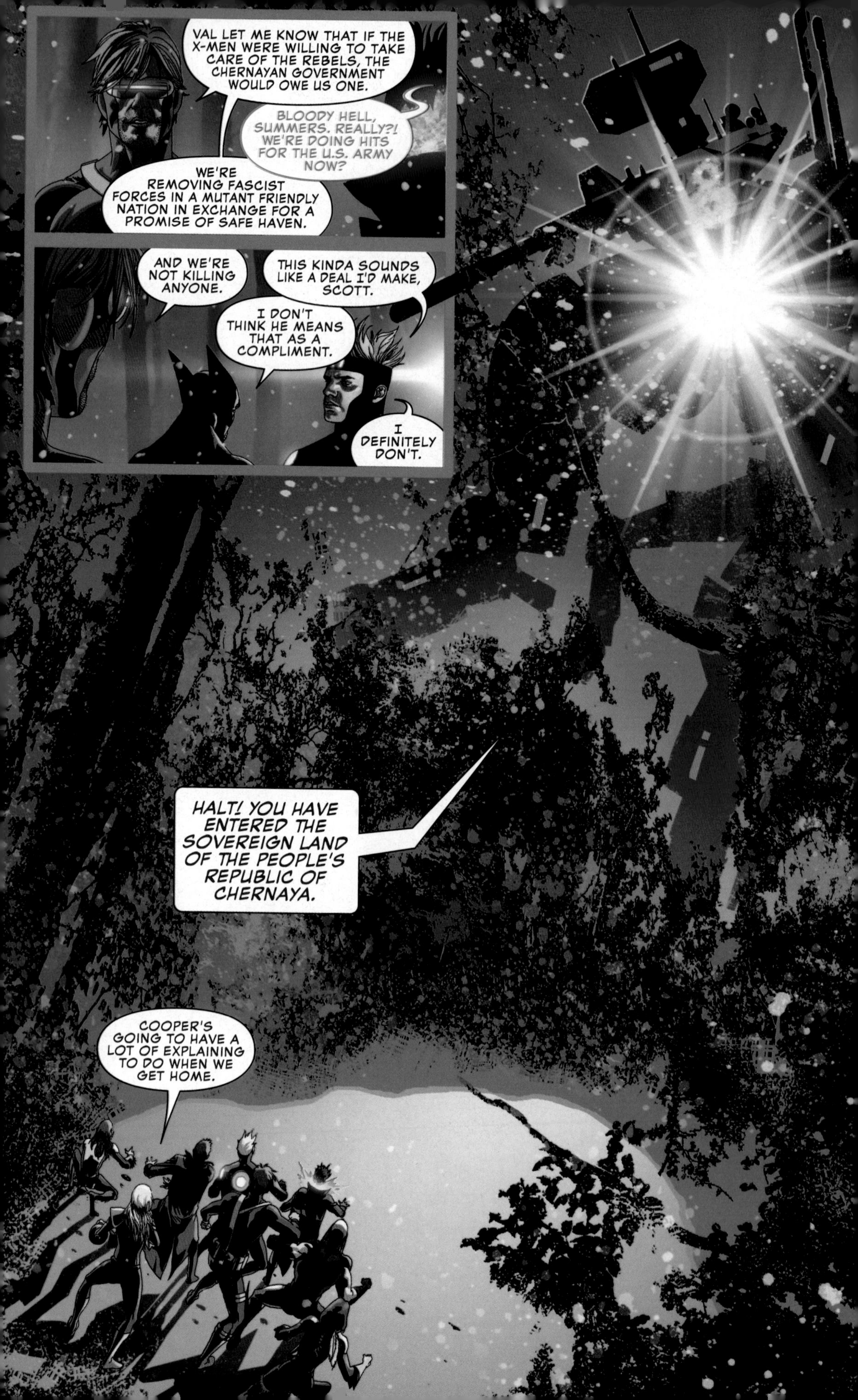
VAL LET ME KNOW THAT IF THE X-MEN WERE WILLING TO TAKE CARE OF THE REBELS, THE CHERNAYAN GOVERNMENT WOULD OWE US ONE.
BLOODY HELL, SUMMERS. REALLY?! WE'RE DOING HITS FOR THE U.S. ARMY NOW?
WE'RE REMOVING FASCIST FORCES IN A MUTANT FRIENDLY NATION IN EXCHANGE FOR A PROMISE OF SAFE HAVEN.
AND WE'RE NOT KILLING ANYONE.
THIS KINDA SOUNDS LIKE A DEAL I'D MAKE, SCOTT.
I DON'T THINK HE MEANS THAT AS A COMPLIMENT.
I DEFINITELY DON'T.
HALT! YOU HAVE ENTERED THE SOVEREIGN LAND OF THE PEOPLE'S REPUBLIC OF CHERNAYA.
COOPER'S GOING TO HAVE A LOT OF EXPLAINING TO DO WHEN WE GET HOME.

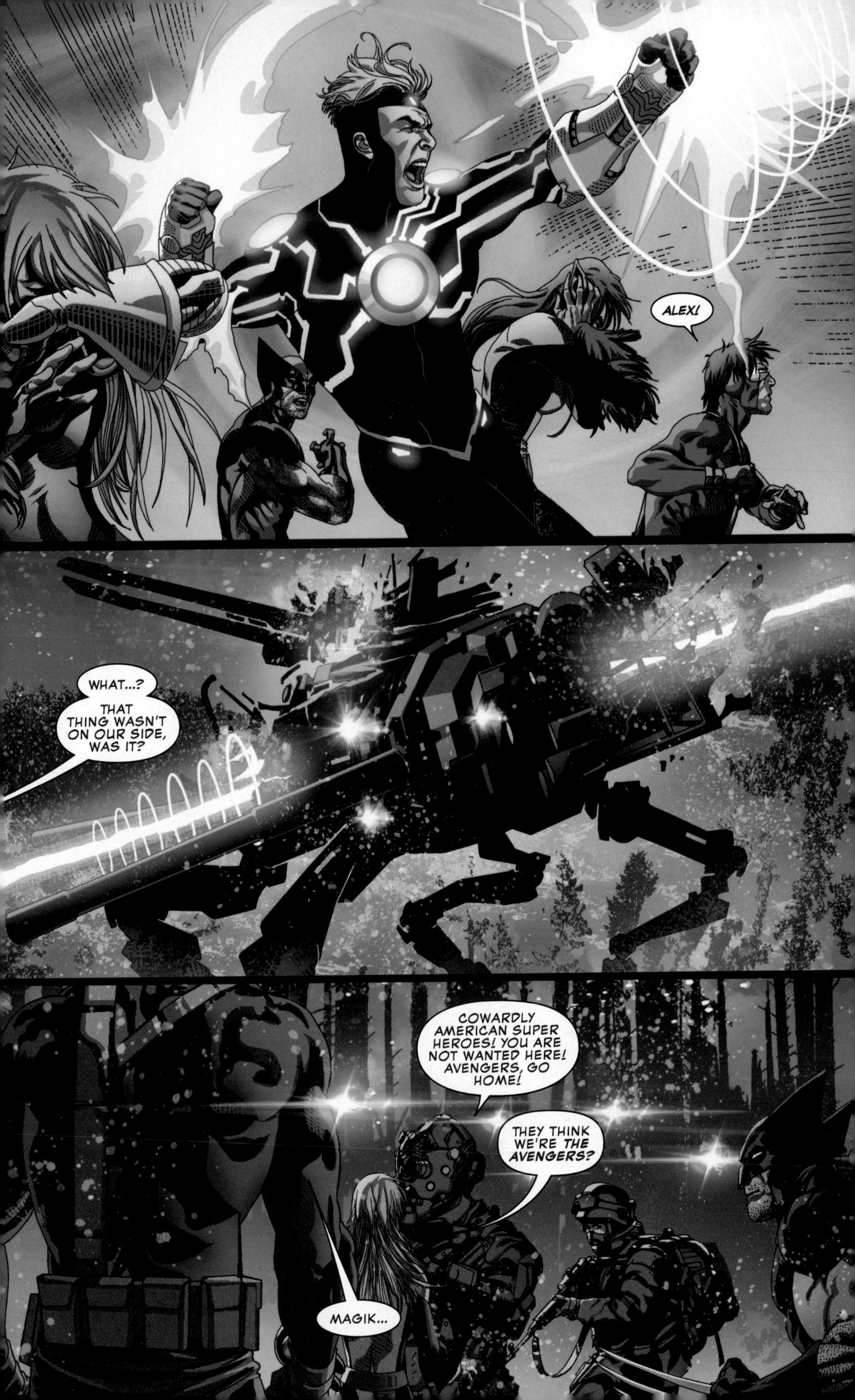
ALEX!
WHAT...? THAT THING WASN'T ON OUR SIDE, WAS IT?
COWARDLY AMERICAN SUPER HEROES! YOU ARE NOT WANTED HERE! AVENGERS, GO HOME!
THEY THINK WE'RE THE AVENGERS?
MAGIK...

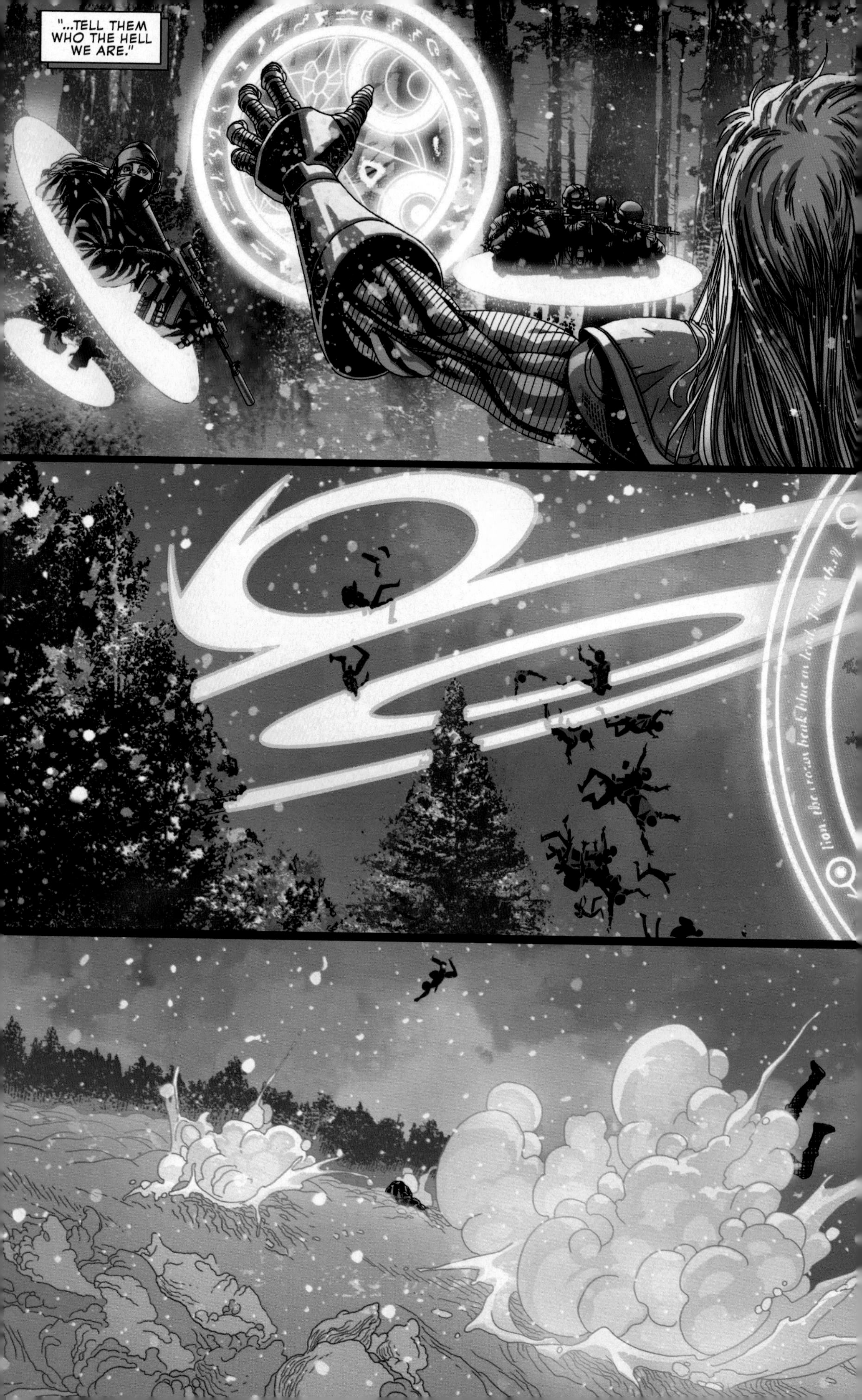
"...TELL THEM WHO THE HELL WE ARE."

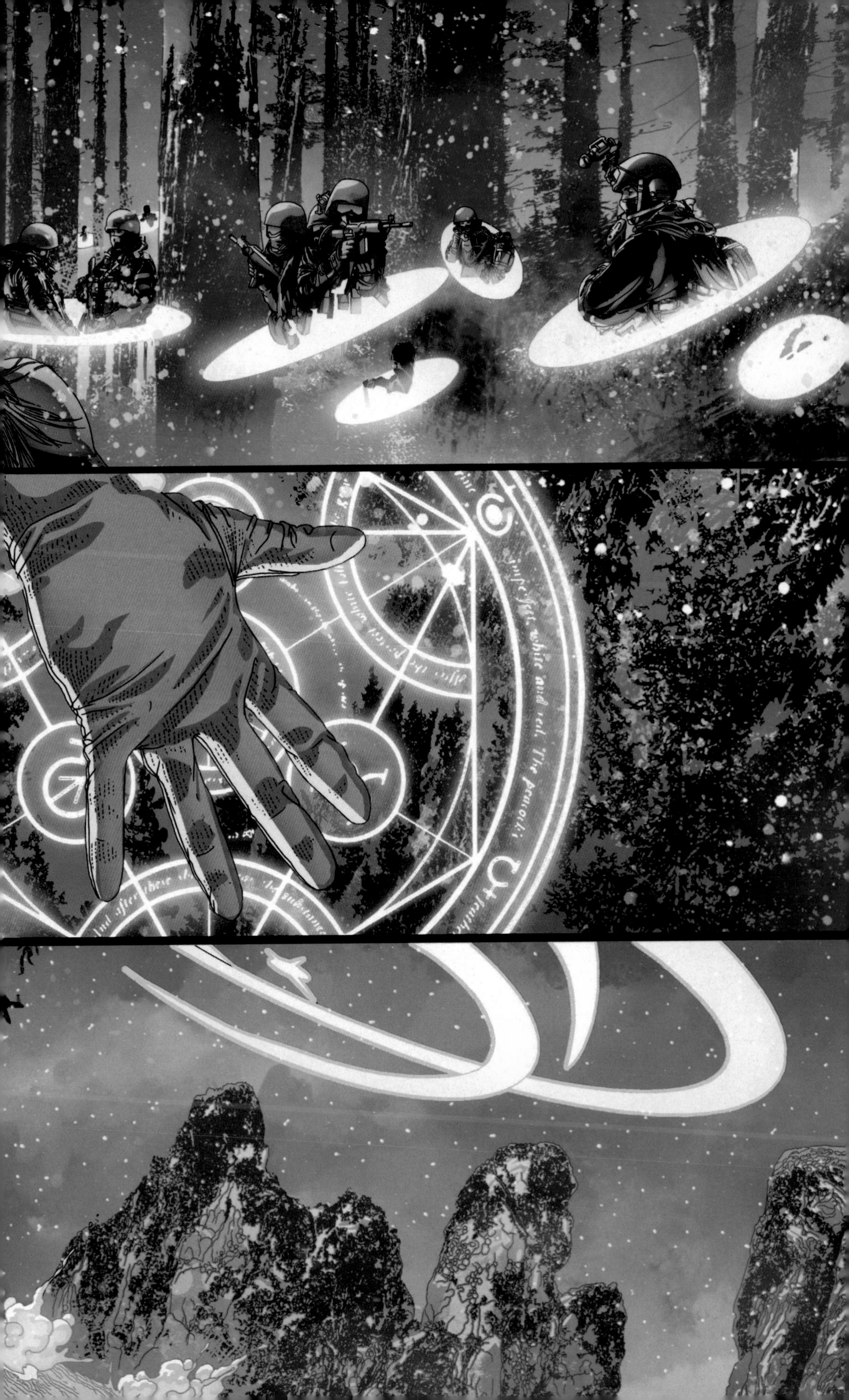
white and red. The peacock's

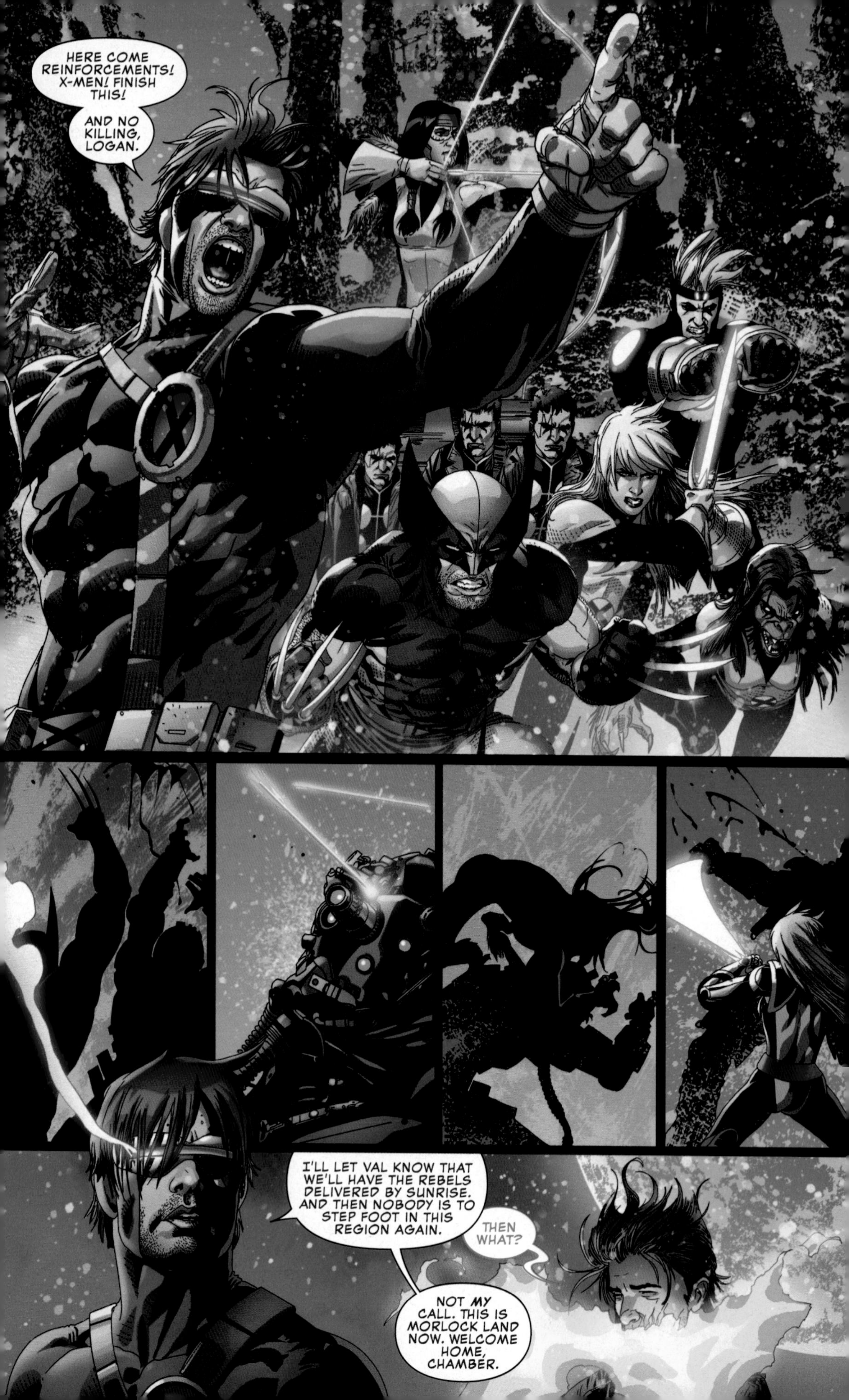
HERE COME REINFORCEMENTS! X-MEN! FINISH THIS!
AND NO KILLING, LOGAN.
I'LL LET VAL KNOW THAT WE'LL HAVE THE REBELS DELIVERED BY SUNRISE. AND THEN NOBODY IS TO STEP FOOT IN THIS REGION AGAIN.
THEN WHAT?
NOT MY CALL. THIS IS MORLOCK LAND NOW. WELCOME HOME, CHAMBER.

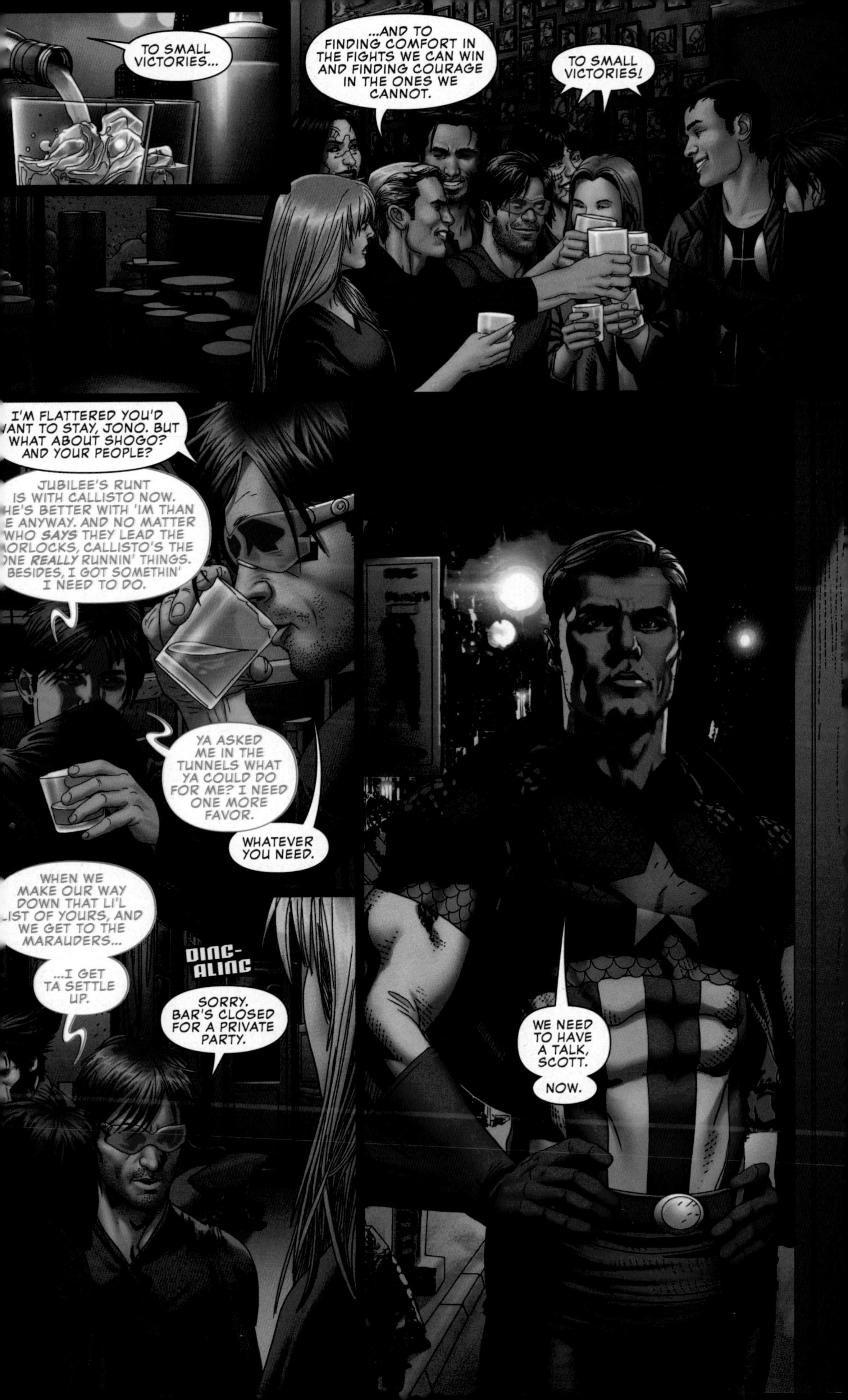

TO SMALL VICTORIES...
...AND TO FINDING COMFORT IN THE FIGHTS WE CAN WIN AND FINDING COURAGE IN THE ONES WE CANNOT.
TO SMALL VICTORIES!
I'M FLATTERED YOU'D ANT TO STAY, JONO. BUT WHAT ABOUT SHOGO? AND YOUR PEOPLE?
JUBILEE'S RUNT IS WITH CALLISTO NOW. HE'S BETTER WITH 'IM THAN E ANYWAY. AND NO MATTER WHO SAYS THEY LEAD THE ORLOCKS, CALLISTO'S THE NE REALLY RUNNIN' THINGS. BESIDES, I GOT SOMETHIN' I NEED TO DO.
YA ASKED ME IN THE TUNNELS WHAT YA COULD DO FOR ME? I NEED ONE MORE FAVOR.
WHATEVER YOU NEED.
WHEN WE MAKE OUR WAY DOWN THAT LI'L IST OF YOURS, AND WE GET TO THE MARAUDERS...
...I GET TA SETTLE UP.
DING-ALING
SORRY. BAR'S CLOSED FOR A PRIVATE PARTY.
WE NEED TO HAVE A TALK, SCOTT.
NOW.

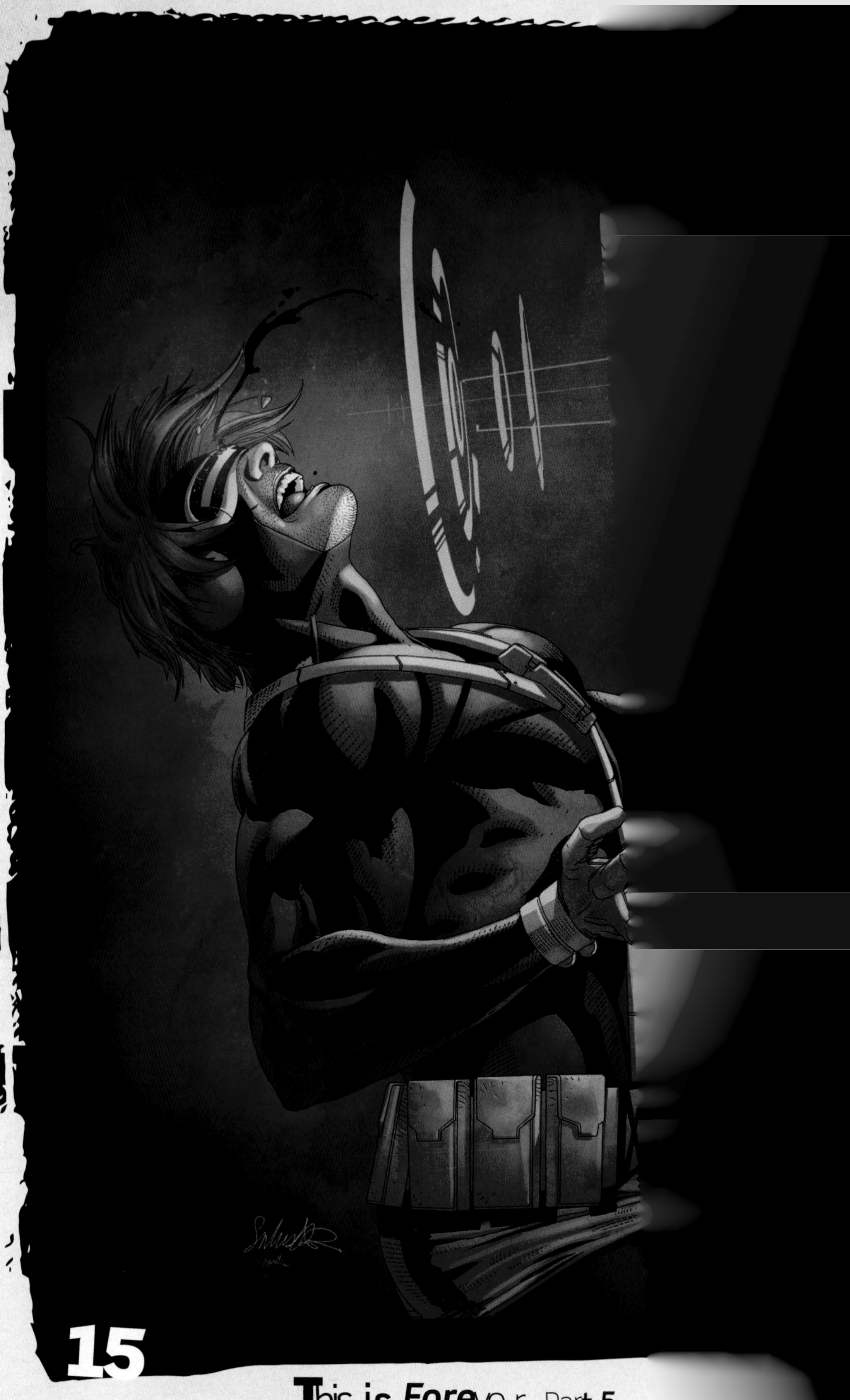

15

This is Forever Part 5

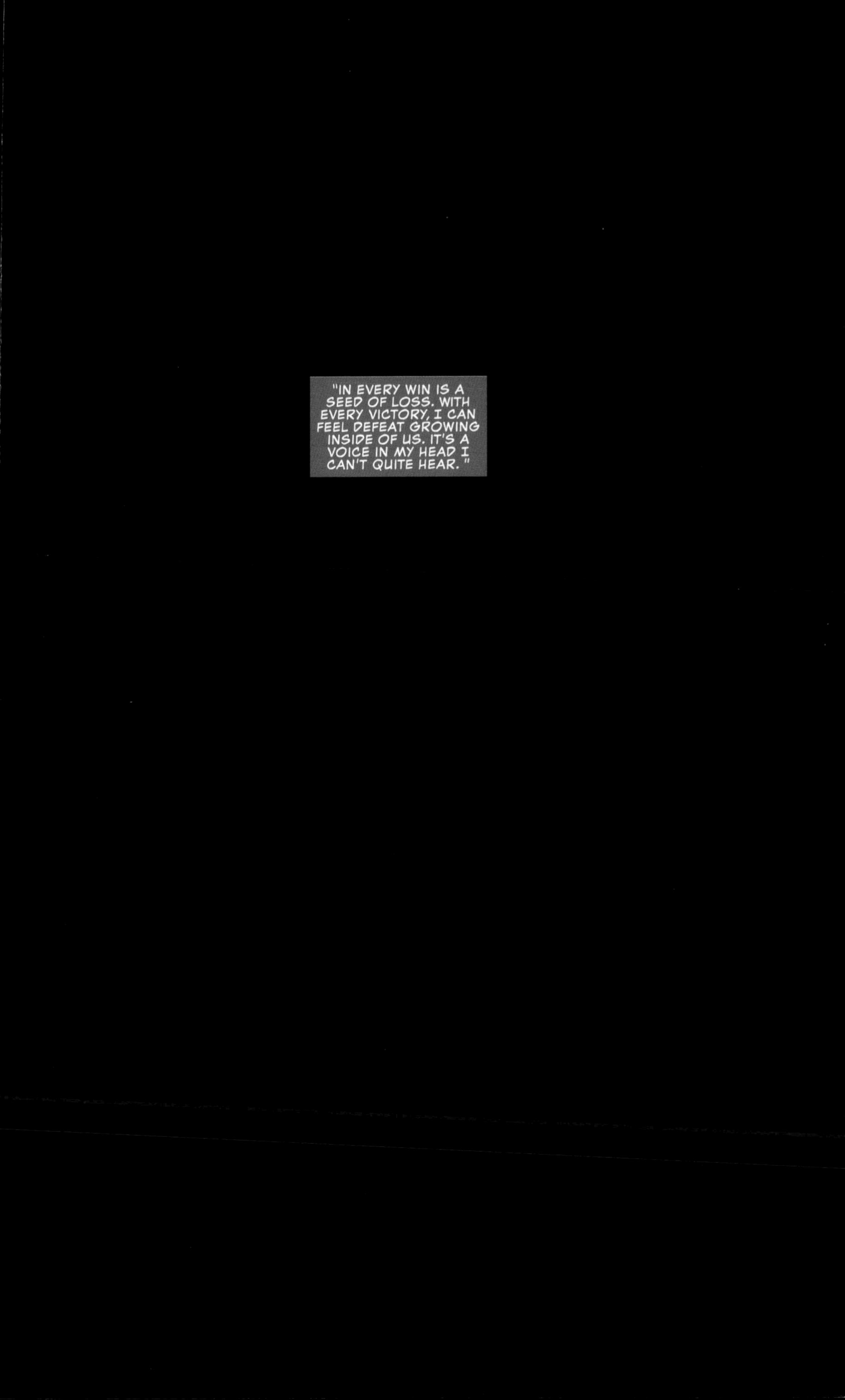
"IN EVERY WIN IS A SEED OF LOSS. WITH EVERY VICTORY, I CAN FEEL DEFEAT GROWING INSIDE OF US. IT'S A VOICE IN MY HEAD I CAN'T QUITE HEAR."

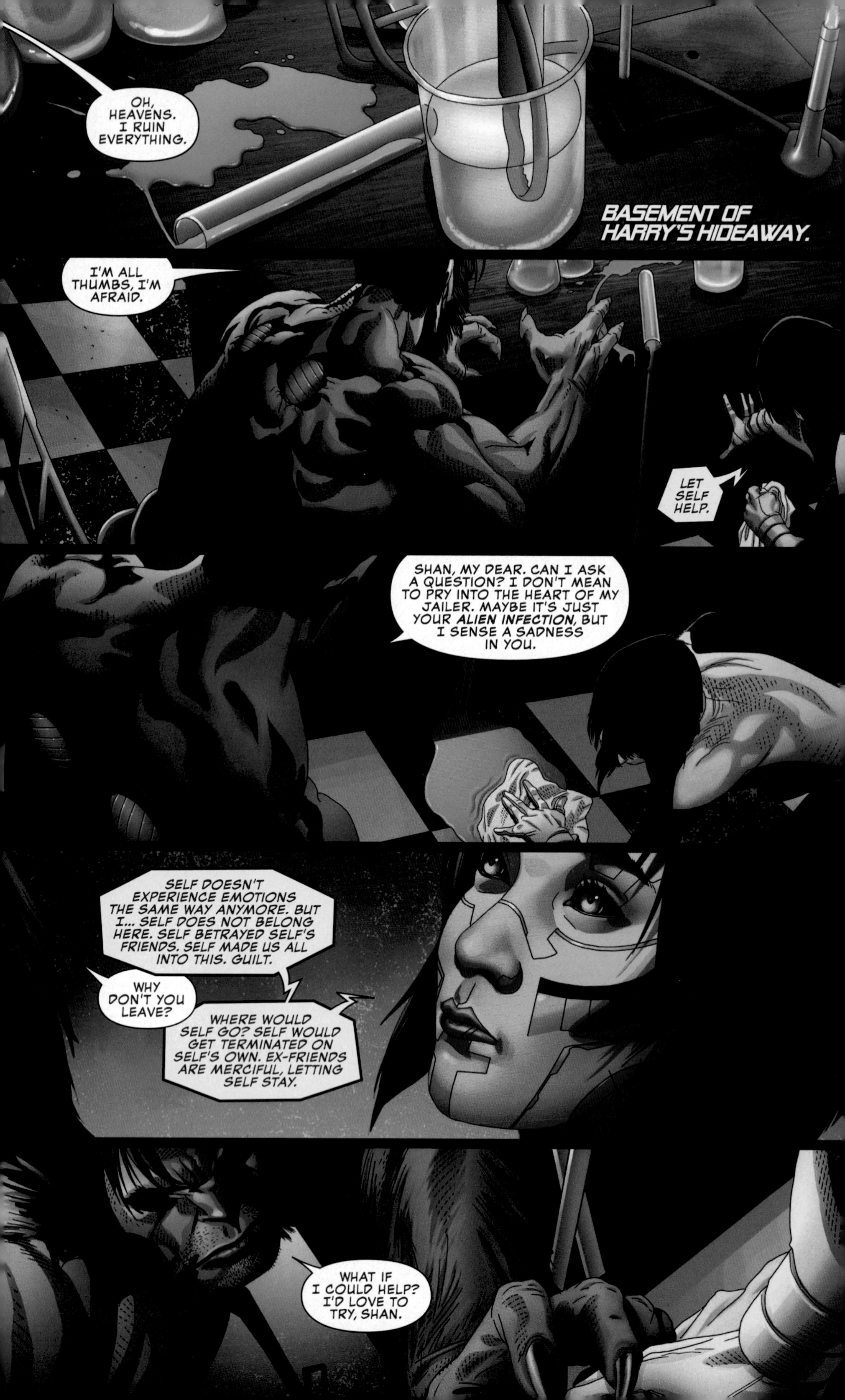

OH, HEAVENS. I RUIN EVERYTHING.
BASEMENT OF HARRY'S HIDEAWAY.
I'M ALL THUMBS, I'M AFRAID.
LET SELF HELP.
SHAN, MY DEAR. CAN I ASK A QUESTION? I DON'T MEAN TO PRY INTO THE HEART OF MY JAILER. MAYBE IT'S JUST YOUR ALIEN INFECTION, BUT I SENSE A SADNESS IN YOU.
SELF DOESN'T EXPERIENCE EMOTIONS THE SAME WAY ANYMORE. BUT I... SELF DOES NOT BELONG HERE. SELF BETRAYED SELF'S FRIENDS. SELF MADE US ALL INTO THIS. GUILT.
WHY DON'T YOU LEAVE?
WHERE WOULD SELF GO? SELF WOULD GET TERMINATED ON SELF'S OWN. EX-FRIENDS ARE MERCIFUL, LETTING SELF STAY.
WHAT IF I COULD HELP? I'D LOVE TO TRY, SHAN.

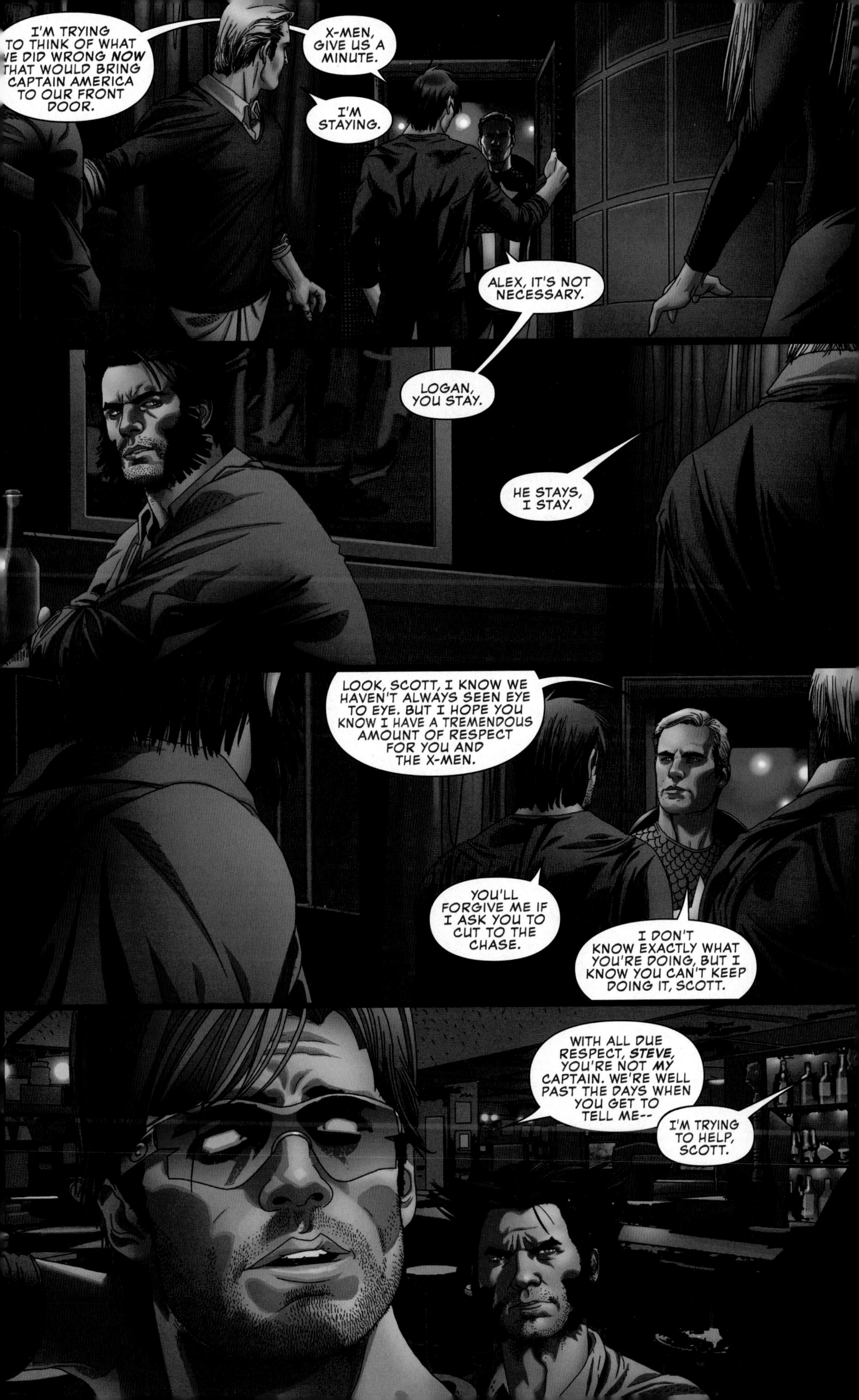

I'M TRYING TO THINK OF WHAT WE DID WRONG NOW THAT WOULD BRING CAPTAIN AMERICA TO OUR FRONT DOOR.
X-MEN, GIVE US A MINUTE.
I'M STAYING.
ALEX, IT'S NOT NECESSARY.
LOGAN, YOU STAY.
HE STAYS, I STAY.
LOOK, SCOTT, I KNOW WE HAVEN'T ALWAYS SEEN EYE TO EYE. BUT I HOPE YOU KNOW I HAVE A TREMENDOUS AMOUNT OF RESPECT FOR YOU AND THE X-MEN.
YOU'LL FORGIVE ME IF I ASK YOU TO CUT TO THE CHASE.
I DON'T KNOW EXACTLY WHAT YOU'RE DOING, BUT I KNOW YOU CAN'T KEEP DOING IT, SCOTT.
WITH ALL DUE RESPECT, STEVE, YOU'RE NOT MY CAPTAIN. WE'RE WELL PAST THE DAYS WHEN YOU GET TO TELL ME--
I'M TRYING TO HELP, SCOTT.

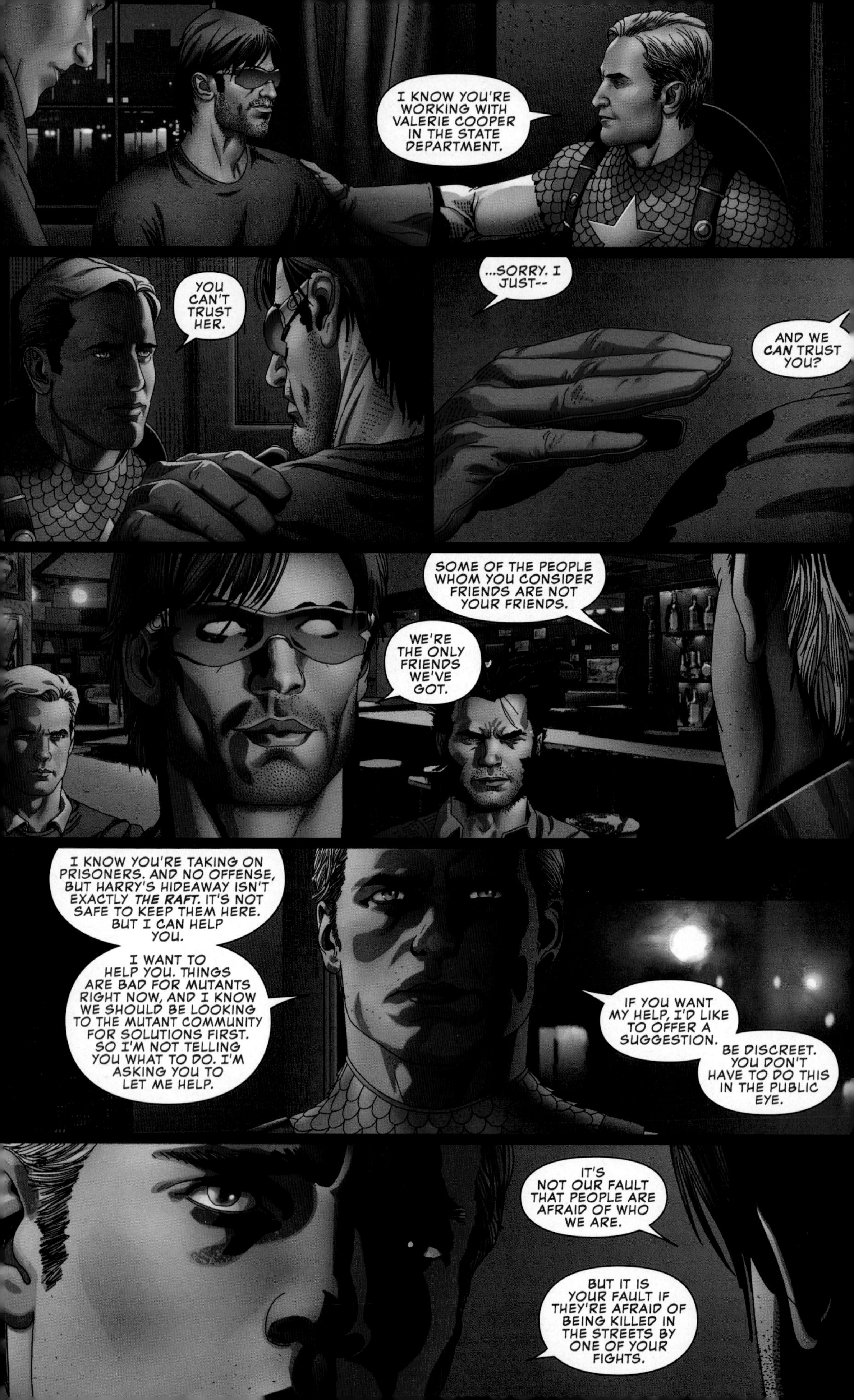
I KNOW YOU'RE WORKING WITH VALERIE COOPER IN THE STATE DEPARTMENT.
YOU CAN'T TRUST HER.
...SORRY. I JUST--
AND WE CAN TRUST YOU?
SOME OF THE PEOPLE WHOM YOU CONSIDER FRIENDS ARE NOT YOUR FRIENDS.
WE'RE THE ONLY FRIENDS WE'VE GOT.
I KNOW YOU'RE TAKING ON PRISONERS. AND NO OFFENSE, BUT HARRY'S HIDEAWAY ISN'T EXACTLY THE RAFT. IT'S NOT SAFE TO KEEP THEM HERE. BUT I CAN HELP YOU.
I WANT TO HELP YOU. THINGS ARE BAD FOR MUTANTS RIGHT NOW, AND I KNOW WE SHOULD BE LOOKING TO THE MUTANT COMMUNITY FOR SOLUTIONS FIRST. SO I'M NOT TELLING YOU WHAT TO DO. I'M ASKING YOU TO LET ME HELP.
IF YOU WANT MY HELP, I'D LIKE TO OFFER A SUGGESTION.
BE DISCREET. YOU DON'T HAVE TO DO THIS IN THE PUBLIC EYE.
IT'S NOT OUR FAULT THAT PEOPLE ARE AFRAID OF WHO WE ARE.
BUT IT IS YOUR FAULT IF THEY'RE AFRAID OF BEING KILLED IN THE STREETS BY ONE OF YOUR FIGHTS.

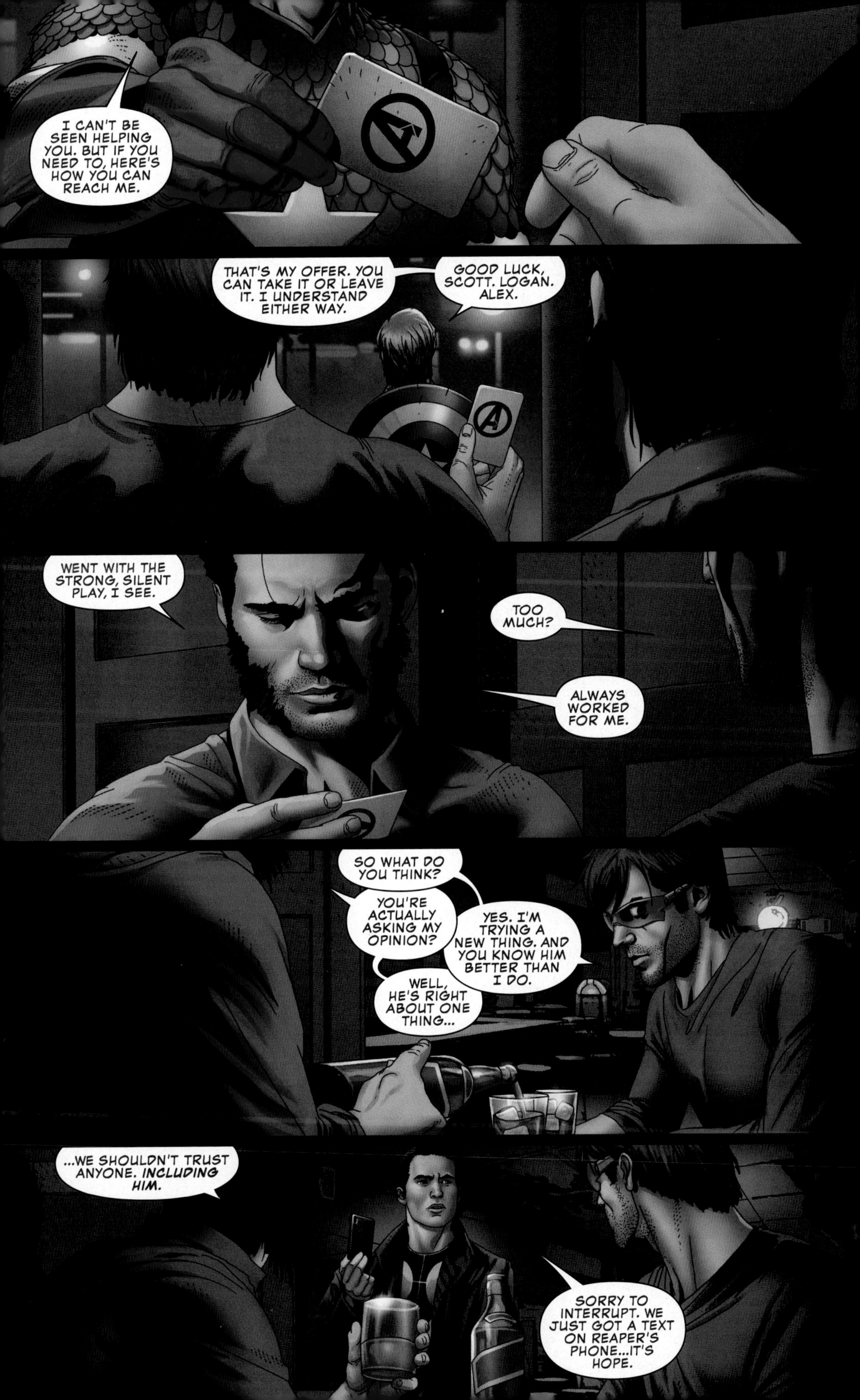
I CAN'T BE SEEN HELPING YOU. BUT IF YOU NEED TO, HERE'S HOW YOU CAN REACH ME.
THAT'S MY OFFER. YOU CAN TAKE IT OR LEAVE IT. I UNDERSTAND EITHER WAY.
GOOD LUCK, SCOTT. LOGAN. ALEX.
WENT WITH THE STRONG, SILENT PLAY, I SEE.
TOO MUCH?
ALWAYS WORKED FOR ME.
SO WHAT DO YOU THINK?
YOU'RE ACTUALLY ASKING MY OPINION?
YES. I'M TRYING A NEW THING. AND YOU KNOW HIM BETTER THAN I DO.
WELL, HE'S RIGHT ABOUT ONE THING...
...WE SHOULDN'T TRUST ANYONE. INCLUDING HIM.
SORRY TO INTERRUPT. WE JUST GOT A TEXT ON REAPER'S PHONE...IT'S HOPE.

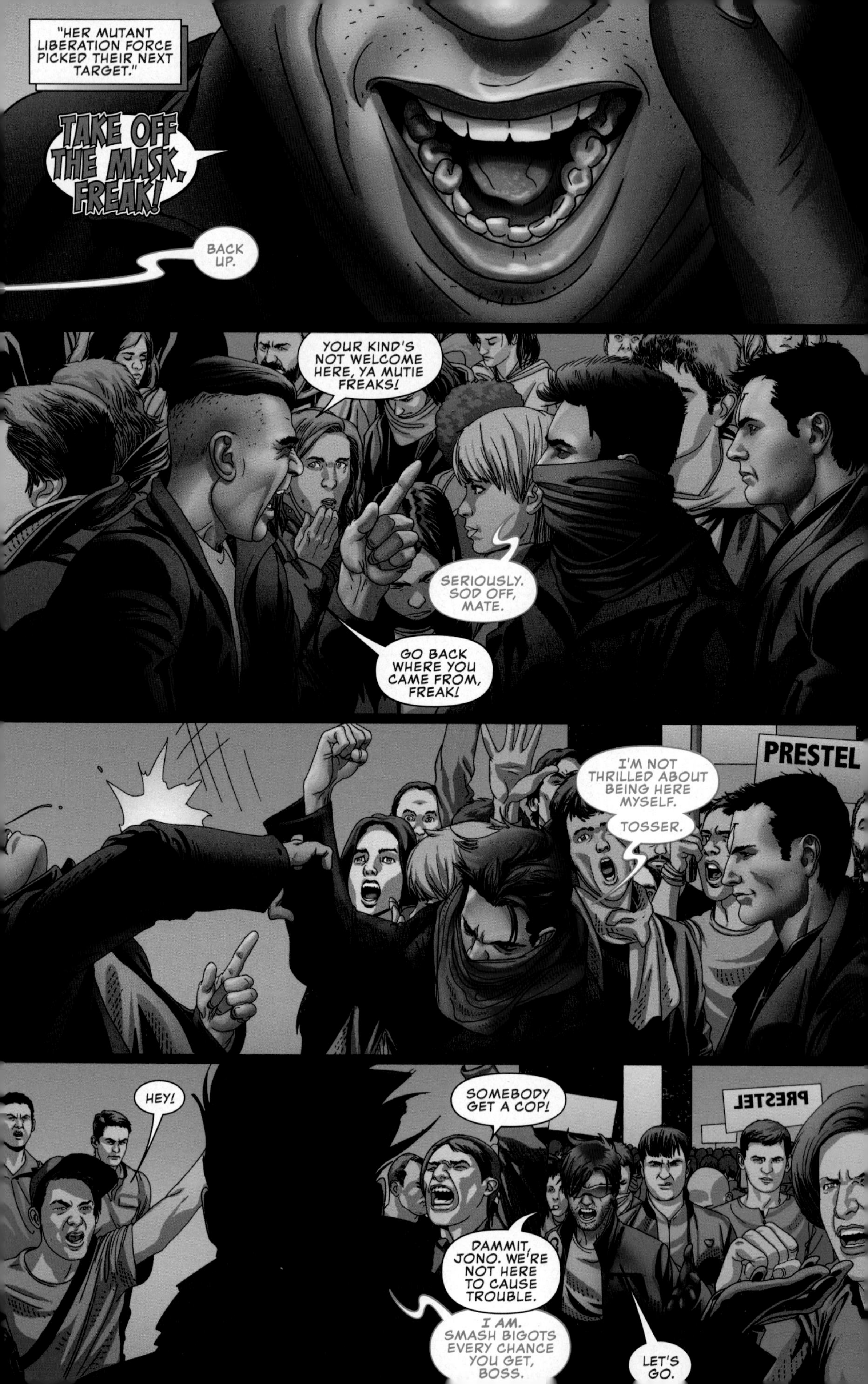

"HER MUTANT LIBERATION FORCE PICKED THEIR NEXT TARGET."
TAKE OFF THE MASK, FREAK!
BACK UP.
YOUR KIND'S NOT WELCOME HERE, YA MUTIE FREAKS!
SERIOUSLY. SOD OFF, MATE.
GO BACK WHERE YOU CAME FROM, FREAK!
PRESTEL
I'M NOT THRILLED ABOUT BEING HERE MYSELF.
TOSSER.
HEY!
SOMEBODY GET A COP!
PRESTEL
DAMMIT, JONO. WE'RE NOT HERE TO CAUSE TROUBLE.
I AM. SMASH BIGOTS EVERY CHANCE YOU GET, BOSS.
LET'S GO.

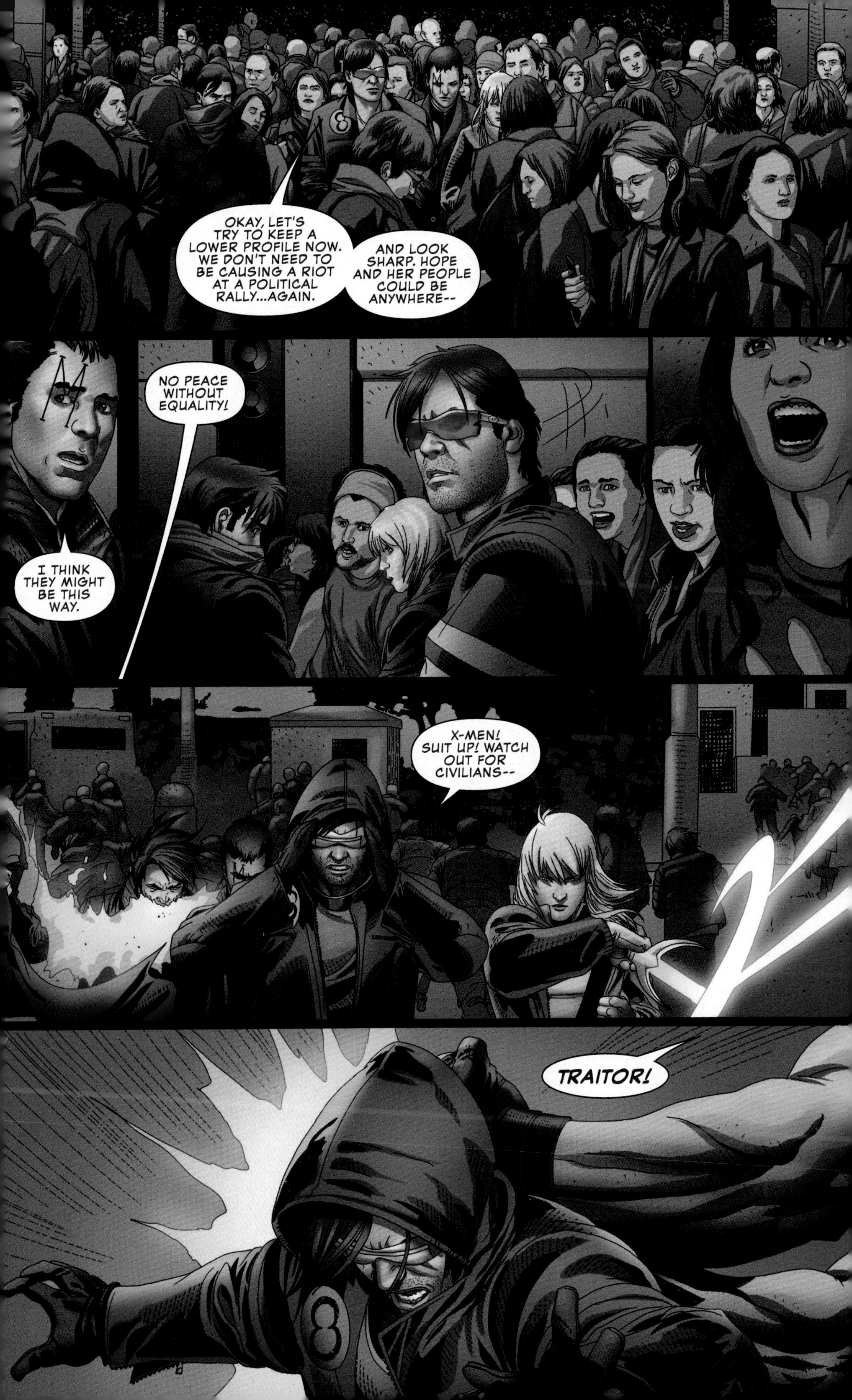
OKAY, LET'S TRY TO KEEP A LOWER PROFILE NOW. WE DON'T NEED TO BE CAUSING A RIOT AT A POLITICAL RALLY...AGAIN.
AND LOOK SHARP. HOPE AND HER PEOPLE COULD BE ANYWHERE--
NO PEACE WITHOUT EQUALITY!
I THINK THEY MIGHT BE THIS WAY.
X-MEN! SUIT UP! WATCH OUT FOR CIVILIANS--
TRAITOR!

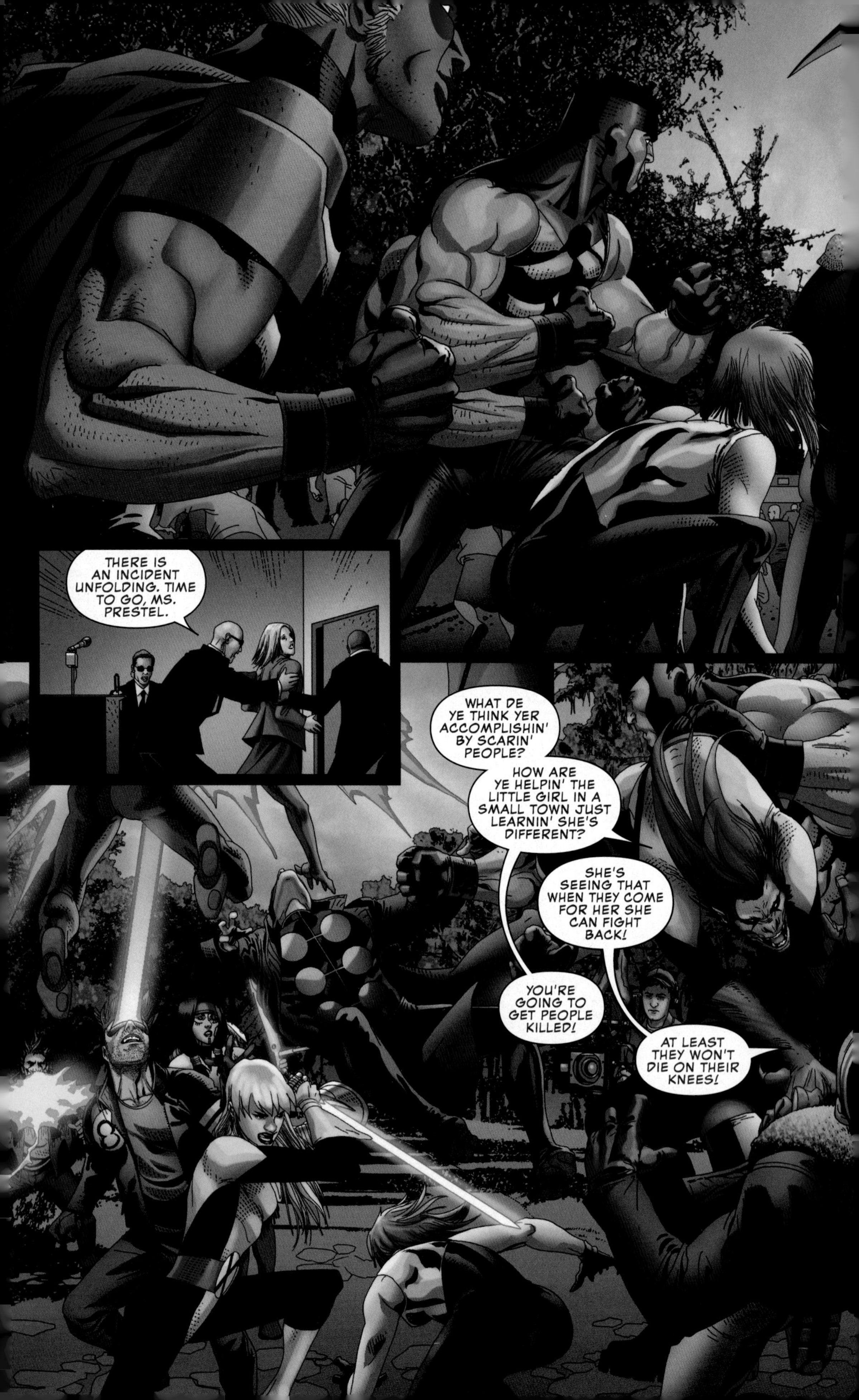
THERE IS AN INCIDENT UNFOLDING. TIME TO GO, MS. PRESTEL.
WHAT DE YE THINK YER ACCOMPLISHIN' BY SCARIN' PEOPLE?
HOW ARE YE HELPIN' THE LITTLE GIRL IN A SMALL TOWN JUST LEARNIN' SHE'S DIFFERENT?
SHE'S SEEING THAT WHEN THEY COME FOR HER SHE CAN FIGHT BACK!
YOU'RE GOING TO GET PEOPLE KILLED!
AT LEAST THEY WON'T DIE ON THEIR KNEES!

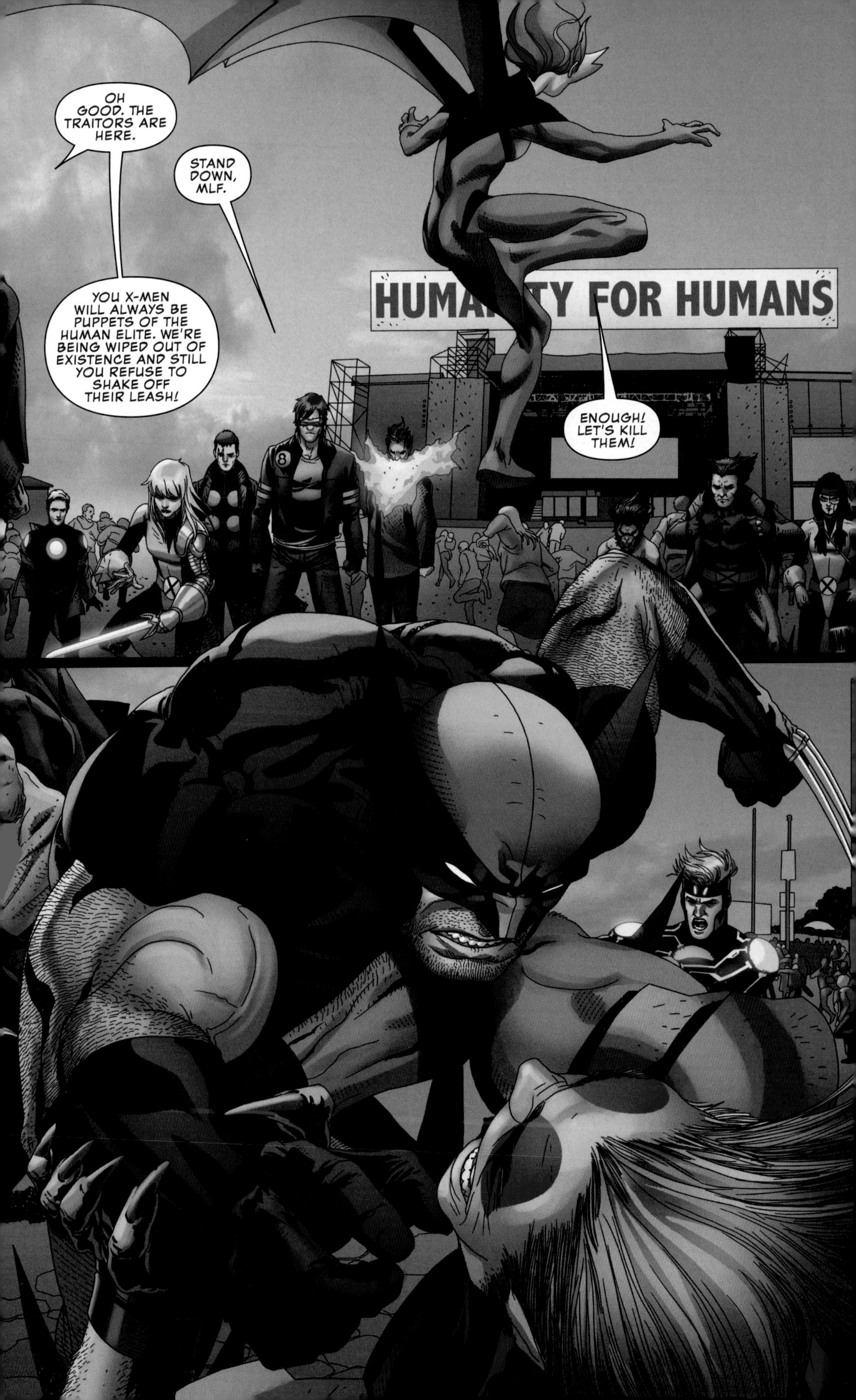
OH GOOD. THE TRAITORS ARE HERE.
STAND DOWN, MLF.
YOU X-MEN WILL ALWAYS BE PUPPETS OF THE HUMAN ELITE. WE'RE BEING WIPED OUT OF EXISTENCE AND STILL YOU REFUSE TO SHAKE OFF THEIR LEASH!
ENOUGH! LET'S KILL THEM!

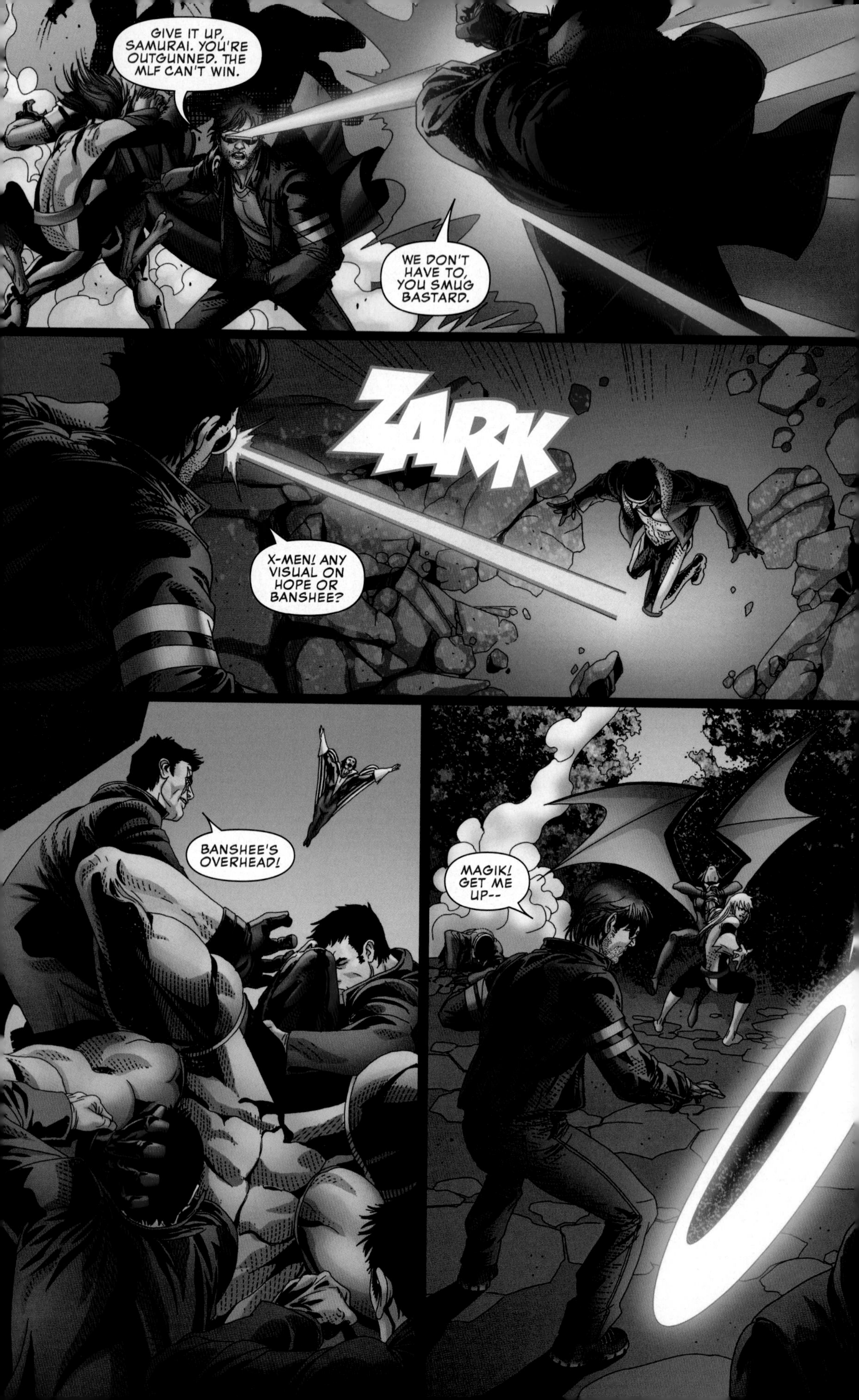
GIVE IT UP, SAMURAI. YOU'RE OUTGUNNED. THE MLF CAN'T WIN.
WE DON'T HAVE TO, YOU SMUG BASTARD.
ZARK
X-MEN! ANY VISUAL ON HOPE OR BANSHEE?
BANSHEE'S OVERHEAD!
MAGIK! GET ME UP--

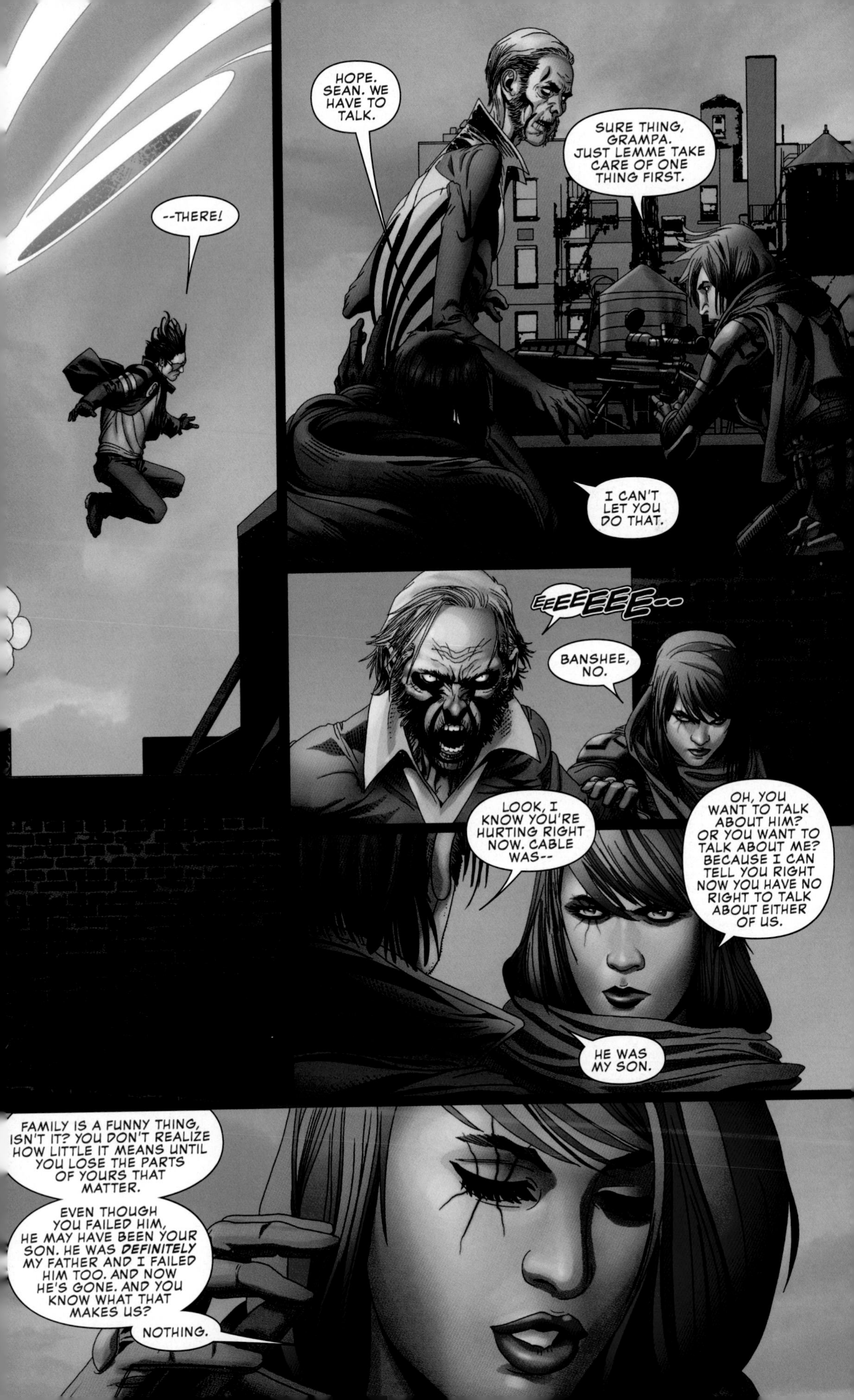
--THERE!
HOPE. SEAN. WE HAVE TO TALK.
SURE THING, GRAMPA. JUST LEMME TAKE CARE OF ONE THING FIRST.
I CAN'T LET YOU DO THAT.
EEEEEEE--
BANSHEE, NO.
LOOK, I KNOW YOU'RE HURTING RIGHT NOW. CABLE WAS--
OH, YOU WANT TO TALK ABOUT HIM? OR YOU WANT TO TALK ABOUT ME? BECAUSE I CAN TELL YOU RIGHT NOW YOU HAVE NO RIGHT TO TALK ABOUT EITHER OF US.
HE WAS MY SON.
FAMILY IS A FUNNY THING, ISN'T IT? YOU DON'T REALIZE HOW LITTLE IT MEANS UNTIL YOU LOSE THE PARTS OF YOURS THAT MATTER.
EVEN THOUGH YOU FAILED HIM, HE MAY HAVE BEEN YOUR SON. HE WAS *DEFINITELY* MY FATHER AND I FAILED HIM TOO. AND NOW HE'S GONE. AND YOU KNOW WHAT THAT MAKES US?
NOTHING.

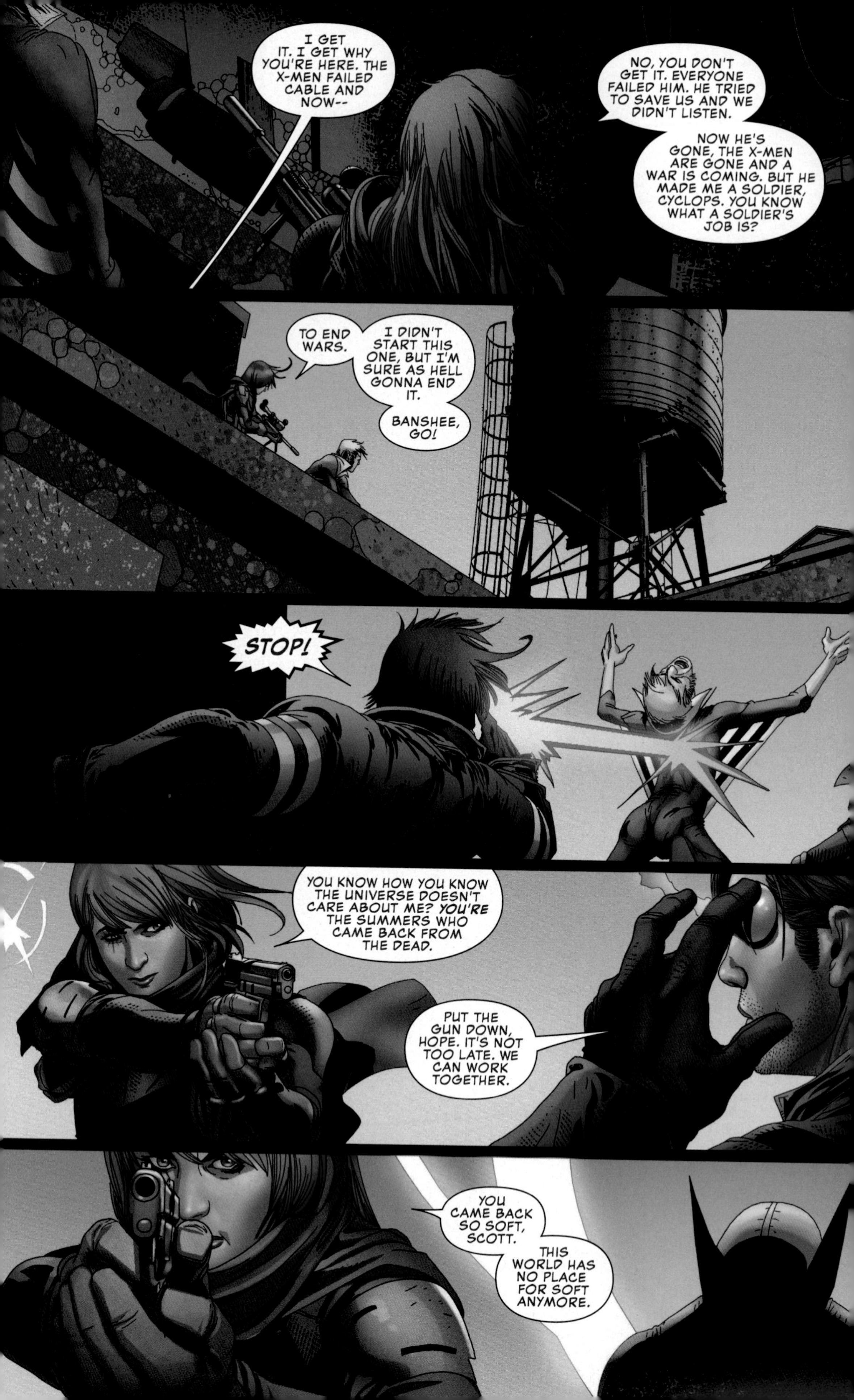
I GET IT. I GET WHY YOU'RE HERE. THE X-MEN FAILED CABLE AND NOW--
NO, YOU DON'T GET IT. EVERYONE FAILED HIM. HE TRIED TO SAVE US AND WE DIDN'T LISTEN.
NOW HE'S GONE, THE X-MEN ARE GONE AND A WAR IS COMING. BUT HE MADE ME A SOLDIER, CYCLOPS. YOU KNOW WHAT A SOLDIER'S JOB IS?
TO END WARS.
I DIDN'T START THIS ONE, BUT I'M SURE AS HELL GONNA END IT.
BANSHEE, GO!
STOP!
YOU KNOW HOW YOU KNOW THE UNIVERSE DOESN'T CARE ABOUT ME? *YOU'RE* THE SUMMERS WHO CAME BACK FROM THE DEAD.
PUT THE GUN DOWN, HOPE. IT'S NOT TOO LATE. WE CAN WORK TOGETHER.
YOU CAME BACK SO SOFT, SCOTT.
THIS WORLD HAS NO PLACE FOR SOFT ANYMORE.

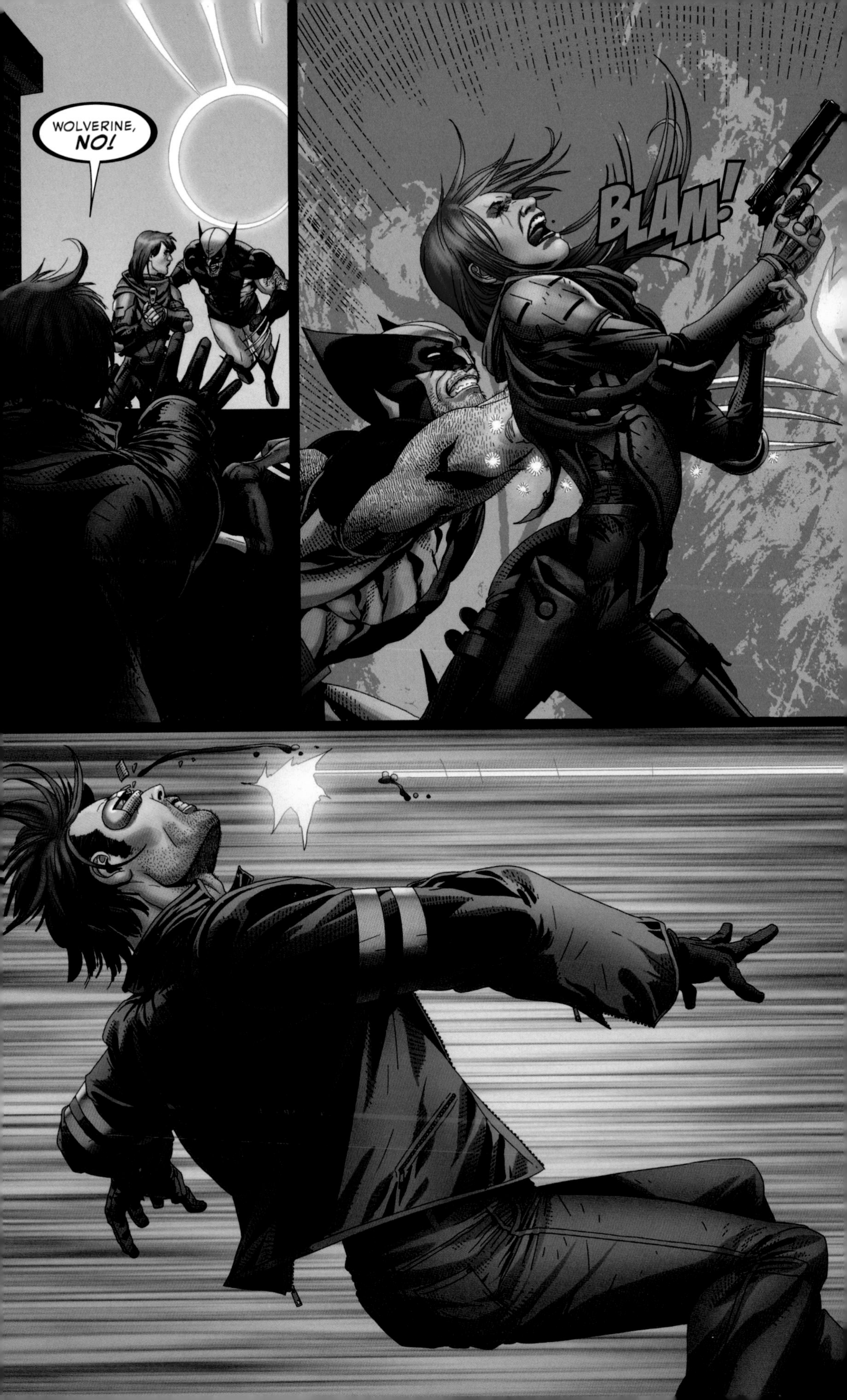
WOLVERINE, NO!
BLAM!

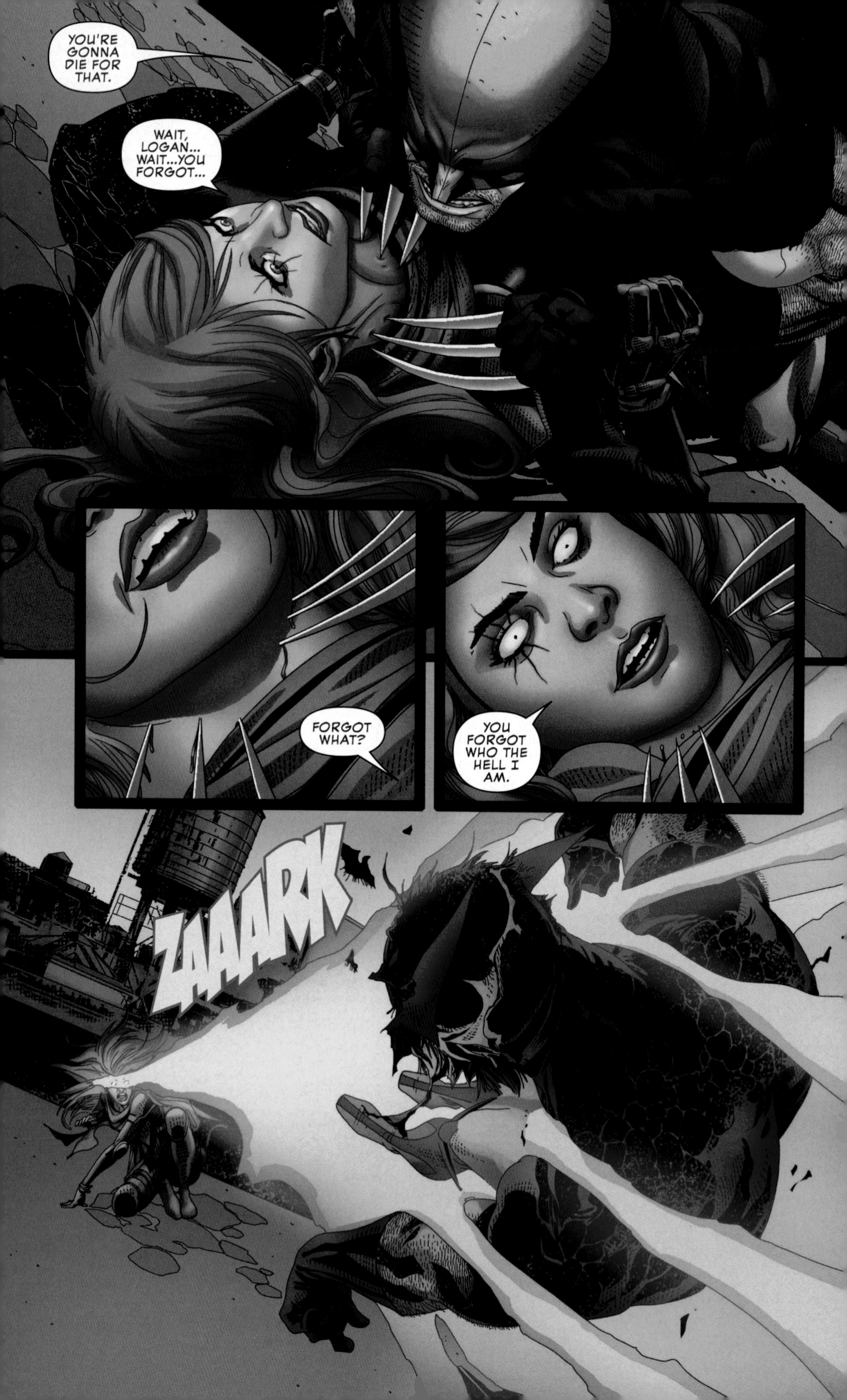
YOU'RE GONNA DIE FOR THAT.
WAIT, LOGAN... WAIT...YOU FORGOT...
FORGOT WHAT?
YOU FORGOT WHO THE HELL I AM.
ZAAARK

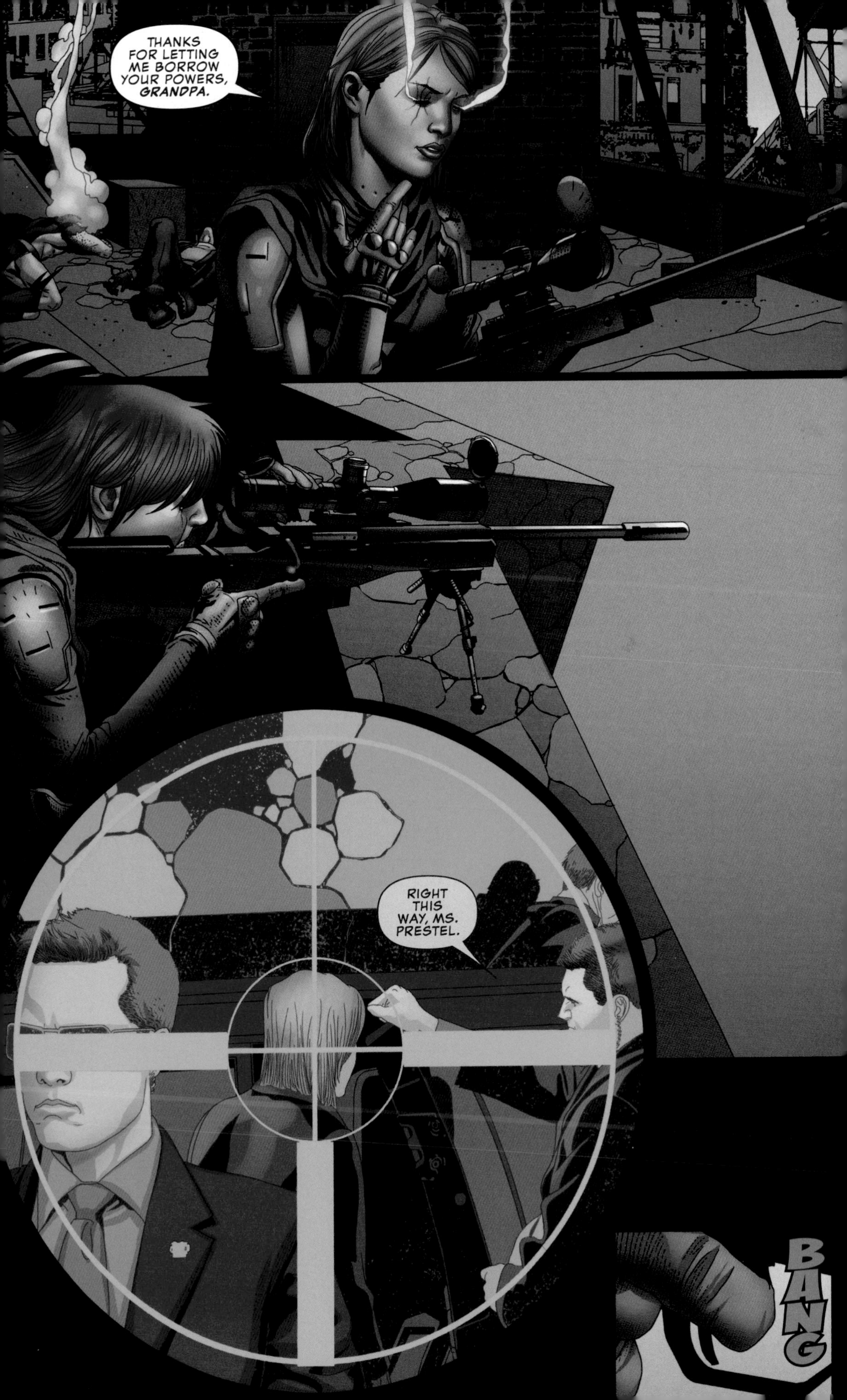
THANKS FOR LETTING ME BORROW YOUR POWERS, GRANDPA.
RIGHT THIS WAY, MS. PRESTEL.
BANG

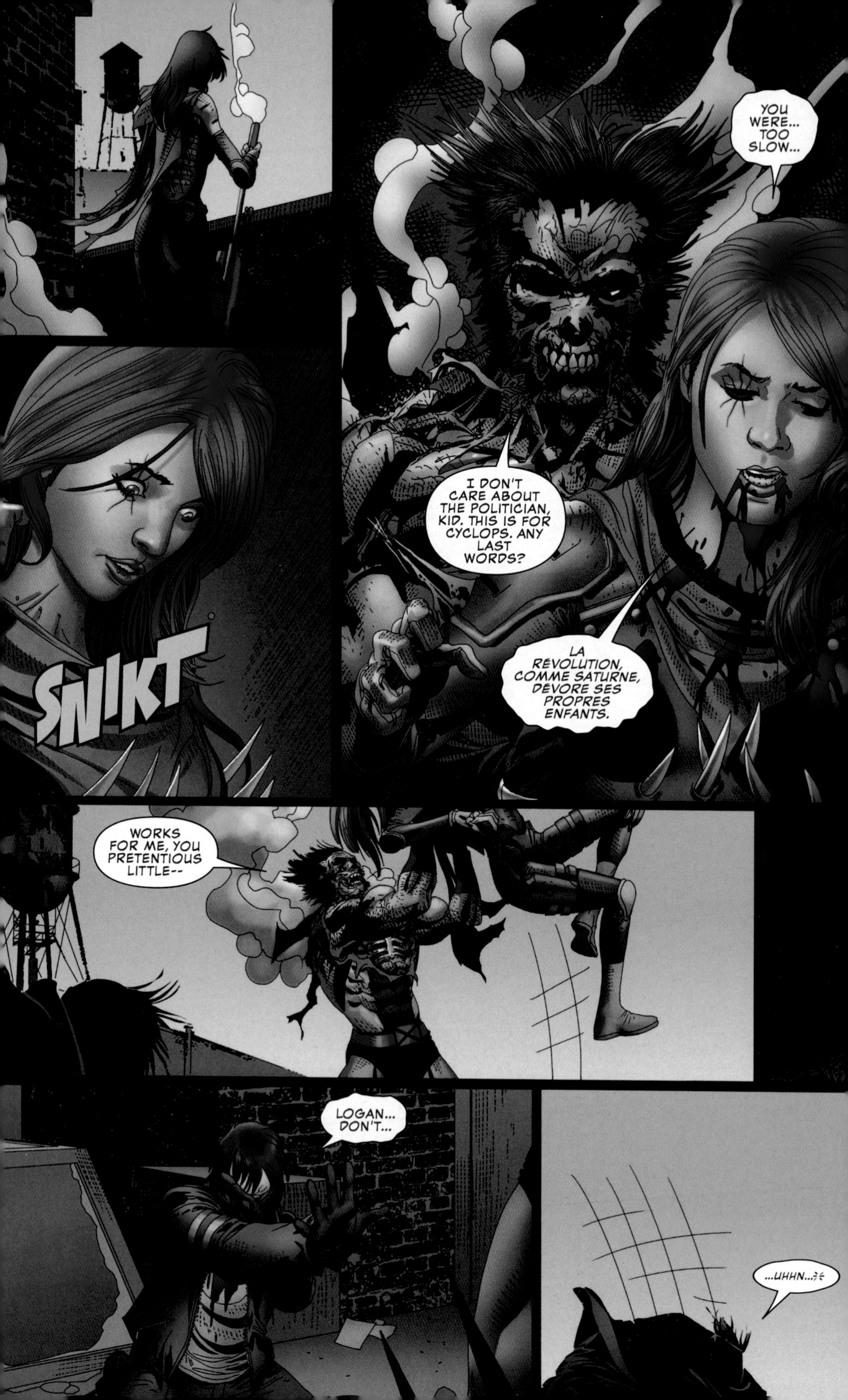
YOU WERE... TOO SLOW...
SNIKT
I DON'T CARE ABOUT THE POLITICIAN, KID. THIS IS FOR CYCLOPS. ANY LAST WORDS?
LA REVOLUTION, COMME SATURNE, DÉVORE SES PROPRES ENFANTS.
WORKS FOR ME, YOU PRETENTIOUS LITTLE--
LOGAN... DON'T...
...UHHN...

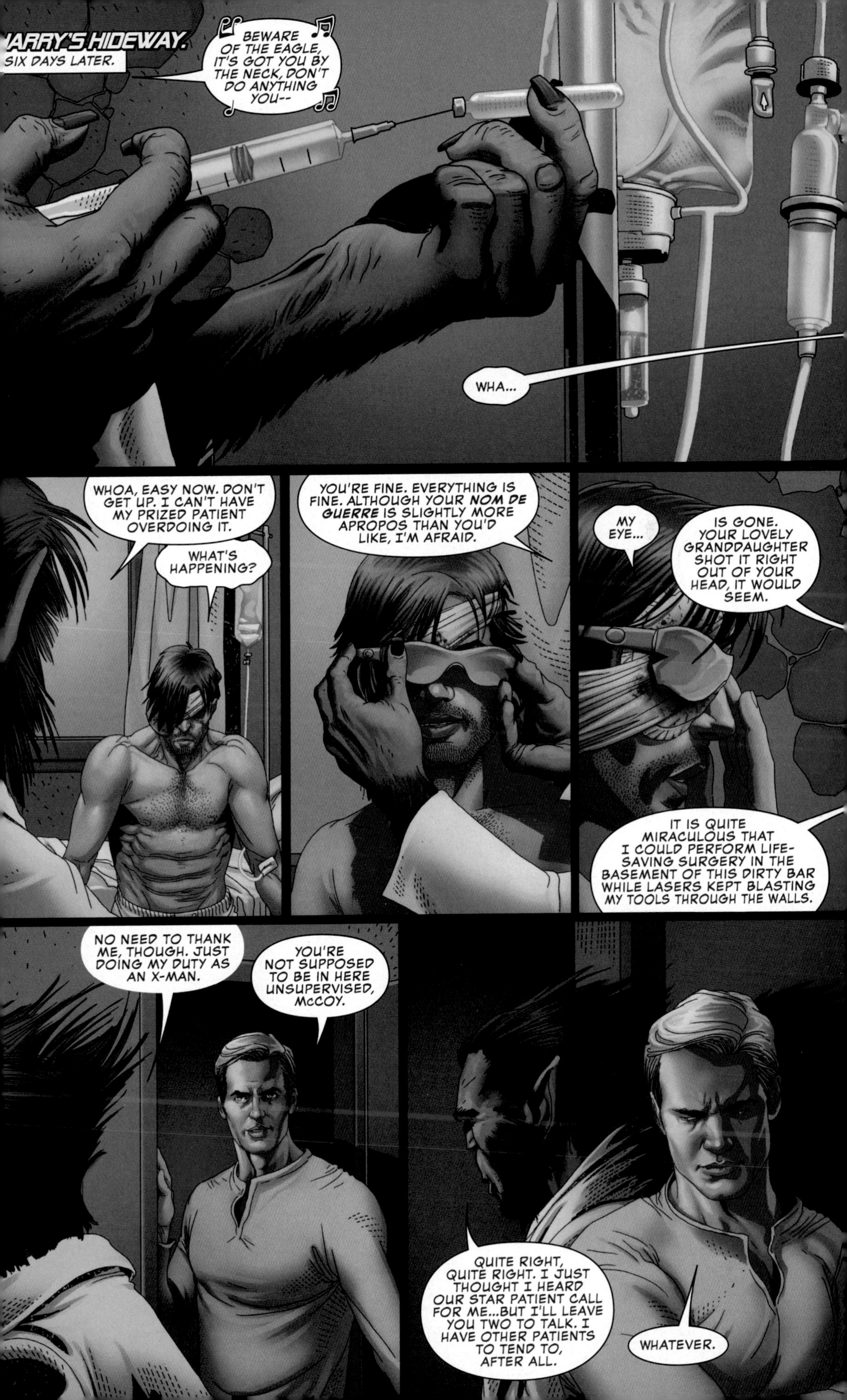

HARRY'S HIDEWAY.
SIX DAYS LATER.
BEWARE OF THE EAGLE, IT'S GOT YOU BY THE NECK, DON'T DO ANYTHING YOU--
WHA...
WHOA, EASY NOW. DON'T GET UP. I CAN'T HAVE MY PRIZED PATIENT OVERDOING IT.
WHAT'S HAPPENING?
YOU'RE FINE. EVERYTHING IS FINE. ALTHOUGH YOUR NOM DE GUERRE IS SLIGHTLY MORE APROPOS THAN YOU'D LIKE, I'M AFRAID.
MY EYE...
IS GONE. YOUR LOVELY GRANDDAUGHTER SHOT IT RIGHT OUT OF YOUR HEAD, IT WOULD SEEM.
IT IS QUITE MIRACULOUS THAT I COULD PERFORM LIFE-SAVING SURGERY IN THE BASEMENT OF THIS DIRTY BAR WHILE LASERS KEPT BLASTING MY TOOLS THROUGH THE WALLS.
NO NEED TO THANK ME, THOUGH. JUST DOING MY DUTY AS AN X-MAN.
YOU'RE NOT SUPPOSED TO BE IN HERE UNSUPERVISED, McCOY.
QUITE RIGHT, QUITE RIGHT. I JUST THOUGHT I HEARD OUR STAR PATIENT CALL FOR ME...BUT I'LL LEAVE YOU TWO TO TALK. I HAVE OTHER PATIENTS TO TEND TO, AFTER ALL.
WHATEVER.

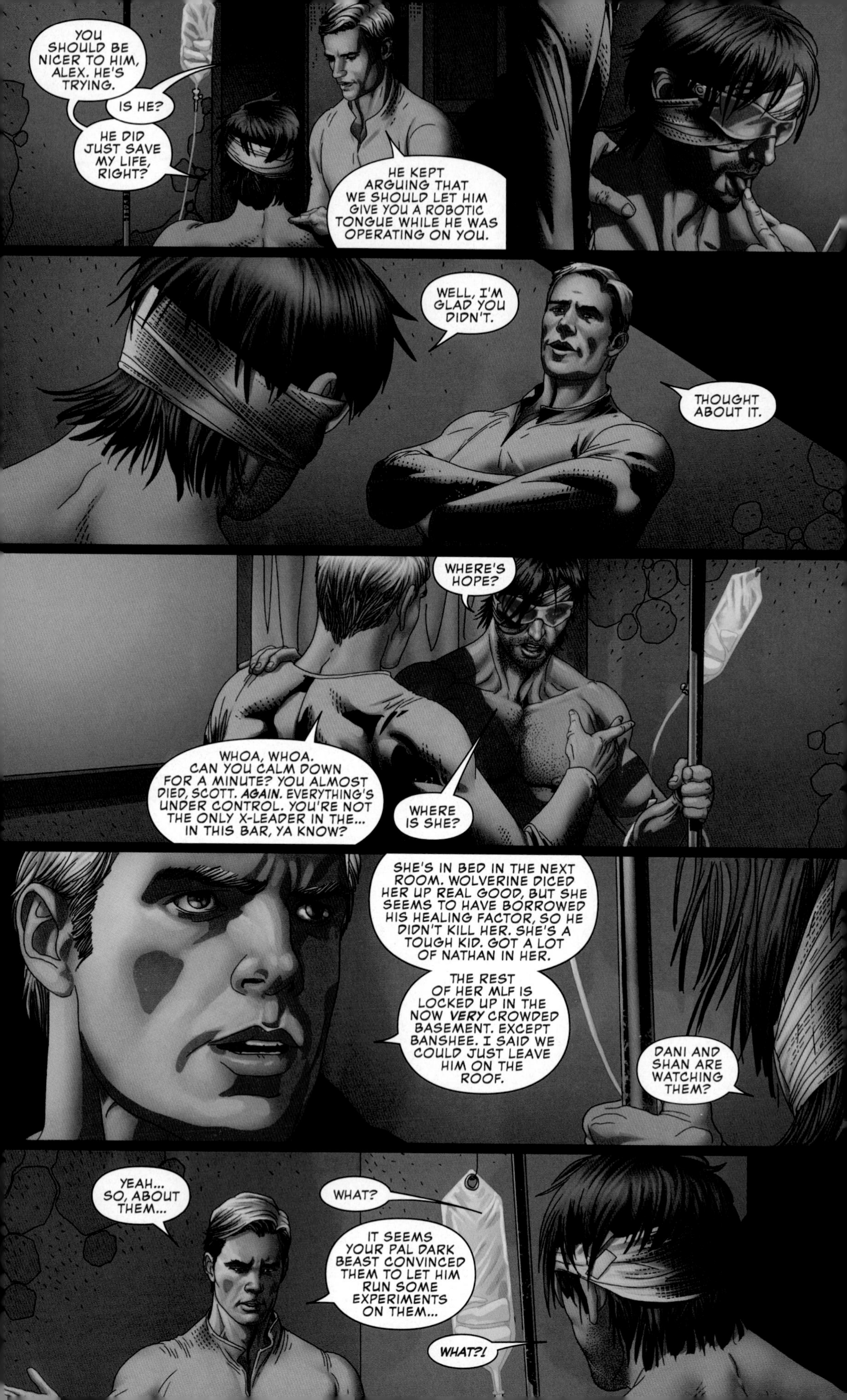
YOU SHOULD BE NICER TO HIM, ALEX. HE'S TRYING.
IS HE?
HE DID JUST SAVE MY LIFE, RIGHT?
HE KEPT ARGUING THAT WE SHOULD LET HIM GIVE YOU A ROBOTIC TONGUE WHILE HE WAS OPERATING ON YOU.
WELL, I'M GLAD YOU DIDN'T.
THOUGHT ABOUT IT.
WHERE'S HOPE?
WHOA, WHOA. CAN YOU CALM DOWN FOR A MINUTE? YOU ALMOST DIED, SCOTT. AGAIN. EVERYTHING'S UNDER CONTROL. YOU'RE NOT THE ONLY X-LEADER IN THE... IN THIS BAR, YA KNOW?
WHERE IS SHE?
SHE'S IN BED IN THE NEXT ROOM. WOLVERINE DICED HER UP REAL GOOD, BUT SHE SEEMS TO HAVE BORROWED HIS HEALING FACTOR, SO HE DIDN'T KILL HER. SHE'S A TOUGH KID. GOT A LOT OF NATHAN IN HER.
THE REST OF HER MLF IS LOCKED UP IN THE NOW VERY CROWDED BASEMENT. EXCEPT BANSHEE. I SAID WE COULD JUST LEAVE HIM ON THE ROOF.
DANI AND SHAN ARE WATCHING THEM?
YEAH... SO, ABOUT THEM...
WHAT?
IT SEEMS YOUR PAL DARK BEAST CONVINCED THEM TO LET HIM RUN SOME EXPERIMENTS ON THEM...
WHAT?!

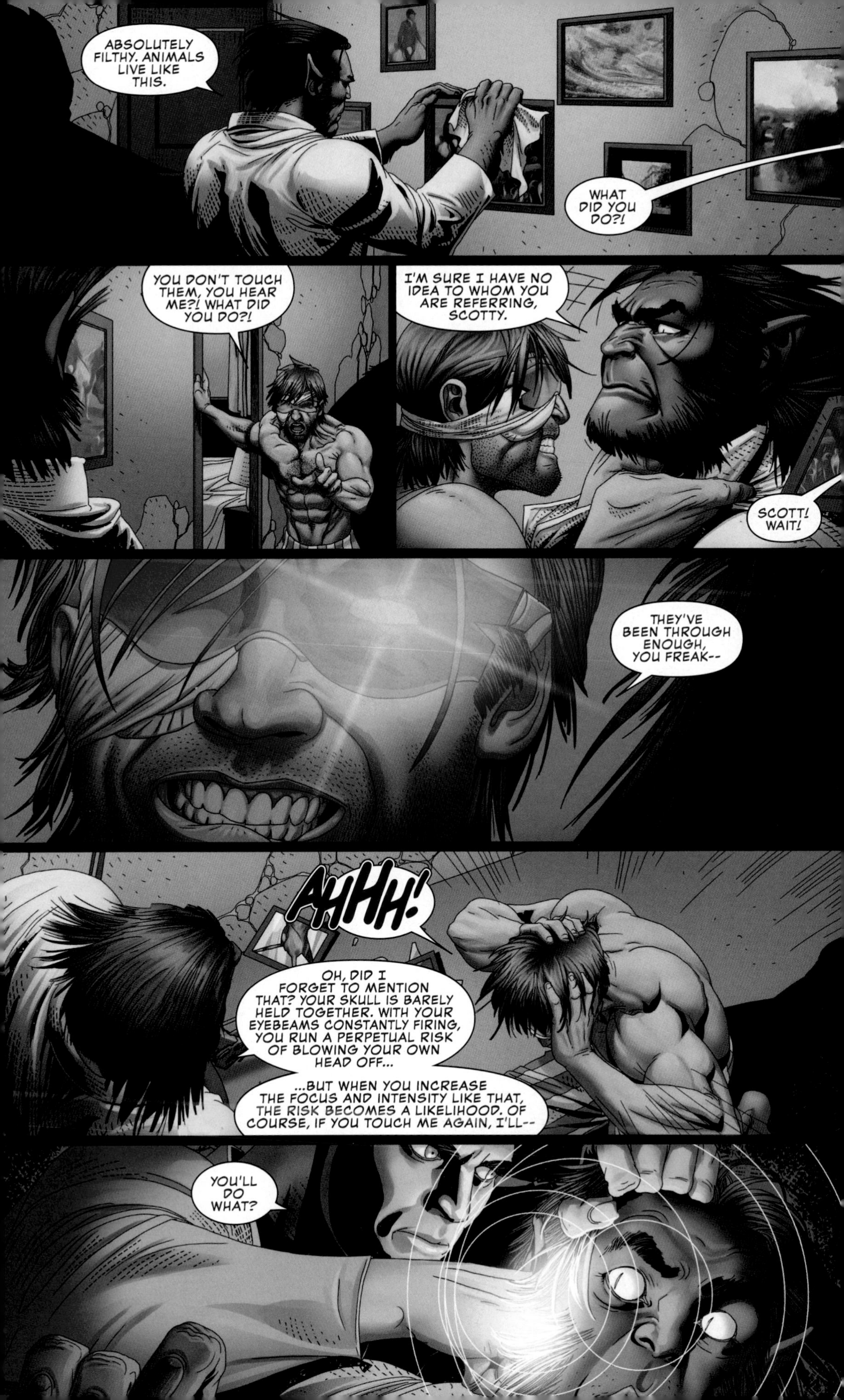
ABSOLUTELY FILTHY. ANIMALS LIVE LIKE THIS.
WHAT DID YOU DO?!
YOU DON'T TOUCH THEM, YOU HEAR ME?! WHAT DID YOU DO?!
I'M SURE I HAVE NO IDEA TO WHOM YOU ARE REFERRING, SCOTTY.
SCOTT! WAIT!
THEY'VE BEEN THROUGH ENOUGH, YOU FREAK--
AHHH!
OH, DID I FORGET TO MENTION THAT? YOUR SKULL IS BARELY HELD TOGETHER. WITH YOUR EYEBEAMS CONSTANTLY FIRING, YOU RUN A PERPETUAL RISK OF BLOWING YOUR OWN HEAD OFF...
...BUT WHEN YOU INCREASE THE FOCUS AND INTENSITY LIKE THAT, THE RISK BECOMES A LIKELIHOOD. OF COURSE, IF YOU TOUCH ME AGAIN, I'LL--
YOU'LL DO WHAT?

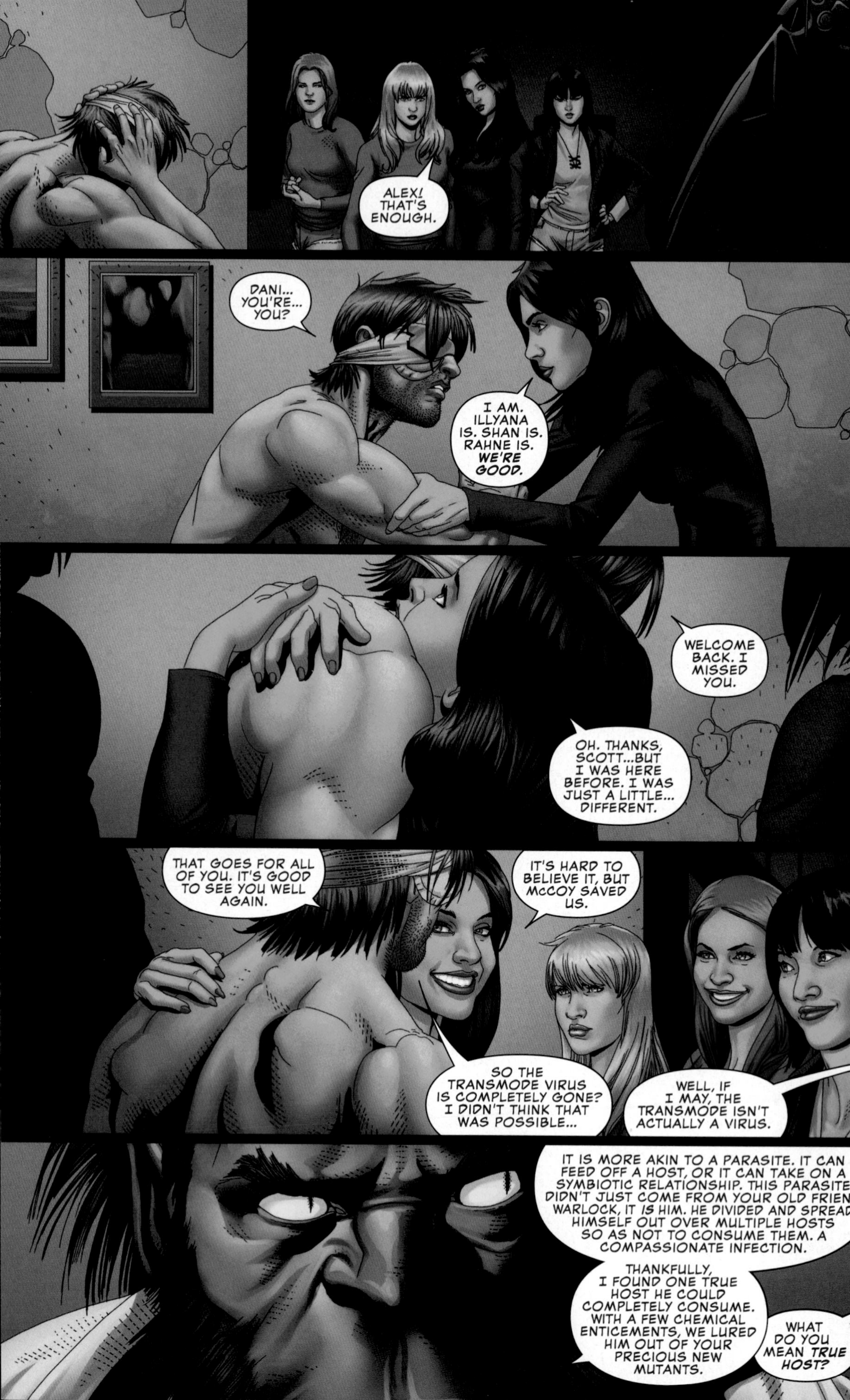

ALEX! THAT'S ENOUGH.
DANI... YOU'RE... YOU?
I AM. ILLYANA IS. SHAN IS. RAHNE IS. WE'RE GOOD.
WELCOME BACK. I MISSED YOU.
OH. THANKS, SCOTT...BUT I WAS HERE BEFORE. I WAS JUST A LITTLE... DIFFERENT.
THAT GOES FOR ALL OF YOU. IT'S GOOD TO SEE YOU WELL AGAIN.
IT'S HARD TO BELIEVE IT, BUT McCOY SAVED US.
SO THE TRANSMODE VIRUS IS COMPLETELY GONE? I DIDN'T THINK THAT WAS POSSIBLE...
WELL, IF I MAY, THE TRANSMODE ISN'T ACTUALLY A VIRUS.
IT IS MORE AKIN TO A PARASITE. IT CAN FEED OFF A HOST, OR IT CAN TAKE ON A SYMBIOTIC RELATIONSHIP. THIS PARASITE DIDN'T JUST COME FROM YOUR OLD FRIEN WARLOCK, IT IS HIM. HE DIVIDED AND SPREAD HIMSELF OUT OVER MULTIPLE HOSTS SO AS NOT TO CONSUME THEM. A COMPASSIONATE INFECTION.
THANKFULLY, I FOUND ONE TRUE HOST HE COULD COMPLETELY CONSUME. WITH A FEW CHEMICAL ENTICEMENTS, WE LURED HIM OUT OF YOUR PRECIOUS NEW MUTANTS.
WHAT DO YOU MEAN TRUE HOST?

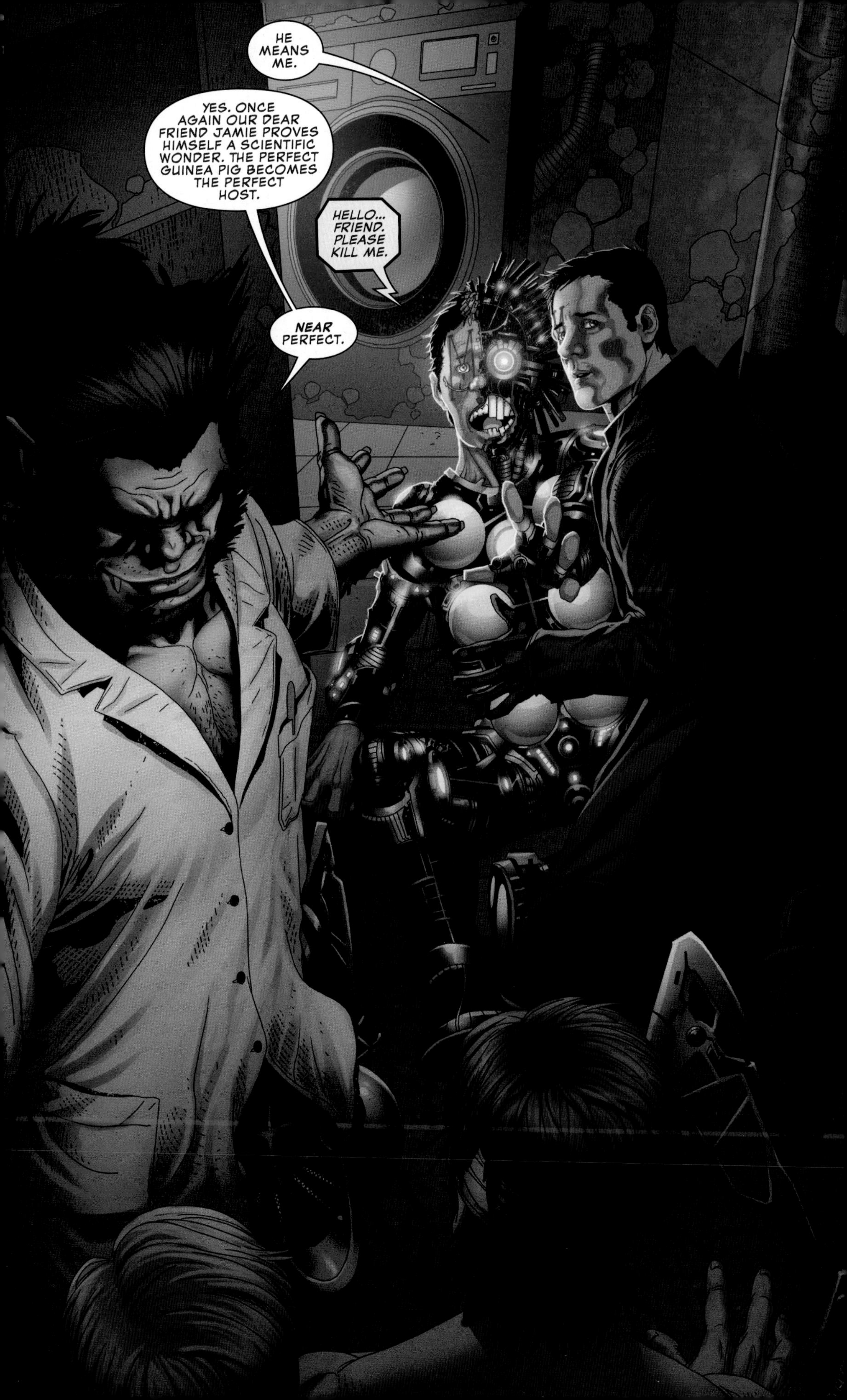
HE MEANS ME.
YES. ONCE AGAIN OUR DEAR FRIEND JAMIE PROVES HIMSELF A SCIENTIFIC WONDER. THE PERFECT GUINEA PIG BECOMES THE PERFECT HOST.
HELLO... FRIEND. PLEASE KILL ME.
NEAR PERFECT.

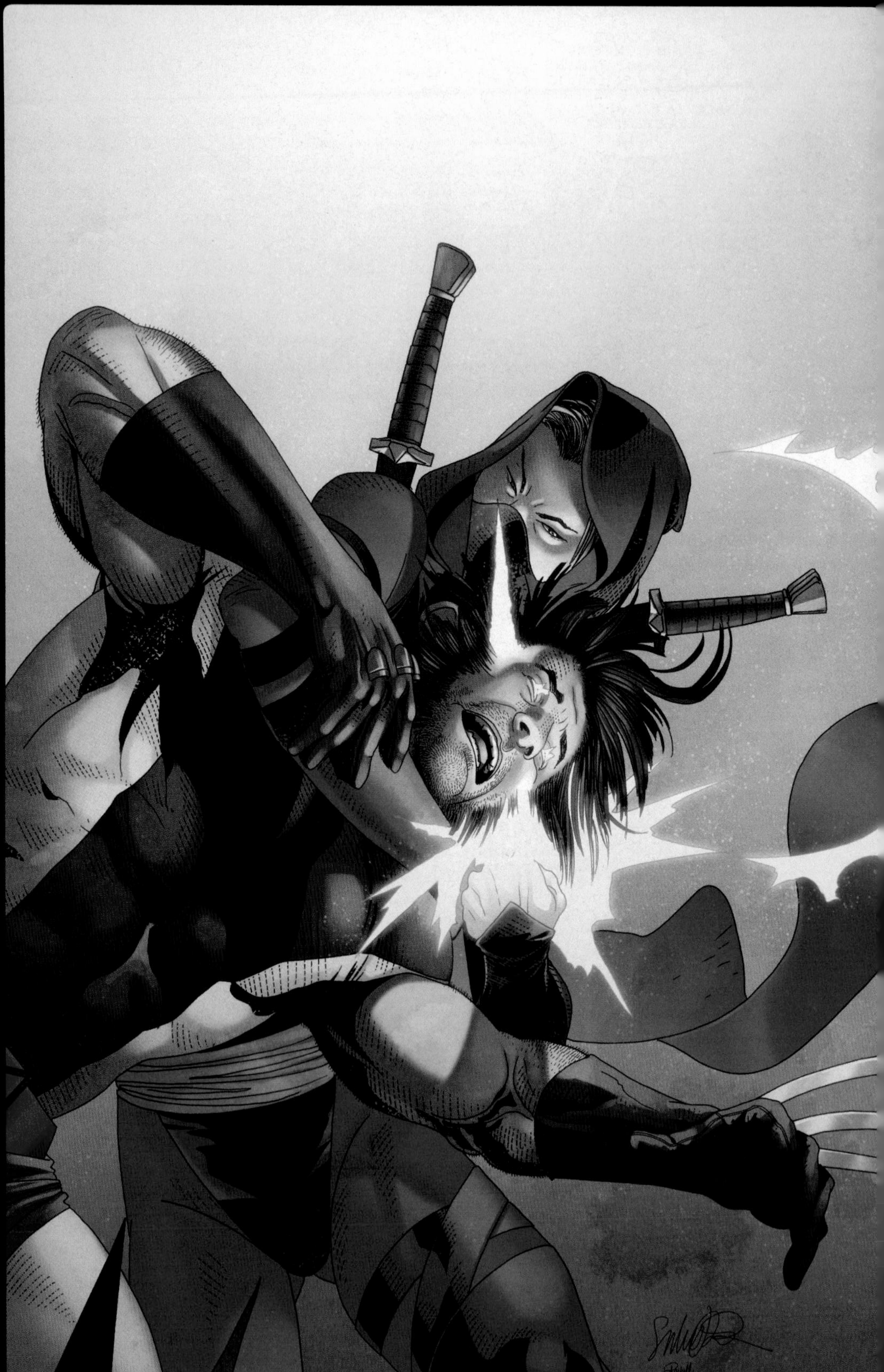

16

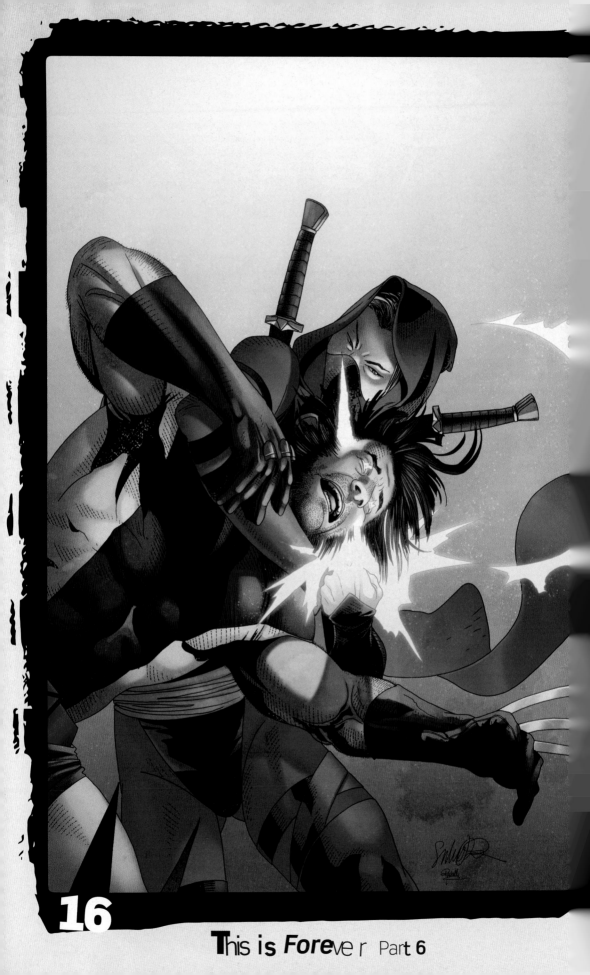

This is Forever Part 6

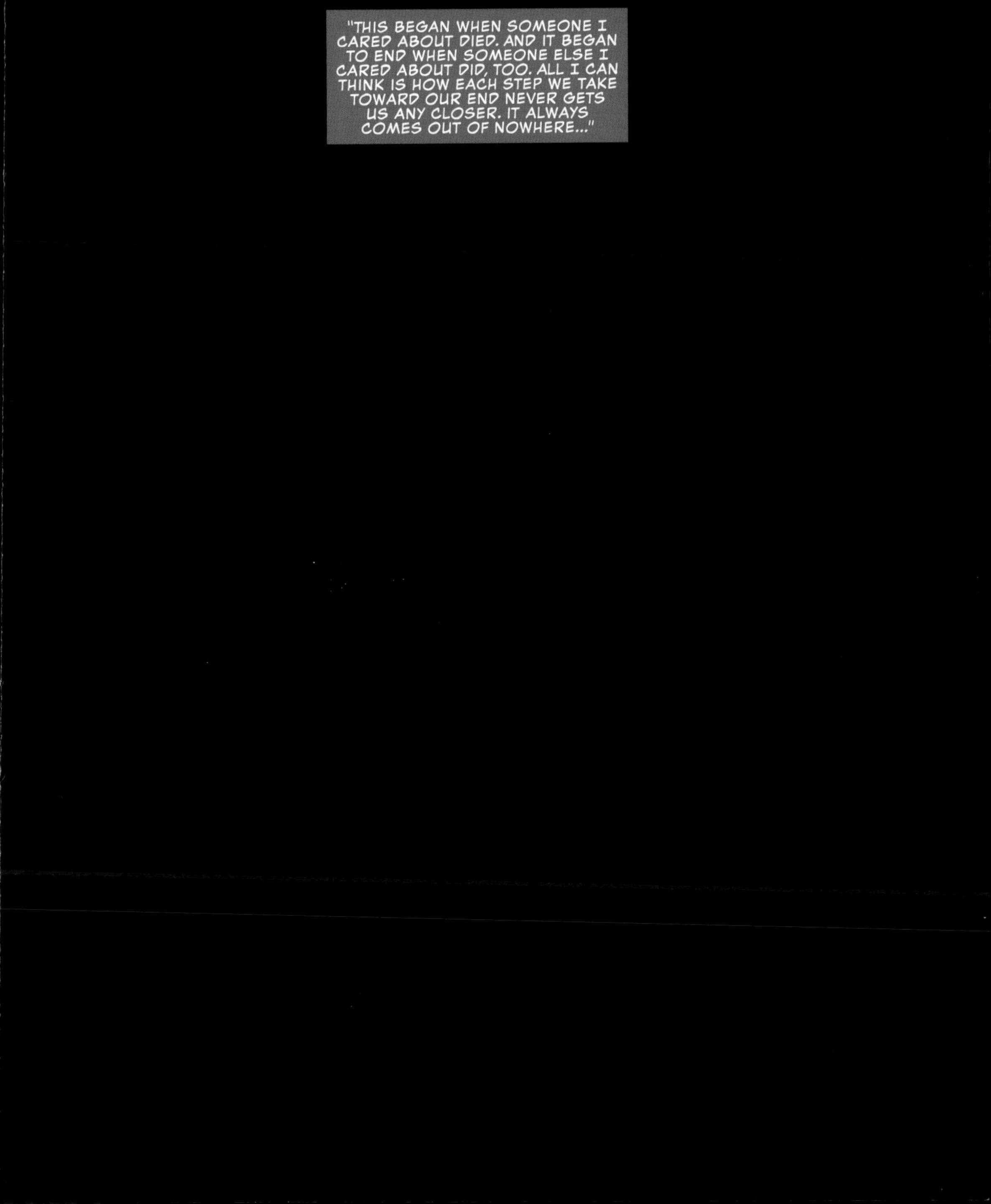
"THIS BEGAN WHEN SOMEONE I CARED ABOUT DIED. AND IT BEGAN TO END WHEN SOMEONE ELSE I CARED ABOUT DID, TOO. ALL I CAN THINK IS HOW EACH STEP WE TAKE TOWARD OUR END NEVER GETS US ANY CLOSER. IT ALWAYS COMES OUT OF NOWHERE..."

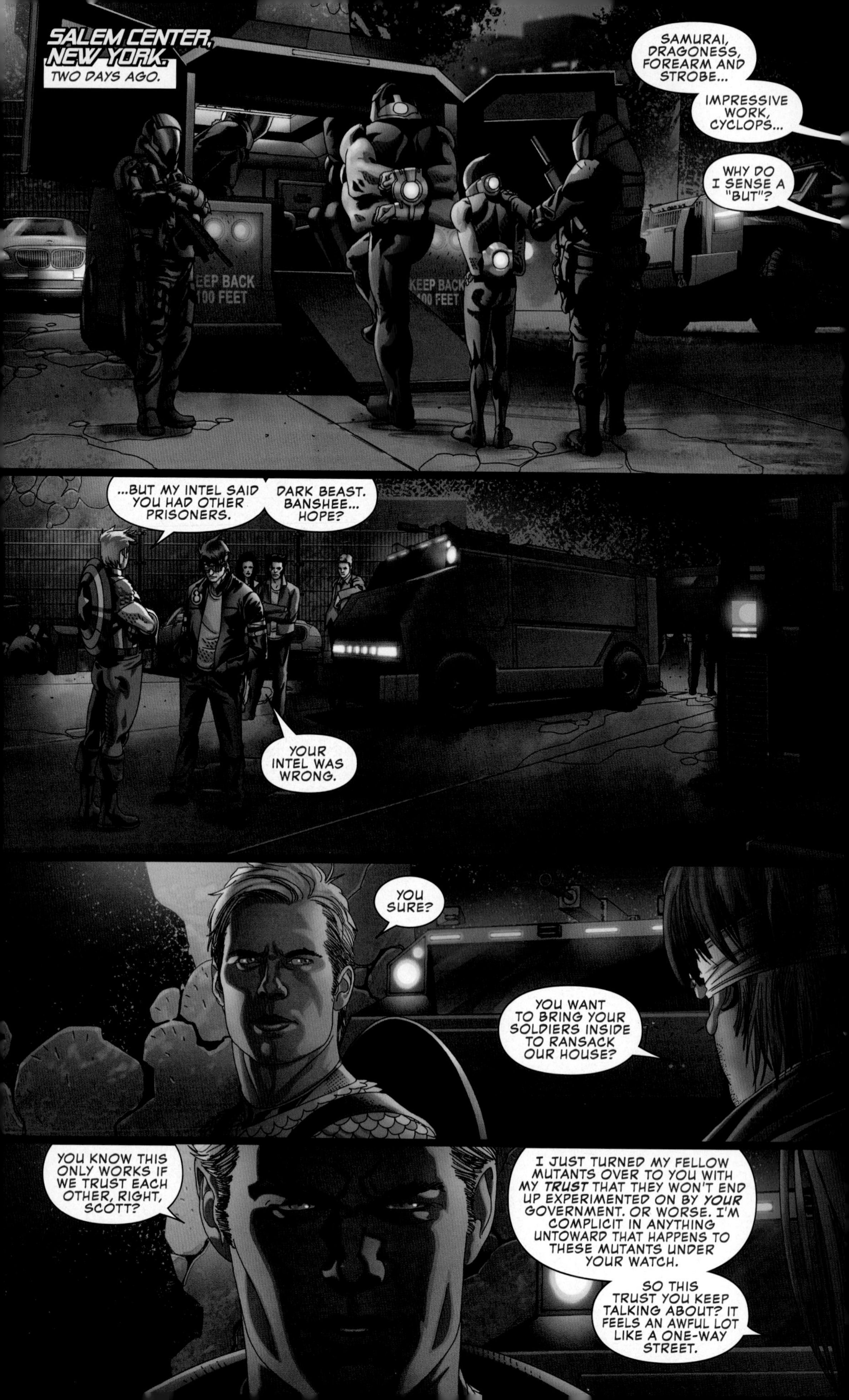
SALEM CENTER, NEW YORK.
TWO DAYS AGO.
SAMURAI, DRAGONESS, FOREARM AND STROBE...
IMPRESSIVE WORK, CYCLOPS...
WHY DO I SENSE A "BUT"?
KEEP BACK 100 FEET
KEEP BACK 100 FEET
...BUT MY INTEL SAID YOU HAD OTHER PRISONERS.
DARK BEAST. BANSHEE... HOPE?
YOUR INTEL WAS WRONG.
YOU SURE?
YOU WANT TO BRING YOUR SOLDIERS INSIDE TO RANSACK OUR HOUSE?
YOU KNOW THIS ONLY WORKS IF WE TRUST EACH OTHER, RIGHT, SCOTT?
I JUST TURNED MY FELLOW MUTANTS OVER TO YOU WITH MY *TRUST* THAT THEY WON'T END UP EXPERIMENTED ON BY *YOUR* GOVERNMENT. OR WORSE. I'M COMPLICIT IN ANYTHING UNTOWARD THAT HAPPENS TO THESE MUTANTS UNDER YOUR WATCH.
SO THIS TRUST YOU KEEP TALKING ABOUT? IT FEELS AN AWFUL LOT LIKE A ONE-WAY STREET.

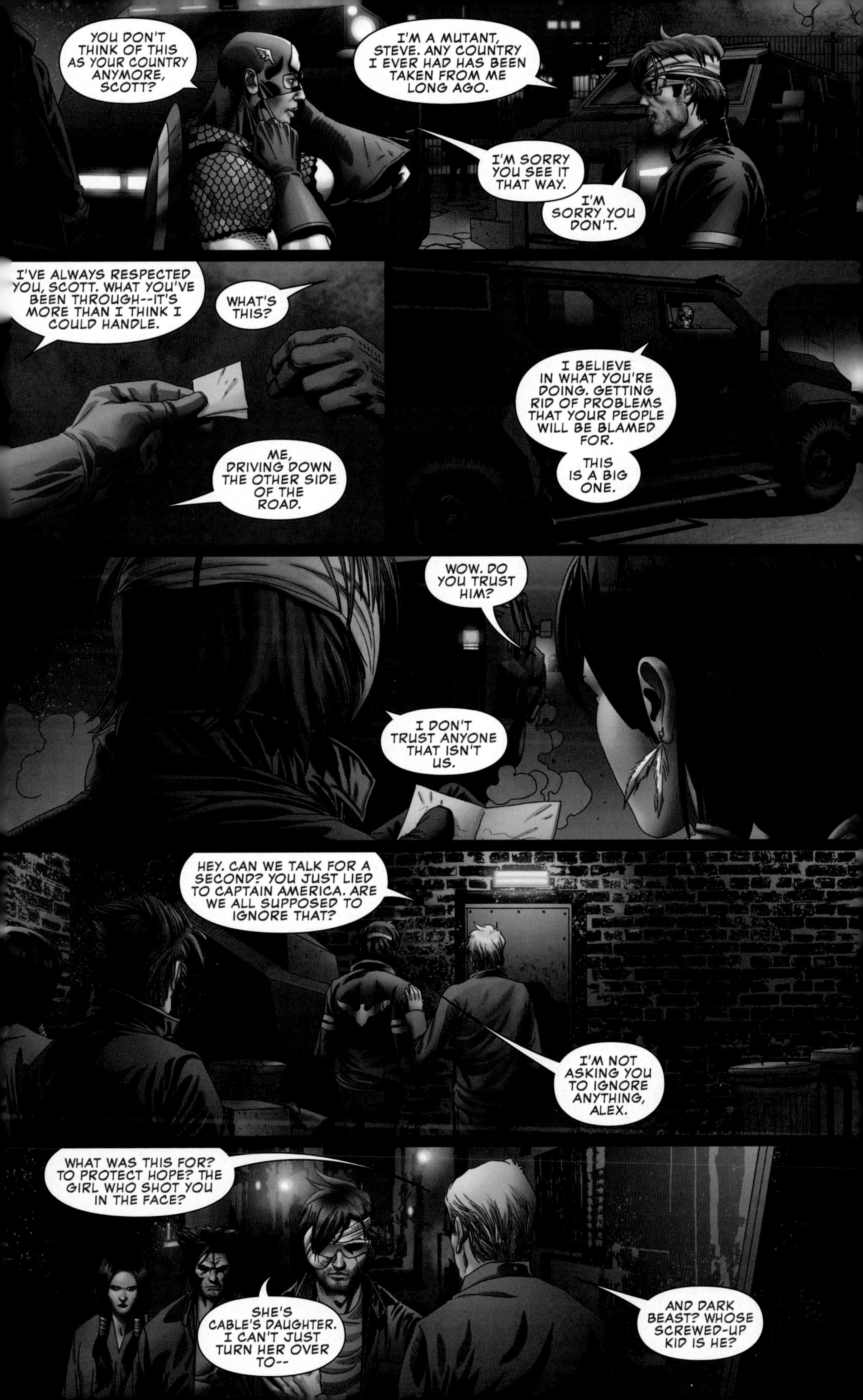
YOU DON'T THINK OF THIS AS YOUR COUNTRY ANYMORE, SCOTT?
I'M A MUTANT, STEVE. ANY COUNTRY I EVER HAD HAS BEEN TAKEN FROM ME LONG AGO.
I'M SORRY YOU SEE IT THAT WAY.
I'M SORRY YOU DON'T.
I'VE ALWAYS RESPECTED YOU, SCOTT. WHAT YOU'VE BEEN THROUGH--IT'S MORE THAN I THINK I COULD HANDLE.
WHAT'S THIS?
ME, DRIVING DOWN THE OTHER SIDE OF THE ROAD.
I BELIEVE IN WHAT YOU'RE DOING. GETTING RID OF PROBLEMS THAT YOUR PEOPLE WILL BE BLAMED FOR.
THIS IS A BIG ONE.
WOW. DO YOU TRUST HIM?
I DON'T TRUST ANYONE THAT ISN'T US.
HEY. CAN WE TALK FOR A SECOND? YOU JUST LIED TO CAPTAIN AMERICA. ARE WE ALL SUPPOSED TO IGNORE THAT?
I'M NOT ASKING YOU TO IGNORE ANYTHING, ALEX.
WHAT WAS THIS FOR? TO PROTECT HOPE? THE GIRL WHO SHOT YOU IN THE FACE?
SHE'S CABLE'S DAUGHTER. I CAN'T JUST TURN HER OVER TO--
AND DARK BEAST? WHOSE SCREWED-UP KID IS HE?

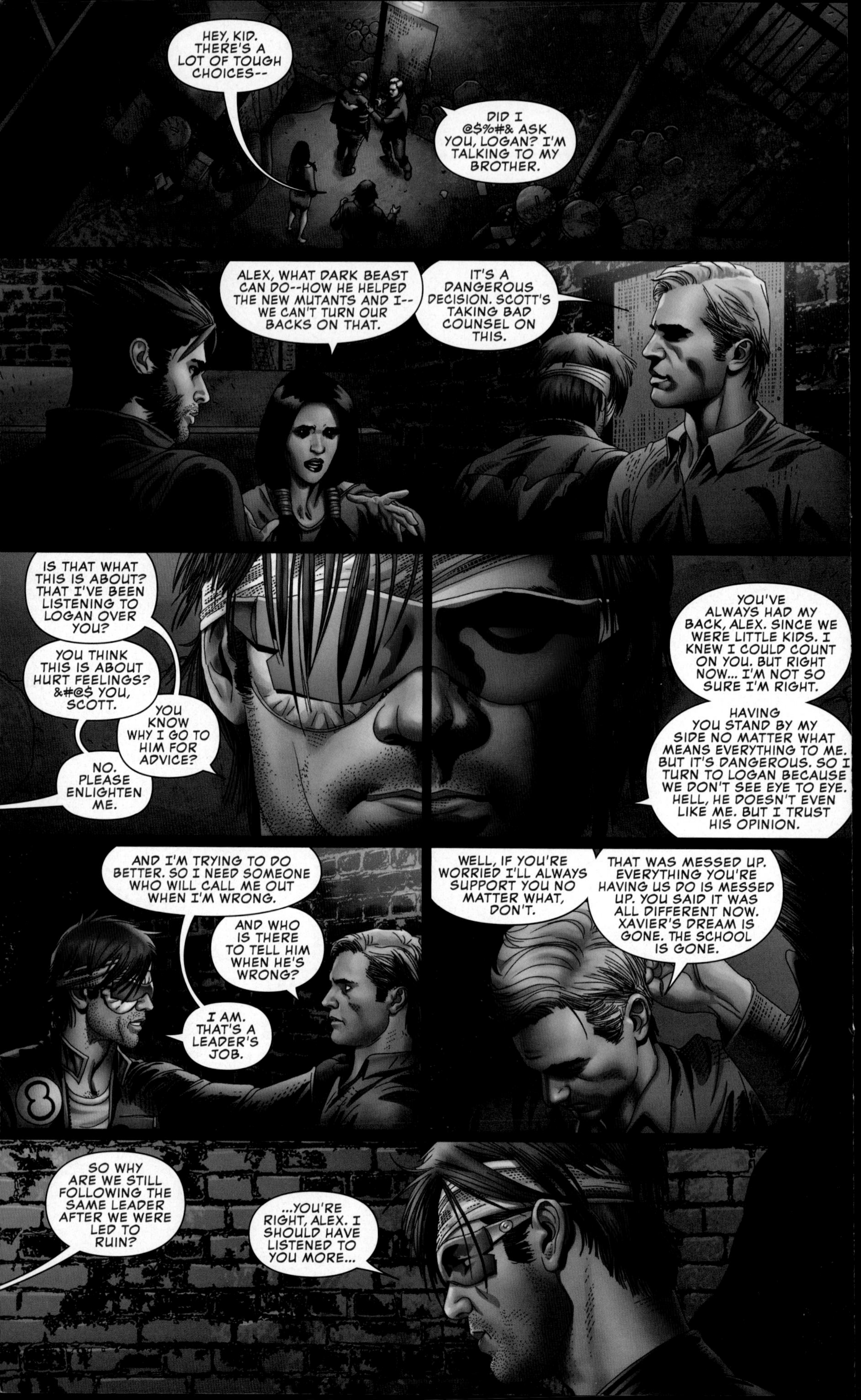
HEY, KID. THERE'S A LOT OF TOUGH CHOICES--
DID I @$%#& ASK YOU, LOGAN? I'M TALKING TO MY BROTHER.
ALEX, WHAT DARK BEAST CAN DO--HOW HE HELPED THE NEW MUTANTS AND I-- WE CAN'T TURN OUR BACKS ON THAT.
IT'S A DANGEROUS DECISION. SCOTT'S TAKING BAD COUNSEL ON THIS.
IS THAT WHAT THIS IS ABOUT? THAT I'VE BEEN LISTENING TO LOGAN OVER YOU?
YOU THINK THIS IS ABOUT HURT FEELINGS? &#@$ YOU, SCOTT.
YOU KNOW WHY I GO TO HIM FOR ADVICE?
NO. PLEASE ENLIGHTEN ME.
YOU'VE ALWAYS HAD MY BACK, ALEX. SINCE WE WERE LITTLE KIDS. I KNEW I COULD COUNT ON YOU. BUT RIGHT NOW... I'M NOT SO SURE I'M RIGHT.
HAVING YOU STAND BY MY SIDE NO MATTER WHAT MEANS EVERYTHING TO ME. BUT IT'S DANGEROUS. SO I TURN TO LOGAN BECAUSE WE DON'T SEE EYE TO EYE. HELL, HE DOESN'T EVEN LIKE ME. BUT I TRUST HIS OPINION.
AND I'M TRYING TO DO BETTER. SO I NEED SOMEONE WHO WILL CALL ME OUT WHEN I'M WRONG.
AND WHO IS THERE TO TELL HIM WHEN HE'S WRONG?
I AM. THAT'S A LEADER'S JOB.
WELL, IF YOU'RE WORRIED I'LL ALWAYS SUPPORT YOU NO MATTER WHAT, DON'T.
THAT WAS MESSED UP. EVERYTHING YOU'RE HAVING US DO IS MESSED UP. YOU SAID IT WAS ALL DIFFERENT NOW. XAVIER'S DREAM IS GONE. THE SCHOOL IS GONE.
SO WHY ARE WE STILL FOLLOWING THE SAME LEADER AFTER WE WERE LED TO RUIN?
...YOU'RE RIGHT, ALEX. I SHOULD HAVE LISTENED TO YOU MORE...

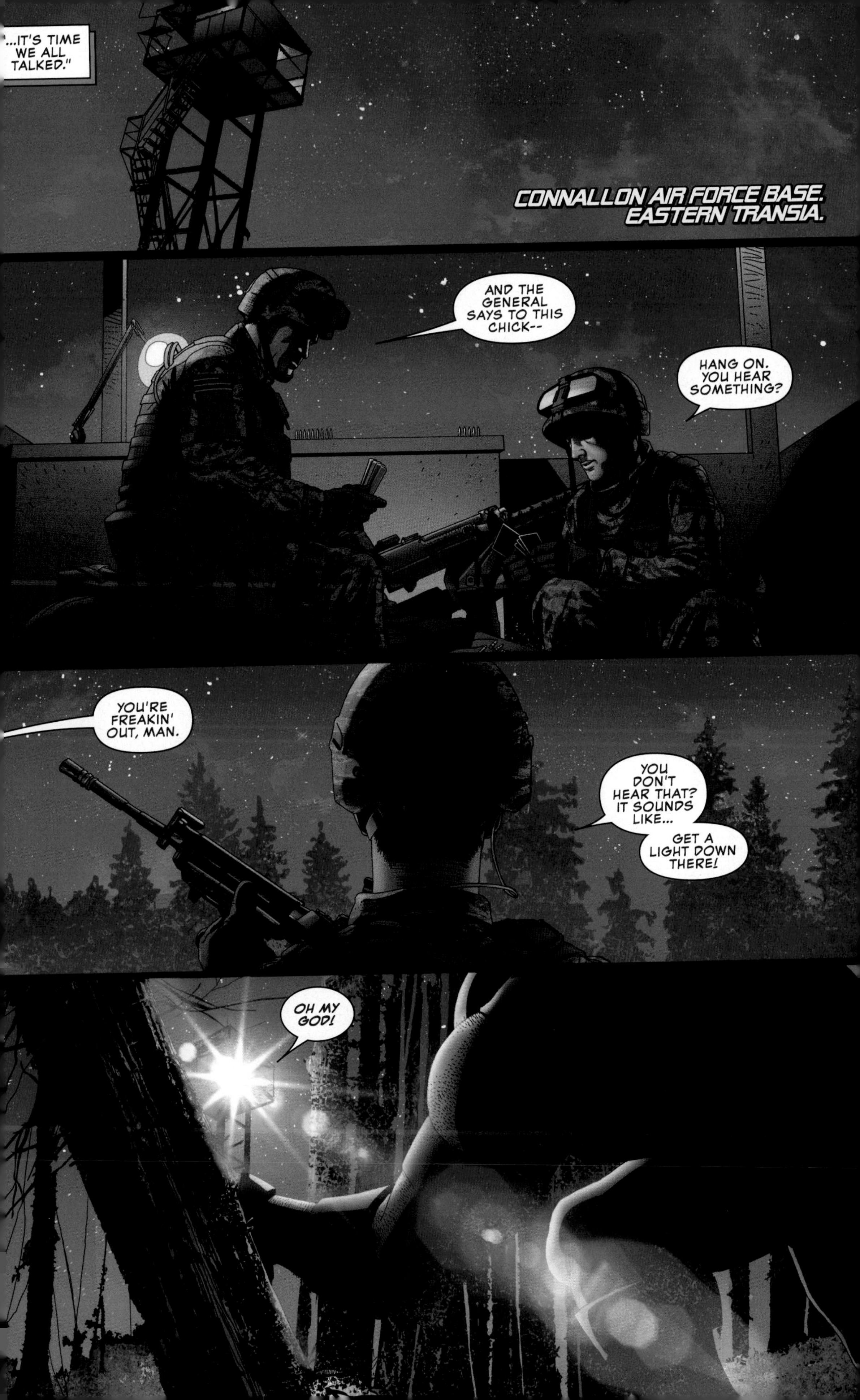
"...IT'S TIME WE ALL TALKED."
CONNALLON AIR FORCE BASE. EASTERN TRANSIA.
AND THE GENERAL SAYS TO THIS CHICK--
HANG ON. YOU HEAR SOMETHING?
YOU'RE FREAKIN' OUT, MAN.
YOU DON'T HEAR THAT? IT SOUNDS LIKE...
GET A LIGHT DOWN THERE!
OH MY GOD!

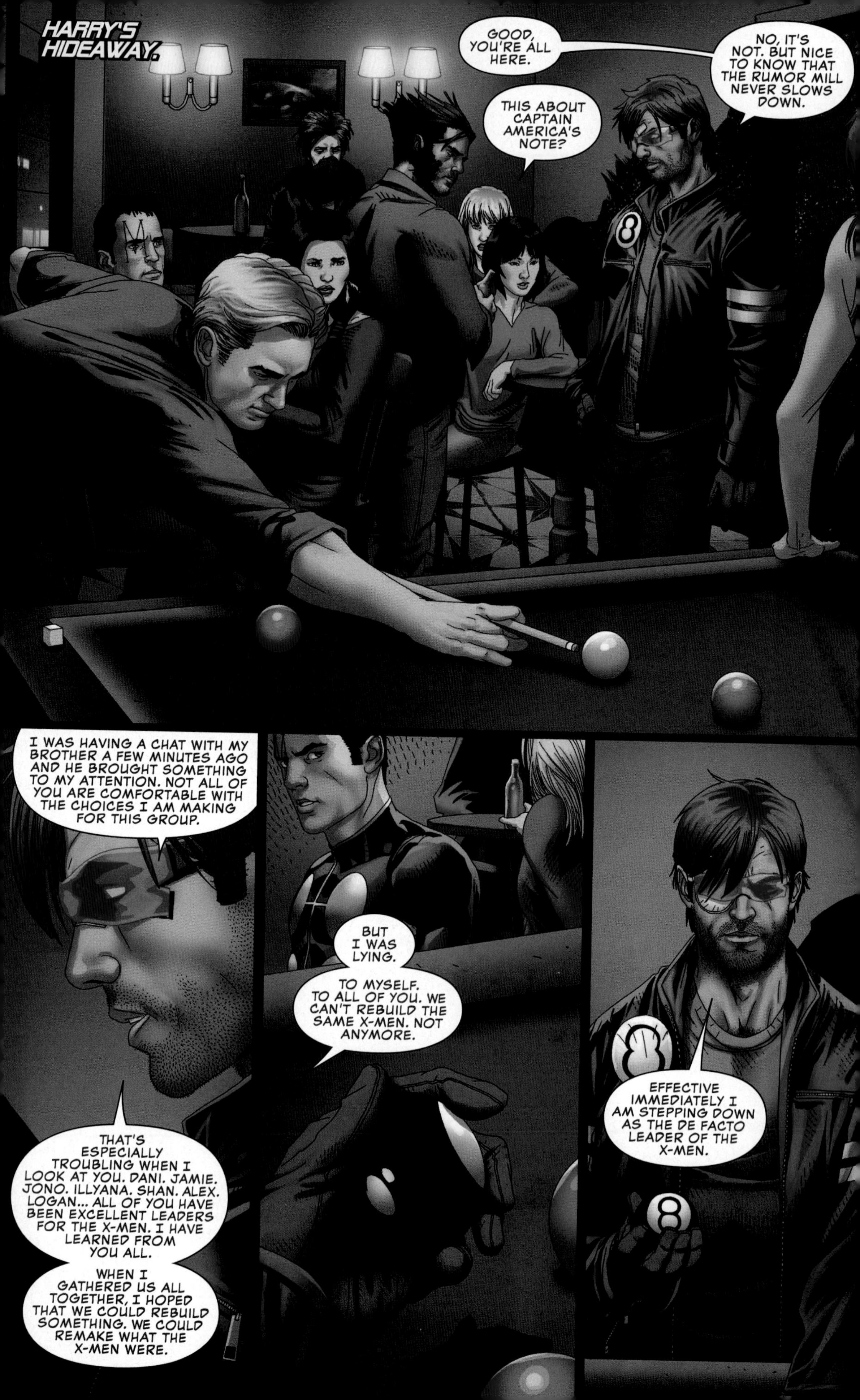
HARRY'S HIDEAWAY.
GOOD, YOU'RE ALL HERE.
THIS ABOUT CAPTAIN AMERICA'S NOTE?
NO, IT'S NOT. BUT NICE TO KNOW THAT THE RUMOR MILL NEVER SLOWS DOWN.
I WAS HAVING A CHAT WITH MY BROTHER A FEW MINUTES AGO AND HE BROUGHT SOMETHING TO MY ATTENTION. NOT ALL OF YOU ARE COMFORTABLE WITH THE CHOICES I AM MAKING FOR THIS GROUP.
THAT'S ESPECIALLY TROUBLING WHEN I LOOK AT YOU. DANI. JAMIE. JONO. ILLYANA. SHAN. ALEX. LOGAN... ALL OF YOU HAVE BEEN EXCELLENT LEADERS FOR THE X-MEN. I HAVE LEARNED FROM YOU ALL.
WHEN I GATHERED US ALL TOGETHER, I HOPED THAT WE COULD REBUILD SOMETHING. WE COULD REMAKE WHAT THE X-MEN WERE.
BUT I WAS LYING.
TO MYSELF. TO ALL OF YOU. WE CAN'T REBUILD THE SAME X-MEN. NOT ANYMORE.
EFFECTIVE IMMEDIATELY I AM STEPPING DOWN AS THE DE FACTO LEADER OF THE X-MEN.

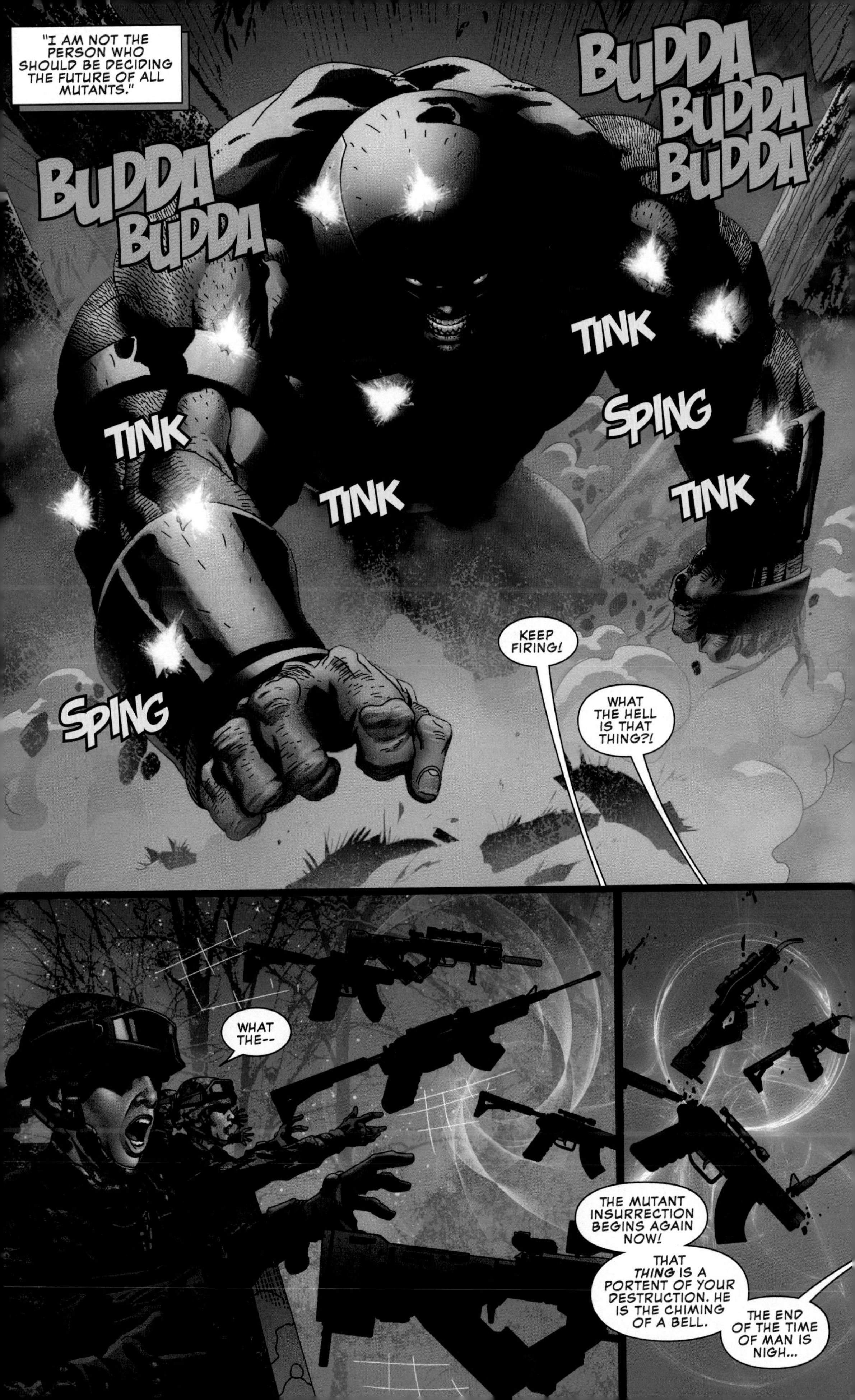

"I AM NOT THE PERSON WHO SHOULD BE DECIDING THE FUTURE OF ALL MUTANTS."
BUDDA BUDDA BUDDA
BUDDA BUDDA
TINK
SPING
TINK
TINK
TINK
SPING
KEEP FIRING!
WHAT THE HELL IS THAT THING?!
WHAT THE--
THE MUTANT INSURRECTION BEGINS AGAIN NOW!
THAT *THING* IS A PORTENT OF YOUR DESTRUCTION. HE IS THE CHIMING OF A BELL.
THE END OF THE TIME OF MAN IS NIGH...

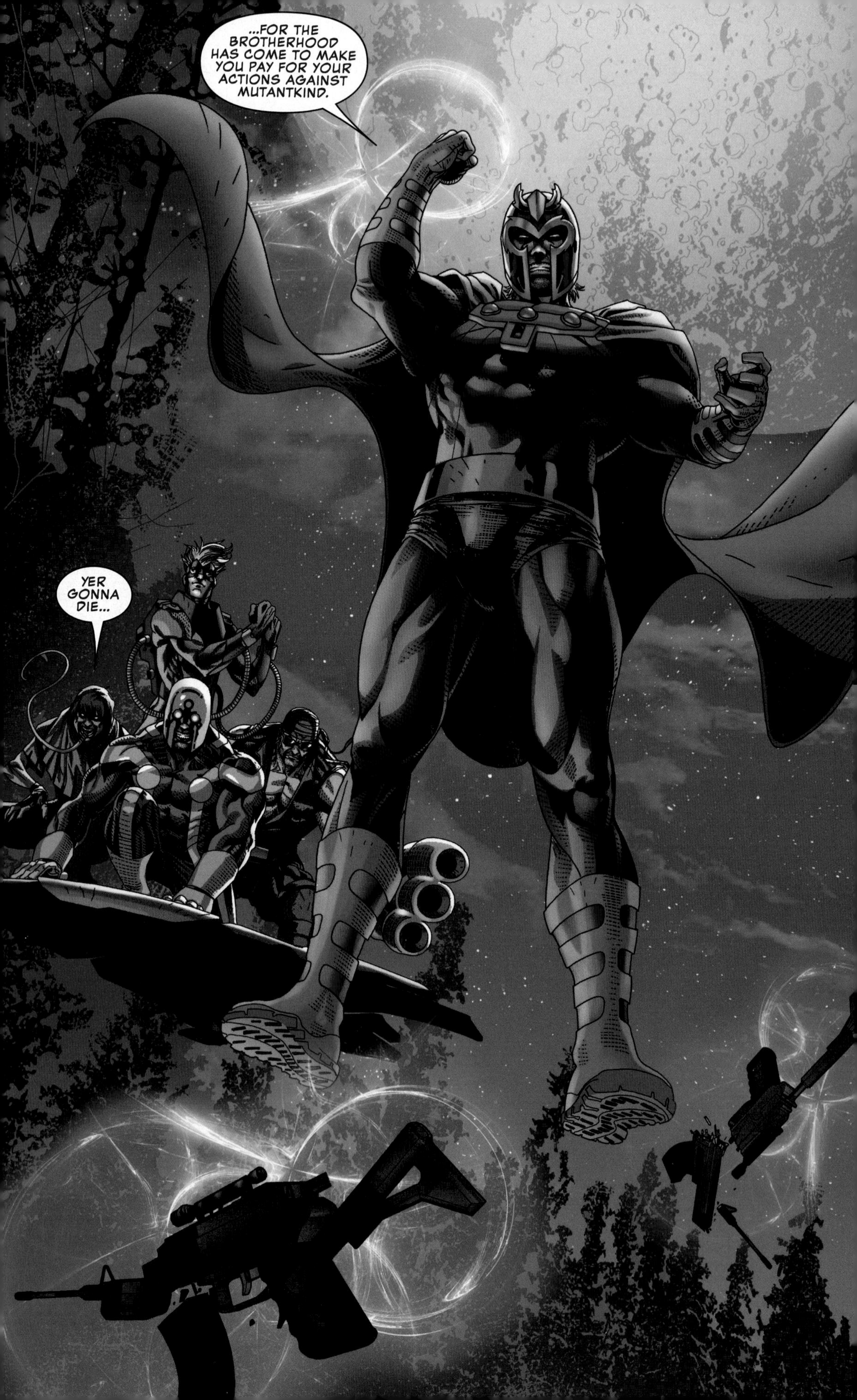
...FOR THE BROTHERHOOD HAS COME TO MAKE YOU PAY FOR YOUR ACTIONS AGAINST MUTANTKIND.
YER GONNA DIE...

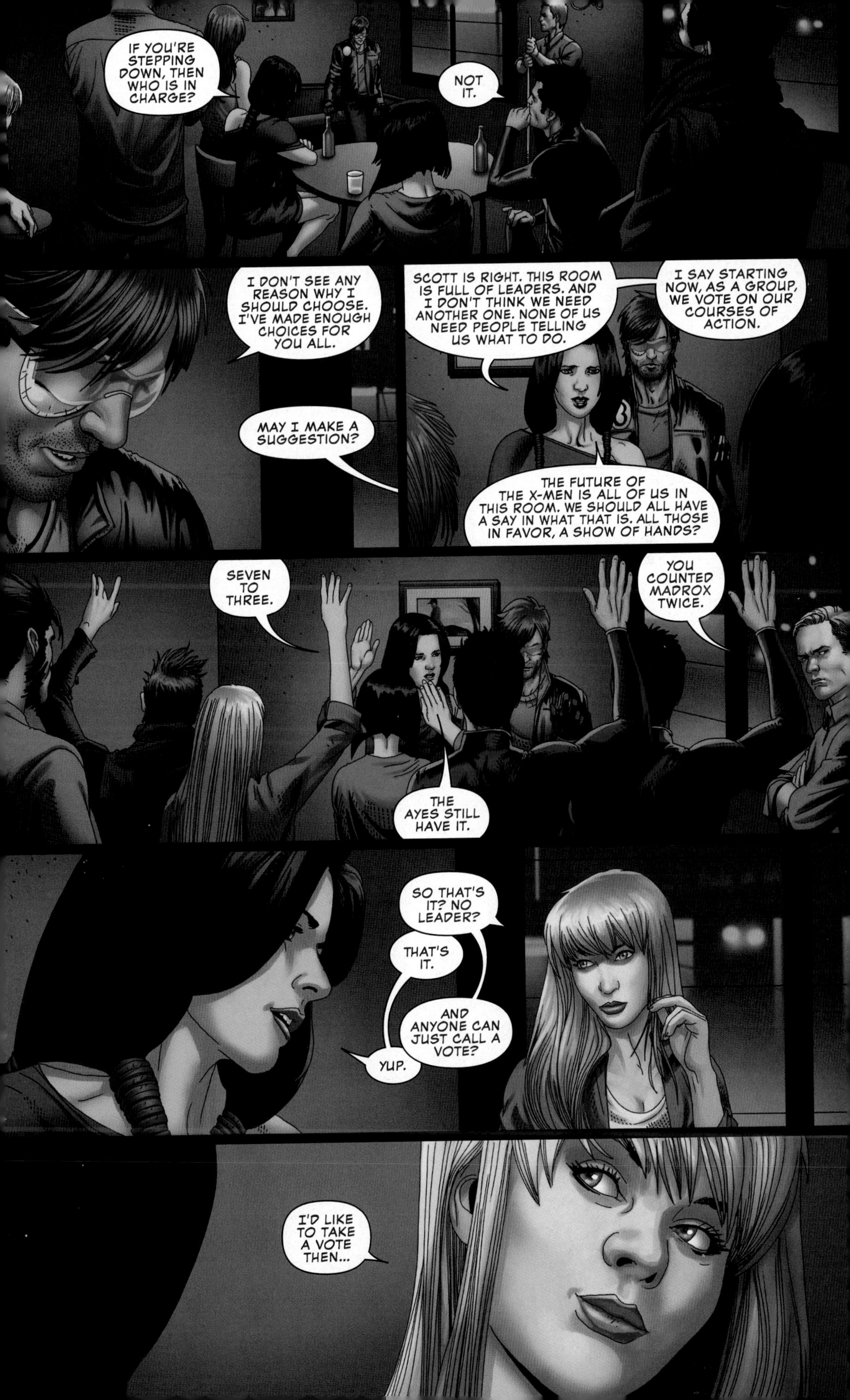
IF YOU'RE STEPPING DOWN, THEN WHO IS IN CHARGE?
NOT IT.
I DON'T SEE ANY REASON WHY I SHOULD CHOOSE. I'VE MADE ENOUGH CHOICES FOR YOU ALL.
MAY I MAKE A SUGGESTION?
SCOTT IS RIGHT. THIS ROOM IS FULL OF LEADERS. AND I DON'T THINK WE NEED ANOTHER ONE. NONE OF US NEED PEOPLE TELLING US WHAT TO DO.
I SAY STARTING NOW, AS A GROUP, WE VOTE ON OUR COURSES OF ACTION.
THE FUTURE OF THE X-MEN IS ALL OF US IN THIS ROOM. WE SHOULD ALL HAVE A SAY IN WHAT THAT IS. ALL THOSE IN FAVOR, A SHOW OF HANDS?
SEVEN TO THREE.
YOU COUNTED MADROX TWICE.
THE AYES STILL HAVE IT.
SO THAT'S IT? NO LEADER?
THAT'S IT.
AND ANYONE CAN JUST CALL A VOTE?
YUP.
I'D LIKE TO TAKE A VOTE THEN...

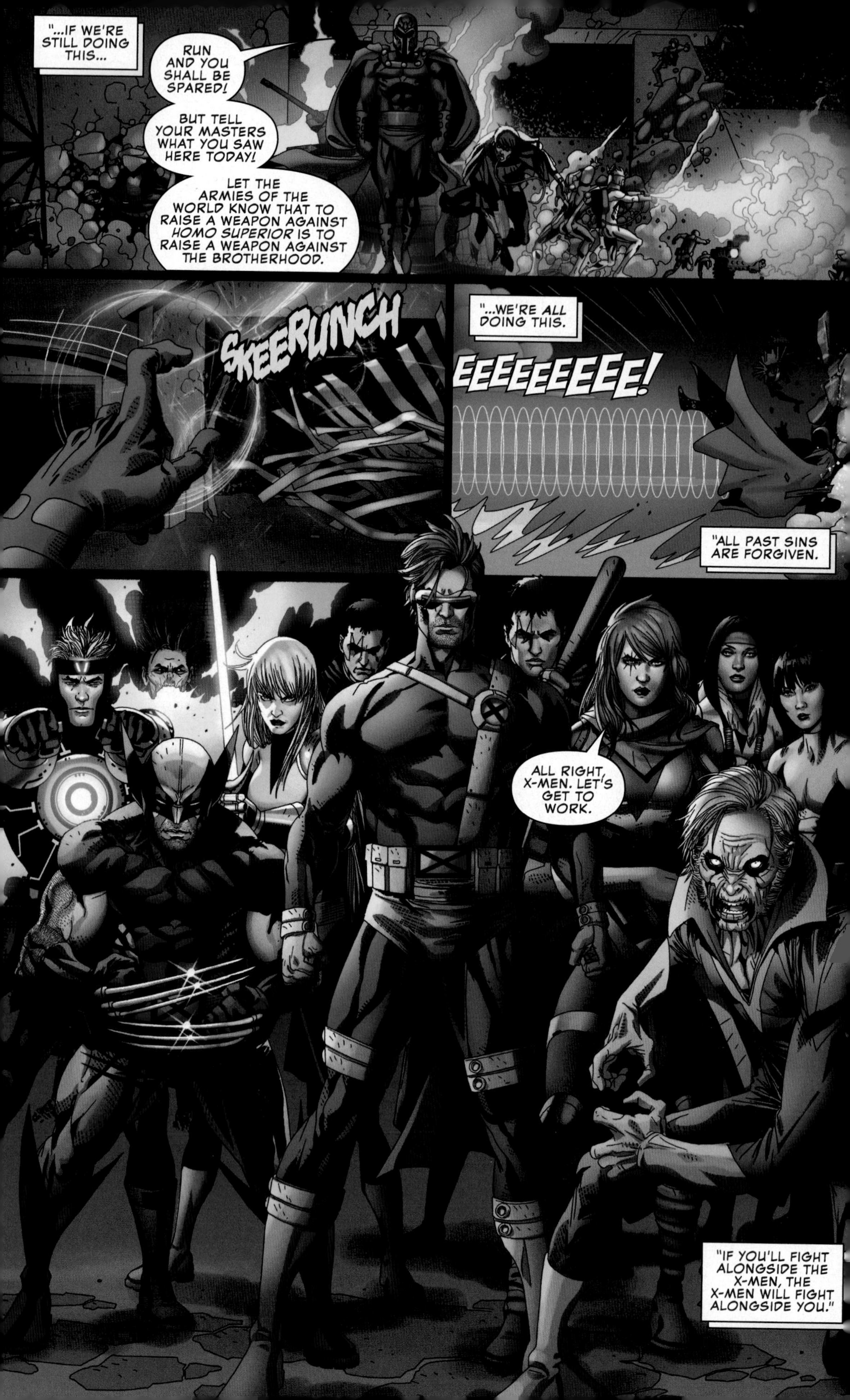
"...IF WE'RE STILL DOING THIS...
RUN AND YOU SHALL BE SPARED!
BUT TELL YOUR MASTERS WHAT YOU SAW HERE TODAY!
LET THE ARMIES OF THE WORLD KNOW THAT TO RAISE A WEAPON AGAINST *HOMO SUPERIOR* IS TO RAISE A WEAPON AGAINST THE BROTHERHOOD.
SKEERUNCH
"...WE'RE *ALL* DOING THIS.
EEEEEEEEE!
"ALL PAST SINS ARE FORGIVEN.
ALL RIGHT, X-MEN. LET'S GET TO WORK.
"IF YOU'LL FIGHT ALONGSIDE THE X-MEN, THE X-MEN WILL FIGHT ALONGSIDE YOU."

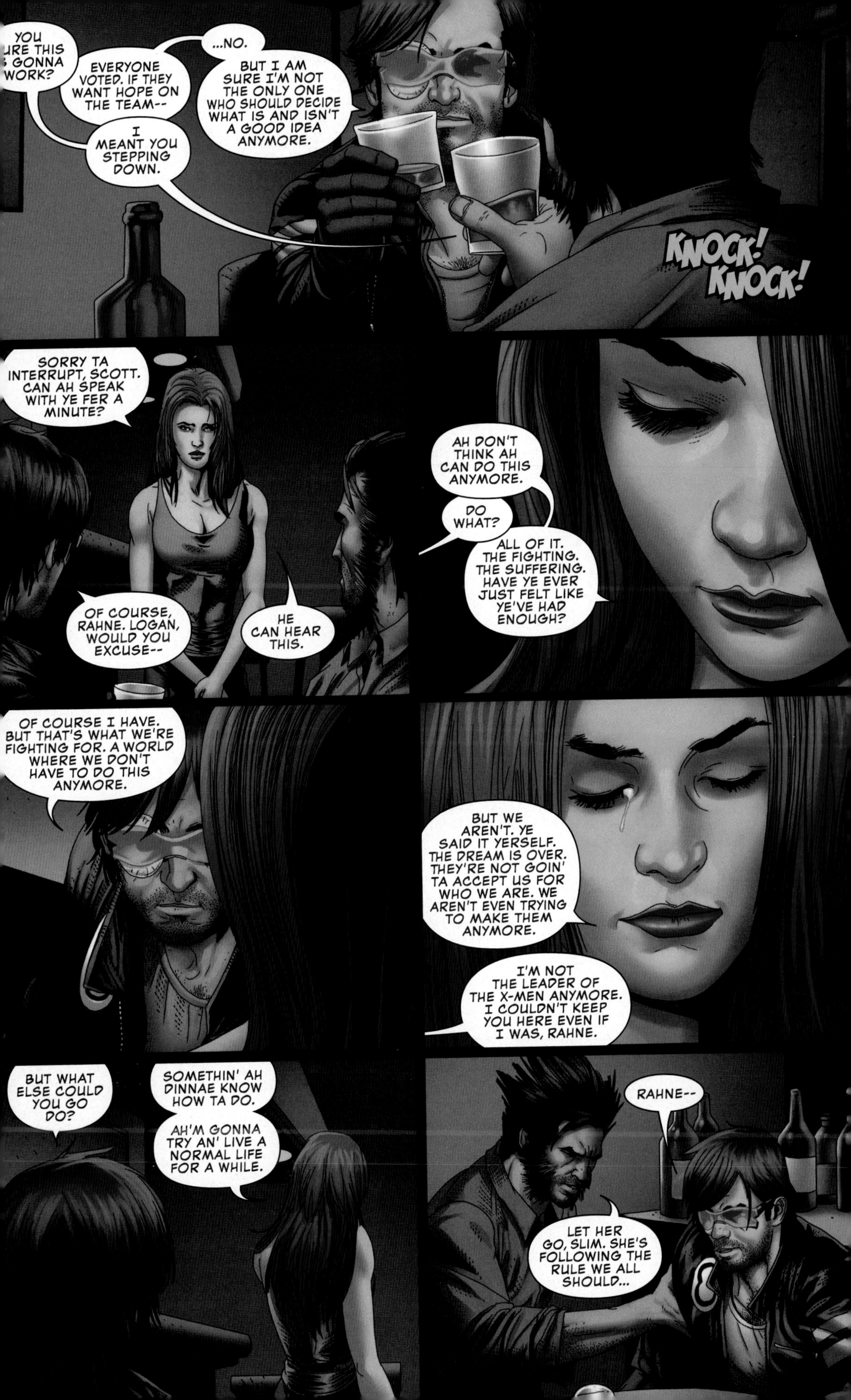

YOU SURE THIS 'S GONNA WORK?
EVERYONE VOTED. IF THEY WANT HOPE ON THE TEAM--
I MEANT YOU STEPPING DOWN.
...NO.
BUT I AM SURE I'M NOT THE ONLY ONE WHO SHOULD DECIDE WHAT IS AND ISN'T A GOOD IDEA ANYMORE.
KNOCK! KNOCK!
SORRY TA INTERRUPT, SCOTT. CAN AH SPEAK WITH YE FER A MINUTE?
OF COURSE, RAHNE. LOGAN, WOULD YOU EXCUSE--
HE CAN HEAR THIS.
AH DON'T THINK AH CAN DO THIS ANYMORE.
DO WHAT?
ALL OF IT. THE FIGHTING. THE SUFFERING. HAVE YE EVER JUST FELT LIKE YE'VE HAD ENOUGH?
OF COURSE I HAVE. BUT THAT'S WHAT WE'RE FIGHTING FOR. A WORLD WHERE WE DON'T HAVE TO DO THIS ANYMORE.
BUT WE AREN'T. YE SAID IT YERSELF. THE DREAM IS OVER. THEY'RE NOT GOIN' TA ACCEPT US FOR WHO WE ARE. WE AREN'T EVEN TRYING TO MAKE THEM ANYMORE.
I'M NOT THE LEADER OF THE X-MEN ANYMORE. I COULDN'T KEEP YOU HERE EVEN IF I WAS, RAHNE.
BUT WHAT ELSE COULD YOU GO DO?
SOMETHIN' AH DINNAE KNOW HOW TA DO.
AH'M GONNA TRY AN' LIVE A NORMAL LIFE FOR A WHILE.
RAHNE--
LET HER GO, SLIM. SHE'S FOLLOWING THE RULE WE ALL SHOULD...

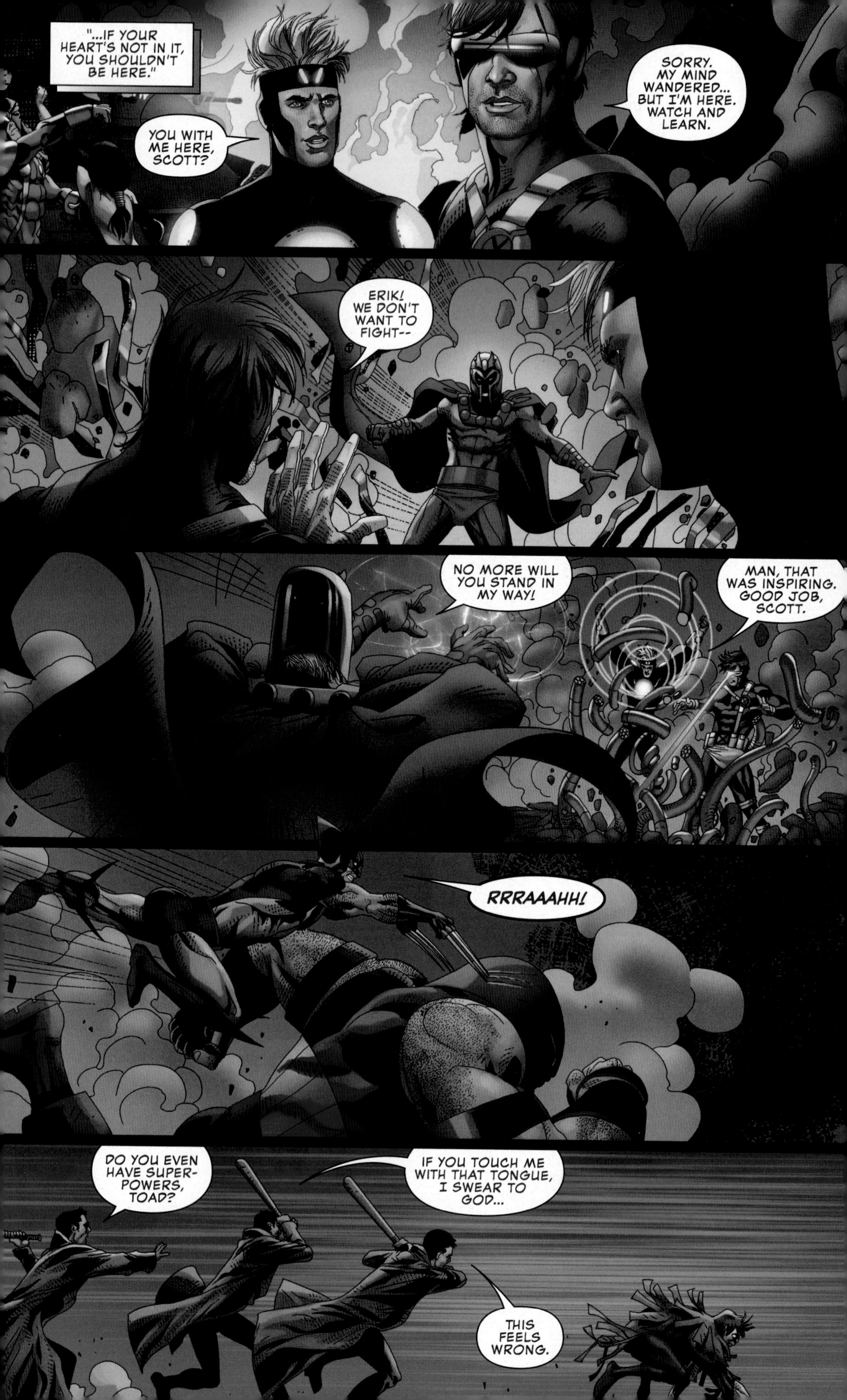
"...IF YOUR HEART'S NOT IN IT, YOU SHOULDN'T BE HERE."
YOU WITH ME HERE, SCOTT?
SORRY. MY MIND WANDERED... BUT I'M HERE. WATCH AND LEARN.
ERIK! WE DON'T WANT TO FIGHT--
NO MORE WILL YOU STAND IN MY WAY!
MAN, THAT WAS INSPIRING. GOOD JOB, SCOTT.
RRRAAAHH!
DO YOU EVEN HAVE SUPER-POWERS, TOAD?
IF YOU TOUCH ME WITH THAT TONGUE, I SWEAR TO GOD...
THIS FEELS WRONG.

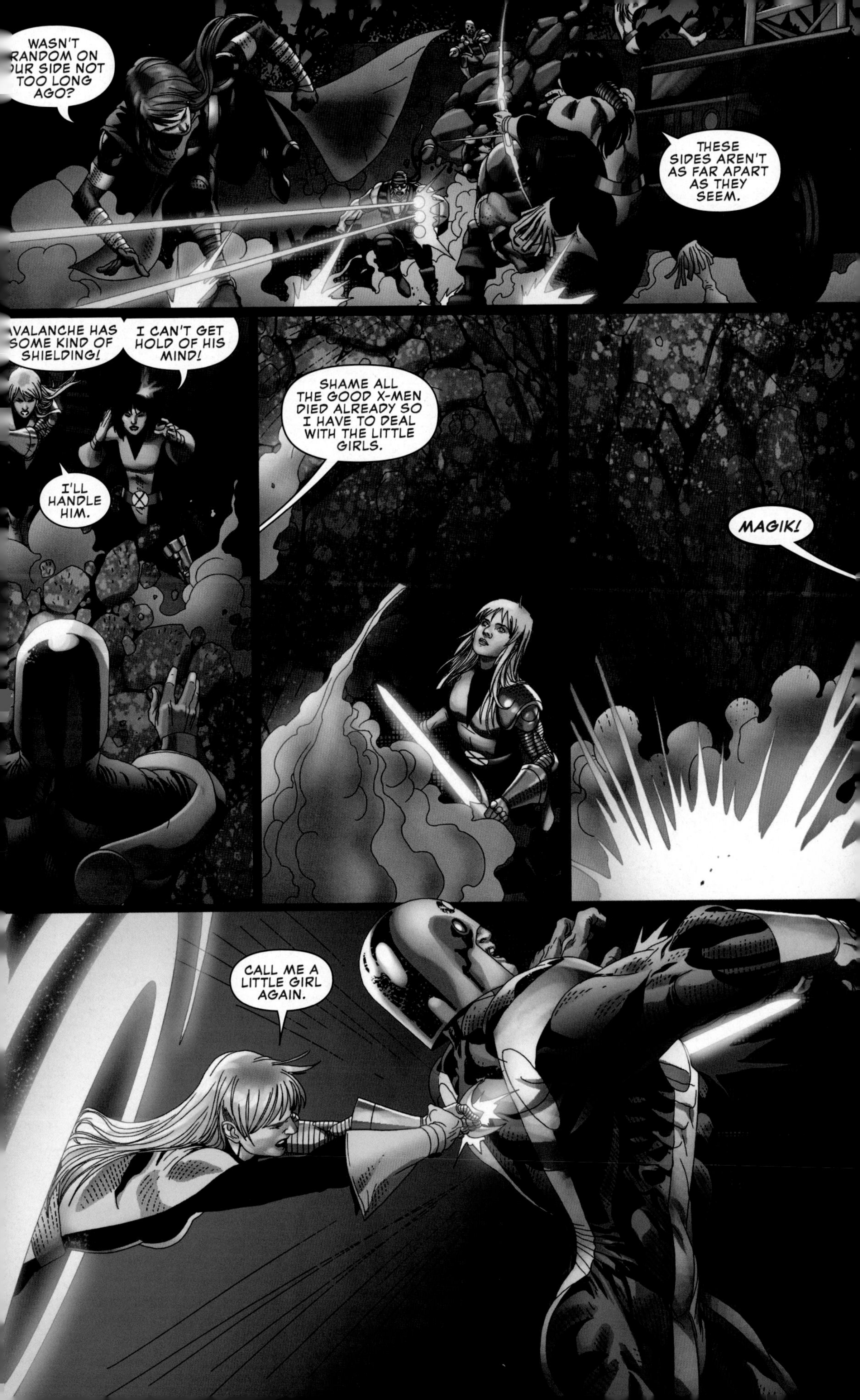

WASN'T RANDOM ON OUR SIDE NOT TOO LONG AGO?
THESE SIDES AREN'T AS FAR APART AS THEY SEEM.
AVALANCHE HAS SOME KIND OF SHIELDING!
I CAN'T GET HOLD OF HIS MIND!
I'LL HANDLE HIM.
SHAME ALL THE GOOD X-MEN DIED ALREADY SO I HAVE TO DEAL WITH THE LITTLE GIRLS.
MAGIK!
CALL ME A LITTLE GIRL AGAIN.

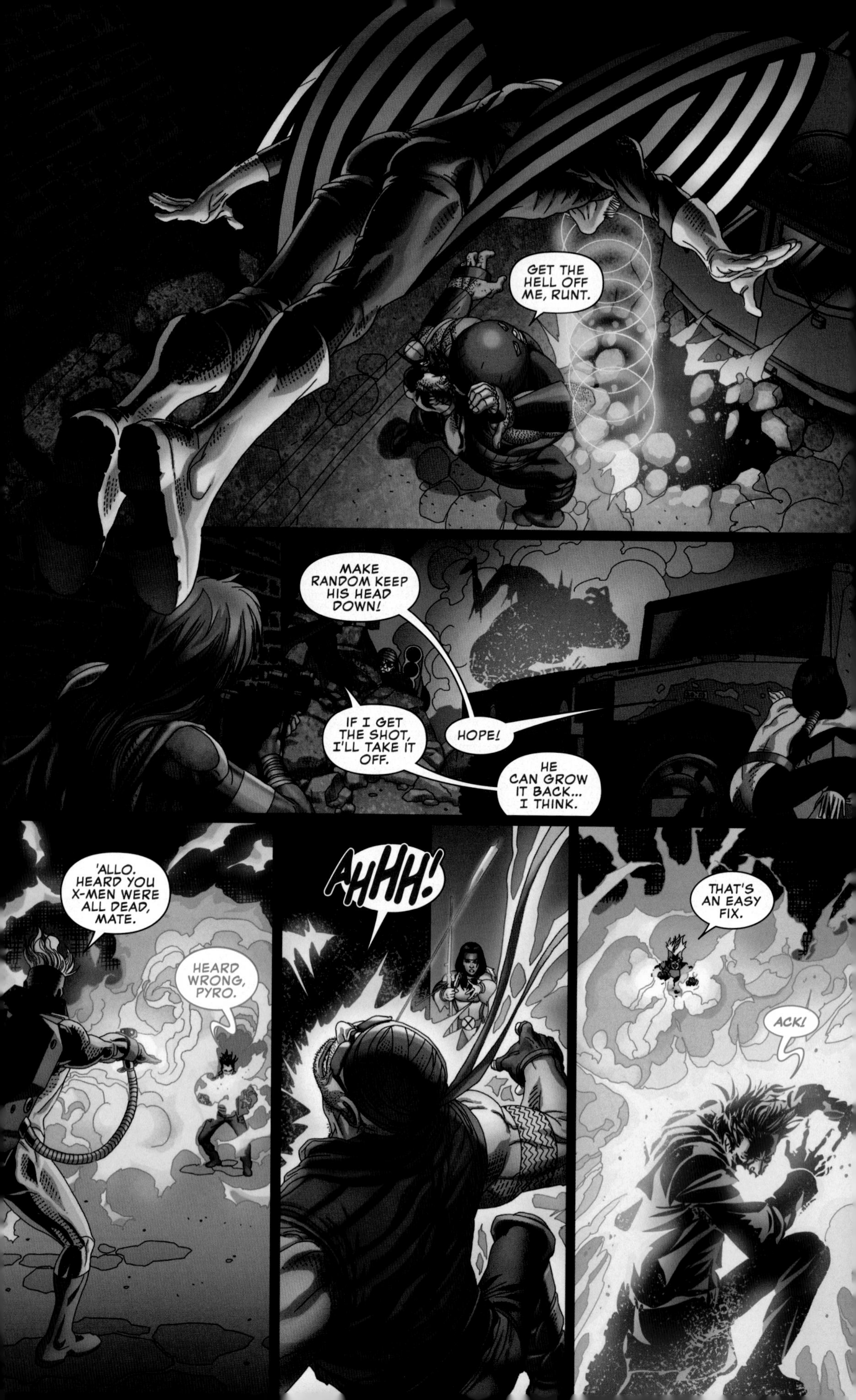
GET THE HELL OFF ME, RUNT.
MAKE RANDOM KEEP HIS HEAD DOWN!
HOPE!
IF I GET THE SHOT, I'LL TAKE IT OFF.
HE CAN GROW IT BACK... I THINK.
'ALLO. HEARD YOU X-MEN WERE ALL DEAD, MATE.
HEARD WRONG, PYRO.
AHHH!
THAT'S AN EASY FIX.
ACK!

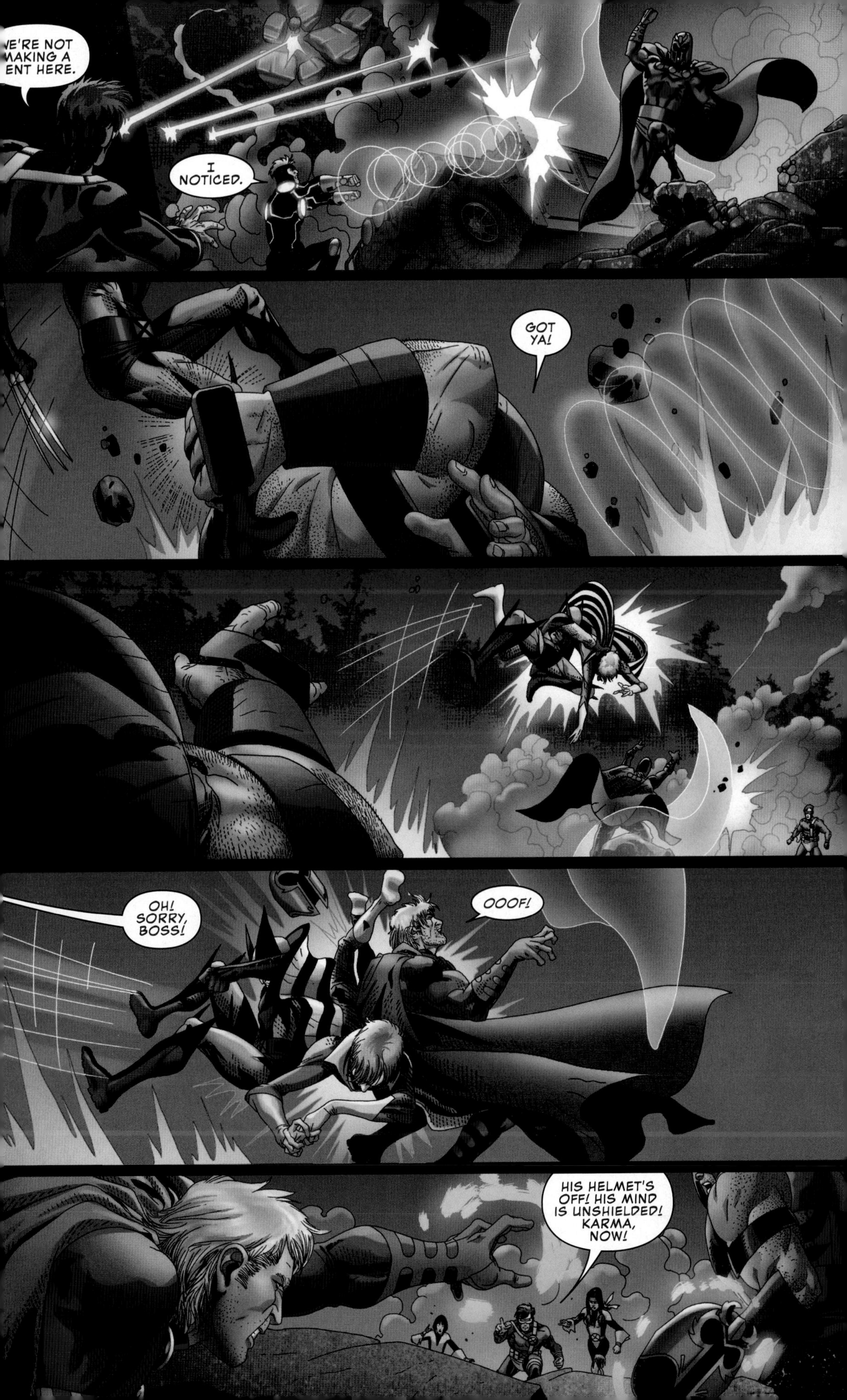

WE'RE NOT MAKING A ENT HERE.
I NOTICED.
GOT YA!
OH! SORRY, BOSS!
OOOF!
HIS HELMET'S OFF! HIS MIND IS UNSHIELDED! KARMA, NOW!

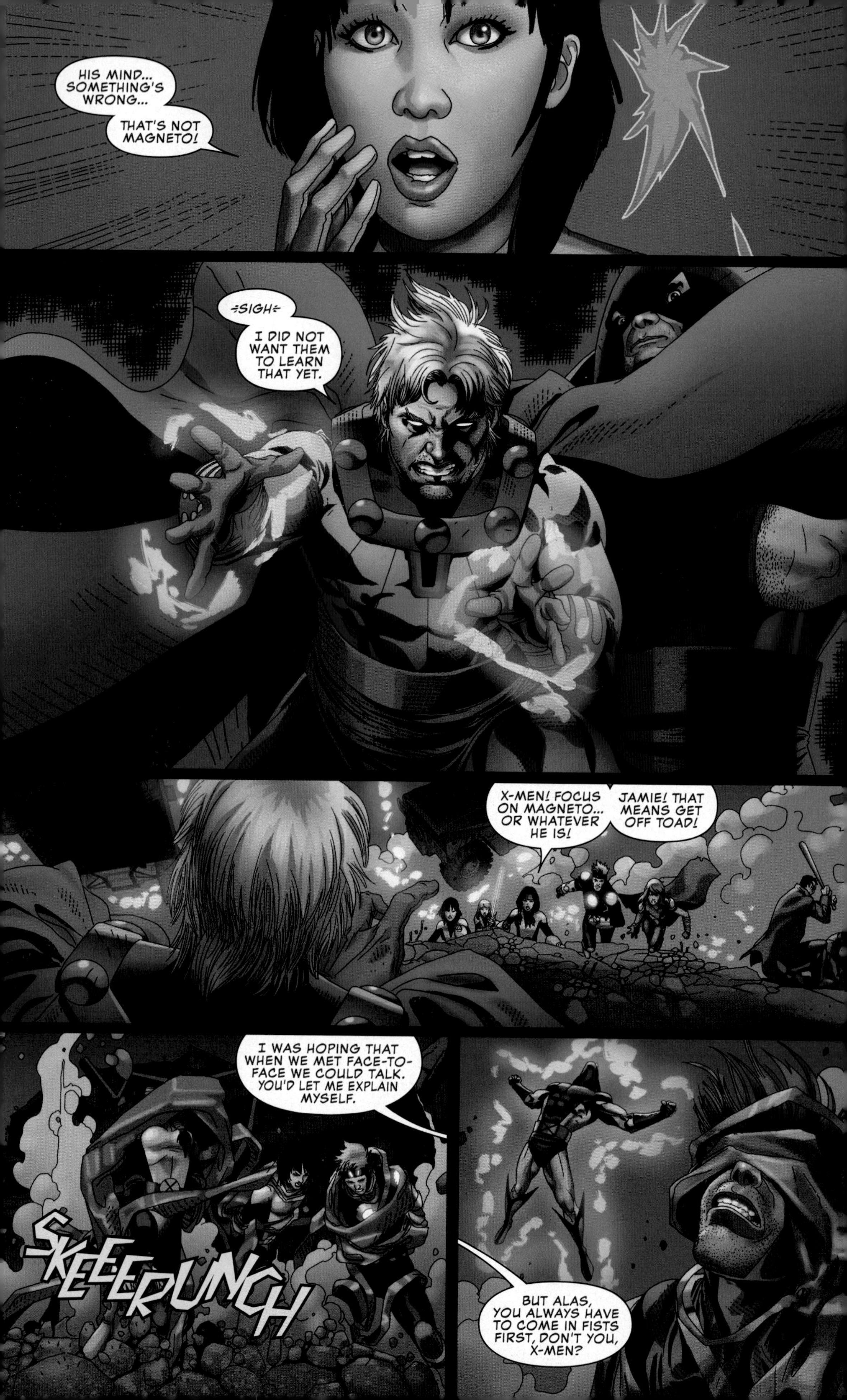
HIS MIND... SOMETHING'S WRONG...
THAT'S NOT MAGNETO!
=SIGH=
I DID NOT WANT THEM TO LEARN THAT YET.
X-MEN! FOCUS ON MAGNETO... OR WHATEVER HE IS!
JAMIE! THAT MEANS GET OFF TOAD!
I WAS HOPING THAT WHEN WE MET FACE-TO-FACE WE COULD TALK. YOU'D LET ME EXPLAIN MYSELF.
SKEEERUNCH
BUT ALAS, YOU ALWAYS HAVE TO COME IN FISTS FIRST, DON'T YOU, X-MEN?

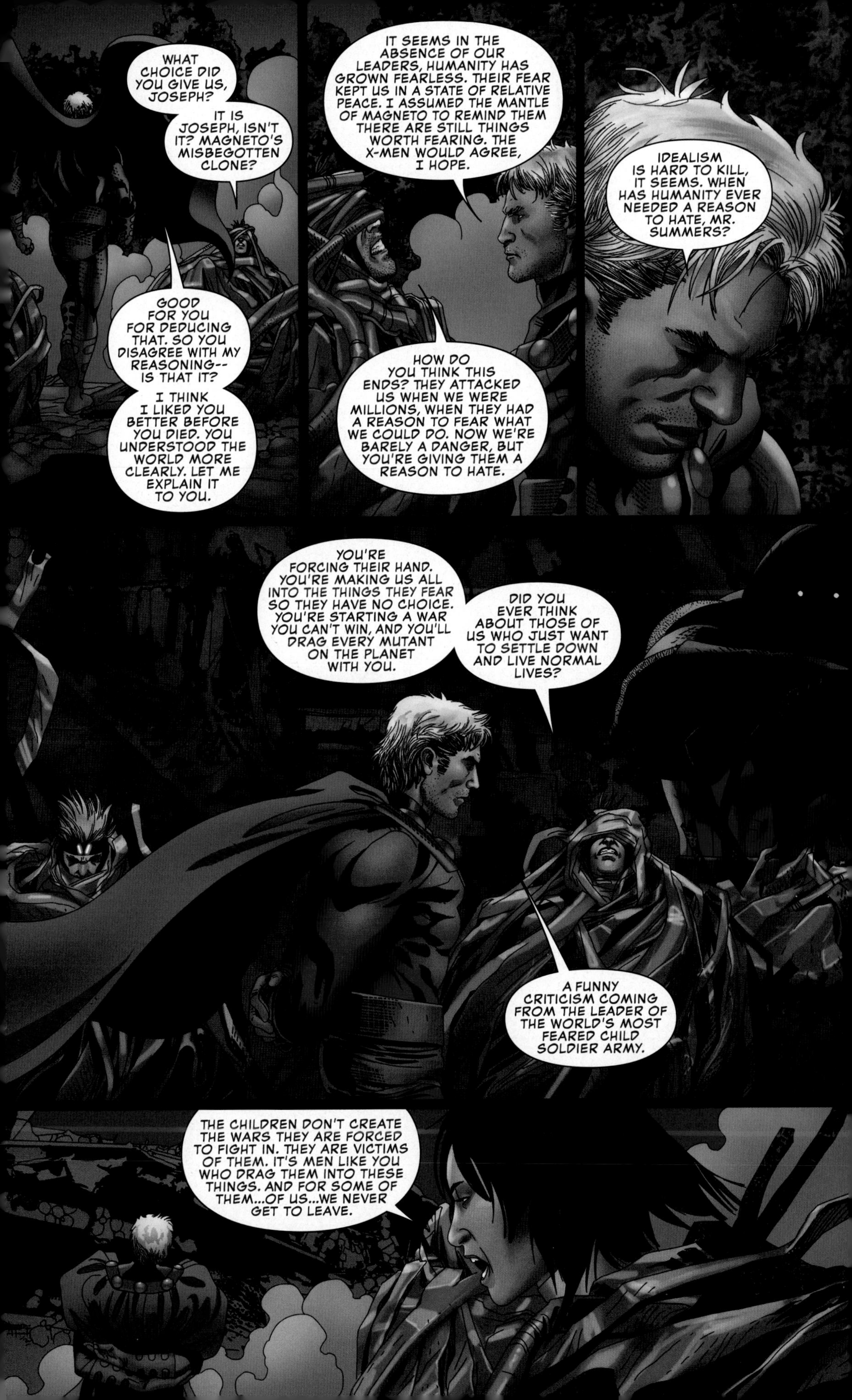

WHAT CHOICE DID YOU GIVE US, JOSEPH?
IT IS JOSEPH, ISN'T IT? MAGNETO'S MISBEGOTTEN CLONE?
GOOD FOR YOU FOR DEDUCING THAT. SO YOU DISAGREE WITH MY REASONING-- IS THAT IT?
I THINK I LIKED YOU BETTER BEFORE YOU DIED. YOU UNDERSTOOD THE WORLD MORE CLEARLY. LET ME EXPLAIN IT TO YOU.
IT SEEMS IN THE ABSENCE OF OUR LEADERS, HUMANITY HAS GROWN FEARLESS. THEIR FEAR KEPT US IN A STATE OF RELATIVE PEACE. I ASSUMED THE MANTLE OF MAGNETO TO REMIND THEM THERE ARE STILL THINGS WORTH FEARING. THE X-MEN WOULD AGREE, I HOPE.
HOW DO YOU THINK THIS ENDS? THEY ATTACKED US WHEN WE WERE MILLIONS, WHEN THEY HAD A REASON TO FEAR WHAT WE COULD DO. NOW WE'RE BARELY A DANGER, BUT YOU'RE GIVING THEM A REASON TO HATE.
IDEALISM IS HARD TO KILL, IT SEEMS. WHEN HAS HUMANITY EVER NEEDED A REASON TO HATE, MR. SUMMERS?
YOU'RE FORCING THEIR HAND. YOU'RE MAKING US ALL INTO THE THINGS THEY FEAR SO THEY HAVE NO CHOICE. YOU'RE STARTING A WAR YOU CAN'T WIN, AND YOU'LL DRAG EVERY MUTANT ON THE PLANET WITH YOU.
DID YOU EVER THINK ABOUT THOSE OF US WHO JUST WANT TO SETTLE DOWN AND LIVE NORMAL LIVES?
A FUNNY CRITICISM COMING FROM THE LEADER OF THE WORLD'S MOST FEARED CHILD SOLDIER ARMY.
THE CHILDREN DON'T CREATE THE WARS THEY ARE FORCED TO FIGHT IN. THEY ARE VICTIMS OF THEM. IT'S MEN LIKE YOU WHO DRAG THEM INTO THESE THINGS. AND FOR SOME OF THEM...OF US...WE NEVER GET TO LEAVE.

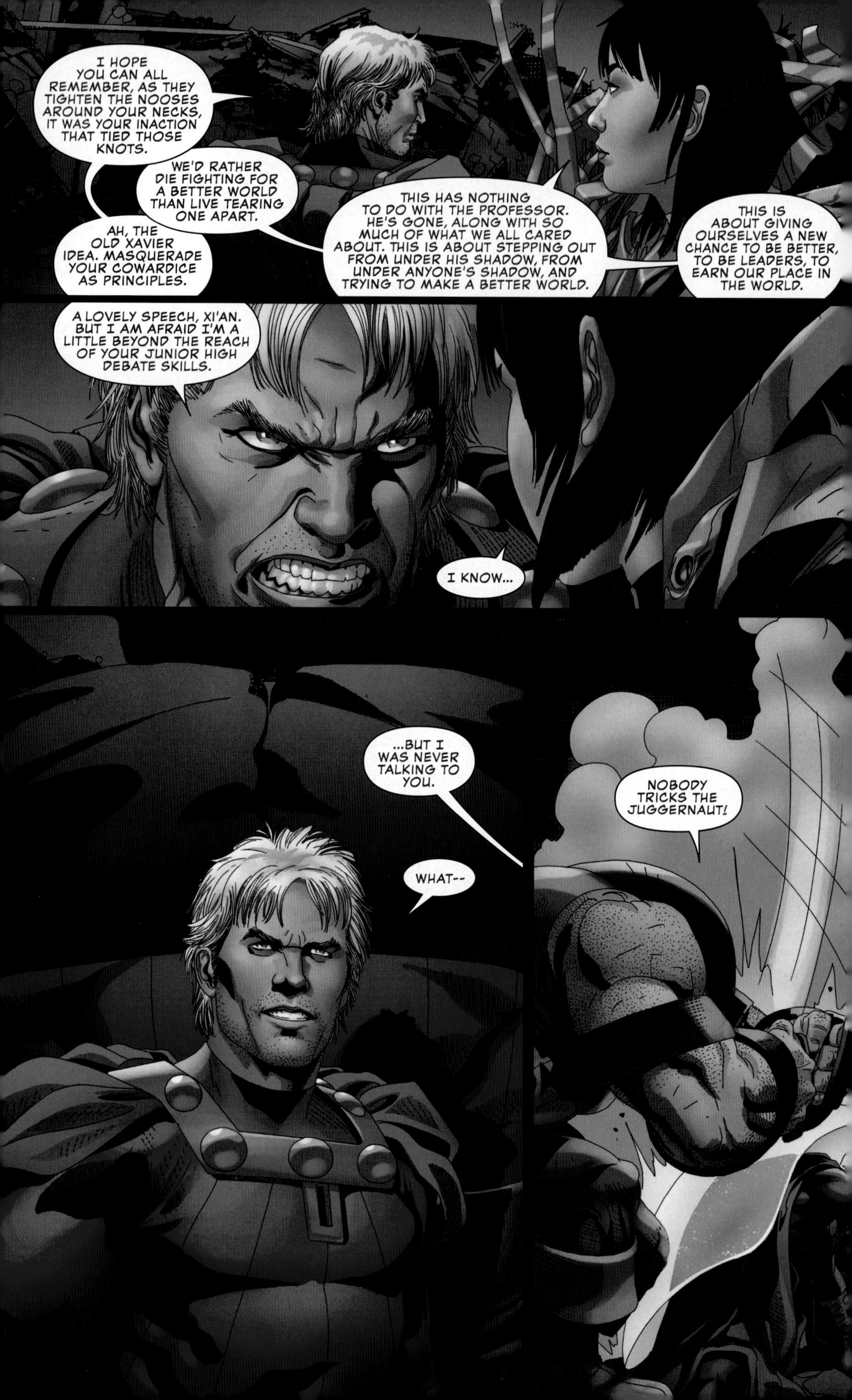
I HOPE YOU CAN ALL REMEMBER, AS THEY TIGHTEN THE NOOSES AROUND YOUR NECKS, IT WAS YOUR INACTION THAT TIED THOSE KNOTS.
WE'D RATHER DIE FIGHTING FOR A BETTER WORLD THAN LIVE TEARING ONE APART.
AH, THE OLD XAVIER IDEA. MASQUERADE YOUR COWARDICE AS PRINCIPLES.
THIS HAS NOTHING TO DO WITH THE PROFESSOR. HE'S GONE, ALONG WITH SO MUCH OF WHAT WE ALL CARED ABOUT. THIS IS ABOUT STEPPING OUT FROM UNDER HIS SHADOW, FROM UNDER ANYONE'S SHADOW, AND TRYING TO MAKE A BETTER WORLD.
THIS IS ABOUT GIVING OURSELVES A NEW CHANCE TO BE BETTER, TO BE LEADERS, TO EARN OUR PLACE IN THE WORLD.
A LOVELY SPEECH, XI'AN. BUT I AM AFRAID I'M A LITTLE BEYOND THE REACH OF YOUR JUNIOR HIGH DEBATE SKILLS.
I KNOW...
...BUT I WAS NEVER TALKING TO YOU.
WHAT--
NOBODY TRICKS THE JUGGERNAUT!

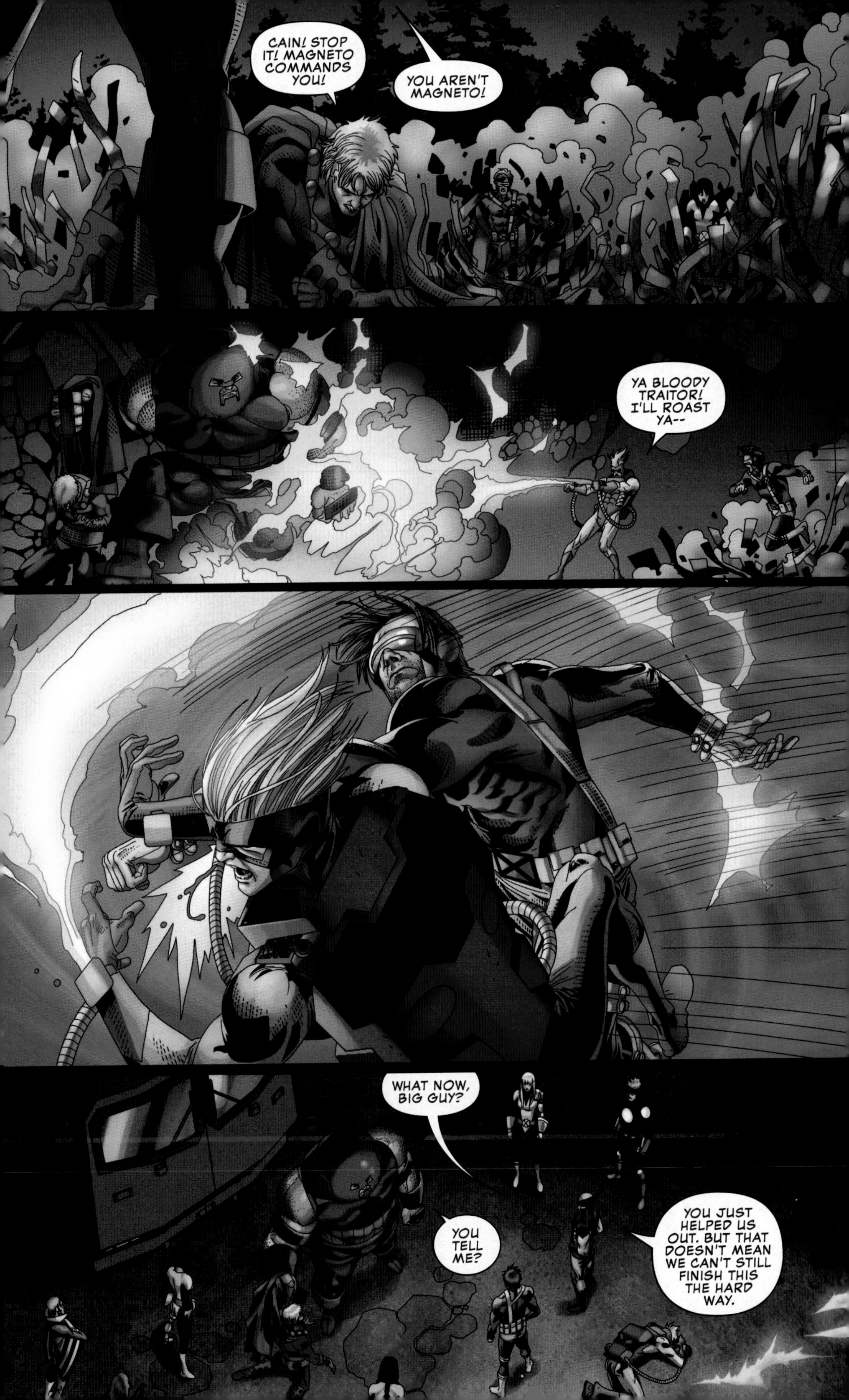
CAIN! STOP IT! MAGNETO COMMANDS YOU!
YOU AREN'T MAGNETO!
YA BLOODY TRAITOR! I'LL ROAST YA--
WHAT NOW, BIG GUY?
YOU TELL ME?
YOU JUST HELPED US OUT. BUT THAT DOESN'T MEAN WE CAN'T STILL FINISH THIS THE HARD WAY.

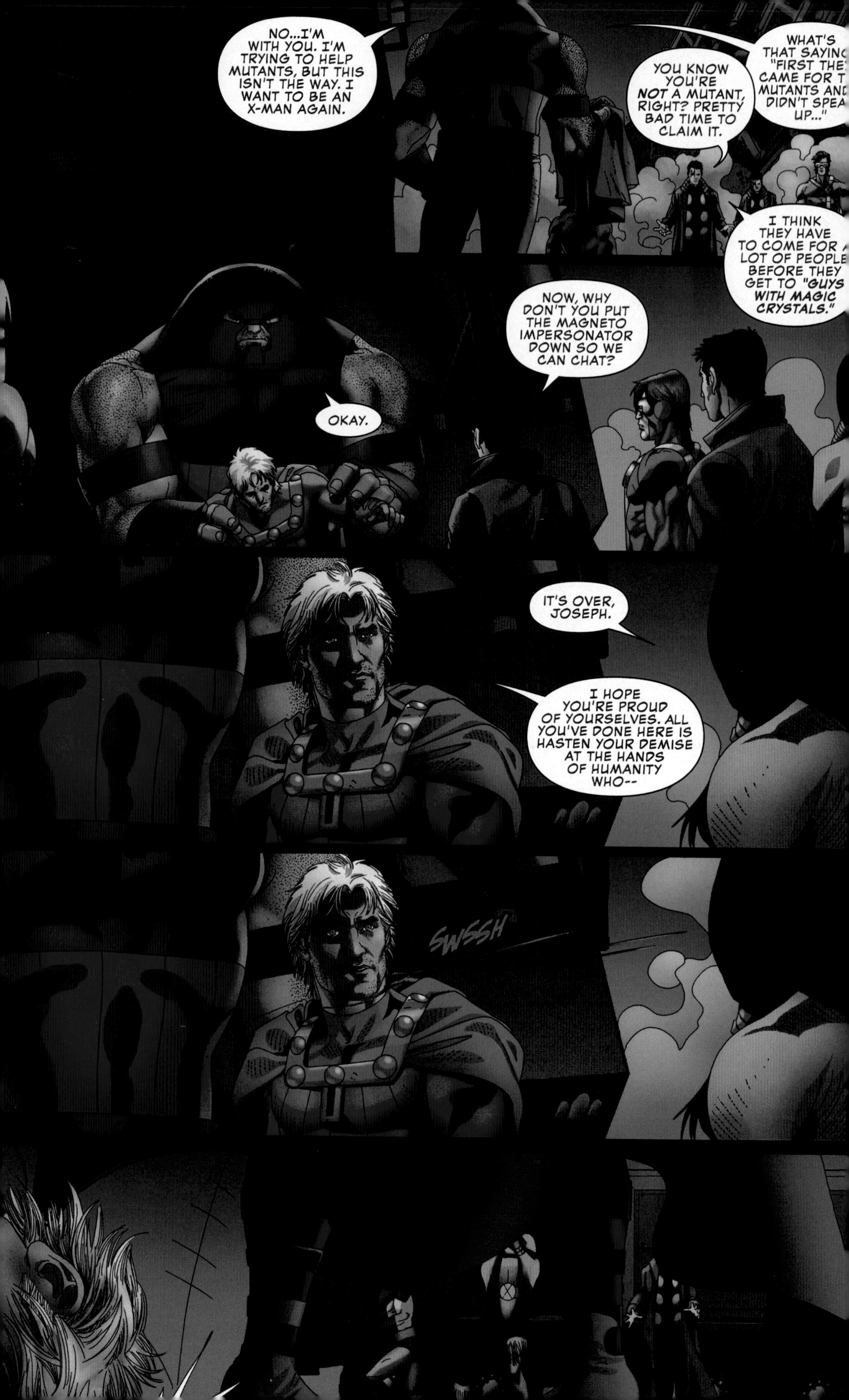
NO...I'M WITH YOU. I'M TRYING TO HELP MUTANTS, BUT THIS ISN'T THE WAY. I WANT TO BE AN X-MAN AGAIN.
YOU KNOW YOU'RE NOT A MUTANT, RIGHT? PRETTY BAD TIME TO CLAIM IT.
WHAT'S THAT SAYING "FIRST THE CAME FOR TH MUTANTS AND DIDN'T SPEA UP..."
I THINK THEY HAVE TO COME FOR A LOT OF PEOPLE BEFORE THEY GET TO "GUYS WITH MAGIC CRYSTALS."
NOW, WHY DON'T YOU PUT THE MAGNETO IMPERSONATOR DOWN SO WE CAN CHAT?
OKAY.
IT'S OVER, JOSEPH.
I HOPE YOU'RE PROUD OF YOURSELVES. ALL YOU'VE DONE HERE IS HASTEN YOUR DEMISE AT THE HANDS OF HUMANITY WHO--
SWSSH

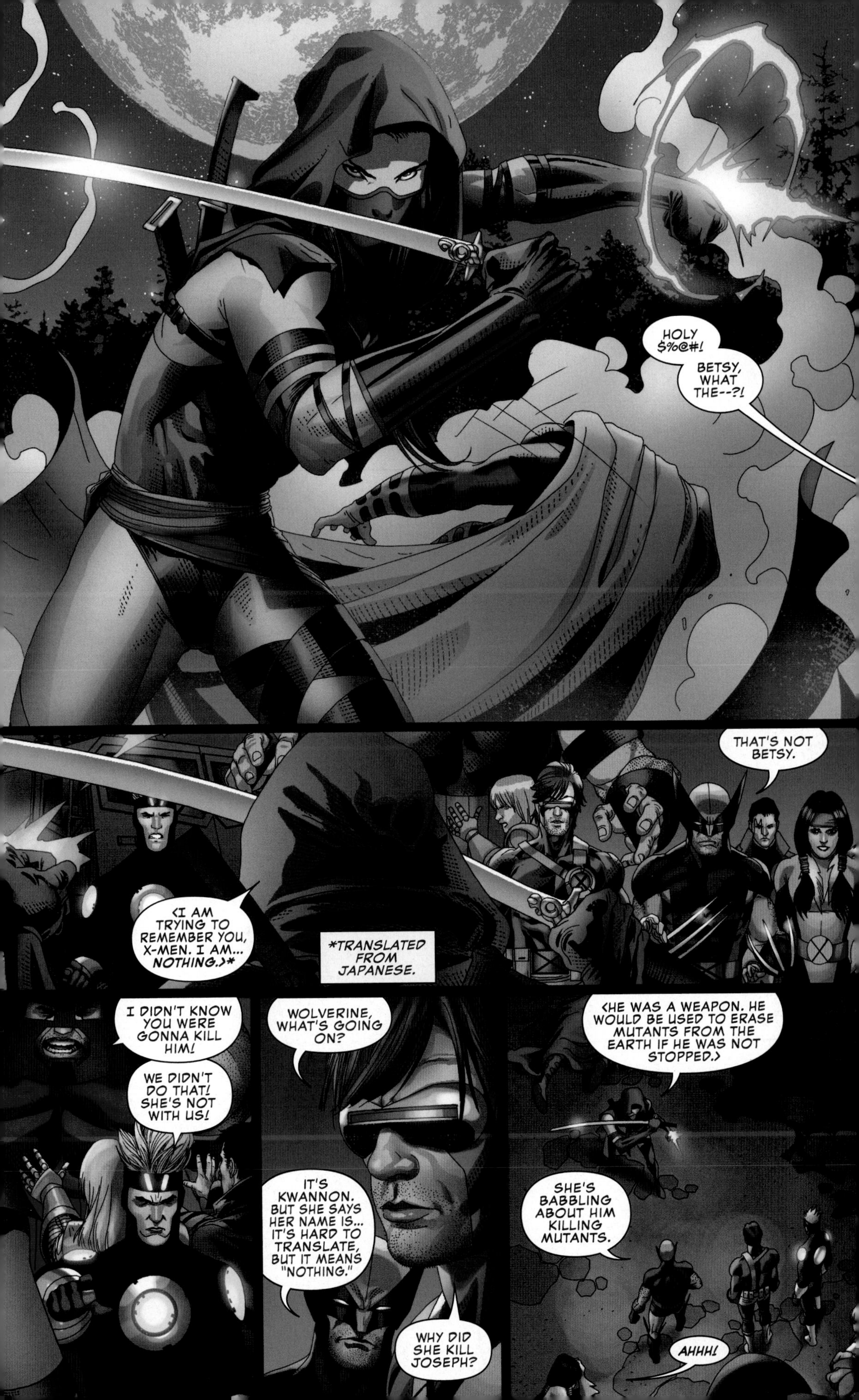

HOLY $%@#!
BETSY, WHAT THE--?!
THAT'S NOT BETSY.
<I AM TRYING TO REMEMBER YOU, X-MEN. I AM... NOTHING.>*
*TRANSLATED FROM JAPANESE.
I DIDN'T KNOW YOU WERE GONNA KILL HIM!
WE DIDN'T DO THAT! SHE'S NOT WITH US!
WOLVERINE, WHAT'S GOING ON?
IT'S KWANNON. BUT SHE SAYS HER NAME IS... IT'S HARD TO TRANSLATE, BUT IT MEANS "NOTHING."
WHY DID SHE KILL JOSEPH?
<HE WAS A WEAPON. HE WOULD BE USED TO ERASE MUTANTS FROM THE EARTH IF HE WAS NOT STOPPED.>
SHE'S BABBLING ABOUT HIM KILLING MUTANTS.
AHHH!

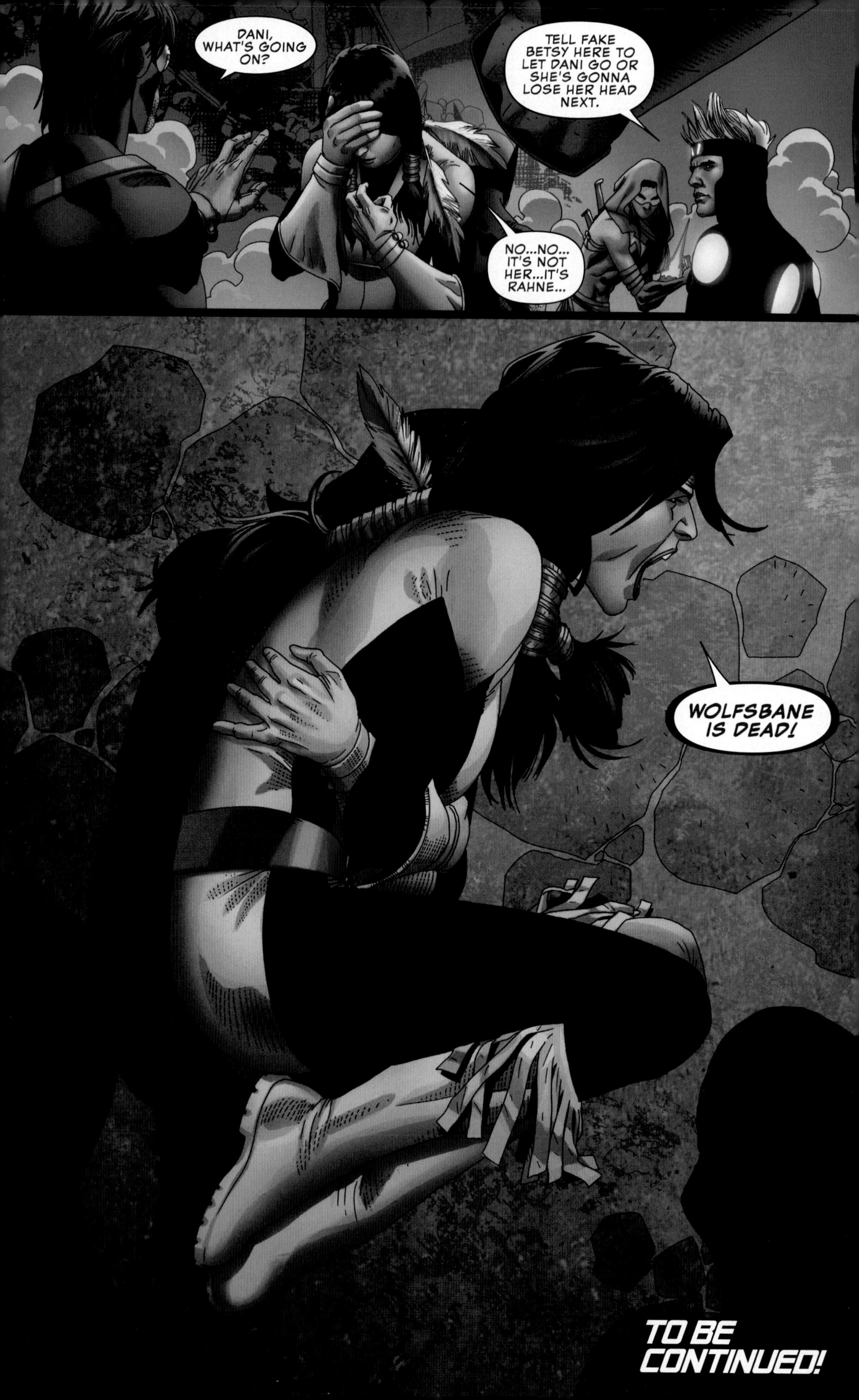
DANI, WHAT'S GOING ON?
TELL FAKE BETSY HERE TO LET DANI GO OR SHE'S GONNA LOSE HER HEAD NEXT.
NO...NO... IT'S NOT HER...IT'S RAHNE...
WOLFSBANE IS DEAD!
TO BE CONTINUED!

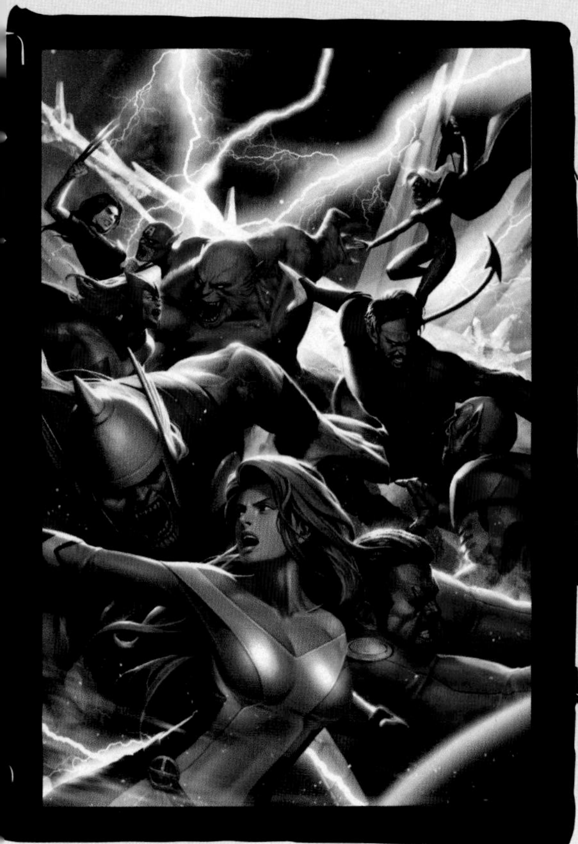

#11 SKRULLS VARIANT COVER BY
INHYUK LEE

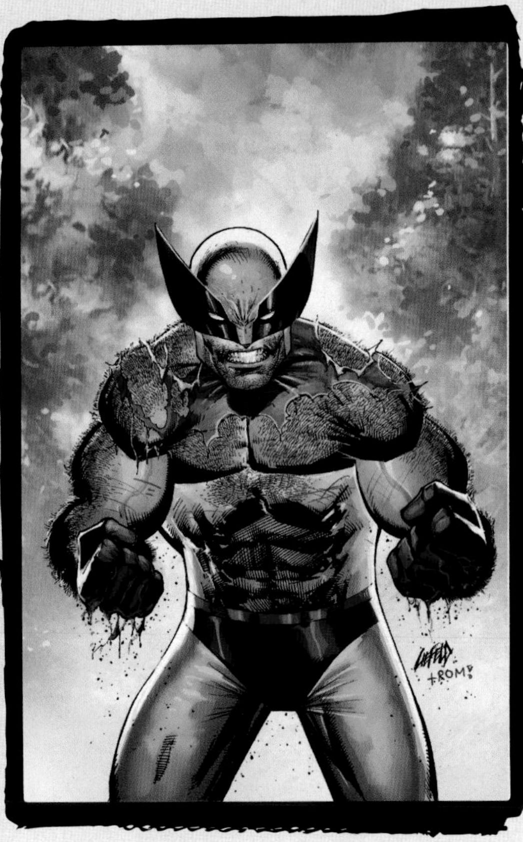

#11 VARIANT COVER BY
ROB LIEFELD & **ROMULO FAJARDO JR.**

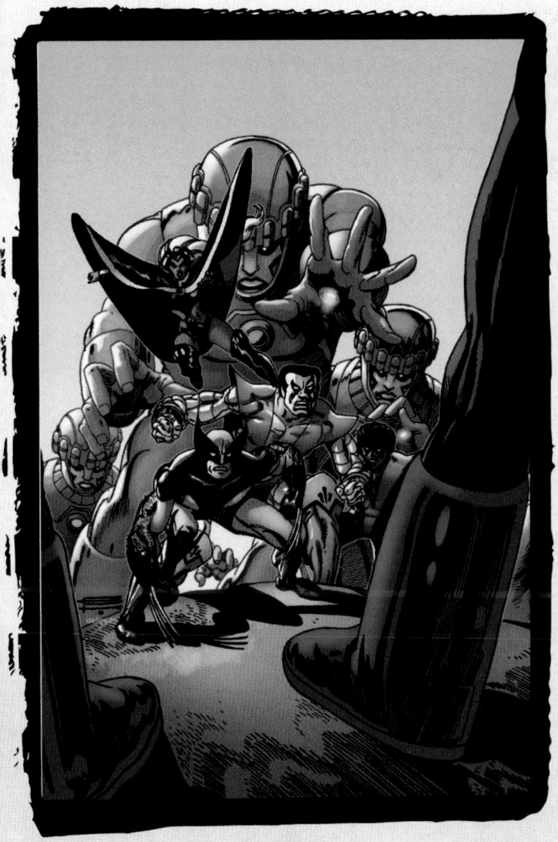

#11 HIDDEN GEM VARIANT COVER BY
GIL KANE & **EDGARDO DELGADO**

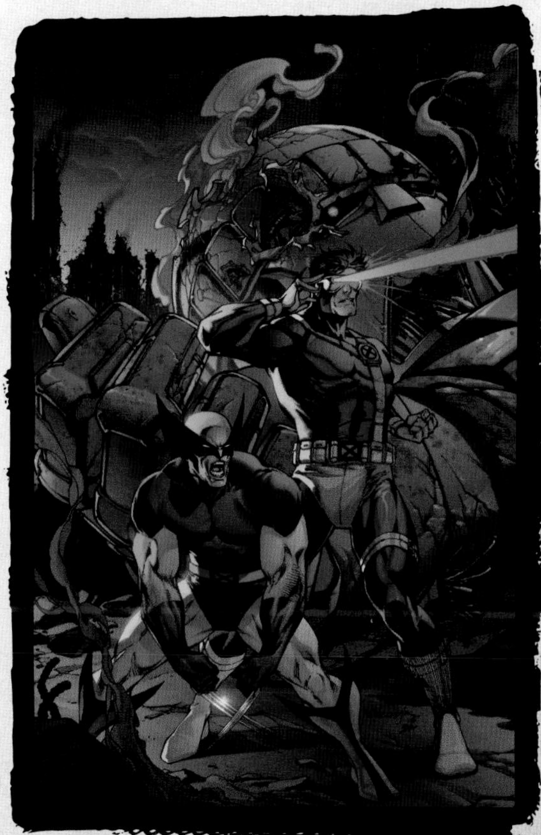

#11 VARIANT COVER BY
SCOTT WILLIAMS & **BRAD ANDERSON**

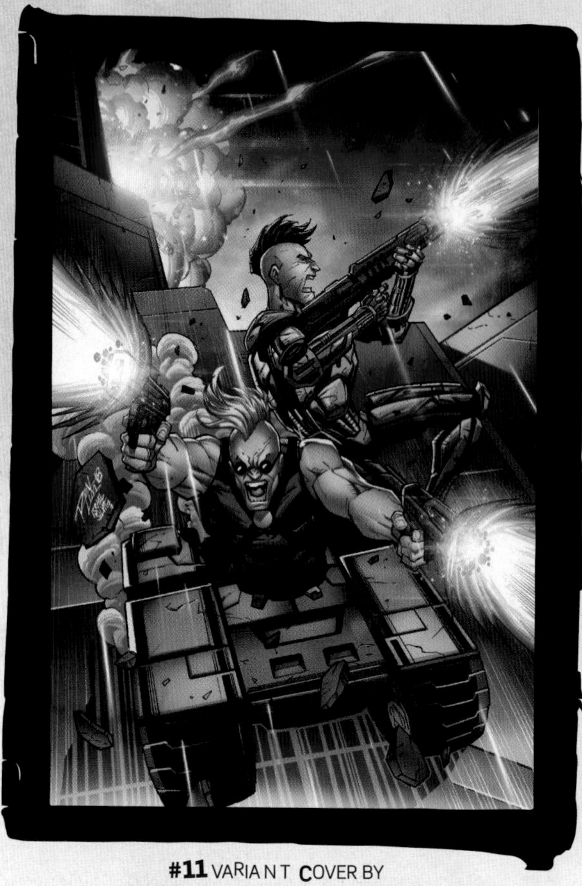

#11 VARIANT COVER BY
RON LIM & **ISRAEL SILVA**

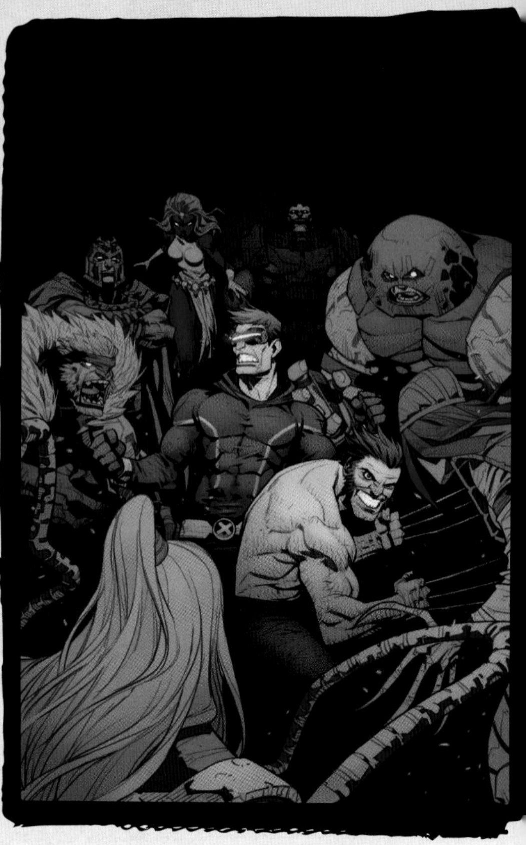

#11 VARIANT COVER BY
EDUARD PETROVICH

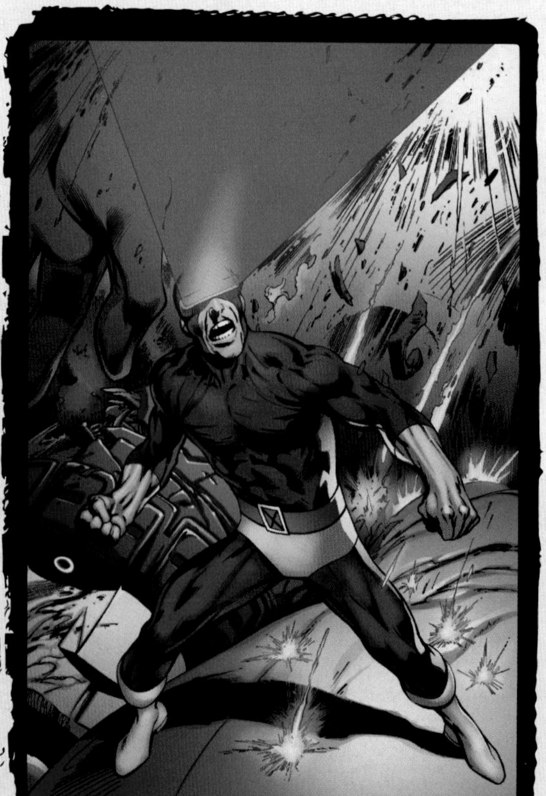

#11 VARIANT COVER BY
ALAN DAVIS, MARK FARMER
& **CHRIS SOTOMAYOR**

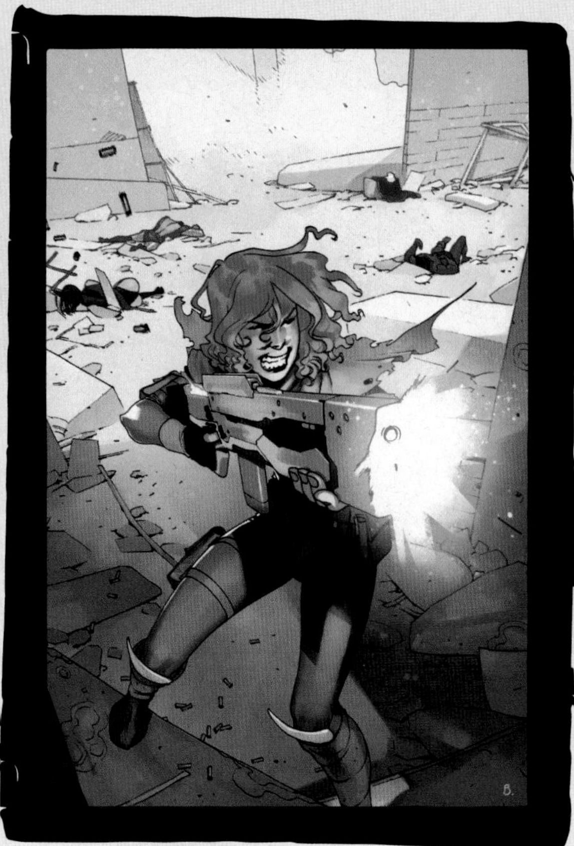

#13 VARIANT COVER BY
BENGAL

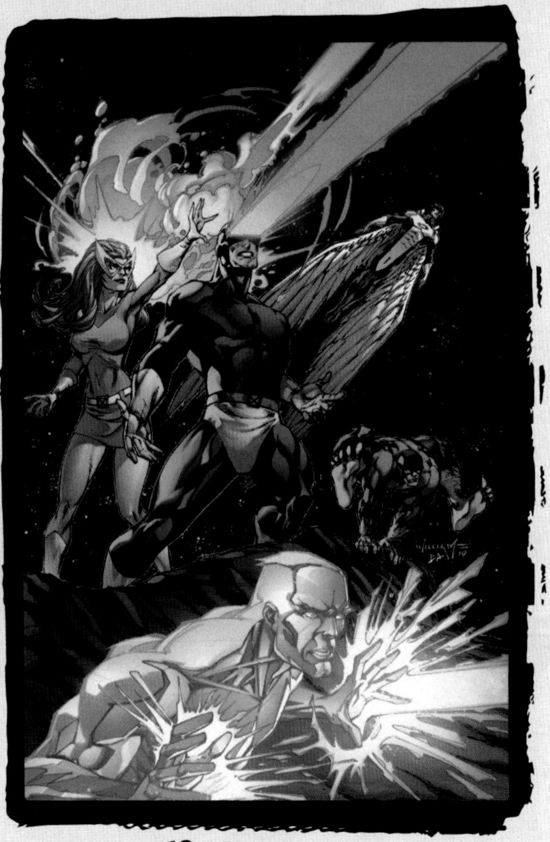

#13 VARIANT COVER BY
SCOTT WILLIAMS & BRAD ANDERSON

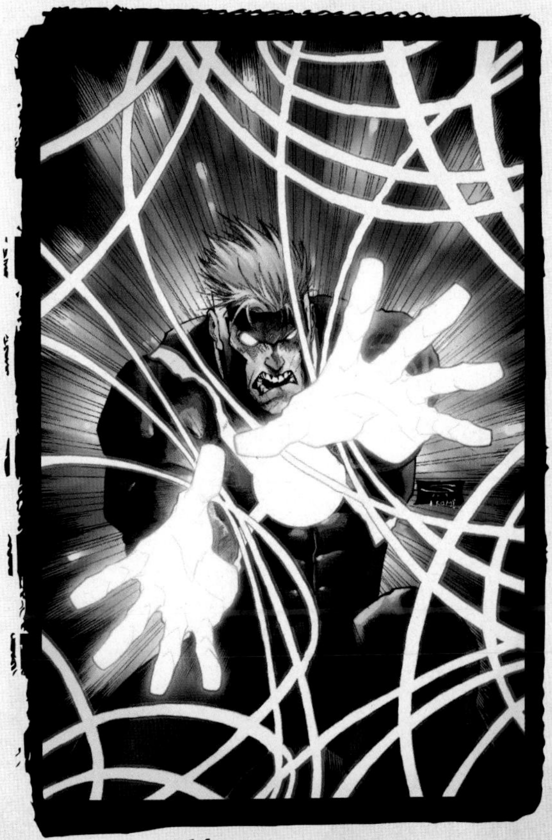

#14 VARIANT COVER BY
GERARDO SANDOVAL & ROMULO FAJARDO JR.

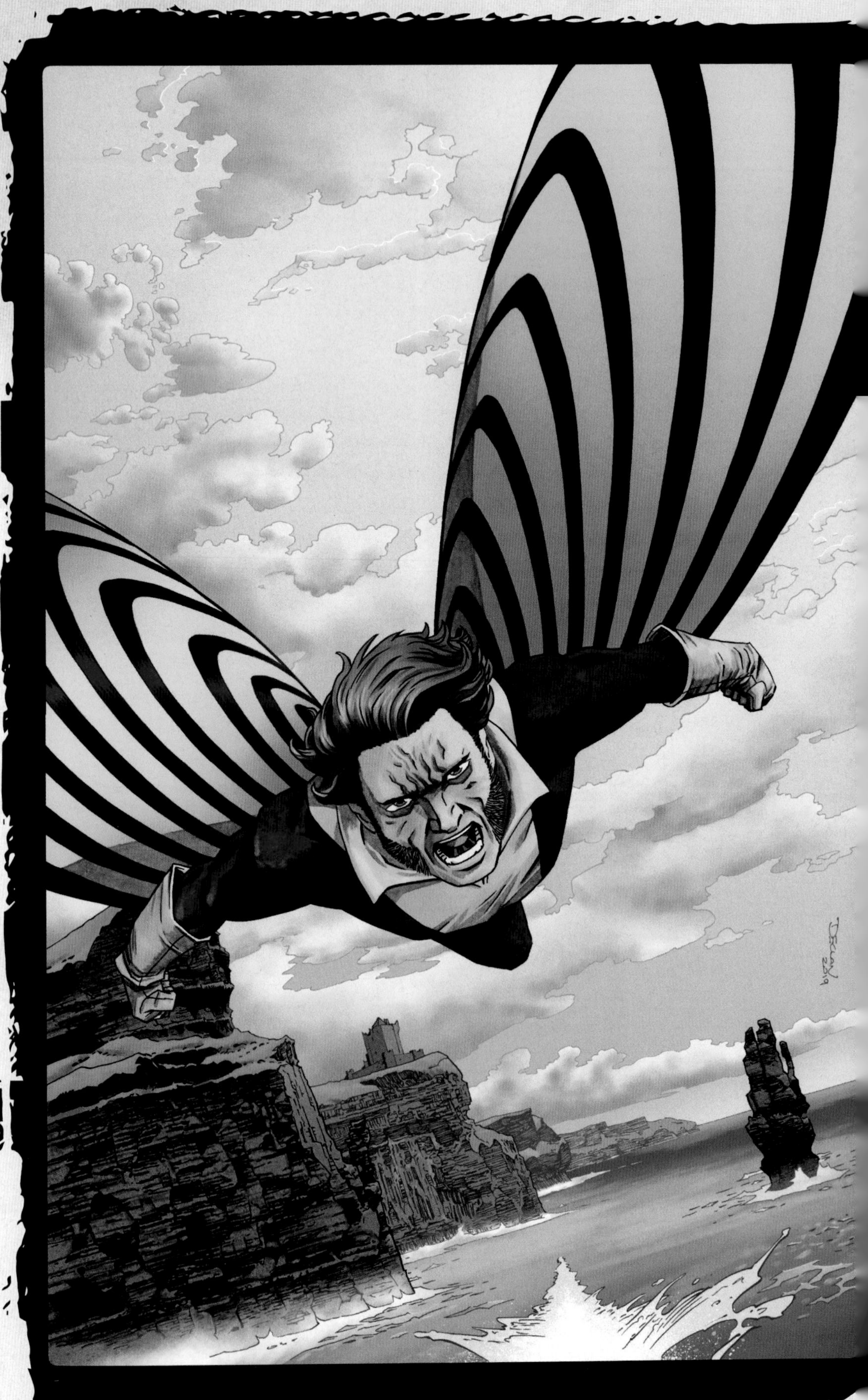

#15 VARIANT COVER BY **DECLAN SHALVEY**

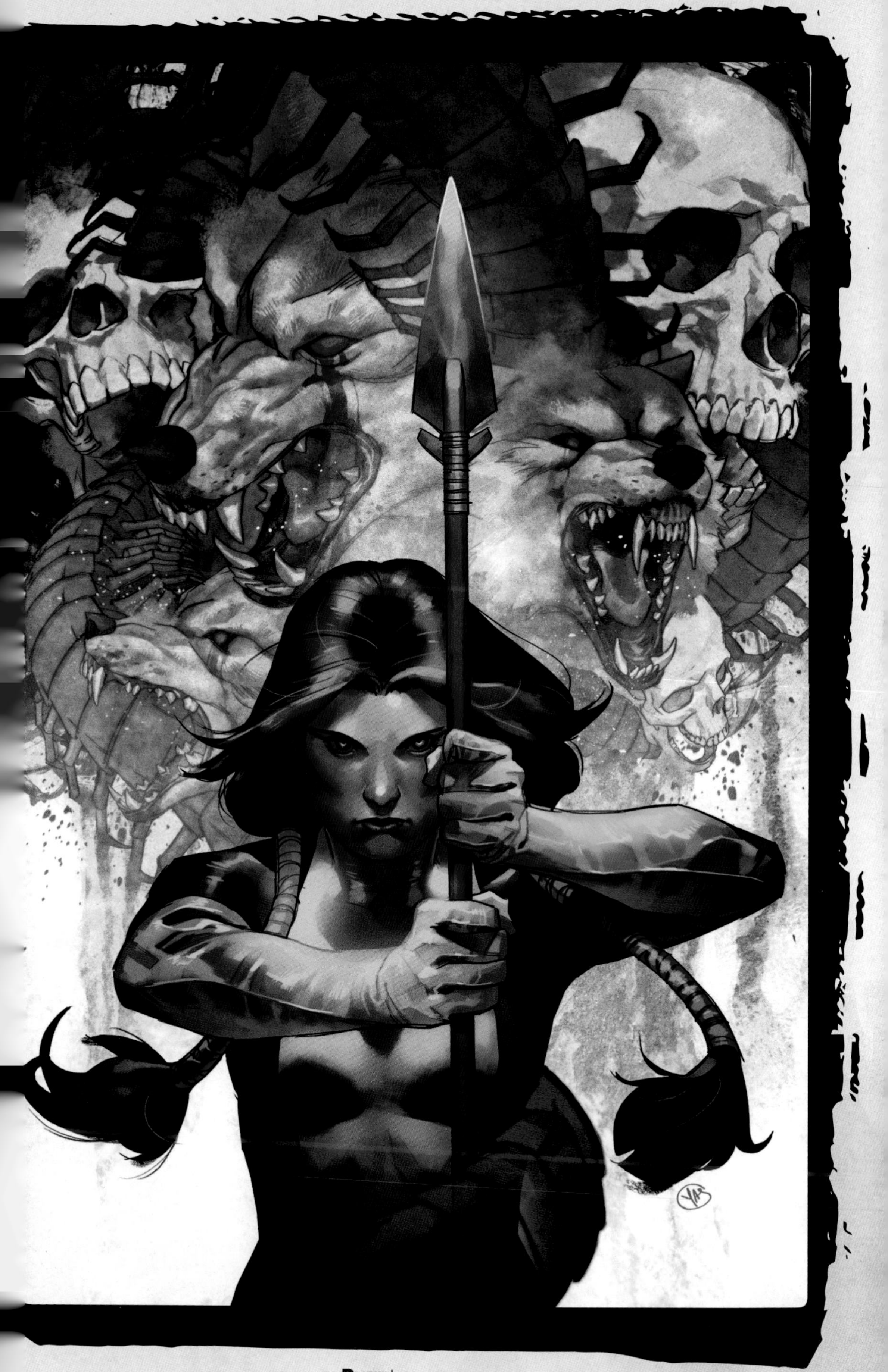
YAS

#16 VARIANT COVER BY **YASMINE PUTRI**

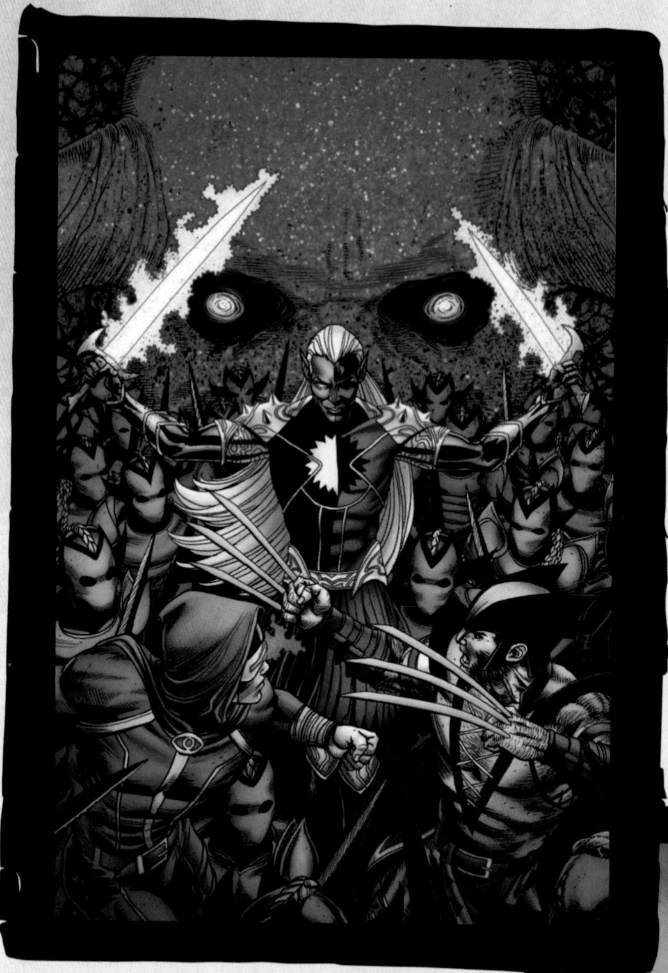

#15 ASGARDIAN VARIANT COVER BY
PATCH ZIRCHER & MORRY HOLLOWELL

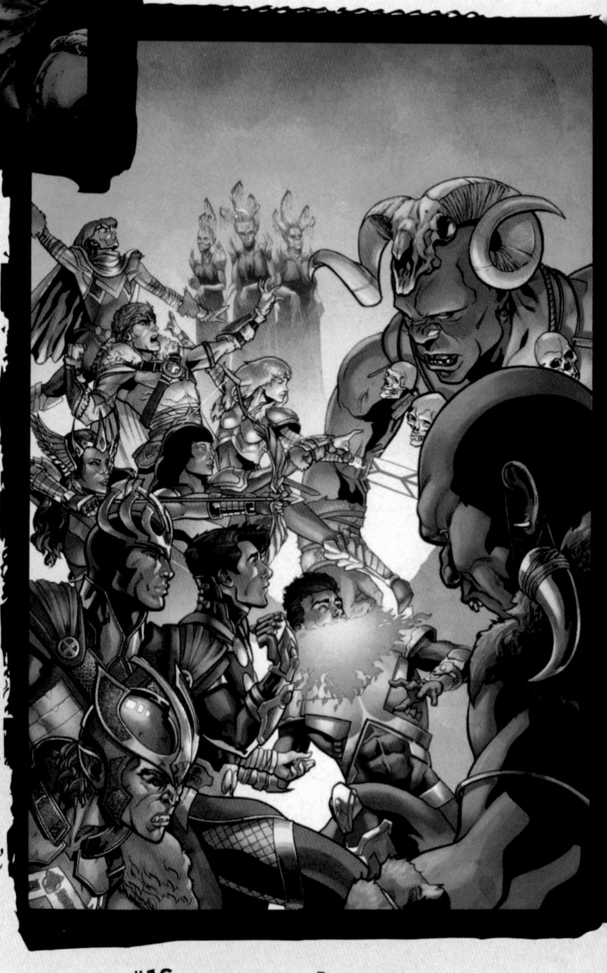

#16 ASGARDIAN VARIANT COVER BY
WILL SLINEY & RACHELLE ROSENBERG